FRANK MOORHOUSE

strange paths

FRANK MOORHOUSE

strange paths

KNOPF

KNOPF

UK | USA | Canada | Ireland | Australia
India | New Zealand | South Africa | China

Knopf is part of the Penguin Random House group of companies whose addresses can be found at global.penguinrandomhouse.com

First published by Knopf, 2023

Copyright © Matthew Lamb, 2023

The moral right of the author has been asserted.

All rights reserved. No part of this publication may be reproduced, published, performed in public or communicated to the public in any form or by any means without prior written permission from Penguin Random House Australia Pty Ltd or its authorised licensees.

Correspondence between Frank Moorhouse and Michael Wilding, and between Moorhouse and Wendy James, is quoted with their kind permission.

Every effort has been made to acknowledge and contact copyright holders for permission to reproduce material contained in the book. Any copyright holders who have been inadvertently omitted from acknowledgements and credits should contact the publisher and omissions will be rectified in subsequent editions.

Cover design by Adam Laszczuk © Penguin Random House Australia
Typeset in Adobe Garamond by Midland Typesetters, Australia

Printed and bound in Australia by Griffin Press, an accredited ISO AS/NZ 14001 Environmental Management Systems printer.

 A catalogue record for this book is available from the National Library of Australia

ISBN 978 0 14378 612 2

penguin.com.au

We at Penguin Random House Australia acknowledge that Aboriginal and Torres Strait Islander peoples are the first storytellers and Traditional Custodians of the land on which we live and work. We honour Aboriginal and Torres Strait Islander peoples' continuous connection to Country, waters, skies and communities. We celebrate Aboriginal and Torres Strait Islander stories, traditions and living cultures; and we pay our respects to Elders past and present.

For Tess

*the relief of biography — we are not alone
others have gone this way before us*

— Frank Moorhouse, undated index card

Contents

Author's Note		xi
1	A Prehistory of Frank Thomas Moorhouse Jr	1
2	'Fuck Father Christmas!'	46
3	'This is it; This Is Failure or Success in Life!'	73
4	'I Feel Like Some Other Species Looking at Humans'	111
5	'Is This You, Moorhouse?'	147
6	'There Are Those Who Kick, Those Who Get Kicked, and Those Who Kick Back'	186
7	'I Am More Confused Now'	225
8	'Writes Short Stories and Does Not Intend to Write a Conventional Novel'	263
9	'The Stories Aren't Dirty Enough'	303
10	'But the Important Thing I Want You to Know Is That I'm Trying to Be an Honest Craftsman'	337
11	'Contrary to Popular Misconception, Banned Writing Doesn't Pay'	377
12	'No, That Is Called a Discontinuous Narrative'	410
Coda: 'Reading Biographies to Overcome Loneliness'		443
Sources		451
Acknowledgements		461

Author's Note

This is the first in a projected two-volume cultural biography of Frank Moorhouse. *Strange Paths* covers the period 1938–74, following Frank's youth, his long writing apprenticeship, and his breaking into the literary establishment, on his own terms.

It draws heavily on archival material: letters, notes, drafts and uncollected works published in small magazines. Where possible these have been cited faithfully from the original, including idiosyncratic forms of expression, syntax and spelling.

Regarding the use of titles in depicting the stages of Frank's various writing projects: titles in Roman connote the broad process of researching, note-taking, working with other people, contract negotiations, funding, and so on (for example, the Between Wars project); the working title of a manuscript draft or film script that is the outcome of such a project, but which is not yet published, is referred to in Roman in single quote marks (for example, the 'Between Wars' script); and when a work is published or released, the title is italicised (for example, *Between Wars* refers to the film).

Foreign-language books referenced are dated according to the English translations available to Frank. Historically contemporaneous verbiage is maintained throughout, with changes in language acting as markers for cultural changes occurring throughout Frank's life.

This biography is a supplement to Frank's own books and writings, not a substitute for them. For this reason, stories or articles collected in Frank's published books are referenced for context, but given minimal description – these are otherwise available to readers. Stories, essays or articles that remain uncollected or unpublished – and so not widely available to the reader – are outlined in more detail.

The second volume, *Ways of Going*, will cover the second half of Frank's life, 1975–2022. This includes his mature works and the culmination of his lifelong reflections on the foundations of Australian history and culture.

This is an ongoing project, anchored in, but not exhausted by, these two books. To access additional material, paratexts, outtakes from the books and further reflections on the topics that interested and occupied the critical imagination of Frank Moorhouse, join me at publicthings.substack.com.

I

A Prehistory of Frank Thomas Moorhouse Jr

'The limits of our narrative are the limits of our experience.' Frank Moorhouse added that handwritten line to the typescript of a talk he gave to the Nowra Historical Society in the late 1980s. Frank argued in the talk that 'the need to be shown how to see is related to the need to have the right words or a new vocabulary to accurately describe and visually catalogue what we see'. Regarding Australian prehistory, Frank said: 'The Aboriginals as we know covered the landscape with stories, dance, and song and painting to make it theirs – narratives which were maps, history, archives, and mythology – the narratives of why we exist.' To which he added: 'Those of us who arrived after 1788 are still making our stories, songs and dances to help us to be at home here.'

In another set of typescript notes, Frank outlined what he called the 'Characteristics of the Australian Style', the ways literary imagination contributed to the making of these narratives. He suggested a fourfold historical sequence: an initial fractured attachment to the British and European cultural tradition, a fracture welded with storytelling, a storytelling deeply encrusted by the weld, resulting in 'a storytelling which is about the need for storytelling'. Frank was deeply concerned with finding his place within that fractured tradition, the better to orient himself towards his own experiences, his own literary imagination, in order to plot a path forward.

At the time he gave this talk to the Nowra Historical Society, he was also researching a book about the League of Nations. In an interview he described how the book he was working on was motivated by the idea of looking back at the generations who lived before he was born. 'It is part of the thesis that our lives, or parts of our lives, are formed before we are born,' he said. 'In some ways we are a walking archive of antiquated beliefs and genetic and cultural baggage ... So this book looks at the archival ghosts we carry with us.'

It is necessary, in order to adequately introduce the subject of *this* book, to examine the archival ghosts Frank Moorhouse carried within himself, to consider the constituent parts of his life and times that were formed before he was born, if only to show how he had later been haunted, had exorcised or had come to terms with these 'archival ghosts'.

Much of the material for this introductory chapter – fragmented, overlapping, seemingly unrelated historical stories – is drawn from Frank's own archives, both public and private, including tape-recorded interviews he made with his parents, Frank Osborne Moorhouse Sr and Purthanry Thanes Mary Moorhouse (née Cutts), various political, legal and technological histories, together with cultural and familial genealogies, collected and consulted over decades, and a marginalia of books and pamphlets he read throughout his life, in an attempt to understand the world before he was born, the world he had been born into and how culture is transmitted from generation to generation. Additional material comes from the private archives of his family, supplemented by scholarly sources only in order to corroborate and provide context for this otherwise impressionistic prehistory of Frank Thomas Moorhouse Jr.

The titular heroine of Charlotte Brontë's first novel, *Jane Eyre* (1847), in fleeing her past, spends a cold night on the West Yorkshire moors, before being rescued by the inhabitants of Marsh End. 'Some calls it Marsh End, and some calls it Moor House,' Jane is told. And for the rest of her tale she refers to her new home as 'Moor House'.

In reality, there were many Moor Houses in West Yorkshire, and 'Moorhouse' – meaning 'the house on the moor' – was a common family name in that part of rural England in the early nineteenth century. One figure was John Midgley Moorhouse, born in 1807, in Keighley, two miles north of Haworth, where Charlotte Brontë would be born nine years later, followed soon after by her sisters. What was uncommon about this Moorhouse was that his surname, against custom, was passed on to him by his mother, Mary Moorhouse. She became pregnant to a man named John Midgley, who died before their son was born; they had not married. John Midgley Moorhouse grew to become a farmer. In 1835, he married Hannah Cook, and over the next fifteen years she bore him nine children. The fifth, born in 1843, was christened David Addeman Moorhouse.

Meanwhile, on the other side of the Earth, a penal colony had been established by the British. Sailing south of Botany Bay, the explorer George Bass made landfall and, noting the shoals of sand along the coast, called the area 'Shoals Haven'. He later reported to the governor that it would make a fine 'nursery for cattle'.

In 1822, taking advantage of a colonial land-grant system, a man named Alexander Berry was assigned 10,000 acres in the Shoalhaven, occupying the traditional lands of the Yuin nation, constituting thirteen tribal groups. The original inhabitants told a story of a great deluge, when the floodwaters were said to have reached higher than the mountains. Such stories indicated areas of relative safety. A creek off the Shoalhaven River supplied fresh water, and the nearby area was high and flat enough for a serviceable campsite. 'Ngurra', meaning 'camp', was corrupted by the Europeans to become 'Nowra'. But the flood warnings were unheeded, the intruders having to learn by their own mistakes. Berry failed with various crops, mainly due to rust disease and flooding. He had more luck with dairy cattle, as Bass had predicted. By September 1824, surplus butter was sent by ship to Sydney, followed by cheese in December.

Another settlement opened up 75 miles (120 kilometres) inland, along the Shoalhaven River, a village later known as Braidwood. Land grants were awarded to settlers. They were assigned convicts, to work and occupy the land, in order to validate the grants. One convict, arriving in 1830, was Thomas Keivel. Born in Somerset, England, in 1797, he married Patience Sidwell. They had six children. The first, Caroline, was born in Wiltshire, England, in 1825. The family was illiterate. Five years later, Thomas Keivel was convicted of robbery and sentenced to twenty-one years' transportation. His family followed him to Braidwood. In 1841, sixteen-year-old Caroline Keivel married a 34-year-old man named James Lynn. Her parents acted as witnesses.

Another Braidwood convict, John Boden Yates, had also arrived recently. Born in 1812, he could read and write. A shoemaker by trade, he was convicted of larceny and sentenced to seven years' transportation. He was assigned to work for Dr Robert Huntley, a Quaker. Huntley had come from Cork, Ireland, and was travelling with a 25-year-old Irishwoman named Mary O'Driscol, who was bonded to Huntley as a housemaid and cook.

In 1838, Huntley's maid married his convict. A year later, John Boden Yates was accused of obscenity by Dr Huntley, and charged by the local magistrate. Huntley testified that he had witnessed Yates accidently stepping on a dog, exclaiming: 'Damn your b—— eyes' (the language was censored in the court documents). He also witnessed Yates in the kitchen using an expression considered unprintable in the court papers, referenced only as '——'. The court reprimanded Yates, but he escaped the lash.

Prohibitions against obscenity and blasphemy, and the use of the lash, were only some of the measures deployed to maintain moral order in a community that was predominantly male and criminal. In February 1787, Governor Arthur Phillip had written to the colonial secretary, Lord Sydney, stating 'there are two crimes that would merit death; murder and sodomy'. By the time David Addeman Moorhouse was born in 1843, at least ten men had been officially executed, four in New South Wales and six in Van Diemen's Land, for the crime of sodomy.

In the Shoalhaven, new lease-holding arrangements saw Berry's land broken up into more manageable family plots, given over to a growing influx of settlers. Berry built family houses on the plots, in exchange for half the produce from each plot being returned to his estate. This division of labour increased the production of butter and cheese.

Families poured their daily milk into large, shallow dishes, where it was left to stand for several hours. The cream was skimmed off the top and put into wooden churns, turned by hand to create butter. Wooden kegs, carrying the butter and cheese, were sent by ship to Sydney. Hygiene and quality were a constant problem: the butter and cheese were washed with whatever water was at hand, and heavily salted. The transport kegs, which were reused over and over, were unsanitary, and the scrapings in the wood ran rank in the summer months.

In 1846, local production was increased by milking cows twice a day, instead of only each morning.

There was no underlying harmony of interests in the colonies. The patterns and codes imported from Britain fractured against the shoals of this strange reality. Conflicts occurred between the colonists and the land, and between the colonists and the first inhabitants of the land, permanently intruded upon. Conflicts occurred within the penal system, between convicts and gaolers, and afterwards between the emancipated seeking equal rights and status and the freeborn and voluntary immigrants. No hard lines existed within these conflicts, wives and children travelling voluntarily to be with their convict or emancipated husbands, convict parents giving birth to freeborn children.

Such was the case with the convict Thomas Keivel and his free wife and children, the first two (including Caroline) born in England, the remaining four in New South Wales. Complications compounded as new generations arrived. As in 1841, when John Boden Yates and Mary had a son, Joseph Thomas Yeates (his last name changed perhaps to distance him from his convict heritage).

Or in 1847, when Caroline and James Lynn had a daughter, Fanny Lynn.

Until 1824, there were only four government newspapers, after which independent newspapers were permitted. They remained subject to various forms of control and censorship, which kept their views within proscribed bounds. They required a licence to operate, for example, which could be withdrawn at will. Libel charges became a useful legal tool to bankrupt precarious editors, shuttering publications in their infancy. The first independent newspaper in 1824, *The Australian* was also the first to have its publisher charged with sedition. *The Australian* never reached more than 800 in circulation, and closed its doors in 1848 due to loss of subscription revenue.

Out of this foment came something of an official narrative, enough to sustain a governing elite and local commercial interests, as long as the threads were not picked over. Beyond this, a much richer oral storytelling culture emerged, one not requiring literacy. It began as anecdotes, spread as rumours, shared as yarns and ended up in song. Cultural fractures welded into simplistic moralities, pitching ordinary people against colonial governments, itinerant working men against the 'squattocracy'.

Between the official narrative of government decrees and newspaper columns and these unofficial oral subplots was a space in which literary fiction and poetry could emerge. Newspapers serialised imported novels, but there were few local publishers, editors or readers who might support the development of a domestic literary culture. Writing fiction and poetry was an individual and private pursuit, among a particular class, and only made public through private means. This accounts for the first collection of short stories in the colonies, *Our First Lieutenant, and Fugitive Pieces, in Prose* by David Burn (Hobart Town, 1842), followed by *Tales for the Bush* by Mary Vidal (Sydney, 1845). Periodicals would sprout and wilt after several issues. The editors were amateurs, enthusiasts driven by passion, quickly exhausted. They did, however, establish a long tradition of not paying contributors.

In Great Britain in 1710, under the Statute of Anne, an author's ownership over their work was first recognised, allowing them to share with printers and booksellers the economic gains from selling their work. The original purpose of the statute was to encourage writing and foster an intellectual and literary culture in England. It was only superseded by various copyright acts, in 1814 and 1842, extending each time the copyright protection of a work – eventually it covered the lifetime of the author plus seven years, or a minimum of forty-two years.

This recognition of an author's copyright stretched throughout the Empire – but only on condition that the work was first published in Britain. Such laws, in their colonial context, became an instrument for promoting imperial ambitions and loyalty to Britain, at the cost of developing a local publishing infrastructure. The effect was to inhibit an Australian intellectual and literary culture from forming. The books of Burn and Vidal, for example, were not covered by these acts.

The *Literary Copyright Act 1842* met with opposition among British publishers, whose businesses were built upon the practice of exporting into the colonies cheap editions of out-of-copyright works (from recently deceased authors) and uncopyrighted works (usually those not first published in Britain, including foreign translations). Factoring in the cost of paying an author led to an increase in production costs, and so the price of books to readers. The new act authorised the customs division of each colony to search for, seize and destroy pirated books or unauthorised foreign reprints. An unintended consequence was the creation of competing book markets: a black market for cheaper imports that eluded customs, and a secondary market for second-hand books. Sales in these markets brought no economic benefit to the original authors.

One response to this situation was the introduction of 'colonial editions' in 1843. These were books published in a uniform series and imported into the colonies. Although they were the same titles available to the domestic British market, colonial editions were cheaper, printed on a lighter-weight paper – which lowered printing and freight costs – and bound in 'colonial cloth', a darkly dyed strawboard or esparto cardboard. Their purpose was to enforce British copyright throughout the Empire, and to counter the importation of foreign and pirated books. In the background was a publishing regime selling such books wholesale to colonial importers at 50 per cent less than the cost of the same works to English booksellers, with a generously extended six-month payment period.

Until then, the lack of publishing infrastructure in the colonies could be seen as the outcome of benign neglect. Colonial assemblies were more focused on maintaining a convict system, developing an agricultural base to sustain that system, and then managing the transition from penal colony to industrious free settlement in the service of Britain. Even so, other colonies such as Canada, New Zealand and India had during the 1830s and 1840s created local copyright legislation, to foster local literary cultures. The Australian colonial authorities persistently thwarted similar attempts and would continue to do so for decades to come.

The successful introduction of legislation recognising and protecting patents, beginning in 1852 in New South Wales, suggested that colonial assemblies understood how incentives for the development of local technical and scientific inventions were linked to the legal protection of those inventions. So when those selfsame assemblies rejected attempts to foster an equivalent publishing infrastructure, it can only be considered as conscious opposition to the development of any local literary culture that might deviate from imperial British ideology.

John Midgley Moorhouse travelled to New Zealand from Liverpool in 1860, at age fifty-three. With him was his eldest son, nineteen-year-old William. Passing through Melbourne, they heard talk of a gold rush, and so soon after arriving in New Zealand they returned to the Australian colonies, William staying to try his luck on the goldfields. His father returned alone to England.

Gold was also discovered in Braidwood in 1851 – a year after the initial rush in Victoria – but this was quickly mined out. One man who followed the gold to Braidwood was Charles Isaac Watson.

Born in 1830 in Parramatta's Female Factory, Watson was the illegitimate son of a convict, Susannah Watson. He was an unsuccessful prospector, but when the gold rush receded, he turned to various newspaper ventures, establishing the Braidwood *Dispatch*, the Braidwood *Observer* and, in 1856, the Braidwood *Daily News* – the first daily newspaper outside Sydney.

In 1861, Watson married a local girl, Eliza Yeates, the older sister of Joseph Thomas Yeates. Their father, John Boden Yates, had died in 1861. Two years later, 22-year-old Joseph Yeates married fifteen-year-old Fanny Lynn, the daughter of James and Caroline Lynn.

Meanwhile, the dairy industry continued to grow in the Shoalhaven. Alexander Berry built a butter factory, using horsepower to churn the cream in bulk. In 1855, five years after the butter factory opened, the first freehold land sale occurred in Nowra. Berry, who had monopolised and benefitted from prior property arrangements, resisted this change.

Newspapers fanned the debate, with libel laws once more used to manage the fallout. In 1859, Reverend John Dunmore Lang wrote two letters to nearby newspapers, the *Mercury* and the *Kiama Examiner* – Shoalhaven did not have a newspaper of its own – arguing that Berry's land ought to be rezoned as a local government area. He referred to Berry as 'The Shoalhaven Incubus', to which Berry took exception, suing Lang and the newspapers in five separate libel actions. The financial damage shuttered the *Examiner* completely. But it was not enough to halt progress.

The Nowra Public School opened in 1862. By then, telegraphy had arrived in the area. Over the next decade, every colony had some form of telegraphy, and many were linked by this rapidly developing technology. Its installation across the landscape was in lockstep with the extension of the railway, the telegraph running along the same routes.

This had an enormous impact on the material and administrative development of the continent, the main users being government, business and the colonial press. By 1867, Charles and Eliza Watson moved to the Shoalhaven and launched the region's first newspaper, *The News, Shoalhaven*. They were involved in building local communities and associated infrastructures. She joined the Ladies' Working Society. He participated in establishing the first savings bank and the first literary society, supported various sporting organisations and advocated for a public library. Following major floods in 1860, 1864, 1865 and 1870, a number of smaller townships folded, their residents migrating to Nowra, which grew accordingly. It was finally incorporated as a government town in 1871.

When the 1870 flood destroyed his stock of black ink, Watson printed the next edition of his newspaper using his reserves of green ink.

An important work of local literature emerged from this period, Marcus Clarke's historical reconstruction of the brutality of the convict system and the origins of the Australian settlement. The first instalment of 'His Natural Life' was published in March 1870, in the pages of *The Australian Journal*, operated by Clarson, Massina & Co. in Victoria. It continued for two and a half years, reaching its conclusion in June 1872.

The year before Clarke's serial launched, Victoria introduced the first Australian copyright legislation. The Victorian *Copyright Act 1869* replicated Britain's *Literary Copyright Act 1842*, except in one detail: the territory in which copyright was protected was limited to the colony of Victoria. Such copyright was not recognised in any other colony in Australia, or indeed anywhere else in the British Empire.

Newspaper publishers retained the copyright of content they commissioned, meaning Clarson, Massina & Co. held the copyright in Clarke's serial novel – albeit only in the colony of Victoria. But a distinction could be made between the serial and book forms of a novel, if there were enough substantive changes between the two forms to establish each as a different work. So when Melbourne bookseller and publisher George Robertson agreed to publish Clarke's serial as a book, Clarke spent two years revising the manuscript, halving the word count and substantially altering the story.

Clarke secured the copyright to his own work in 1874 – but again only in Victoria.

In 1875, *His Natural Life* was published in England by Richard Bentley and Son. As the book was first published outside of England, Clarke's Victorian copyright was not recognised and Bentley asserted his own copyright claim upon publication. Bentley used the title as the first in his new collection of colonial editions distributed throughout the Empire, including the Australian colonies, where his version of Clarke's book competed with the Victorian edition – and overwhelmingly outsold it. Consequently, no royalties went to Clarke for his own book being a bestseller in his own country. Robertson, as both a bookseller and importer of books, continued to earn from the sale of both editions of Clarke's book.

When Clarke died in 1881, at age thirty-five, he was financially ruined, even as his work continued to sell. One month after his death, Clarson, Massina & Co. reprinted 'His Natural Life' in *The Australian Journal*, the first instalment running one month after Clarke's death. They reprinted the serial novel twice more, from September 1886 and from June 1913, flexing their original copyright. By the time of the second reprint, Clarke's widow and children were destitute. The Victorian Legislative Assembly placed £1000 in trust for the family, in recognition of Marcus Clarke's literary esteem.

Clarke is portrayed as a bohemian figure, a heavy drinker who was never good with money and who lived beyond his means – and this, more than anything else, contributed to the fact that, when he died young, he left his family near poverty. But his means were severely constricted by the copyright conditions, the imperial publishing regime, political neglect, social obstruction and the lack of adequate local literary infrastructure. It would be more correct to say Clarke's talent reached beyond the capacity of his own society to justly reward that talent.

Over the two and a half years readers followed the original serial publication of 'His Natural Life', they also followed the equally arduous saga of the construction of the Overland Telegraph Line between Adelaide and Darwin, from there to connect with Indonesia. In October 1872, the Australian colonies were telegraphically connected to the world. In June 1875 New South Wales and New Zealand began working together on a shared telegraph line, with the trans-Tasman link coming into operation the following February.

So enamoured were people by this new technology that the word 'telegraph' began to be used in dispatches and mastheads – such as *The Daily Telegraph,* launched in Sydney in 1879 – to signal the new and efficient, the medium itself promoted as integral to the message and its social value. As news agencies, government and business – along with private messages – began spreading more quickly around the British Empire, so too did people.

Around this time, the Moorhouse family made a permanent move to New Zealand from England. In 1865, 22-year-old David Addeman Moorhouse – the fifth child of John Midgley and Hannah Moorhouse – had married 28-year-old Ellen Curtis. Together, they had six children. The first, born in 1866, was Frederick Curtis Moorhouse, and the fifth, born in 1877, was David Moorhouse. In 1881, fourteen-year-old Frederick and his father travelled to New Zealand.

The rest of the family followed: Ellen and the remaining five children, along with the grandfather, John Midgley Moorhouse, and his second wife, Mary. Typhoid fever struck during their gruelling 234-day trip, and so, when they finally made landfall in January 1882, they were placed in quarantine. One of their children died from the fever. It was an inauspicious start to their new life in New Zealand.

They moved to Rangiora, on the South Island. John became a farmer, David a cattle dealer and Frederick a horse trainer. In 1883, a family dispute erupted between John and David. The father had defrayed the costs of bringing the extended family out from England, on the understanding that his son would repay him after they settled. But the family was not prospering, and the unpaid debt became a point of contention. The situation remained unsettled in

1884 when the patriarch fell from a straw cart pulled by a dray and died. He left his estate to one of his daughters in England, and not to his son and family in New Zealand.

In 1880, John Archibald and John Haynes set up shop on Castlereagh Street, Sydney, where they wrote, edited and printed a weekly paper called *The Bulletin*. It was originally going to be called *The Lone Hand*, a reference to the itinerant bush workers between whom the newspaper aimed to create a sense of solidarity, regardless of where they were across the continent. It very nearly did not survive its first year, as it was the target of a libel action.

One figure who made repeated appearances in *The Bulletin* in its early years was Charles Watson, of *The Shoalhaven News*. On one occasion, the Sydney paper reported that Watson had been 'fined at the local police court for having used abusive language to a policeman'. When Watson died in 1886, aged fifty-six, an obituary appeared in *The Bulletin*, declaring that 'as a journalist he had many enemies, but as a private citizen he was much esteemed by the thousands with whom he was acquainted', and that Watson was 'remarkable for his outspokenness, and was eternally in trouble with his many journals – in the matter of libel actions he was undoubtedly top scorer'. And the highest esteem, for *The Bulletin*, regarding Watson's character: 'the weary tramp was never known to pass his office unassisted'.

The same year Watson died in Shoalhaven, two Scotsmen in Sydney entered into a partnership to run a bookshop. George Robertson and David Angus met while working in the Sydney division of a bookshop owned by George Robertson (no relation) from Melbourne – the publisher of the Victorian edition of *His Natural Life*. In 1884 Angus started a rival bookshop, and was joined later by Robertson. And so, in 1886, Angus & Robertson was born.

That year saw two advances in copyright law, influencing the prospects of both *The Bulletin* and Angus & Robertson. The Berne Convention for the Protection of Literary and Artistic Works was an international treaty designed to harmonise, coordinate and reciprocate copyright between nations. It included the British Empire, but not the United States of America. Britain also enacted the *International Copyright Act 1886*, which, finally, recognised the copyright of works first published in each of the colonies within the Empire. Together with the Berne Convention, this provided copyright protection for Australian colonial authors across much of the world – in theory, at least.

Such acts and agreements aided the sale and distribution of British books outside the Empire, but it was the reciprocal influx of foreign literature that caused concern. One way this was dealt with was through increasing censorship. Since early in the nineteenth century, societies in Britain opposed to vice had grown in influence, populated by clergy, businessmen, lawyers and civil servants. In 1829 the first Vice Squad was established within the police service to aid and abet the moral vigilantism of these societies.

In 1857 such activities were legitimated under the *Obscene Publications Act*. 'Obscenity', however, remained undefined in law. In practice, the act was only arbitrarily applied, used as a tool for class control, to curb certain sexual instincts among an uncouth working class, to preserve conventional family structures and to protect the Empire from foreign influence.

An important development in 1868 was the introduction of what became known as the Hicklin test. In a ruling against a religious pamphlet, the intent of a publication was deemed irrelevant; what mattered was how a work could be interpreted and, alternatively, used 'to deprave and corrupt those whose minds are open to such immoral influences, and into whose hands a publication of this sort might fall'. The Hicklin test left the definition of 'obscenity' to the discretion of individual magistrates, providing a justification for arbitrary decisions to be reached. The removal of intent as a defence against obscenity meant works of scientific or educational intent could also be suppressed, alongside openly pornographic material. Literature became suspect.

In this climate, in 1887, a shipment of novels by Émile Zola was seized on the Melbourne docks. The customs minister was authorised to seize and destroy obscene material, but after some prevarication the books were allowed through. But matters were about to change. The very next year, in England, the publisher Henry Vizetelly was charged with obscenity over his English translations of Zola's novels. He was fined and ordered not to publish the books in their unexpurgated form. The following year he was back before the court, for his expurgated Zola translations as well as his translation of, among other French novels, Gustave Flaubert's *Madame Bovary*. He was fined and jailed for three months.

Only a few weeks after the second trial, the customs department in Melbourne seized another consignment of French novels. News of the Vizetelly trial had arrived via telegraph more quickly than the ship carrying the cargo of foreign literature. This time the offending books were immediately destroyed. The door had been opened for customs to assert more fully their search, seize and destroy powers.

The Shearers' Strike of 1891 was telegraphed across the continent and did much to galvanise the union movement in Australia, and aided, later, the formation of the Australian Labor Party.

The early 1890s was a period of economic depression, exacerbating the plight of working men and their families. Print workers and compositors were often in union and strike leadership roles, and they were among the hardest hit. William Lane wrote his 1892 novel *The Workingman's Paradise* to raise funds for unionists, and to propagandise for the movement, and founded the newspaper *The Worker*, published out of Brisbane and Wagga Wagga.

This convergence of unionism, print technology and telegraphy was a boon to *The Bulletin*. During that same decade, political elites from each of the colonies met, in a series of constitutional conventions, to discuss federating into a collection of states under a national constitution. *The Bulletin* was undertaking a similar project, but from the bottom up and in a more populist style. Its journalists papered over the complexities and unresolved conflicts of the previous century, channelling them into a simplified, coherent set of figures that readers could be either for or against. The white working man and his family were on the positive side, and the British monarchy, political elites and the bosses were on the other. On the other side too were non-white people, especially Chinese immigrants and First Nations people. *The Bulletin* would soon adopt variations of the motto 'Australia for the White Man'.

The Bulletin tapped into the oral culture of the country, giving it the imprimatur of the official print culture, while at the same time challenging its authority. The paper turned the vernacular into a mass media. The tone was irreverent and gossipy. The critic A.G. Stephens joined *The Bulletin* in 1894, establishing the Red Page, a literary supplement that gave locally produced literature a prominent place. The literary forms favoured were the ballad and the short story, the heirs of oral poetry, bush songs and a culture of oral yarns. A stock of characters, situations and motifs informed each.

Behind the irreverence and spiteful humour of its public image, the serious intent of *The Bulletin* was reflected in its editorial discipline and tireless efforts to professionalise writing and publishing. This was its lasting impact. The publication sought submissions from its readers, rejecting much of it but providing writers with reasons for that judgement, as well as advice and encouragement. What was included in its pages went through a rigorous editing process, developing local talent. Archibald's writing credo was: 'Be terse; give forceful word-pictures; and omit as many words as you can. Edit your work severely.' Most importantly, *The Bulletin* gave Australian writers an appreciative, if self-congratulatory, audience.

Such efforts were reinforced by the agenda of Angus & Robertson, which began unabashedly publishing books from Australian authors who had already proven themselves in the pages of *The Bulletin*. Angus & Robertson shared *The Bulletin*'s professionalism, especially with regard to marketing.

One early success for Angus & Robertson was *The Man from Snowy River and Other Verses* in 1895, by Andrew Barton 'Banjo' Paterson, who epitomised *The Bulletin*'s ballad tradition. The title poem from this collection was first published in 1890, when he was twenty-six years old.

The short-story tradition emerging from *The Bulletin* was epitomised by Henry Lawson. He was born in 1867 – one year after Frederick Moorhouse – on the goldfields at Grenfell, New South Wales. In 1887, Henry's mother, Louisa, ran a newspaper called *The Republican*, where Henry had his first taste of journalism; eventually he co-edited the paper with her. In 1888, he had his first short story published in *The Bulletin*. So at just twenty-one years old, Henry Lawson was already a published short-story writer, a journalist, and newspaper editor. His most famous collection of stories and sketches, *While the Billy Boils*, was published in 1896 by Angus & Robertson.

After the death of John Midgley Moorhouse, the family continued to struggle in New Zealand. David tried to make the farm work, while Ellen supplemented their income by operating a roadside eatery called 'Mrs Moorhouse's A.1. Dining Rooms'. In October 1890, David was charged with stealing horses. The following year he was fined for grazing cattle on somebody else's land, and when he refused to pay the fine he was again taken to court, compounding his financial difficulties. Then, in March 1892, he was charged with stealing two cows.

That same year, in Sydney, Henry Lawson also struggled. John Archibald paid for him to travel to inland New South Wales, surveying the social and economic degradation caused by the recent drought. These experiences gave Henry a store of material to write about in various stories, sketches and poems.

Adding to his stock of experience were his sojourns to New Zealand. In November 1893, Henry Lawson joined nearly 10,000 unemployed Australians who were crossing the Tasman in search of work. He arrived in Auckland, and made his way down to Wellington in time to witness New Zealand women voting for the first time. He travelled the country, working as a house painter and as a linesman, installing the telegraph. Single men were often passed over for jobs in favour of married men, and New Zealanders chosen over Australians. In Australia, workers protected themselves against foreigners taking local jobs, but in New Zealand the Australians *were* the foreigners.

Henry was ready to leave by July 1894, and so was excited to receive a job offer in Sydney, editing the *Daily Worker* newspaper, an offshoot of William Lane's *The Worker*. It was to be published daily, but only for a limited period, in the lead-up to the New South Wales election. By the time the offer found Henry in New Zealand, the details were lost, so when he returned to Sydney he was too late. The election was over. He was offered a provisional position editing *The Worker* in Wagga, after which he became a regular contributor.

Henry left New Zealand the same month David Addeman Moorhouse, pushed to the limit and with creditors swarming, abandoned his family, absconding with the last of their savings. He was never seen again. Ellen Moorhouse, with her five surviving children, faced the creditors and was forced to sell the farm and all their assets. She was permitted to keep their furniture and her diner. She was helped by Frederick, her eldest son, who a few months earlier had married a local girl. By the time of his parents' bankruptcy, she was pregnant; they would have a son, Frederick Jr.

Frederick Moorhouse was also in financial difficulty. In 1896, he too declared bankruptcy. That year, Henry Lawson travelled again to New Zealand, returning to Australia almost immediately to marry Bertha Bredt Jr. The following year, after Angus & Robertson published *While the Billy Boils*, Henry and Bertha travelled back to New Zealand, with Henry telling the press he was leaving Australia for a long time, maybe forever. This was an effort to escape his drinking haunts in Sydney, to get his life in order.

They arrived in Wellington, where Henry was offered a job in Kaikōura, on the South Island, as a schoolteacher for a Māori community. He lasted six months. He was unsuited to the job, his partial deafness – the result of a childhood illness – compounding his social distance from the children and their community. There were no nearby pubs in which he might find solace, and he was unsuited to domestic life. He sank into a deep depression.

Bertha had become pregnant before he took up the job, which only increased the marital tensions. Their son, Jim, was born in Wellington in February, and as soon as mother and son were well enough to travel, they returned, defeated, to Sydney. There, Henry fell back into old patterns, and by November 1898 he was installed in a home for inebriates.

That year Frederick Moorhouse's wife died. He left his infant son with relatives and went looking for work in Wanganui, on the west coast. The township, on the Whanganui River, was once a major Māori settlement. The first European traders had arrived in 1831, followed by missionaries in 1840, collecting signatures for the Treaty of Waitangi. That same year a town was established, becoming Wanganui in 1854.

Meanwhile, Frederick's younger brother, David Moorhouse, was working on the North Island. When his father abandoned the family and they lost the house and farm, he headed north in search of work, ending up at a sawmill near Woodville. He drank at a local hotel, where he met the proprietor's daughter, a waitress named Ethel May Osborne. She was the same age as David, but born in New Zealand to Welsh parents.

When in 1898 David heard of his older brother's move to Wanganui, he travelled to join him. Ethel followed soon after, the expectation being she would marry David. But for reasons unknown, it was his brother Frederick, eleven years her senior, whom Ethel ended up marrying.

Joseph Thomas Yeates and Fanny Lynn had been married in Braidwood in 1863. Over the years they had fourteen children – including, in 1869, a daughter named Mary Caroline Yeates. When Mary was fifteen years old, she was sent to Balmain, in Sydney, to work as a servant girl and cook. In 1894, 25-year-old Mary Caroline Yeates married London-born Thomas George Cutts, ten years her senior. Cutts was a fireman. After they married in Balmain, he was transferred to a station in Pyrmont. Firemen lived at the station houses, in single men's or married quarters. In 1901 – the year of

Australia's Federation – Mary and George had their first and only child, Purthanry Thanes Mary Cutts. They called her Purth.

The family moved wherever the fire service sent George Cutts, and Purth went to infant school in Crows Nest, primary school in Stanmore, then middle school in Mosman. At middle school, she became the editor of the school newspaper, which was handwritten rather than printed. She grew up to be methodical and deliberate in both action and bearing. Her parents were the same way, a fire station needing to be a well organised space, with no obstructions or distractions. It was no place for a child to play. Before her father went to bed each night he laid out his clothes and boots such that if the fire bell sounded in the night, he could leap out of bed and be dressed, ready for action, as efficiently as possible.

In 1908, in England, Lord Robert Baden-Powell had started the Boy Scouts, transferring what he had learned during the Boer War to building the character of boys. Scouting groups appeared in Australia, New Zealand and India by the end of that first year. In 1910, Agnes Baden-Powell, Lord Robert's sister, formed the Girl Guides, adapting the training program for girls, with the first branch in Australia starting in 1911. Purthanry Cutts, in Mosman, became involved with the Guides soon after they formed in New South Wales.

A branch of the British Red Cross was established in Australia in 1914, nine days after the start of the Great War. By November that year, New South Wales had 337 branches, including a Shoalhaven–Nowra branch. Mrs Cutts and her teenage daughter, Purth, were among the thousands of Australian women involved with the Red Cross during the war.

At the same time, Purth started a job as a counter girl at Farmer's Department Store, a Sydney institution established in 1839 as a drapery business before it grew into a retail empire. Located on Pitt Street, Farmer's would later expand to incorporate several buildings behind a single facade. Angus & Robertson originally occupied part of the same block. Purth walked by there each day, to and from work. She stayed at Farmer's for the next six years. The store had so many people working there that it became its own community. There was a choir group, for example, which Purth joined.

It was in Mosman that another national civic organisation was born. Dr Richard Arthur, a local doctor, started writing articles in 1904, advocating for women on the land, for their health and social wellbeing. After the war, he pushed for a bush conference for country women. In 1921, Florence Gordon joined in Dr Arthur's crusade, and in April 1922 a five-day conference was held in Sydney, at Castlereagh Street. Within six days of this conference, the first Country Women's Association (CWA) had formed. Six months later, there were sixty-eight branches across the country. They established restrooms, spaces where country women could meet when they came to town. It was a place for respite, where women could socialise with other women with similar experiences, overcome the isolation of their situation, and plan and organise social and political activities. This included advocating for an improved water supply, electricity, and a telephone service – communications technology being the very heart of any community, particularly one spread out over a large regional area.

Recuperating in Sydney in late 1898, Henry Lawson penned a bitter indictment of the conditions facing Australian writers. In '"Pursuing Literature" in Australia', published in *The Bulletin* in January 1899, he argued that publishing practices in the colonies conspired against writers earning a just living from their literary efforts. Over the previous twelve years he had earned less than half the living wage of the very workingmen he defended in his writing. Many newspapers still did not pay for material, others only a bare minimum. The broader problem was 'clipping', in which material from one publication would be reprinted in another publication without consent or payment. Technically, writers had copyright protection, but practically it was unenforceable.

Domestic book publishing was not much better. Two options for an author were to make a one-off sale and transfer of their rights to the publisher, or to contract their rights to the publisher for a fixed amount per copy sold. The former option was the norm, as writers usually sought payment to cover their immediate needs. They could not afford to wait for payment on sales, which could take months or even years to come through. Publishers took advantage of this situation. Henry Lawson, for example, sold the rights of his first two books – including *While the Billy Boils* – to Angus & Robertson but thereafter made no money from these books' great success during his lifetime.

Having a book published first in Australia was still a disadvantage for an Australian writer. Regardless of recent copyright acts, which theoretically protected the rights of any Commonwealth writer, the Publishers' Association of Great Britain and Ireland prohibited Australian writers from publishing in Great Britain if they had a prior publishing contract in the colonies. And even here colonial writers were disadvantaged: after 1894, the standard rate offered to Australian writers on colonial editions was four pence per book sold, while English writers were offered eleven pence.

An Australian writer's options were limited. In '"Pursuing Literature" in Australia', Lawson weighed these options:

> My advice to any young Australian writer whose talents have been recognised, would be to go steerage, stow away, swim, and seek London, Yankeeland, or Timbuctoo – rather than stay in Australia till his genius turned to gall, or beer. Or, failing this – and still in the interests of human nature and literature – to study elementary anatomy, especially as applies to the cranium, and then shoot himself carefully with the aid of a looking glass.

Following Federation, the Australian parliament passed the *Copyright Act 1905*, accepting UK copyright as domestic law. Technically, this provided parity for Australian writers within the Commonwealth, but in practice the prior imbalances continued.

This situation was recognised by an informal meeting in 1907 of influential men, who discussed what assistance could be provided to poor writers and their families. This led to the creation of the

Australian Men of Letters Fund, which, a year later, under the auspices of the federal government, became the Commonwealth Literary Fund. On the proposal of the bill, the federal member for Parramatta said: 'It is our first recognition – and a very small one – of Australian Literature and as such we should pass it unanimously.'

Although the Commonwealth Literary Fund would, for several decades to come, award pensions to elderly, sick or otherwise impoverished Australian writers of note, little was done to alleviate, or even to begin to consider, the underlying conditions that meant such a fund was required in the first place, or why writers in Australia generally remained impoverished.

In December 1902, Henry Lawson attempted suicide. The previous year he had published *Joe Wilson and His Mates*, which contained a story called 'The Loaded Dog', a farce about a dog fetching a stick of dynamite, its owner and friends fleeing the playful dog. It showed that Lawson was still able to write humour even as his own world was collapsing around him.

Meanwhile, in New Zealand, Frederick and Ethel Moorhouse had three children together. The firstborn, in 1904, was Frank Osborne Moorhouse, followed by Sylvia and Leslie, at two-year intervals. Frederick was a dairy farmer who had continuing financial troubles. Like Henry Lawson in Australia, he turned to drink. Dr John Anderson, who knew Frederick for about five years, said he was 'a morbid kind of man constantly worrying'.

In Sydney, legally separated from his wife, Henry Lawson was often gaoled for not paying child maintenance, which he could not afford to do. From 1907 he was regularly admitted into various mental hospitals. Otherwise, he haunted the Sydney streets and pubs, bumming a drink from his ever dwindling circle of friends, a loaded dog of sorts himself.

For much of 1909, Frederick Moorhouse was also unwell, in body and mind. He had trouble sleeping and worried over money matters. Ethel said he was 'low spirited'. He thought he was going to die. On 4 August, after several days without sleep, he went to bed, but could not sleep. He told Ethel he was hypnotised and someone was willing him to leave the house and go to town. At 2 am, he dressed and walked out of the house in which his children were sleeping. Ethel followed him for about a quarter of a mile, but when he discovered her following him he started running from her, into the dark of the night. That was the last time she saw him.

Frederick went into town and broke into the Masonic Hotel. The breaking glass had awoken the licensee, who called the police. Frederick was handcuffed, taken into custody and charged with helpless drunkenness, based on his behaviour. Strangely, the constable later recounted, he 'never smelt of liquor'.

The following afternoon, Anderson came to see him in the gaol, later reporting that Frederick said 'some impulse had come over him'. He was prescribed a sleeping draught and some pills, which the gaoler was told to give him around 7 pm. But at around 5 pm Frederick started hammering on his cell door, wanting to get out. The gaoler called upon two other prisoners to help him move Frederick into a padded cell. He was not violent, and allowed them to remove his boots and braces. At 6.30 pm, he was given a sleeping draught, and a mattress, blankets and a pillow were put in the cell with him.

'Here's to good health,' said Frederick. 'You all seemed very much concerned about me tonight – I'm all right.'

At 6.10 am the next morning Frederick was found off the mattress, his feet facing the door, his shirt tied tightly around his neck. The body of the shirt was at the front, the sleeves wrapped twice around his neck and knotted at the front. Frederick Moorhouse was forty-five years old. 'Deceased strangled himself whilst temporarily insane,' the inquest concluded.

In Australia, Henry Lawson likewise spiralled. In 1910, he was once more committed to a mental hospital. His condition worsened. In 1920 the Commonwealth Literary Fund provided him with a pension of £1 per week. He died two years later, on 2 September 1922, from a cerebral haemorrhage.

Nowra Public School established its first classroom library in 1902: a few shelves, a few dozen books. It was an important enough milestone to warrant an opening ceremony and speeches, with Mr Bridges, the Chief Inspector of Schools, stating: 'There could be no thinker without a reader, and as they learnt from their school books, *reading maketh the man*.'

The flipside was a growing concern that the wrong types of books could undo the man, morally. Since the 1880s each colony had become more vigilant, with customs blocking, as best as they could, obscene, offensive or blasphemous literature. The 1904 *Report of the New South Wales Royal Commission on the Decline of the Birth Rate* claimed the nation was 'wallowing in obscene literature' and 'preventives to conception'. Customs banned imported contraception devices, but also literature that drew undue attention to the natural functions of the human body, which was seen as leading to sex or crime or both. Unofficial forms of censorship proved successful. Libraries, churches and schools made available the right sort of material, and made admonitions against the wrong sort, while temperance and vice societies sought out and condemned deviant behaviours. Positive behaviours were modelled by such civic organisations as the Scouts and Girl Guides, the Red Cross, Rotary and the CWA.

Such 'deviant' behaviours included homosexuality. Although the last man officially executed for the crime of sodomy was in 1863, the death penalty remained on the books in New South Wales until the *Criminal Law Amendment Act 1883*. There were publicised arrests in Hyde Park during the 1870s, an early beat. In the 1890s, following the arrest and trial of Oscar Wilde in England, a salacious interest of the Sydney gutter press was to point out streets and parks where such men were known to gather. Violence against these men, including murder, often went unreported, uncharged or misclassified. Homosexuality was still considered a criminal act in New South Wales, with the *Crimes Act 1900* consolidating the laws against same-sex male relations.

These laws were accompanied by forms of censorship that assumed such sexual activities would be diminished if they were not directly written or read about. When Louis Becke and Walter Jeffery, for example, published *Admiral Phillip: The Founding of New South Wales* in 1899, they cited the letter Arthur Phillip had written to Lord Sydney in 1787, censoring it so the word 'sodomy' was replaced: 'there are two crimes that would merit death – murder and another'. The word itself could no longer be uttered, as if this perlocutionary act erased an undesirable reality. Certain four-letter words – such as 'damn', but even 'blast' or 'lousy' – were banned from print in the 1890s. Usually a dash or a blank space was used instead of the word 'bloody'. *The Bulletin* coined 'blanky' as an awkward substitute.

In 1910, the Agreement for the Suppression of Obscene Publications was enacted, by which nations in Europe and elsewhere would cooperate in limiting the international trade of obscene literature. It provided further justification for what the Australian federal government was already doing.

In literary terms, *The Bulletin* did much to establish professionalism, editorial guidance and critical feedback among Australian writers, and to develop and promote local literary talent – even as they, along with Angus & Robertson, exploited that talent. Yet this new approach quickly solidified as a set of stale literary conventions that otherwise restricted the range and scope of characters, situations and emotions permitted in print. As with all conventions, though, *The Bulletin*'s also stood as a model from which an innovative writer could deviate. One figure who did so was Joseph Furphy.

Furphy was born to Irish immigrant parents in Victoria in 1843, one year after his brother, John Furphy. As children, they were taught to read, write and recite from both the Bible and Shakespeare. When they were in their early twenties, Joseph took up farming, while John, completing an apprenticeship, began a blacksmithing and wheelwright business. When the farm failed, Joseph became a bullock-driver in the Riverina, transporting between New South Wales and Victoria. Meanwhile, John added a furnace and established an iron foundry, adapting agricultural machinery to the tough local conditions. He invented new implements and contraptions, which he patented and manufactured in the foundry.

When the 1883 drought ended Joseph's tenure as a bullock-driver, he – unemployed at last – returned to Shepparton and found work in his brother's foundry. By night he wrote stories, as much essays as works of narrative fiction, based on his experiences in the Riverina but also incorporating his reflections on those experiences. The motifs and characters and events he wrote about suggested further yarns, further ideas, which he finally, by 1897, federated into a manuscript nearly 1200 pages in length. Here was a storytelling about the need for storytelling.

Furphy had published in *The Bulletin* – his favourite Australian writer was Henry Lawson – so he wrote to A.G. Stephens, inquiring how to get his manuscript published.

Stephens' reply: 'Send the animal for inspection.'

The work was titled *Such Is Life*. Stephens loved it, but Archibald hated it, for obvious reasons: the manuscript violated every one of his rules for writing, overturned every convention upon which *The Bulletin* stood. The book was passed over by other publishers, in part because of four chapters considered politically extreme, in which Furphy advocated for a radical form of socialism in Australia.

Furphy also nudged against the limits of censorship. In writing dialogue, he replaced four-letter words with phrases such as '(adj.)' or '(irrelevant expletive)', or else the narrator used circumlocution to draw attention to the otherwise absented or suppressed words. Characters spoke with 'unprintable emphasis' or 'with a similar potency of adjective'. Instead of omitting an obscenity or passing over it with a brief, embarrassed substitute, Furphy lingered over the moment, drawing it out, forcing the reader to ventriloquise the omitted words, with their sexual or scatological connotations, whether they wanted to or not. He also pushed against the limits of sexual and gender proprieties: the protagonist's male horse was named Cleopatra, while a character introduced as a man might later be revealed as a woman, cross-dressed. Nosey Alf, a boundary-rider, turns out to be Molly, and Jim becomes Miss Jemima.

There is a crooked path that leads from Rabelais in the fifteenth century, Montaigne and Cervantes in the sixteenth century, Laurence Sterne in the eighteenth and Herman Melville in the nineteenth centuries to the work of Joseph Furphy, which he adapted to the tough Australian conditions, inventing a few new linguistic implements and literary contraptions along the way. Furphy took the literary landscape of Henry Lawson and Banjo Paterson, popped the rivets off their texts and revealed the discontinuities that lurked beneath this burgeoning national literature. An expurgated version of *Such Is Life* was finally released by *The Bulletin* in 1903. Stephens had won, with some concessions, but Archibald was initially vindicated: the book sold poorly and *The Bulletin* lost money. Meanwhile, John Furphy's manufacturing business continued to grow.

The two brothers' circumstances starkly showed the difference between the effectiveness of various legislative regimes. A strong patent system advantaged the growth of one local industry, while a copyright and publishing regime disadvantaged another. Joseph Furphy's literary career confirmed what his contemporary Lawson and their forebear Marcus Clarke knew only too well. Australia was no place to make a living in literature.

In 1886 – the year Charles Watson died – the first linotype printing machines arrived. Soon after, in Nowra, newspapers were being printed with this new technology on Kinghorne Street, and later on Junction Street. Watson's son, Charles Watson Jr, had worked on the family newspapers in Braidwood and Kiama, so when his father died he moved to Nowra to take over the whole enterprise.

The area was rapidly developing and the newspapers had much to report on. The longstanding method of separating cream from the whey, by placing milk in large trays, was based on the assumption that cream floated to the top, where it could be skimmed off. But cream is made of fat globules, lighter than the rest of the milk, and so it is more the case that the whey sinks to the bottom. This led to the invention, in Sweden in 1878 by Gustaf de Laval, of a machine that used centrifugal force to separate cream more efficiently and more thoroughly than previous methods, resulting in a purer product, in less time, with less effort. The first Laval cream separator arrived in Australia in 1882. Two years later, Shoalhaven had its first large-scale, steam-powered cream separator.

Primitive refrigeration and the manufacture of ice had since been developed in Australia, with dairy and milk products now being transported without needing to be heavily salted. A bridge was finally constructed over the Shoalhaven River, and by the early 1890s a railway line ran from Berry, on the north side of the river, direct to Sydney. The transportation of dairy products could now take hours by rail instead of days by ship.

But during this period of rapid expansion and technological efficiency, one challenging aspect remained: the milking of cows was still done by hand. Even as mechanical milking machines became available, Australian dairy farmers objected that the machines had a deleterious effect on the cows, injured the udders and affected the quality of the milk. These concerns had been proven unwarranted, but dairymen remained unconvinced. They continued to milk by hand, holding back the industry.

Another by-product of refrigeration was the growth in various drinks products. By 1879 Nowra newspapers were carrying advertisements for a local cordial and aerated drink, manufactured out of premises on Kinghorne Street. Over the next decades, other cordial and soft drink factories opened on the same street. By 1911 these various factories had merged to create the Nowra Cordial & Ice Works, which became a mainstay in the district for the next several decades.

In 1896, moving pictures came to Australia, first demonstrated in Nowra the following year. The early projectors were hand-operated, like the old butter churns. Over the coming years, advances in cinema technology were advertised, as much as the content of the films, to promote moving pictures. In 1908 a short film was made based upon Marcus Clarke's *His Natural Life*, and in 1911 a feature film based upon the play adaptation of the novel was produced.

In 1918, the first cinema in Nowra, the Crown Theatre, was constructed. Until 1914, *The Shoalhaven News* was published each Saturday, and *The Nowra Colonist* each Wednesday. That April he combined the two into a larger weekly edition of *The Shoalhaven News*, consolidating the business, before selling it and retiring.

Soon after the death of Frederick Moorhouse, his younger brother, David, moved in with Ethel, to help raise his niece and nephews. In November 1911 they married, and together they had five more children. But David shared his brother's disposition, his low spirits and his drinking. He became increasingly abusive towards his brother's three children.

Frank Osborne Moorhouse was only five years old in 1909, when his father died. As a child he never knew the circumstances: suicide was not spoken about. One of his earliest memories, a year before his father's death, was his father taking him to the moving picture shows at Hayward's Theatre in Wanganui. He was fascinated by the lights, his first electrical experience.

The year his mother and uncle married, Frank enrolled in Queen's Park School. The family still had the dairy farm. Unlike Australian dairy farmers, those in New Zealand had embraced milking machines. The efficiency of these mechanical milkers meant Frank had time to deliver milk before and after school. He was shy but could forget himself when he became involved in a task, and he could get others involved as well. He organised his schoolfriends to help him with his milk deliveries.

When not in school or working on the farm, he explored the countryside on his own, in part to escape the oppressive atmosphere at home. In 1917, after six years of schooling, he graduated from Queen's Park. Thirteen years old, he rode a horse eight miles into town, one evening a week, to attend night school at the Wanganui Technical College. He started a correspondence course in electrical engineering. At home, he studied electricity by candlelight; the power lines had not yet reached the family farm.

When he graduated, Frank Osborne Moorhouse was only the fourth licensed electrician in New Zealand. He secured an apprenticeship at C.H. Davis & Co., Electrical & Mechanical Engineers and Dairy Experts. The proprietor, Charles Davis, was an Australian. Like John Furphy, Davis had started out as a blacksmith, but then became an engineer and an inventor. Davis had invented the milking machines Frank used as a child, the same machines he now worked on and helped install as an apprentice.

After his apprenticeship, Frank's first job was as an assistant engineer at the Wanganui Base Hospital. The hospital had previously generated its own electricity, but after the hydroelectric Mangahao Power Station opened in 1923, the hospital needed rewiring, retrofitted for the new energy source. Frank's introduction to charitable work, meanwhile, was installing gratis electricity at a local community centre.

Nettie and Vance Palmer were married in 1914, in England. Both were born in 1885. Vance came of age reading *The Bulletin* at the peak of its influence. He was a pupil of A.G. Stephens, who in 1901 had edited the anthology collection *The Bulletin Story Book*. 'The literary work which is Australian in spirit, as well as in scene or incident, is only beginning to be written,' Stephens wrote, noting the poor economic conditions for Australian writers. 'A mere two or three of them have been able to earn a living by the profession of literature, and even these have been obliged to make the perilous compromise with journalism.'

In 1905, the nineteen-year-old Vance Palmer had published 'An Australian National Art', which reiterated Stephens' position – and the general ethos of *The Bulletin* – while also outlining the principles Palmer would pursue for the rest of his life. He called for Australian writers to be 'ardent nationalists', culturally speaking, avoiding the negative nationalism of the previous generation.

In England, the Palmers associated with various modernist writers, including Katherine Mansfield. Born in 1888 in New Zealand,

Mansfield worked in the short story form, publishing three collections, absorbing the early modernist experiments, and the work of Oscar Wilde, which she fused with her own experiences growing up in New Zealand. Her writing inquired into the interior nature of individuality, gender and sexuality – including same-sex desire, which she alternately embraced and suppressed throughout her short life, the accompanying anxiety providing the atmosphere for many of her stories. She associated with the Bloomsbury Group, especially D.H. Lawrence. They shared an interest in Freudian psychoanalysis. In 1917, Mansfield was diagnosed with tuberculosis, dying in 1923, the same year a final collection of her short stories was published.

D.H. Lawrence published *Kangaroo* in 1923. He was the same age as Vance and Nettie Palmer. The previous year, Lawrence and his wife, Frieda, travelled to Australia, settling for three months in Thirroul, 55 miles (90 kilometres) north of Nowra. There he wrote most of *Kangaroo*, about a character, Benjamin Cooley – nicknamed 'Kangaroo' – an ex-soldier and lawyer, and leader of the Diggers Club, a secret, proto-fascist, anti-communist militia.

As a portrait of Australian society two decades after Federation, *Kangaroo* was unflattering: it was a culture anaemic and shallow. Lawrence's sense of cultural declension drew on his recent experiences in Europe, where Mussolini had come to power in Italy. Although the secret right-wing militia Lawrence sketched in his novel was a transposition of European fascism, it reflected real undercurrents in Australia, the novel prefiguring such groups as the Australia First Movement, the seeds of which were sown in the late 1930s, when in some circles admiration for Mussolini had given way to admiration for Hitler.

After Federation, individuals wanted to know what was happening across the country during any given day or week. The Great War broadened those horizons to include international affairs. The communications technology facilitating this curiosity, creating this sense of a shared reality, was only enhanced when publications adapted themselves to commercial imperatives, and the optimal relationship between advertising, circulation and revenue.

The scope and focus of newspapers were levelled to the capacities of the average person, who wanted a general sense of everything happening, at a glance, on their way to work. The structure and layout of newspapers became like Farmer's Department Store, where Purthanry Cutts still worked: the best wares in the window display, drawing customers in, and an internal layout designed to keep them moving through, lured by novelty and excitement. By the 1920s, it was clear that the average person who consumed these publications was not so much the husband, who worked and made the money, but the wife, who spent the money according to the needs of the household budget. The husband might read the newspapers first, but it was the wife who lingered over its pages – and advertisements – longer.

This culminated in June 1933 with the launch of *The Australian Women's Weekly*, published by Frank Packer's Sydney Newspapers. They covered national current affairs, through the lens of the average Australian household, with an emphasis on lifestyle, cooking, fashion, beauty, parenting and relationships – and plenty of advertising. It was an immediate and growing success, effectively replacing *The Bulletin* in the national culture. Although *The Bulletin* continued to publish, its initial moment had passed, its circulation dropping considerably since the Great War. The lone hands of the Australian bush had since become domesticated into the urban household. In response to the success of *The Australian Women's Weekly*, a new magazine, *Man*, was launched in 1936, but it never reached the same level of circulation or had similar purchase upon the culture.

In 1936 Consolidated Press was formed, with Packer acquiring *The Daily Telegraph*, giving it a fresh design and style, based on the success of *The Australian Women's Weekly*. They hired firebrand journalist Brian Penton, who quickly became news editor, then general editor. Penton was intelligent and fiercely independent, opposing all censorship. He was also a novelist, and friends with Norman Lindsay and Ethel Florence Richardson – an expatriate writer, publishing under the pen name Henry Handel Richardson. Penton's literary sensibility contributed to his skill as a journalist and editor. By that stage, the newspaper industry was entering into competition with an emerging media: radio. Although experiments with radio went back to the 1890s, it was only in the 1920s that the first public broadcast happened in Sydney, after which the technology spread exponentially. In July 1932 the federal government established the Australian Broadcasting Commission (ABC), modelled on the British Broadcasting Corporation (BBC), giving it statutory powers that provided it with a degree of independence from government interference. For the first time, radio allowed the news to be truly national, the same stories being heard everywhere at the same time.

During the Great War, the Attorney-General's Department acquired sweeping powers, centrally coordinating the censorship activities of the departments of customs, police and post – directed mainly at what was considered seditious material. In 1921 these wartime powers were belatedly revoked, only to be replaced by Proclamation 24 under the *Customs Act*, effectively continuing wartime censorship measures during peacetime. The activities of the attorney-general became more covert, kept not only from the public but also from other arms of government. The list of banned books was itself restricted.

Along with sedition, the censors targeted obscene literature. This culminated in 1929 with the banning of Radclyffe Hall's *The Well of Loneliness* (1928), James Joyce's *Ulysses* (1922) and D.H. Lawrence's *Lady Chatterley's Lover* (1928). The Department of Customs applied the 'householder test', a variation of the Hicklin test: is this material the average householder would allow his family to read? The 'average householder' being white, heterosexual and male.

This test rippled through society, including Nowra. In January 1929, *The South Coast Register* published an article that asked, 'What books should be kept off the shelves of the circulating library?' Modern fiction had a 'much greater degree of frankness on subjects that a generation ago would have been mentioned with bated breath', it reported. 'One safeguard against this is to know the authors who have good or reasonably good reputations and purchase within the limits of such a compass.'

During the period 1927–29, the number of books banned doubled, from 120 to 240. By 1936 the restricted list had around 5000 books. In 1933 the federal government created the Book Censorship Advisory Committee, which was to advise the government, but only as and when it was asked to do so; moreover, the advice was often ignored.

In 1937 this was replaced by the Literature Censorship Board. Its advice was accepted slightly more often than that of its predecessor. *The Well of Loneliness*, for example, was released in 1939, but it was an exception, a pressure-release valve on a regime that was beginning to come under public scrutiny.

A 1935 article in *The Australian Quarterly* outlined the ironies emerging from this system. All of Stalin's books were banned, for example. Australians were told that communism was a threat, but they were unable to come to their own understanding of why or how. And yet, at the same time, Russia was a member of the League of Nations, and Stalin was being courted by the British prime minister, Anthony Eden. 'It is strange that the States should spend so much money on compulsory education,' the author concluded, 'while the Federal Government seeks to build its authority on compulsory ignorance.'

The colonial publishing and bookselling regime only compounded the absurdities of censorship. Norman Lindsay, for example, could not get his 1930 novel, *Redheap*, published in Australia, but managed to do so in England, thanks to the efforts of Brian Penton. But when the publisher attempted to import the book into Australia, the customs department banned it. The *Daily Guardian* (Sydney) planned to obviate the ban by serialising the novel in its pages. When this plot was discovered, the Post and Telegraph Department informed the newspaper publisher the offending editions would not be circulated within Australia, and the newspaper could lose its registration. This latter tactic had successfully worked since the first independent newspapers were licensed in the 1820s. In the 1930s, it still worked: the *Daily Guardian* acquiesced and *Redheap* was not serialised.

The national censorship regime operated independently of the British censorship regime, so there were often overlapping restrictions placed on a particular title in both Britain and Australia. But when these were not overlapping, one side or the other of this export–import supply chain might have a restriction in place. So if a book was banned in England, it was effectively banned in Australia – but that book could also be banned in Australia while being available in England, and vice versa.

The Well of Loneliness, for example, was banned in England from 1928 until 1949. It was banned in Australia from 1929 until 1939, but as it was still banned in England for another decade, the book remained difficult to access in Australia for ten years after it was technically available.

Wanganui had come a long way since Frank Osborne Moorhouse's father arrived in the area in 1898. It was the first provincial town to have an electric tramway. In 1924, it was formally declared a city. Frank was raised, educated and reached adulthood during a period of rapid social expansion, technological advancement and commercial opportunity. These experiences personally enthused him, and he had played a minor role in it, modernising the local dairy industry, installing electricity in the region. His old boss, Charles Davis, sold his milking machine patent to the Diabolo Separator Company in Sydney, moving back to Australia to work for Diabolo. The Davis family moved to Mosman.

In 1925, not quite twenty-one years old, Frank left New Zealand for Sydney. He travelled light, only taking his tools and a small library of technical books. He wanted to strike out on his own, to escape his abusive uncle-cum-stepfather. That same year, Frank's sister, Sylvia, aged nineteen, suffered a nervous collapse. Like her father and uncle, she had long suffered depression and anxiety.

Frank also inherited this predisposition, which accounted for his shyness around other people. But it also drove his work ethic, as a way to keep himself distracted from, and always one step ahead of, his dark humours. His mother, Ethel, the moral backbone of the family, could only do so much coping with the moods, drinking and behaviour of her Moorhouse husbands. She had a fatalistic demeanour, a stoicism expressing itself in various maxims and refrains, a habit inculcated into her children, who subsequently lived by such rules and simple moral guidelines. *What cannot be cured must be endured.* Frank carried a head full of such phrases and rules with him to Australia.

In Sydney, it took eighteen months for Davis to secure Frank a job. Diabolo had been bought out by Alfa Laval – the Swedish company that invented the cream separator in 1878 – and so in 1927 Frank commenced work as a sales representative for the Alfa Laval Separator Company. He was assigned the South Coast region, including the Shoalhaven.

For such a shy person, becoming a travelling salesman – which meant meeting new people and winning them over in order to make a sale – filled Frank with horror. He had confidence in his experience and technical skills, but needed to overcome his shyness in order to communicate that confidence to other people. He discovered *Efficiency* magazine, which was concerned with a managerial movement that used 'scientific' methods to combine professional and personal improvement. The magazine was largely written by Canadian writer Herbert Casson, who had written dozens of books, histories of various businesses and technologies, as well as titles focused on efficient business practices. Frank collected these books and subscribed to *Efficiency* magazine, where he found tips on public speaking, the role of courtesy in business and other practical topics.

He was selective of the ideas he took, adapting them to local conditions and turning them into pithy maxims and sayings, integrated with his mother's maxims and refrains. *Selling depends more on selling yourself. Do the things the other fellow appreciates. Doing the small things well. Always walk up to a man as if he owes you ten pounds*. He then travelled the South Coast, selling and installing cream separators, while trying and often failing to sell milking machines. One of the first Shoalhaven dairy farmers he met told him there were only two bad things in the world: communism and milking machines.

In 1925, the Producers' Co-op Distributing Company (PDS) was established in the Shoalhaven, supplying milk to Sydney from the dairy farms in the region. But the actual supply of milk had not proportionately increased since the regime of two milkings per day was introduced in 1846. By 1910, few farmers used milking machines. Labour shortages during the war provided the impetus for more machines to be adopted, but manual methods were still the main well into the 1920s. Many machines used during the war were abandoned afterwards, left to rust on various properties, scarecrows against innovation. When Frank left New Zealand, the dominant local trademark was the L.K.G. Milking Machine. Now he liked to say, 'In New Zealand we had the L.K.G. machine and in Australia they have the D.M.K. milking machine – Dad, Mum and Kids.'

Behind the humour – which Herbert Casson advised was a good way to break the ice – Frank Osborne Moorhouse saw a challenge to be met.

In 1924, Nettie Palmer published *Modern Australian Literature 1900–1923*. She argued that literature prior to Federation was characterised by 'the colonial attitude', described as 'showing off Australia to an outside audience'. Marcus Clarke's *His Natural Life* represented this attitude. In the 1890s, this had been 'superseded by the short story of the intimate and natural type, written as though for people who knew their own country'. *The Bulletin* represented this, embodied by Henry Lawson.

The monograph established Nettie's credentials as a literary critic, allowing her to publish regularly in newspapers and periodicals across the country. She wrote thousands of words each week, cobbling together a semi-regular, if insecure, income to support her family. In 1928 Nettie edited *An Australian Story Book*, published by Angus & Robertson. It was the most important anthology of Australian short fiction since *The Bulletin Story Book*, explicitly designed, as she wrote in her diary, to 'begin where A.G. Stephens left off'.

But the short story form was already in decline. Authors were turning more to the novel, preferably written while living and publishing overseas. This was a period marked by a number of relatively successful expatriate Australian novelists, such as 'Henry' Handel Richardson and Christina Stead. In her earlier monograph, Nettie cited the phenomenon of the expatriate writer, while noting no serious developments in the locally produced novels. She cited Lawrence's *Kangaroo* as a notable ring-in. 'In its pictures of our landscape, seen through friendly, alien eyes, as well as in its revelation of our national character and social habits, it is a boon to us, and we may consider it a brilliant gift from overseas,' Nettie wrote. 'Or perhaps we may take it as compensation for the loss of those of our writers who have been forced to go abroad.'

By the end of the 1920s, Vance Palmer had published eight novels and a collection of plays. By the end of the next decade, a further five novels and three collections of short stories. But he struggled to make a living from literature, the Palmer family remaining dependent on Nettie's journalism.

When Frank Osborne Moorhouse first arrived in Australia in 1925, Purthanry Cutts was in England, visiting her father's relatives for the first time. She was away for sixteen months, returning to her family home in Mosman in October 1925, where she resumed working at Farmer's Department Store and continued her involvement with the Girl Guides. In 1927, visiting Charles Davis in Mosman, Frank was waiting for a ferry when two Girl Guides tried selling him tickets to a dance. He did not have anybody to take to the dance, so the Guides – being prepared, as per their motto – colluded with Frank to have him come along and meet their captain, who also did not have a date for the dance.

Frank and Purth were married soon after, on 14 January 1928, in Sydney. That same year, the Moorhouses moved to Nowra, into a little house on East Street, centrally located within Frank's sales territory on the South Coast. Houses in Nowra did not yet have designated numbers, and the streets were dirt and frequently muddy. There was no sewerage system. But it was their first married home. He named it 'Aramoho', after a settlement on the Whanganui River.

Soon after, Purth fell pregnant. Her parents, recently retired, moved to Nowra to help the Moorhouses with the birth of their first child, especially as Frank had to travel for work. On Christmas Eve of 1928, Owen George Moorhouse was born.

That was the year electricity had come to Nowra, as if to mark Frank's arrival. One of the first milking machines he managed to sell had a petrol engine, which the farmer did not like. Frank put an offer to him: if the farmer could get power lines to the farm and into the milking shed, Frank would install an electric motor and do the wiring free of charge.

This was also the year Frank had his big idea. One of the main problems facing the Producers' Co-Op supplying milk to Sydney was quality control. Milk was often rejected due to a high bacteria count or a rubber flavour created by poor sterilisation of equipment. Driving along the highway one day, between Nowra and Eden, Frank imagined what would become the Moorhouse Dairy Boiler. Sterilisation required boiling water, but it was difficult to produce a sufficient volume close to the milking sheds quickly and efficiently. His invention addressed each of these problems.

At home that weekend, he built a working model on his verandah, tinkered with it, then built a full-scale version out of copper. It resembled a Ned Kelly mask on a plinth, the top section holding ten gallons of water, the plinth being where a fire could be safely raised, fed by light fuel – woodchips, bark or corn cobs. The boiler was compact, occupying a single square foot of floor space, boiling ten gallons of water in only ten minutes. A simple, inexpensive solution to the hygiene and sterilisation problem was precisely what the dairy farmers on the South Coast needed.

He started making copper boilers on his own time, selling them to farmers as he travelled around distributing cream separators and milking machines.

Frank became so well-known over his first few years in Nowra that one day he received a letter from a farmer who, not knowing they lived on East Street, simply addressed the envelope to 'Moorhouse the Machinery Man'. The letter reached him, and the name stuck.

Over the next decade, the Moorhouses consolidated their standing in the local community. In 1930, Purth rekindled her association with the Girl Guides, joining the Nowra branch. She also joined the CWA. Their first campaign in 1931 was to to agitate for the town to acquire an ambulance. The following year they got one. The next step was to establish an ambulance station.

In August 1932, Frank and Purth's second child, Arthur Osborne Moorhouse, was born.

The opportunities for an Australian literature were still being largely stifled by censorship and the imperial publishing regime, economically disadvantaging Australian writers, even as other local industries continued to develop.

In 1935, the Victorian branch of the Fellowship of Australian Writers joined with other literary and library groups to form the Book Censorship Abolition League. The vice-president of the league was Dr Reginald Spencer Ellery, a 38-year-old psychiatrist and author.

As an adolescent, Ellery had harboured literary ambitions, but his strict father wanted him to become a doctor. His first professional appointment was at the Kew Hospital for the Insane, where he became involved in a public controversy over the various reforms he wanted to implement. The staff retaliated, making false accusations about his conduct, which led to a royal commission in 1924, at which Ellery was exonerated. He transferred to another hospital for the 'insane', while also contributing to *The Medical Journal of Australia* articles on, among other topics, psychoanalysis.

By the time Ellery joined the Book Censorship Abolition League, his broader intellectual concerns were with studying the underlying social, political and economic causes of war. The truly insane, he believed, were those individuals – politicians, military leaders, ideologues – who created abnormal social situations, placing otherwise perfectly sane citizens at risk. Ellery felt that censorship contributed to a general lack of understanding, creating a barrier to addressing the social problem of war.

In 1930, 21-year-old Beatrice Davis began working as a proofreader and assistant editor at *The Medical Journal of Australia*. She would have edited Reginald Ellery's articles. In 1937 she started working at Halstead Press – Angus & Robertson's printing company – while also working as an assistant bookseller. Soon after, she became their first full-time book editor. This was the first full-time book editor's role in Australian publishing. She was only twenty-eight years old.

Meanwhile, Vance Palmer, among others, tackled the imperial publishing regime. British book imports still dominated the local market, and colonial editions remained an influential part of the system. Since the Great War, the previously observable physical distinction between the colonial and English editions had collapsed, but the underlying regime was still in operation. The colonial royalty rate to Australian authors published through a British publisher was fixed at 10 per cent of the retail price, not graded to volume of sales. This was still substantially less than what authors in Britain earned for the same number of sales.

In 1935, Australian authors, including Vance, agitated to get the same deal as British authors, but to no avail. Domestically, they tried to secure transparent and fair contributor rates for freelance writers in Australian newspapers and periodicals, but failed, their efforts blocked by the Australian Journalists' Association. Finally, although many Australian writers were publicly known figures, this did not translate into book sales. Many readers used their local and state library services to access books, which produced only a single, one-off royalty payment for the author from the library's initial purchase of the book, and nothing for the many readers, over many years, having free access to the book.

Nowra in the 1930s went through a period of rapid modernisation. Although in an economic depression, the local council began supplying indoor plumbing and sewerage, improving hygiene and health, while also preparing the town for the installation of surfaced roads.

The first 'talkie' film shown in Nowra was in 1931. The Roxy Theatre opened on Berry Street in 1935, an Art Deco cinema seating over 800 people. The Moorhouse family attended the Roxy, Frank having lost none of his fascination with moving pictures since he saw the lights of Hayward's Theatre as a boy. He wanted his own boys to have the same experience, so the family had permanent pre-booked seats for every Saturday-night screening.

The local cinema was a barometer of changing attitudes regarding race and gender. In the nineteenth century, the Yuin people were culturally deracinated and forced onto missions. Such segregation only incrementally gave way to limited but controlled assimilation. Aboriginal people were initially not permitted in the cinemas in Nowra. Meanwhile, white men and women would sit separately. Over the coming decades, during a period of 'assimilation', when Aboriginal people were finally permitted to enter the cinemas, they were restricted to seats in the first few rows of the stalls. White men and women were then permitted to commingle in the gallery.

Surfaced roads were installed in Nowra, but the bitumen always ran out before they reached the missions.

The Nowra Rotary Club was launched in 1934, the inaugural meeting minuted by its first secretary, Mr Frank O. Moorhouse. A year later, the Moorhouses sold their East Street property, moving to a larger block on the corner of Kinghorne and Worrigee streets, containing a house and a large workshop. Frank named this house 'Rangimarie', a Māori word for 'peaceful place'. The success of his dairy boiler necessitated a workshop and staff to manufacture the product. This was part of an old industrial site, which in the 1880s had housed the printing works and the first cordial and soft drink manufacturers.

Rotary met weekly, the men sharing a light supper and listening to lectures. In 1936, the first talk Frank gave was titled 'Are milking machines a success?'. He laid out the case for the advantages of milking machines, addressing the long-held concerns of farmers, and how to overcome problems associated with hygiene and sterilisation. Frank had won the trust of the local farmers, the success of his dairy boiler affording him a certain authority. He also understood the best strategy to enact change – *If a man is convinced against his will / He is of the same opinion still* – and knew the power of the media to amplify a message.

The Moorhouse family read *The Daily Telegraph*, *The Sydney Morning Herald* and *The Shoalhaven News*. Purth subscribed to *The Australian Women's Weekly*. After giving his Rotary talk, Frank arranged for the text to be printed in the local newspaper, and it was syndicated across many country newspapers throughout the region. As a result, milking machines began to sell more quickly.

Now the only bad thing in the world was communism.

In April 1937, Purth's father, George Cutts, died. Twelve months later she became pregnant with her third child. One generation passing to the next, and what was carried over, each to each, from generations past, was some chance combination of genetic and cultural baggage.

It came from the West Yorkshire moors, where the child John Midgley Moorhouse was given his mother's last name, her gift to him which he passed down the line. It came from Thomas Keivel and Patience Sidwell, and the unintended consequences of a single criminal act transporting them to some unknown, distant land. It came from England, Ireland and Wales, by way of New Zealand, down through penal colonies, empires, nations built, wars fought and economies depressed. A direct heritage of convicts and free settlers, both literate and illiterate, obscene and righteous; farmers and servants, cattle dealers and cooks; horse trainers, landlords and newspapermen; inventors, adventurers and deserters; the libellous and the bankrupt, the low-spirited and the determined, the generous and the public-minded. And it came from the stories, dances and songs of each, handed down to this particular Nowra family: mother, father and two children, with another on the way.

An average Australian household in 1938.

But that December, with the new baby due, Frank and Purth Moorhouse were probably concerned with more immediate affairs, the more mundane events of the nine months prior. An ambulance station had finally been built on Kinghorne Street, down the road from the Moorhouse residence, willed into being by the CWA. A Nowra factory had won the World Butter Championship, bringing international recognition to the South Coast. It was a reward for all the efforts over the decades building a quality dairy industry, backed by a patent system, in which Frank Osborne Moorhouse's inventiveness and advocacy had played no small part. Meanwhile, in Sydney, the first Coca-Cola factory had opened. First made in the United States in 1886, and imported into Australia, it was only in 1938 that Coca-Cola began working to take market share from local cordial and soft drink manufacturers.

On the evening of Tuesday, 20 December, the Roxy Theatre had a special repeat screening of Steele Rudd's *On Our Selection*, starring Bill Bailey. The next day, Wednesday, 21 December, Frank filed an application towards securing a patent for the proprietary technology behind the Moorhouse Dairy Boiler. That same day, in hospital, Purth's only hope was that, after two boys, she would finally be blessed with a baby girl.

'December 21, at Edmon private hospital, Nowra, to Mr and Mrs F.O. Moorhouse, Rangimarie, Nowra,' the birth notice in *The Sydney Morning Herald* read that Christmas Eve, adding only: '– a boy.'

2

'Fuck Father Christmas!'

December 1938 marked the longest dry spell the Shoalhaven had experienced in eighteen years. Although it rained briefly over the New Year period, it was not enough for the grass to lose its yellow hue. The landscape remained tinder-dry. A few days before the baby was born, the temperature had reached 104 degrees Fahrenheit (40 degrees Celsius). A couple of days later, *The Shoalhaven News* warned of bushfires. The warning was repeated in early January.

Meanwhile, from 29 December, on the Lane Cove River in Sydney was the largest gathering to date of Boy Scouts in New South Wales, with Frank and his eldest son, Owen, in attendance. Arthur, not yet old enough to join the Cub Scouts, was enjoying his final days of childhood freedom before entering the first grade at Nowra Primary School. Purth and the baby were one of four households to be visited by a sister from the Nowra Baby Health Centre that January.

They named the baby Frank Thomas Moorhouse Jr. They would call him Young Frank.

By the end of January 1939, the anticipated bushfires had burned through the territory. Residents could smell the smoke from the burning eucalypts in Kangaroo Valley. The fires were not seen as a portent of greater conflagrations to come.

During the week of the bushfires, an anonymous columnist, under the pseudonym 'Freelance', wrote a front-page article titled 'Who IS the Lunatic?'. In England, the author H.G. Wells had said Adolf Hitler and Benito Mussolini were 'lunatics'. 'Freelance' took exception to this characterisation of Hitler, in particular, providing a point by point defence of Hitler's achievements in the 'mental world', in diplomacy and in the commercial realm, concluding that, as 'he marches on from victory to victory', he clearly cannot be considered a lunatic. 'I fully expected I should be able to scoff,' 'Freelance' wrote, referring to Hitler's 1925 manifesto, *Mein Kampf*, 'but, after reading it, I reluctantly was forced to praise it. Has Mr H.G. Wells done so well in the literary world as this certifiable lunatic?'

War was considered only a remote possibility. And yet, by March, the mood was beginning to change, when the inaugural meeting of the Women's Voluntary Services (WVS) was called. Its aim was to provide a 'trained body of women to be available at any time of national emergency'. In particular, this coordinating body would draw on already established local organisations, such as the CWA, the Girl Guides and St John Ambulance – with all of which Purth was deeply involved. The Nowra Red Cross had folded in recent years, but the impetus of the WVS movement and the rumours of war quickly revived it.

On Good Friday, 7 April, Prime Minister Joseph Lyons, leader of the United Australia Party, had a heart attack in Sydney and died. Robert Menzies had resigned as Lyons' deputy leader a few weeks earlier, so the leader of the coalition Country Party, Earle Page, became interim prime minister. Menzies soon contested the leadership of the United Australia Party, winning narrowly to become prime minister on Wednesday, 26 April. That same day, in Nowra, 'Freelance' was once more trying to downplay the possibility of war.

Scout Week was held in May 1939, part of an effort to maintain some semblance of normalcy. At the end of the month was Scouts and Guides' Day, with over 300 Cubs, Scouts, Brownies and

Girl Guides gathered at the Diggers' Hall. Frank Sr, as the Pageant Marshall, ran the event. Purth, as District Guide Commissioner, sat on the stage with several other local dignitaries from the Scouts' and Guides' movement, surrounded by flags from the thirty-two different nations in which the movements operated. The Renewal of Promises was made by all the assembled children, including Owen, before there was a procession along Junction Street. Crowds gathered on both sides of the street to watch and cheer.

At the Scouts' annual meeting in 1939, it was decided that the organisation would sell a block of land it owned on Osborne Street and use the proceeds to build a hall on its other property, on the corner of Shoalhaven and Jervis streets. Frank Sr supported the motion, arguing the current site was unsuitable because it was close to residential areas. 'Boys would be boys,' *The Shoalhaven News* reported him as saying, 'and the resultant noise on meeting nights would become an annoyance to nearby residents.'

'It should be music to their ears!' said a Mr Hewett.

'Maybe for the first few nights,' replied Frank Sr, the father now to three young boys, 'but not afterwards.'

That August, the Nowra Co-op Dairy Company's new factory opened in Bomaderry, along the trainline connecting the South Coast to Sydney. The new premises were state-of-the-art, including an onsite laboratory for the dairy chemist. Over the previous twelve months, the Co-op had handled over 2.5 million gallons (nearly 9.5 million litres) of milk, supplying one-third of Sydney's milk consumption, 12 per cent of its butter and 70 per cent of its cheese. In size, the dairy industry nationally was third only to wool and gold. This new factory meant the region was poised to grow its dairy industry once more, with Moorhouse the Machinery Man well placed to benefit.

Frank Sr had arranged with Alfa Laval that he would leave their direct employment on the first Friday in September and strike out on his own. He wanted to give his full attention to his private company, which manufactured and sold the Moorhouse Dairy Boiler as well as a growing catalogue of agricultural equipment. He would continue to operate as Alfa Laval's agent, working on commission, while independently servicing his old territory, without additional competition.

The cinema was closed on Sundays, so most people would have been home when, at 8 pm, on the wireless, via BBC short-wave, the British prime minister, Neville Chamberlain, announced that Britain was at war with Germany. At 9.15 pm, an announcer cut through all ABC and commercial stations, saying: 'Here is the Prime Minister, the Right Honourable RG Menzies.' Sitting in the Postmaster-General's office in Melbourne, before an ABC microphone, there was an audible rustle of pages before the prime minister spoke.

'Fellow Australians,' he said, 'it is my melancholy duty to inform you officially that in consequence of a persistence by Germany in her invasion of Poland, Great Britain has declared war upon her, and that, as a result, Australia is also at war.'

The next day, *The Sydney Morning Herald* provided a sober summary of these events on its front page, under the heading 'Overseas News'. Beneath the fold, under 'Home News', Australia's declaration of war was noted, including the preparations already made over the weekend in anticipation. These included coastal fortifications, the placing of the Royal Australian Navy on standby and the calling-up of over a thousand men in New South Wales for sixteen days' militia training.

Frank Sr's old manager called him on that Monday morning to give him the opportunity to reconsider his plan of leaving Alfa Laval, considering the economic uncertainty the war seemed likely to bring, and the relative security Alfa Laval could provide his family. But Frank Sr politely declined, being determined to follow through with his plan.

And that week, as Australia lurched into war, 'Freelance' in *The Shoalhaven News* – who, until then, had been sceptical of the prospect – suddenly shifted from politics to literature and began a front-page series on Australian poets. The first to be showcased was Will Ogilvie. *The South Coast Register*, which came out every Thursday, left the story of the declaration of war for its inside pages, under the header 'Business As Usual'.

Over the following weeks, *The Shoalhaven News* continued its poetry series. A.B. Paterson was given his own treatment on 27 September, with 'Freelance' stating that 'Banjo' was arguably the 'most popular of our Australian poets'. And while the Moorhouse family, along with other Nowra residents, sat down to read over breakfast that Wednesday morning 'The Man from Ironbark' and 'Frying Pan's Theology', 10,000 miles (16,000 kilometres) away, in Poland, Warsaw was only hours away from surrendering to Nazi invaders.

By October 1939, all the local civic organisations in the Shoalhaven had amalgamated into a Central Committee, with two representatives from each organisation tasked with coordinating and mobilising the district's war effort and patriotic activities. Three hundred troops were stationed at the Nowra Showground, at the end of Worrigee Street, about five blocks down from the Moorhouse residence. A martial air pervaded the town and all activities became reconfigured around the war effort. A woollen sock pattern was included in the local newspapers, for women of the town to knit for the local militia. The reformed Red Cross began making camouflaged netting. By November, the showground had become a permanent training ground, with the 2nd Armoured Car Regiment camped there through to early December.

Dairy was a protected industry during the war, so Frank Sr was not required for military service. Even had this not been the case, it was unlikely he would have been called up. Although the cut-off age for recruitment was forty, that was only for single men. The cut-off age was thirty-five for men with families, and in October 1939 he had reached that age. He did not treat that as a relief, though, and increased his efforts on the home front. There were domestic labour shortages, and the increased need for a steady milk supply created the impetus for more milking machines to be installed, and higher vigilance around hygiene and quality. This meant more dairy boilers had to be manufactured. At the same time, Frank Sr's workshop was commissioned to manufacture headlight masks and hoods for cars and trucks, so they could be driven during blackouts.

But it was not just through his business that Frank Sr contributed to the war effort. By July 1941, a Volunteer Defence Corps had been formed. The Moorhouse workshop was their makeshift armoury, storing all the single shot, lever-action .310 rifles, which had been confiscated from the district's school cadet corps. At shooting practice, with fifteen points being the minimum qualifying score, Frank Sr came in third with twenty points. There were three platoons, No. 1 and No. 2 from Nowra, and No. 3 from Cambewarra. The recreation field in Nowra was used every Tuesday evening at 7.30 pm for training. By August 1941, Officer Moorhouse was leading the men through their regular drill.

Frank Sr was equally busy with the Boy Scouts. In 1940, the new clubhouse opened a few blocks from the Moorhouse residence. The opening ceremony occurred on the first Saturday of June, with Frank Sr in the lead, and a formation of Cubs and Scouts – including Arthur and Owen – marching from Diggers' Hall in town to the reserve, accompanied by the Berry Band.

In the early days of Moorhouse the Machinery Man, Purth managed the administrative side of the business, including bookkeeping. Her volunteer work in the community also stepped up during the war years, particularly now her two elder sons were in school. In February 1941, in *The Shoalhaven News*, a letter received by Purth on behalf of the Red Cross was published. The 1st Australian General Hospital, based in Palestine, thanked the Nowra branch for its work and support. Every convalescing soldier had received a Christmas parcel from Nowra, as part of a fundraising campaign by the Red Cross to send goods, mainly food parcels, to soldiers in the field.

At the 1943 Girl Guides' annual meeting, Purth spoke about the work being done by the Guides' International Service. The Girl Guides had run the tuckshop at the school to raise funds, but they'd had to stop when sugar rationing was introduced. Each Guide was expected to donate a penny every week to the war effort.

And so Purth was not as present in the family home as she had been when her first two boys were infants. Young Frank was often left with his grandmother, who had grown into a very stern widower. At other times he was left to his own devices in one room while his mother hosted a meeting or fundraiser in another.

Sometime during the war years, Purth engaged a maid to take care of the house and look after Young Frank. Belle McLeod, a Yuin/Wandandian woman, was sixteen years old when she came to work for the Moorhouses. She had finished high school and had been working at the local private hospital in Nowra. She moved into the Moorhouse home during the week, returning to her own family on weekends. She had her own room at 'Rangimarie', which Purth had decorated in pink. She bought dresses for Belle and doted on her. Years later, Belle would say Mrs Moorhouse was like a second mother to her; for Purth, it almost seemed like Belle was the daughter she had always wanted.

In the first edition of *The Shoalhaven News* following the declaration of war, an editorial cited 'strict censorship' as the reason there was little solid information regarding its progress. The editorial concluded that such censorship was a necessary wartime measure.

In May 1940, nine communist newspapers in Australia were banned, on the pretext that they were opposed to the war effort. In 1942, the newspaper of the Australia First Movement was shuttered in a series of raids, and its leaders interned. Throughout the war years, the censors from the newly formed Department of Information and Censorship would send instructions to all the newspapers in Australia – often up to seven times a day – which were duly followed.

The ABC was heavily censored too, with all news being vetted to ensure no information that might aid the enemy went to air. Meanwhile, opinions were carefully crafted to support the war effort and domestic morale, which meant – as with the print media – not criticising the government or undermining public confidence in Australia's political leadership.

From the beginning of the war, newspaper proprietors and editors agreed to abide by these censorship measures, even though, as the war progressed, it was becoming clear many instructions were less about the war effort and national security, and more about shoring up the federal government's domestic control. A number of American correspondents had left Australia during this period because of the paucity of actual news available to them to report on.

This came to a head in April 1944, when some US senators criticised the Australian government over a decision regarding Australian troop deployment. Rupert Henderson, general manager of *The Sydney Morning Herald* and president of the Australian Newspaper Proprietors' Association, issued a statement arguing the Americans would have been better informed had the government not been so heavy-handed with its press censorship.

The Minister of the Department of Information and Censorship, Arthur Calwell, attacked Henderson for making false statements regarding the government's actions. Already Henderson had broken the agreement by publicly discussing the process of censorship. But Calwell had also made false statements in his attack on Henderson, so Henderson felt obliged to reply by citing examples of political censorship.

Since all newspaper copy was vetted by the censor before publication, Henderson's reply was itself severely cut. Rather than pull the piece from publication, Brian Penton decided *The Daily Telegraph* would publish Henderson's reply but leave blank spaces where text had been censored. This made it clear to the public that Henderson had offered evidence to back up his claims but it had been censored – which dramatically reinforced his original claim.

As a result, the newspaper was placed under censure. Henderson issued a further statement, which was again censored. *The Sunday Telegraph* attempted to publish the blank column inches under Henderson's by-line, but before it was made public the police arrived and seized all the trucks carrying the printed newspaper.

Now Sydney's newspaper proprietors, editors and lawyers met, agreeing to publish in their Monday editions an outline of these events, including all of Henderson's statements in full, plus an editorial statement of support. That Monday, Commonwealth police seized all copies of the four Sydney dailies – *The Daily Telegraph*, *The Sydney Morning Herald*, *The Sun* and *The Daily Mirror* – along with the Melbourne *Herald* and the Adelaide *News*. Among the consequences of these events was a libel lawsuit Calwell brought against Penton; it was ultimately settled out of court.

Literary censorship on the grounds of obscenity continued unabated during the war. Soon after the seizure of the newspapers in 1944, Max Harris, editor of the short-lived literary journal *Angry Penguins*, was charged with obscenity over his publication of the poetry of Ern Malley, a fictional figure created as a hoax by James McAuley and Harold Stewart. Harris took the hoax seriously and published the poems, but matters took a turn when an Adelaide police detective saw the issue and suspected obscenity.

At the trial, a number of literary and academic critics were called for the defence. The defence also called the psychiatrist Dr Reginald Ellery, who testified that the poems would not unduly excite the average reader sexually. The former vice-president of the Book Censorship Abolition League had since co-founded the Melbourne Institute for Psycho-Analysis, and had become more interested in communism.

The result of the trial saw Harris fined £5 for indecency.

The early years of the war brought fears of a Japanese invasion. There was an air raid in Darwin in February 1942, midget submarines in Sydney Harbour a few months later. Closer to home, Japanese submarines were sited off Jervis Bay.

In December, a state of emergency was declared in the Shoalhaven. Near the Moorhouse residence, additional troops and equipment occupied the Nowra Showground. There were three squadrons of the 6th Australian Motor Regiment – formerly the Light Horse Regiment – in the area. One was stationed off Jervis Bay, Huskisson and Nowra, and the other two squadrons were further inland.

The troops created defensive positions along the coast. Barbed-wire barricades lined the beaches. There were constant military exercises and troop marches around the township. Drill was performed in the paddocks. There was a twenty-four-hour guard patrolling the streets. About 100 men were permanently camped close to Mayfield Hill, from where most of the district could be kept under surveillance. Their encampment, including Bren gun carriers, was camouflaged by the coral trees.

A disused cottage was commandeered for use as staff quarters, while a nearby farm shed was used for rest and recreation. The township had sent lounge chairs for the troops, a ping-pong table, paddles and balls. Purth Moorhouse and the Red Cross had sent over letter-writing materials, playing cards, games and a first-aid kit. The troops would stay on Mayfield Hill until a couple of weeks before Easter in 1943, when they moved to the Nowra Showground, due to excessive flooding in the area.

Rotary remained the central activity in Frank Sr's life. It provided a structure to integrate and articulate all his other activities, private and public, family and business. At the heart of this was the Rotary mantra, the four-way test: *Is it the truth? Is it fair to all concerned? Will it build good will and better friendships? Will it be beneficial to all concerned?* These were the principles by which he measured how he thought, spoke and acted.

The degree to which Frank Sr took Rotary seriously can be seen in his perfect attendance record, and the measures he took to maintain that record. Each year an international directory was distributed listing all the clubs, their schedule of meetings and the contact details of office bearers. Frank and Purth Moorhouse travelled quite extensively, within Australia and, following the war, overseas. They would plan these trips months in advance, plotting their course around the proximity of local clubs and when their meetings were scheduled. Frank Sr would write in advance to request an invitation to the meetings, and would offer himself as a speaker. This was particularly welcome in smaller clubs where it was difficult to secure fresh speakers on a weekly basis. On one occasion, when Frank Sr was hospitalised, he checked himself out of hospital to attend a Rotary meeting, before checking himself back in before lights out.

The Nowra branch of Rotary fell into a temporary recess in 1942, with the energies of its members directed more towards the war effort. But this changed during an enthusiastic meeting at the Moorhouse residence on the evening of 15 October 1943. The outgoing president, Dr Rodway, officially handed the reins of the club back to Frank Sr, who had just returned from the annual Rotary conference in Newcastle. *The Shoalhaven News* reported that Mr Moorhouse 'informed Rotarians that they would be asked to play an important part in post-war planning and in dealing with post-war problems'.

Part of the job of president was to arrange the topic and speaker for each meeting. The very first speaker Frank Sr arranged during his tenure was a Petty Officer Jackson, from the US Navy, who spoke about how peace could be advocated according to Christian principles. This session was held at the Moorhouse residence. Young Frank would have been close to five years old, and was likely either hovering in the room with the Rotarians or in another room, but within earshot, as Jackson spoke about the Japanese attack on Pearl Harbor, and the friendship between Australia and the United States.

That same year, the CWA Annual International Day celebrations focused on the United States. The Moorhouses spent the year researching and exploring all things American. During those war years, there were many Americans in Nowra, visiting or stationed there, and Young Frank became particularly fascinated by them. He was drawn to their accents, which made them seem exotic, visitors from some faraway place.

In October 1944, Frank Sr passed on the Rotary gavel and was happy to take his place back in the audience. He was particularly interested in the four-week lecture series immediately following his tenure, on how to avoid a post-war economic depression.

The distance in age between Young Frank and his older brothers was such that by the time he was only a few months old, Owen was already in Grade Five at school, and Arthur was beginning Grade One. This meant Frank's infant years – which coincided with the war years – were largely spent alone. They shared the sleepout at the side of the house, as well as a room where they kept their clothes and personal belongings. They also shared the house rules, laid down by their mother: set mealtimes, manners and a strict etiquette. The house was a well-organised space, with no obstructions or distractions permitted. She ran it like a fire station, always ready for action, with little room for play.

When Young Frank was nearly three years old, Owen began three years of boarding school in Wollongong. From that time he became a more distant figure in Frank's life. The horizons of the older Moorhouse brothers quickly expanded beyond the home. As he got older, Frank became aware he was missing out on their shared adventures, and increasingly frustrated he could not join them.

The behaviour of the boys was shaped by the practices of the Cubs and Scouts, and the lessons of Sunday School. Their purpose in life was predetermined by an education track starting in Nowra Primary School, with a detour through Wollongong Tech, before returning to Nowra to be apprenticed into the family business. They would work towards a management role and then eventually inherit the operation. Owen beat this path, and it was widened by Arthur. Young Frank, now crawling, now walking, was coming up behind.

The growth of the family business added to the demarcation between Frank and his brothers. When they were much younger, Owen and Arthur were co-opted into helping their father in the workshop. After school they would clean and polish the copper dairy boilers. If Frank Sr was making water tanks, Owen and Arthur were small enough to get inside them with a rivet gun to secure the edges of the corrugated iron together. By the time Young Frank was old enough to follow suit, the business had taken on technical staff who were doing the bulk of this work, so he avoided this initiation. His presence in the workshop was rarely useful.

Family legend has it that for the first few years of his life, Frank thought his name was 'Pissoff', because this is what he constantly heard from his brothers and from the men in the workshop. One December, when Young Frank was probably four or five years old, he ran excitedly into the workshop, calling out, 'Father Christmas is coming! Father Christmas is coming!' One of the tradies responded wryly, under his breath, 'Ah, fuck Father Christmas.' Young Frank picked up on this and started calling out, 'Fuck Father Christmas! Fuck Father Christmas!' The office was nearby, and the office ladies and his mother within earshot, so the tradie chased after Frank to get him to keep quiet, but he escaped and continued shouting, 'Fuck Father Christmas!'

During the early 1940s, Owen and Arthur were more conscious of the war, and the changes it had brought about, than their younger brother. It would be incorrect to suggest that Young Frank was not conscious of the war. He was too young to comprehend the context, but his awareness and personality was very much shaped by the effects of the war years on the family, its routines and activities. He knew about being shushed while adults spoke in hushed tones, or listening to crackly voices on the wireless, footsteps in other rooms, always walking away from him, and the constant brush-offs. He knew about being left alone. He would have caught the mood of patriotic songs, air-raid sirens and darkened streets, and the general oppressive atmosphere, which was characterised by uncertainty and anxiety. He would have recognised everybody as being in uniform, even if he was unable to distinguish between Cub, Scout and Guide uniforms, and between home guard and soldiers' uniforms, Australian and American. His brothers' school uniforms were dyed black, as were the girls' blouses.

For Young Frank, all this was normal. It was a world without colour, often without light, and there was no 'before' to remember. His experiences may have had no common point of reference for Young Frank other than a secret he was not let in on, a conspiracy from which he was always excluded, a wall with only occasional gaps through which he could push to briefly gain somebody's attention.

Young Frank had got into the habit of hiding in order to see how long it took his family to notice he was missing. He came to like the feeling of being lost. On one occasion, probably around the age of four or five, he accompanied his father and Arthur to a property, where Frank Sr needed to fix a piece of machinery. Frank wandered off. Eventually, they realised he was missing and they started searching for him. Several hours later, near dusk, he was found over the road, hiding in the neighbouring farm's cornfield. Frank had heard his father calling for him but had not answered. When he was found, his clothes were dusted by dirt, dropped tassel and corn silk, his skin covered in fleas and ticks. Purth was not happy with any of them.

Frank started at Nowra Primary School in 1945, a few months after turning six years old. He quickly became best friends with his classmate, Keith Paterson, the pair becoming inseparable. Keith lived close by, so finally Frank was able to roam the streets and do all the things his brothers had done without him. Owen was sixteen years old at this stage, living back at home and apprenticed in the workshop. Arthur was twelve, and this was his first year at boarding school.

Although Frank's school was mixed, many of the activities the students undertook were run separately for boys and girls. Even when they played together, these expectations were reinforced in the games they chose and the roles they undertook. Frank was now old enough to join the Cub Scouts, and the separate curricula of the Scouts and Guides, and the badges children were awarded, did much to establish and maintain gender roles.

The war years brought into sharper relief the image of men as soldiers and women as nurses. Many childhood games reflected these stereotypes. One Anzac Day, after the public march and memorial service, Frank was dressed in his father's home service army cap, his outsized Sam Browne officers' belt, leather pistol holster and shoulder strap. The girls were dressed as nurses. The boys enacted imaginary scenes from what they had been told about previous battles, such as Gallipoli, while the girls tended to the wounded.

At the same time, under the cover of such approved play, games of chase and catch would occur – soldiers chasing nurses, and soldiers wrestling other soldiers. From these brief moments of physical contact, Frank would come away breathless and flustered. At other times the children would play doctors and nurses in an empty lot over the road from Moorhouse the Machinery Man. They would perform examinations on each other's clothed bodies. The girls would teach Frank and Keith how to make daisy chains.

Frank Sr soon purchased this empty lot. The grass was cleared in preparation for a larger workshop, showroom and office. With a basement planned, the foundation was dug deep into the ground. A retaining wall was built along the footpath for safety purposes. Over the wall was a 15 foot (nearly 5 metre) drop. After school, Frank and Keith would sometimes climb the retaining wall and leap down onto a mound of dirt in the construction site below. One time Frank leaped awkwardly, and instead of landing on his feet and sliding down, he landed on his back, winding him. As he tumbled into the pit, frightened and gasping for air, Keith ran to his rescue.

The planned building across the street would allow the family business to keep up with the demand for its products and services. By 1945, it was stocking domestic appliances, such as the Breville hand-operated washing machine. 'Although we specialise in selling labour saving devices for the "Man on the Land",' a new advertisement ran, 'it is not often that we can suggest something for the "Woman on the Land".' By the following year it was supplying Hotpoint Electrical Appliances: electric irons, electric toasters and vacuum cleaners.

In March 1947, the new premises of Moorhouse the Machinery Man on Kinghorne Street were officially opened. Local dignitaries and members of the press were invited. The new premises contained a large showroom, which included a model two-unit milking set-up, with two sets of welded steel bails, rump chain in place, and a seat. Near the bails was a stainless-steel rustproof milk vat, including strainer and cooling unit. The galvanised iron draining bench included a steel trough.

The company's signature copper dairy boiler had pride of place. Over a cup of tea, Frank Sr explained to the press that he had sold well over 1750 units to date. Also on display were all the domestic 'electrical gadgets', the toasters and washing machines and other kitchen and laundry appliances. One noted feature of the new premises was the absence of wood in the design. The showroom was all concrete and steel. *The Shoalhaven News* reported that one visitor was heard to quip, 'This reminds you of the model dairy a man dreams about.'

At the rear of the building, one floor down, was the spacious workshop and storeroom. It even had its own underground cinema. This would be used to show reels of the latest agricultural machinery or techniques, for the edification of staff and clients alike. More popularly, the company would hold occasional public events for films and newsreels that were not being shown at the local cinemas.

The same domestic appliances sold out of the Machinery Man premises were used in the Moorhouse family home. When Purth entertained guests – for semi-formal morning or afternoon teas, or for the lunchtime gatherings of the ladies from the Red Cross, the CWA or the Girl Guides – it was as if her kitchen and laundry were showrooms for appliances sold next door. The house always remained impeccably clean, tidy and orderly.

This retail spirit infiltrated the games Frank and Keith played in the backyard. They would set up a table and stock it with discarded appliance boxes from the house and business. They made money from strips of painted paper, and would take turns in the roles of shopkeeper and customer.

The first call for the formation of a Nowra branch of the newly constituted Liberal Party of Australia appeared in *The Shoalhaven News* in February 1945. The stated purpose was 'to champion the cause of the individual – his liberty and his personal dignity – against the rising tide of bureaucracy and regimentation'. Additional advertisements the following year claimed the Labor Party was 'committed to a policy of complete nationalisation', that individuals would not have the right to choose their own jobs, would be denied home ownership and would lose the right to own and run their own businesses. By August 1946, Frank Sr was elected treasurer and chairman of the Finance Committee of the Nowra Liberal Party.

This political turn was due, in large part, to Frank Sr's experiences during the war, and his sense of mission regarding post-war reconstruction. He was, at this stage, a newly elected local alderman. His personal politics were always filtered through his Rotarian principles, guided by the four-way test. When in 1945, for example, water shortages necessitated a special meeting of the Nowra Council, he argued that limitations on water should be placed on all but domestic usage. He argued that industrial users – including his own business – needed to receive permissions and quotas from the Water Committee. This was a position he defended alone against the rest of the business-oriented council and their claims that his suggestion was 'arrant stupidity'. In 1946, the council proposed an electricity subsidy. As a businessman, this would have benefitted Frank Sr personally, but he opposed the measure as it would be unfair to others. His belief that community undergirded business, rather than the other way around, was decisive.

Rotary had actively associated itself with the mission of the United Nations, which had formed in October 1945, and this encouraged Frank Sr to view his local and regional activities from a benevolent international perspective. The nascent Liberal Party provided him with an additional perspective, regarding the perceived malevolent forces at play within national and international politics – communism, in particular – and the promise to keep such forces at bay.

The following year, Nowra Rotary invited the US Ambassador to Australia, Mr Robert Butler, to speak on the topic of Australia–United States relations. At the Annual Rotary Conference, held in Goulburn in March 1947, one of the topics under discussion was 'Should Rotary Enter Politics?'. There was a lecture by Sir Robert

Garran. Then eighty years old, Garran was part of the Federation movement of the 1890s, working alongside Edmund Barton. In 1901, he was the first public servant hired in Australia, as secretary of the Attorney-General's Department.

That weekend in Goulburn, Garran appealed to Rotarians to give serious attention to the fourth aim of Rotary – international peace and goodwill – by affiliating with the United Nations. He argued that every 'sane Government knows that there must not be another war', and although Australian Rotarians were used to thinking and acting locally, it was incumbent upon them to 'train themselves to be citizens of the world, with an outlook beyond their immediate surroundings'.

This point was reinforced six months later, when the president of Rotary International, Ken Guernsey, visited Wollongong for a conference. Frank and Purth Moorhouse heard Guernsey argue that Rotary should work closely with the United Nations Organisation (UNO). 'I urge you to have faith in UNO,' he said. 'Don't be swayed by the disagreements, but remember rather the many matters on which agreement has been reached. Spread your confidence in UNO throughout the communities in which you live.'

Purth Moorhouse soon after became a committee member of the United Nations Association of Australia, Shoalhaven Branch. That same month, Frank Sr was elected secretary of his local Rotary. 'I have been attending these conferences over a number of years,' he was reported as saying, 'but each one that I attend gives me fresh inspiration and something fresh to think of. Rotary is like an inexhaustible well.'

In January 1947, during the school holidays, Frank and Purth Moorhouse went on vacation to New Zealand, to visit family and some old acquaintances. During that vacation, eight-year-old Frank was left in the care of eighteen-year-old Owen. With Arthur boarding in Wollongong, Owen would have seemed more distant to Frank than ever, focused as he was on his apprenticeship and getting ahead in the family business. Their parents' annual holidays were, in part, intended to create space for Owen to take charge.

Young Frank continued to be left more and more on his own, especially after school, when he would often come home to an empty house. For several years he spent a lot of time on his own in the house, usually with the ABC radio as company, the sound of which had become the background of his growing up. A favourite show was the *Children's Session*, which played every afternoon. This included *The Argonauts*, a live radio show that introduced Australian children to the world of art, science, literature and music.

Each week boys and girls around the country recited the Argonauts' oath: 'Before the sun and night and the blue sea, I vow to stand faithfully by all that is brave and beautiful; to seek adventure and having discovered aught of wonder, or delight, of merriment or loveliness, to share it freely with my comrades, the Band of Happy Rowers.'

Sometimes Frank would go over to Keith's house to play. There were always children of various ages at Keith's house who would join in their games. Frank did not register then that this was because Keith's house was, in fact, a foster home of sorts, and each of these children, Keith included, was an orphan.

One afternoon Frank came home from school to an empty house. When it turned dark outside, his family had still not appeared, so he wandered up the street to Keith's house. When he told them of his abandonment, they invited him to join them for supper and he sat down to a meal of bread and butter pudding. Eventually, his parents turned up to fetch him home. They knew by then where they would always find him.

At the end of Frank's first year of school in 1945, he was placed twentieth in his class. By the time he had reached the fourth year, his grades had greatly improved. In his report cards for 1948 he was averaging around 86 per cent, with his highest grades being in social studies. He was doing equally well in English and Arithmetic, but his lowest grade was for writing. The teacher's comment: 'Fine type of lad with all-round ability.'

As Frank and Keith grew older, they drifted apart. After Frank had a playground fight with a boy named Jackson Baker, they became best friends. On the weekend, after Sunday School, Frank would change out of his good clothes and meet up with Jackson, and they would head out into the bush for the day, exploring the natural surrounds.

In the fifth grade Frank became class captain. But what the teachers took to be politeness and good behaviour was in reality shyness and anxiety. Frank was terrified of being called on in class. When other kids were asked a question by the teacher, he found he often knew the answer, but when he was asked a direct question, he became paralysed.

Occasionally Frank was able to let slip his reserve. His teacher read out a story one day about a group of miners who used explosives to catch fish. Their retriever dog took one of the explosive cartridges in its mouth and, running by the fire, ignited it. Every time the dog went close to the men, they ran away, the dog thinking they were playing. Frank did not know the title or author of the story at the time. His focus was on its effect, especially the way the teacher got caught up in the telling of it and had the class enraptured. When they all broke out in laughter, Frank laughed too – and for that moment, albeit briefly, he found relief from his shyness, and for perhaps first time felt relaxed in the classroom.

Such moments lifted the crust from the stultifying atmosphere that had settled over Frank's childhood, from the war years during which he was born.

The annual Moorhouse the Machinery Man staff dinner was held in April of 1948. Staff and family were in attendance, including special guests and members of the local press. These were formal affairs, with a series of toasts, the chairman toasting the King, Frank Sr toasting the staff, one of the staff toasting the firm, and Owen toasting the press. At one point, Frank Sr mentioned

Rotary's four-way test. His secretary, Miss Vera Burne, was leaving her job to get married, and Purth Moorhouse gave her a gift of a complete dinner service, saying she hoped Miss Burne was going to be as happy in her married life as Mr and Mrs Moorhouse were in theirs.

For nine-year-old Frank, sitting patiently through the proceedings, perhaps the most interesting part was when Mr Bray performed some magic tricks. He had probably seen magic tricks before – the Thorpe McConville's 'Wild Australia' Rodeo Circus, for example, which came to Nowra in March the previous year, and would come again in December of 1948, had Ray McConville, billed as a Young Houdini, performing magic and escapology – but this night was perhaps the first time Frank had seen such tricks performed at close quarters. It allowed him to interpret the mysterious advertisements he saw weekly in the metropolitan newspapers – for 'Elusive Spot', 'Mystic Coin' and 'Diminishing Card' – which said he could get a 76-page 'Magic Catalogue' all the way from Sydney by writing to a company called Weirdo.

He sent away for the catalogue, and later joined the Magic Club.

In early September 1949, Purth was in hospital in Sydney for nearly a month for some minor surgery. It was probably during this period that Frank, accompanying his father to Sydney one weekend, visited Weirdo's Magic and Novelty Shop in person. Transferring his bush skills of navigation to the city, Frank set out alone from their apartment in Kings Cross to Pitt Street, where Weirdo's was situated in Piccadilly Arcade. There he bought his first deck of cards.

Frank had studied the instructions for card magic previously, following the hand-drawn illustrations in his head, turning over imaginary decks in his hands, but now he was able to practise with the real thing. All he needed was somebody to practise on.

In the apartment in Kings Cross, Frank asked his father if he could practise card tricks on him. His father said no. His father told him to practise in front of the mirror, and when Frank asked why, his father told him because in front of the mirror you can see what those in the audience can see – so if you can see in the mirror how the trick works, then so can those watching.

Although perhaps offered out of impatience, this was sound advice and contained a useful lesson in the art of sleight of hand: perspective is key. The magician must at all times be self-consciously aware, not just of their own actions, but of what their audience can and cannot see of those actions. If an audience member were sitting a few inches more to one side or the other, then they might spot the mechanics of the trick – the key cards, lifts, palms, crimps, back-slips, overhand shuffles and forces – and so dispel the illusion. It was the performance itself – mysteriously revealing a chosen card in a variety of ways, or making a chosen card disappear – which helped keep the mechanics from view and create the magical effect.

Most importantly, there was the routine itself in which the mechanics and the performance took place, and this was framed by the patter, the verbal commentary the magician gives of their performance as it is occurring. This was actually as important as mastering the mechanics of the trick itself, if not more important, because it created the veneer under which the mechanics were hidden. It helped misdirect the viewer's attention, and so set up their expectations regarding the trick – which then turned into astonishment when the opposite mysteriously occurred.

The patter instructed the viewer as to how they too could participate in the routine. They would be asked to choose a card, for example, and then told what to do with it, while in reality the magician was guiding the routine towards its predetermined conclusion: the effect. This was a practical form of storytelling, with immediate feedback from the audience: amazement, wonderment, incredulity. Or sometimes, as in the case of hearing Henry Lawson's 'The Loaded Dog' read out in class, laughter.

Young Frank spent a lot of time in front of the mirror in that flat in Kings Cross. Later, he did the same at home, in Nowra, and eventually he replaced the mirror with people, finding audiences at school, or at Cubs and Scouts. In the workshop, Arthur fashioned Frank a magic wand, painted black and white, but it was made out of steel Rebar and so weighed considerably more than a shop-bought wand – and was more dangerous when being waved about. Frank wore an old top hat, previously owned by Grandfather Cutts. It was too large for his head, and kept sliding down over his eyes, but Frank worked this into his routine, a way to distract and entertain his audience at the same time. Other times he would throw a handful of confetti to create the necessary cover for a required sleight. All the while he delivered his well-rehearsed patter, receiving immediate response and feedback from those watching on.

The 1949 annual staff dinner was held in December. Young Frank received a personal invitation. His reply was posted to the family home on Worrigee Street. It reads, in full:

18 Nov. 1949.
Dear Dad,
   I thank you for the opportunity of coming to the Staff Dinner, and I am looking forward to meeting you on the 2nd of December.
   Love, Frank

It had been another good year for the business, which had expanded yet again, this time to include trading in Ferguson tractors. The Moorhouse family was in full attendance, as were the staff and their families, along with special clients, local dignitaries and the press. Mr and Mrs Davis – of C.H. Davis and Co., who had first apprenticed Frank Sr in New Zealand, and had hired him again in Sydney – were present as special guests. That year, Arthur had started his apprenticeship at the Machinery Man, just as Owen completed his. Young Frank was next in line.

Frank Sr reminded those assembled that the purpose of these dinners was to reinforce the 'right spirit' between employer and employee. The subtext to this – especially as Frank Sr had become more politicised over the previous few years – was that the 'right spirit' was being disrupted by the Labor Party, and threatened by communism, and so required a more vigilant reinforcement.

After the usual series of toasts, Charles Davis made a special toast to Owen Moorhouse, for his upcoming twenty-first birthday, which he would be celebrating in New Zealand later that month.

The long-planned New Zealand trip involved Owen and Arthur canoeing 127 miles (over 200 kilometres) down the Whanganui River. It was an opportunity for them to visit their father's childhood stomping grounds. Owen's birthday fell on 24 December, which meant they would be away for Christmas and New Year. It also meant they would miss Frank's eleventh birthday. What grated on Frank was not that his brothers would miss his birthday, but that he would miss out on their canoe trip. He desperately wanted to go.

He pleaded his case, but unsuccessfully. Arthur had turned seventeen in August and had completed the first year of his electrical apprenticeship, so he was effectively an adult. Frank was still a child. Moreover, the canoe the older brothers had designed and built especially for the trip was only large enough for two people and their kit. Despite these objections, Young Frank saw his exclusion as unfair and a great injustice.

On 10 January 1950, *The Shoalhaven and Nowra News* published a letter Owen had sent to his parents from New Zealand regarding their experiences. They had arrived at Taurmarani on the evening of 21 December – Frank's birthday – and had reached Wanganui in the late afternoon of 27 December. Along the way they slept on the riverbank, one night in an old railway carriage, another under a sleeper dump. 'As we continued down the river we found the Maori's had a bush telegraph, and they checked us through each little village,' Owen wrote. Christmas day was spent with a large family of Māori who were celebrating with a *hāngi*, meat and vegetables wrapped in leaves and buried in a pit with hot coals.

Most consequentially, on the ship to New Zealand Owen had met a young woman. Her name was Muriel.

Meanwhile, brooding in Nowra, Frank read the letter when his parents received it early in the New Year, and again when it was edited and printed in *The Shoalhaven and Nowra News*. His annoyance at not being allowed to go with his brothers was compounded by the imprimatur of the local newspaper: it was now a real-life adventure existing in print. This authorised Owen and Arthur, when they returned later in January, to take centre stage at the Rotary meeting and tell their story in person, and to answer questions from the men gathered there – all watched over by their proud father.

Young Frank's magic shows did not make quite the same impact.

———

Arthur's New Zealand adventure afforded him further credence within the Scouts, the opening paragraph of the 'Scout News' column in the newspaper for 24 January 1950 welcoming him home: 'He seems very well, too, so the sharks couldn't have been fed.' When Frank made an appearance in the 'Scout News' a few months later, it was for less auspicious reasons.

On Good Friday, Frank Sr and Purth, together with another couple, left for a driving tour to Adelaide, via Melbourne. They were still absent when, on Friday, 19 May, an incident occurred during a Scout Investiture ceremony – in which Cubs are initiated into the Scouts – that took place in a quarry at the back of the Scouts' clubhouse in Nowra. The following week, on 23 May 1950, the 'Scout News' column reported: 'Young Frank Moorhouse met with an accident at the camp fire last Friday evening, necessitating medical attention. From reports, he is progressing satisfactorily, but he will be out of action for a while.'

Eleven-year-old Frank, who had gone through the ceremony the previous year, had climbed a tree in order to gain a better view of the proceedings. Sometime during the ceremony he lost his perch and slid down the rough trunk of the eucalypt, only coming to a halt when his crotch became impaled on a forked branch. He tumbled, bleeding, to the ground, calling for help. He soon found himself in hospital, where the doctor removed splinters from his groin and stitched his torn scrotum. Because Frank had recently eaten, the procedure had to be performed without anaesthetic.

In the hospital waiting room, Arthur could hear Frank's screams echoing down the hall.

Frank stayed home from school while he recuperated. He slept at night with a basket over his groin, in order to keep the weight of the sheets and blankets from rubbing against his stitches. His mother did not feel comfortable changing the bandages each day, so she solicited the help of a neighbour, a stern and frightening woman who did little to assuage any embarrassment or discomfort Frank felt about the situation.

He spent his days practising card tricks and reading. He read adventure stories, such as the Biggles books, written by Captain W.E. Johns. But it was *Alice's Adventures in Wonderland*, by Lewis Carroll, that seized his imagination. It was a get-well gift from Owen's new girlfriend, Muriel. Frank had developed a crush on her, and her red hair.

Reading *Alice* was like experiencing a well-executed card trick, but one that kept going, segueing into another trick, and then another. In the story, the cards themselves – the Queen of Hearts, the King, the Jack – literally come alive. For Young Frank the magician, this was a new type of trick, performed with words alone, and one he desperately wanted to learn for himself. Just as 'The Loaded Dog' had conditioned laughter, this recovery-bed reading stirred other emotions and imaginings.

The most common stories at Frank's disposal during this period were in *The Australian Women's Weekly*. He became interested not so much in the stories themselves, but in how they were put together – how they worked. It was shortly after this incident that Frank wrote his first story, in an attempt to capture that magic in words.

One Saturday in late 1950, after seeing a now forgotten Western film at the Roxy, Frank came home and transposed the plot he had just seen on the screen to the page. Like a good card routine, he was trying to work backwards from the effect to see the underlying mechanics of the trick, to find the performance within the patter, and to set about practising how to do it for himself.

That story no longer exists, so it is impossible to know for certain the film on which it was based. But there were only eighteen

Western films shown at the Roxy in 1950, following Frank's scouting accident. It is tempting to suggest it might have been *The Red Pony*, starring Robert Mitchum, as it is based on the John Steinbeck novel, foreshadowing Frank's later love of Steinbeck. But more likely it was a film that reflected eleven-year-old Frank's interests, such as George Montgomery's *Davy Crockett, Indian Scout*. Or perhaps one of the children's adventure films starring Tim Holt, also showing during this period – *Gun Smugglers*, *Red River Robin Hood* or *Stagecoach Kid*. Western films of this era were very formulaic: a generic adventure plot, binary themes of good guys versus bad guys, a lot of shooting and horse riding, a lady love interest and perhaps some 'Indians' in the background.

What matters more is that Young Frank wrote the story in order to capture the rush of involving oneself in a narrative, whether it be watching it on the big screen, or reading it, or writing it. But when he showed the story to his older brothers, they quickly dismissed it as a plagiarism, a rip-off of the film they had all just seen at the Roxy. Frank was crushed. In a sense, Frank attempted to write an adventure story to rival the adventure story his brothers had written and published in the newspaper earlier that year, based on their New Zealand trip. Yet again, Frank's efforts had fallen short. But the positive feelings associated with the act of writing lingered.

He just needed to have his own adventures to write about. And find a more appreciative audience.

3

'This is it; This Is Failure or Success in Life!'

In February 1951, twelve-year-old Frank Moorhouse began three years of middle school at Wollongong Technical College. As she had for her first two boys, Purth arranged for Frank to board during the week with Miss Merle Churchin in Wollongong. She would cook for Frank and clean his clothes, and give him a place to sleep. She would monitor Frank's behaviour, keeping him to a regular routine, ensuring he studied hard. Eventually, he came to feel more at home in Wollongong, in this working-class household, than he did in Nowra, where at weekends he felt like he was only visiting. Churchin's working-class home provided Frank with a point of comparison from which he could begin to put his own middle-class family life into a more critical perspective.

At college, Frank studied English, social studies, mathematics and science. The main emphasis at the school – and the main reason Frank Sr sent his sons there – was the more technical subjects: metalwork, woodwork and technical drawing. In his midyear report for 1951, Frank's highest grade was for technical drawing. His lowest grade was for English, although he was placed third. He had unanimously positive comments from his teachers. By the end of the year, his highest grades were for science and technical drawing, respectively, and his English grades were improving. He placed first overall for the year.

Although polite and popular among staff and students, Frank was also shy. Mr Allen, his English teacher, took Frank under his wing and helped develop his interest in reading and writing. The stories Frank was writing were calibrated to his audience, using familiarity to increase their effect. He would write about school life, the boys and the teachers, and shared his stories among his classmates. He had been reading books such as *Treasure Island* (1883), by Robert Louis Stevenson, and *Peter Pan and Wendy* (1911), by J.M. Barrie. But Mr Allen had the class read more adult books like John Buchan's *The Thirty-Nine Steps* (1915), after which Frank read all the Buchan novels he could find. Buchan provided Frank with a template for a more realistic, albeit still melodramatic, adventure story.

During his first year at Miss Churchin's, Frank experienced his first wet dream. This was not something he was prepared for, or understood. Such matters were not discussed at the time. What made the experience more disconcerting was that Frank's initial alarmed thought when he woke was that the wounds from his scouting injury had opened – that the sticky substance he could feel between his legs in the dark was blood. It was only after he had cleaned himself off in the light that he realised what had happened. Confusion and shame then set in.

Most weekends, Frank would return by train to Nowra. That not much had changed at home in his absence was perhaps an indication of how little his presence had affected his family's comings and goings. Frank would visit old schoolfriends or spend time on his own, wandering the surrounding bushland. By this time he had left the Scouts, unlike his brothers, who had continued into leadership roles. Frank was learning more bushcraft on his own. Besides, Wollongong Tech had a Cadet Corps, which, by 1952, Frank had joined – and they had rifles.

On his weekends in Nowra, Frank still had to attend church with his mother. On one occasion, at a Sunday School picnic, fourteen-year-old Frank was cajoled into participating in a three-legged race with a thirteen-year-old red-haired girl named Wendy Halloway. They won their race.

One change that had been brought into sharper relief in the Moorhouse home – as over the rest of Australia, and indeed the world – was a particular Cold War mentality. The topic would occupy much of Frank Sr's sometimes one-sided conversations. Prime Minister Robert Menzies, fulfilling an election promise, had introduced the *Communist Party Dissolution Act 1950*. A High Court challenge had been lodged against it. In February 1951, while everybody was waiting for the outcome, Nowra Rotary hosted a talk by an ex-communist. The speaker argued that a new world war had already begun, linking the communist threat to Australia's long-simmering fear of an Asian invasion, manifested in the spectre of the Chinese Red Army hovering close to Darwin. The following month, the High Court ruled the *Communist Party Dissolution Act* unconstitutional. A referendum on the issue was immediately called, to be held on 22 September 1951. The referendum was defeated by the narrowest of margins.

A few months later, Frank turned thirteen. He stayed at home over the summer holidays. As usual, his older brothers were busy elsewhere. Arthur was spending his holidays in Melbourne. Owen was preparing for a twelve-month research trip overseas, where he would visit all the Alfa Laval Separator Company sites across Europe. Before he left, Frank Sr and Purth invited some of Owen's friends, his fiancée, Muriel, and the Machinery Man staff to a 'bon voyage' party.

This event was reported in the newspaper, as was the entertainment: 'Frank Moorhouse, jun. delighted the audience with his card tricks.'

Frank's first year at Wollongong Tech had ended well, but during the second year he began to stall. By the middle of 1952, his best subject was science, and his worst was woodwork. He had dropped back to fifth place in English, with his teacher suggesting he would do better with 'concentrated effort'. His woodwork teacher agreed: 'not enough concentration'. By the end of that year, Frank's highest grade was for English – the only problem he had to solve was 'elimination of spelling errors' – and his lowest grade was for mathematics. He had started to lose interest in the technical subjects. This was reflected in a drop in grades, and in the tenor of his teachers' comments: Frank could 'do better', and was 'not working to capacity'. He was fourteenth overall in his year.

One explanation for Frank's loss of focus was that, during this period, he was sexually molested by an adult male. The details are unclear, but this occurred on at least two separate occasions. One incident occurred on the train between Nowra and Wollongong, although it is unclear if this was the same perpetrator. Frank developed strategies to either avoid this person altogether or else ensure he was not left alone with him. He told nobody about this at the time, trying to cope alone.

A heightened sense of apartness from his family developed. At home, he increasingly found their political opinions disagreeable. During the Cold War, the deviant figure of the homosexual was deployed as a moral scapegoat, in the same way that the figure of the communist was used as a political scapegoat. Both fed an impetus to clamp down upon perceived post-war lapses in moral and political virtue.

This was the context within which Frank nursed the wounds of his molestation, which had compounded the sexual and gender confusions and the anxieties puberty had already stirred within him. But Frank did not openly argue with his family, nor did he display any anger. Instead, he would sink into silence, morose and melancholic. In these moments, he would sit at his old desk out in the sleepout, reading or just thinking. Other times, he would write.

Mr Allen continued to nurture Frank's interest in reading and writing. A student newsletter was established in 1952, called *Elouera*, which Frank co-edited. In August, Frank published what is his earliest extant story, called 'Trouble at the Tech'.

It was about six o'clock on a dark Friday night when tall, sandy-haired Bill Mutton, known to his friends as 'Desert Head', entered the steel gates of the Wollongong Tech. in Gladstone Avenue.

It was unusual for Bill to return to school at this hour, but he had lost his new fountain pen and he simply had to find it.

Fortunately, Bill has brought along his 'flashlight camera', because after he locates his fountain pen, he encounters two would-be burglars trying to steal the school's trophies. Bill uses the camera to take their photo (to give to the police, he thought), but when the burglars see the flash, they chase him.

And so, in 836 tightly packed words, amid much running and leaping, young Bill manages to set a slick-trap of spilled floor polish, have pistols fired at him, lob fire extinguishers in return, climb out of windows, use a 'waddy' to furiously lash the burglars, and entangle them in a volleyball net, before running into two policemen and giving his statement (but not, curiously, giving them his camera film).

After giving a statement, Bill raced off home, but when he got there . . . he discovered that in the chase he had lost his fountain pen again.

However, you may be sure that he did not go back again that night.

Elsewhere in *Elouera*, Frank reviewed the annual Play Night, when different classes performed their own plays or adaptations. The opportunity enabled Frank to form his own critical opinions, while also displaying his sardonic wit. Frank's only experience of the theatre until then had been when he performed in *Robin Hood* at primary school, wearing green tights and a tricornered hat, carrying a bow and arrow on the stage.

The first play he reviewed, *The Lion's Whelp*, was 'lacking in action' but contained 'good, clear speech'. The second, *The Stolen Prince*, was 'a well-rehearsed, fast moving play, conducted in the old Chinese manner'. The best play of the evening was *A Night at the Inn*, because it contained horror elements that 'thrilled the crowd immensely'.

The other two plays – *A Distant Relative* and *Scenes from Twelfth Night* – were notable for the female parts being played by boys. On the former, Frank stated: 'The feminine parts, acted by Paul Evans and Ted Duckett, were capably acted and provided a highlight for the play.' And for the latter: 'The "ladies", Olivia (Jeff Brittin) and Maria (Fred Badman) looked extraordinarily well in their feminine finery. The costumes were very colourful and suited the period.'

The practice of men playing female roles in the theatre has a long history. It was commonplace in the army – the theatrical troupes entertaining soldiers often had 'femmes' in their ensemble. It was also commonplace in all-boys schools, like Wollongong Tech. But cross-dressing also occurred in the broader adult public sphere, especially in Australian country towns, in the form of mock weddings, where men and women switched roles for an evening.

In Nowra, a month following Play Night, a mock wedding was held. The 'bride' was named 'Cherry Peachblossom' and his 'bridesmaids' were 'Lemonelia' and 'Pansy'. The 'groom' was named 'Solomon Plumstone' and her 'groomsmen' were 'Adam Apple' and 'Cecil Bruna Rose'. The guests also cross-dressed, and the proceedings were overseen by 'Professor Tinklebell'.

Such occurrences may have been confusing for Frank at this stage of his development. They may have been intriguing. But he would have been aware of the broader social context: such events were held up as authorised aberrations, done in order to reinforce what 'normal' gender roles looked like. The emphasis of these events, after all, was to mock. 'The usual toasts were honoured and responses made amid much laughter,' the local newspaper reported.

During that same week in Nowra, the 'Father and Son Movement', co-sponsored by Rotary, had three screenings of films, and accompanying lectures, titled *The Facts of Life*. The visiting host of the event was a guest of Clive Hamer – a relatively new schoolteacher at Nowra High. The first two screenings were for men and boys, and the final screening for ladies and girls. The evenings provided the 'Christian answer' to sex education, which was broken down into three phases of 'the sex problem': '(1) the case of the lad with no home training; (2) the case of the young married couple, improperly informed regarding their sex education, and (3) the case of the young woman facing life without proper guidance'.

These films did not cover nocturnal emissions, same-sex attraction or what to do if you were sexually molested by an adult.

An additional project assigned to Frank at *Elouera* was to research the history of writing and printing. The article, with hand-drawn illustrations, surveyed the development of writing, from early 'picture writing' up to the invention of the alphabet, and its transposition from Greek to English. It covered the invention of Gutenberg's sixteenth-century printing press, including the world's first newspaper, 'the "Zeitung" (Daily)' – Frank was referring to the *Einkommende Zeitungen*, launched in 1650 – and the first English printer, William Caxton, leading up to the (then) modern rotary press. The article concluded: 'We can say that the invention of writing and printing has transformed the whole life of man.'

The importance of this project, and the practical experience of designing and printing a newsletter, expanded Frank's understanding of writing: it was not only an imaginative and intellectual activity, but a technical one too. It deepened his interest in writing, now more broadly construed as an activity encompassing editing, printing and publishing – and as an activity with its own history.

In February 1953, after Frank had returned to Wollongong to begin his final year, his father received a handwritten letter from the deputy headmaster: 'Dear Mr Moorhouse, You will be delighted to know that Frank was highly honoured today by being elected school captain for 1953.' Frank Sr had this news published in the newspaper. By midyear, social studies had become Frank's best subject. His worst subject remained mathematics. Admitting defeat, his mathematics teacher allowed Frank to sit at the back of the classroom and read. This paid off, because Frank quickly earned first place in English, a position he would hold through to graduation.

Owen had returned home from his twelve-month trip overseas and was eager to begin selling his father's manufactured goods internationally. Arthur started the year on a high note, having completed his apprenticeship and earning his electrical certificate. Although the business had grown over the years, it was difficult to see how it would sustain four Moorhouse men in management roles. Frank would not have been satisfied in a subordinate role, and in any case had already made up his mind that he did not want to follow his brothers' path. He wanted to complete high school. He just needed to find a way to tell the family.

That year in Wollongong, Frank started dating a girl named Nola Johanson. She was in her final year of high school. At sixteen, she was two years older than Frank, and although they were still both under the legal drinking age, she would take Frank into pubs to drink with her and her friends. Alcohol allowed Frank to overcome his social anxieties, holding in abeyance his inner tensions and recent traumas. It also helped him postpone facing some important life decisions.

It was probably Nola who encouraged Frank to complete high school. She was very supportive of Frank's writing, reading his stories and offering constructive criticism. She encouraged him to submit them for publication. He sent them to *The Australian Women's Weekly*. He also submitted two stories to the *Australian Magazine* – otherwise known as *A.M.* – a pictorial magazine containing feature stories, short stories and reviews. In March 1953, Frank received his first rejection letter, from the editor of *A.M.*, Cyril Pearl. 'I was very interested in your two stories which you sent me though they are not quite suitable for publication in "A.M.",' it read. 'They show that you have a very good idea of story writing and you should certainly continue to write stories.'

For many students in Frank's class, 1953 would be the final year of schooling. To help them decide what line of work to pursue, the school provided vocational guidance. On one occasion a teacher spoke individually with each of the 150 final-year students. When Frank's turn came, the teacher rifled through a stack of cards with details of each of the students, including their grades, teachers' comments and other internal notes. The teacher said advertising was the right job for Frank. It required a sharp intelligence, which, according to these grades and comments, Frank displayed.

The teacher then glanced at Frank and said, 'Wait a minute – what is your name?'

'Moorhouse.'

'Sorry,' the teacher said. 'I had the wrong record.' He shuffled the cards and scanned Frank's for a moment. 'Now, wouldn't you like to go into your father's business?'

The state government provided a more formal Vocational Guidance Service. When Frank fronted the Vocational Officer, he said he wanted to be a fiction writer. The Vocational Officer didn't have a card file for a fiction writer. But after speaking with Frank about his experiences and interests, they suggested he might try his hand at journalism. He could then write fiction on the side.

His parents, although initially disappointed, were supportive of Frank's decision to pursue a career as a journalist. Journalism was not an entirely disreputable occupation (unless it was for a communist newspaper). After all, the Moorhouse family were frequently in the local press, and encouraged and cultivated the relationship. The press was a useful tool for business and community engagement. Frank Sr even harboured some hope that Frank's talents might somehow be deployed in the service of the family business, perhaps in a copywriting, publicity or advertising role.

In the short term, Frank's decision to become a journalist meant he would spend another two years at school. Although a high school certificate was not necessary for securing a journalism cadetship, it was desirable and would make Frank a more competitive candidate. Frank harboured a deeper desire – the possibility of attending university – which for the times was ambitious.

Frank's mother showed her support for Frank's decision in her usual practical and forthright manner. That year, the Commonwealth Literary Fund had arranged for writers to visit regional Australia. The poet Rosemary Dobson visited Nowra at an event held at the School of Arts. This was the first poet – indeed, the first Australian writer – Frank had seen in the flesh. Afterwards, she was sitting on a table. Frank was too shy to approach her, so Purth went up to Dobson and said that she had a fourteen-year-old son who wanted to be a writer. She interrogated Dobson about rates of pay, prospects for getting published, the morality of the literary world, and generally whether she thought it was a good idea for Frank to pursue this course of action. Dobson proved persuasive.

Frank was on the editorial committee of the school magazine that year. The 1953 volume of *Excelsior* included a piece by Frank which displays how his confidence in his writing had developed – perhaps to the point of cockiness. 'As We Would Like It' included an excerpt of William Shakespeare's play *As You Like It*, but translated – as Frank explained in his introduction – for the 'modern school-boy':

> It always puzzles me to understand why teachers say that Shakespeare is England's greatest writer. So I, being a benevolent humanitarian, have decided to write, on behalf of our honourable and esteemed system of education, a modern and up-to-date edition of Shakespeare's work.

What followed was a rewriting of Act 1, Scene 1, set in a pigpen where Orlando had been kept. He complains to his older brother, Oliver, about the way he has been treated. A taste:

> **Oliver:** (seething with anger.) And do you know who you are speaking to?
> **Orlando:** (He knows more grammar than Oliver.) Yes, I do know to whom I am speaking. But listen, elder brother, be a good fellow and take a sensible view of the situation. After all, the United Nations preach 'Freedom of speech and equality,' and you should look after me, you know.

'As you will readily agree,' Frank concluded, 'my version has somewhat livened up the play. Of course, our English teachers may not agree . . . they never do, but any average, broad-minded schoolboy would be interested in the full edition of Moorhouse's Modern "As You Like It". 5/6 everywhere.'

Frank had completed his intermediate studies with a first place in English, and a second place in social studies. During his time at Wollongong Tech, Frank played first-grade Rugby League. In 1953 he was singled out as the most improved player. That year he was one of five non-commissioned officers in the cadets to undergo specialist training, with Cadet Sergeant Frank Moorhouse becoming a qualified signaller.

It was customary at Wollongong Technical College's annual speech day to award the top students in the final year with tools that they might take with them into their future trades. Knowing Frank had decided not to join the family business, Mr Allan – supportive to the end – arranged for Frank to be presented with a copy of *The King's English* (1906), by H.W. Fowler and G.G. Fowler, a handbook of English usage and grammar – an essential tool for Frank's chosen trade of writing.

Frank turned fifteen that December, and he left the residence of Miss Churchin and returned to Nowra to complete his final two years of high school. In many respects, moving back into the family home was like moving into another boarding house. Choosing to complete high school meant Frank had effectively opted out of the family routine.

This situation was not unique to the Moorhouse family. Across the Western world, a cultural shift was taking place during these post-war years, with an extension of adolescence and the emergence of the 'teenager'. This coincided with the rise of rock 'n' roll music and films about disaffected and rebellious youth. That cultural dividing line cut through the Moorhouse family, midway between Owen and Frank, with Arthur teetering on the side of Owen and their parents.

This separation between Frank and his family took on a symbolic legal form during the first half of 1954, when the family business – which until then was a legal partnership between Frank Sr, Purth and Owen (with Arthur as an employee) – had been dissolved and reconstituted in June as a limited liability propriety company: Moorhouse the Machinery Man, Pty Ltd. The four directors and sole shareholders were Frank Sr (governing director), Purth (secretary), Owen (sales director) and Arthur (service director). Frank was excluded – by choice, but excluded nonetheless.

To earn pocket money, Frank arranged with his father that he would wash the utility trucks and vans the business sold. Frank Sr also tested his youngest son by getting him to write an advertorial for a demonstration day for the family business. This became Frank's first published newspaper article, appearing in *The Nowra Leader* in January 1954.

Frank began by describing the background of the Greenhills farm – the site of the demonstration day – from the founding of Nowra in the 1850s to the present, including Alexander Berry and the various advances in dairy technology. Yet he placed the beginning of its history further back: 'This brown sea has had a varied and vigorous history since native tribes held their corroborees on its grassy flats.' The article is similar in outline and approach to Frank's earlier student newsletter article on the history of writing and printing, but transposed the history to farming equipment.

It was a piece of writing Frank did under some duress, but it had the desired effect: afterwards his family let him get on with his reading and writing with little interference. From the outside, it was difficult to tell if what he was doing when he was sitting at his desk in the sleepout was schoolwork, training for journalism or his own short stories and essays. It all looked the same to them. Frank would often use the former sanctioned activities as a cover for private writing.

In his first year at Nowra High School, Frank discovered the work of Ernest Hemingway, finding a copy of *The Fifth Column and the First Forty-Nine Stories* (1938) in a second-hand shop on Berry Street. Although Hemingway's public persona was a man of action, his stories dealt with subtle crises of masculinity, of fear and cowardice and suicide. The young Nick Adams stories provided Frank with a perspective from which to consider more precisely his own adolescent self. Frank was drawn to the fact that Hemingway was a journalist as well as a fiction writer, and this reinforced his resolve to do both.

Further support for Frank's decision to become a writer came from Aunt Sylvie – his father's sister, in New Zealand – who gifted Frank an Imperial typewriter, on which he slowly taught himself how to touch-type. Aunt Sylvie knew about strange paths and encouraged Frank, even from a distance, to follow them. As a guide, she sent him a copy of *The Collected Stories of Katherine Mansfield* (1945). In these modernist stories Frank found a way to begin articulating an inner ambiguity he had always felt.

But while Hemingway helped Frank think about the exteriority of the male self and the craft of writing short stories, and Mansfield opened him up to the possibilities of the interiority of the female self and sexual ambivalences, it was the work of John Steinbeck – especially *The Grapes of Wrath* (1939) and *East of Eden* (1952) – that helped Frank find a balance between lyricism and social realism, a way to look beyond the self towards the world, and a language to make sense of both.

On 4 March 1954, the 28-year-old Queen Elizabeth II, on her first royal visit to Australia since her coronation in 1952, attended an event at the Wollongong Showground. Schoolchildren from the Shoalhaven region were bussed in for a glimpse of the new monarch. The following week, Frank's composition class wrote about the occasion. They had been taught first to plan and structure what they were about to write, with main topics divided into subtopics, with an introduction and conclusion.

'The Queen responded in a tired voice and the Duke stood by, bored but disguising his feelings well,' Frank wrote. 'Perhaps the surf in the background made him wish he was a steelworker at the time.' His teacher crossed out the word 'tired' and placed a red question mark beside the second sentence.

The comments on his weekly composition exercises go some way to indicating Frank's attitude to his schoolwork during his first year back in Nowra. He was frequently thoughtful, but tended not to go back and correct past errors, always preferring to move on to the next thing. After weeks of increasingly exasperated comments, his teacher finally wrote: 'Why don't you correct your errors?'

The month before the Queen's visit, Frank was elected as a school prefect. One of the other prefects that year was his friend

Peter Martin, a year ahead of Frank. They would often go on long bike rides together, usually along the South Coast, sometimes camping out overnight. In 1955, for his final year, Frank was again made a prefect, as well as school captain. His co-captain was Helen Jordan. Technically, Frank was captain of the boys and Helen was captain of the girls. Frank and Helen were briefly high-school sweethearts.

As a prefect, Frank's main tasks included supervising other students and ensuring they stayed within the boundaries of the schoolyard, and that there was no fighting, no bullying and no littering. Prefects were to set an example for other students, and in return enjoyed certain privileges, including having their own recreation room. But they endured extra duties, such as attending regular prefect teas, which were very formal affairs, often including a visiting lecture, to help prepare them for their future leadership roles in the community.

Outwardly, sixteen-year-old Frank played the role of prefect diligently. But inwardly, he was rebelling. This only found expression in his private writing sessions. In an essay titled 'Prefects To-day', written on his Imperial typewriter, Frank argued that schools must seek out any 'obsolete pieces' holding them back from modernising.

'One thing that has outlived its usefulness and is starting to become malignant is the age old system of school prefects, or in other words, school police,' he began. Frank found the electoral process flawed, and the swearing-in process built false expectations. 'The badge on the coat injects the wearer with a false superiority,' Frank wrote, 'and the prefect strides about the school with determination and with a swagger suited to his position.' This all collapses the moment the prefect is confronted by their first instance of wrongdoing and they have to send one of their fellow students to the headmaster's office. Resentful of the teachers above them, in whose authority the prefects are acting as a proxy, and resented by the student body below them, from which they had been involuntarily elevated, the prefects end up keeping company with each other, becoming cynical towards the whole school system.

These ideas informed a short story Frank wrote at the time called 'The Boy Who Did His Duty', about a student who becomes a prefect. It follows the election and the pledge, in similar terms as in the essay. But he then finds three fourth-year students smoking. 'The pledge repeated itself in his head like a tock of a clock.' He tells them to stop smoking, but they don't. 'His badge felt conspicuously large.' They laugh at him when he tells them to go to the office. After some taunts, they acquiesce, but only after finishing their cigarettes. The biggest boy tells the prefect to meet him after school at the vacant allotment for a fight. The prefect agrees, unable to back down.

After school he goes to the allotment. He is the first one there. 'He sat and tried to solve the problem of loyalty to his friends and duty of office.' Finally, he realises the other boys are not coming. 'He mentally triumphed and smiled.' They were all talk, too scared to confront him. 'It was with well-feeling pride that he walked back to his bike,' the final paragraph concludes. 'At his bike he stopped and stared. His jaw clenched. He wheeled the bike away but it did not wheel very well, a bike with the tyres slashed and the spokes trodden out never does.'

In his final year, one of the new prefects from the year below was a young woman named Wendy Halloway, the red-headed girl with whom Frank had once won the three-legged race at a Sunday School picnic. Frank and Wendy had not really crossed paths during the previous year, but when they were both elected as prefects, they were brought into closer orbit.

The prefects had a roster system for gate duty, before and after school as well as during lunch breaks, to check people coming and going. They operated in pairs, with boys and girls together. In this way, Frank and Wendy spent an increasing amount of time together. They would linger before and after their rostered duties, sitting together on the paspalum beside the front gates of the school, talking about everything.

In June 1954, John Landy, an Australian middle-distance runner, was the second person in the world to run a mile in under four minutes. Inspired by this feat, Frank joined the Nowra High athletics team. Outside team sessions, Frank read the latest scientific methods for physical training, and put together his own regime of diet and exercise. He studied race tactics. In September, at an interschool sports carnival in Wollongong, in the under-sixteen division, Frank came third in the 440-yard run and fourth in the mile. The following year, he came first in the 880-yard run and second in the 440. His discipline and training had paid off.

It was a discipline he also applied to his writing. He read Sir Arthur Quiller-Couch's *On the Art of Writing* (1916), based on a series of lectures given at Cambridge University in 1913: 'Literature is not a mere Science, to be studied; but an Art, to be practised.' Any words Quiller-Couch used of which Frank did not know the meaning he looked up in a dictionary and scribbled the definition in the margin. For his own writing, he kept his Fowler & Fowler English usage book close by. In sharp contrast to his classroom composition exercises, his extracurricular writing – both in handwritten and typed drafts – contains frequent corrections, amendments, additions and subtractions, together with a final, clean, typed version, which he kept in a folder.

The only lesson he heeded from composition class was to plan and structure a piece of writing, with set topics and subtopics, a practice he transposed to his short-story writing. Here he outlined a story about going on a date with a girl:

Action
Boy meets girl's eyes
Repeat
Boy discusses girl
Boy attempts to date girl
Boy dates girl
Worries over future date – money
The meeting
Manners and fears, places arm around girl ('Scene: Picture show')
Milkshakes
The Kiss

For Frank, writing was a way to interrogate his own thinking about particular aspects of social life and his place in it. It was a space to rehearse different ways of being in the world.

He turned to writing, for example, to think through his relationship to sport. One essay was called 'Why I Do It', or, in another draft, 'Why I Chose Rugby League as a School Sport'. 'The other day I went onto a rectangular piece of earth bounded by white lines and controlled by a so-called neutral man, to struggle mentally and physically for a leather ball.' The opening paragraphs depersonalise the game, describing it according to its external features – the bodies on the field, the uniforms, the ball and the whistle – in order to expose the strangeness of the ritual.

He then asks himself why he participates, and with each reason he comes a step closer to reimagining the game from within, from the internal perspective of a player for whom the ritual is not so strange after all. He claims he plays for 'personal glory', for the personal satisfaction of doing something well and of hearing the praise of his fellow players. He plays for 'entertainment', which he defines as a wilful distraction from, and a 'means of forgetting', the self and its complications, its 'general tasks and troubles'. He does it for the 'glory of the team and the glory of the school'. It provides a sense of belonging to something greater than the self, and is, Frank surmises, a model for other group belonging, such as to a township or a nation.

This essay too led Frank to write a story on the same topic. It was called 'The Boy Who Tried'. A schoolboy who has never played football before is encouraged to try out for the school team. He worries about the roughness of the sport but agrees to try. The middle section of the story recounts his training schedule – transposed from Frank's actual athletic regimen – his attempts to build his fitness and strength, and to improve his game skills. Finally, game day comes, and after an initial demoralising stint on the bench, he gets his chance. But then, after a dramatic section break in the story, there is an understated epilogue: 'They said it was the other fellows fault but who is to judge? Anyway a broken leg can not be fixed by blame.'

A pattern was beginning to take shape, in which Frank would write an essay on a particular theme, to clarify his thinking, drawing from his own experience. He would then analyse and categorise, positing it as a formal structure, from which he could then gain enough perspective in order to question or criticise it in various ways. And then, from within that formal structure, he would reimagine the theme in terms of character and action, from which he could begin to build a fictional story. Often the only semblance to the real-world experience in which a story had its starting point was in emotion and mood.

One of the boys who played football with Frank was Paul Coombes. Paul was in the grade below Frank – he was Wendy's friend and classmate – but because of his size he was allowed to play with the older boys. There was a natural affinity between Frank and Paul, because Paul hated authority perhaps even more than Frank, and they were both voracious readers.

Reading had become an integral part of Frank's daily regime to become a writer. He had always read, but now he was doing so in an organised, almost systematic manner. Reading was no longer about distracting him from where he was, but became a way for him to plot where he wanted to go. He approached it as a way of gaining more knowledge about the world.

He also considered the form of what he read, to learn how best to communicate that knowledge in writing. There was no public library in Nowra. The School of Arts Library was small and contained mainly romance, adventure and mystery fiction, all of which he had picked over and outgrown. On the shelves at home were his mother's poetry books: Keats, Tennyson, Longfellow. In his father's office there was a series of Herbert N. Casson's books on business and technology, and books by Winston Churchill and Benjamin Franklin. Frank worked his way through most of these, too.

The two most important sources of reading for Frank during this period were the monthly delivery of books from the State Library of New South Wales, and the subscription to the *Current Affairs Bulletin*. Both of these were done on Frank's own initiative. This meant his reading choices could be unsupervised by parents or school. The cardboard carton of books arrived each month on the train from Sydney. He chose works from all subject areas. Meanwhile, the *Current Affairs Bulletin*, which launched in 1942, arrived fortnightly through the post, with each issue dedicated to a topic of political, economic or cultural concern, either national or international.

Frank Sr continued to try to influence Frank during this period by giving him particular reading material. In lieu of suffering through the awkwardness of a father-and-son conversation about sex, he gave Frank the book *Why We Behave Like Human Beings* (1925), by George A. Dorsey. It is a 500-page survey of the biological and psychological bases of human development and adult behaviour, including habit formation, linguistic organisation and sexual instincts. It is unclear if Frank Sr had read the book before giving it to Frank.

Dorsey attempted to demystify sex, undoing the 'confusion and nonsense' leading to puritanism and the belief that marriage 'is a divine institution and the god of Love is a saint, but sex is shameful and Cupid is a carnal beast'. He suggested there was a basic bisexual nature to human beings, in which the 'two sexes differ in degree rather than in kind'.

Dorsey argued against the notion of a natural inequality between men and women, pointing instead to the ways social and cultural forces shaped gender roles. '[T]he vicious element in such phrases as "Woman's proper work" and "Woman's true sphere" is the assumption implied of lack of capacity,' Dorsey wrote. 'To assume that her capacity for intelligent behaviour or human adjustments is less than man's is biologically and physiologically absurd.' For Dorsey, boys and girls become men and women through an upbringing that encourages greater physical freedom for boys, but a more narrow emotional range, while girls have their physical freedom restricted but with a broader emotional leeway. But the freedoms do not necessarily compensate for the restrictions, with the latter often undermining the former.

Implicit in Dorsey's argument was a suggestion that forms of cross-dressing may act as a counterbalance to such social and cultural pressures:

> Men, to 'understand' women, must be brought up as women: play dolls, wear dresses, be coddled, petted, protected, favoured, shielded, guarded, restricted, chucked under the chin, kissed. And thereby driven to such outlets as are open to women and have no more 'expected' of them than men expect of women.

The Dorsey book may have been Frank's introduction to the field of psychology, but around this time he also discovered the Pelican series of paperback psychology books. Frank sought out as many of these as he could. He read, for example, *Uses and Abuses of Psychology* (1953), by H.J. Eysenck, which introduced him to Alfred Kinsey's research on male sexuality. He learned about psychological testing, and then began – from a distance – to analyse and categorise his fellow students, teachers and family.

Eysenck complicated the notion of 'normality' by considering it under three aspects: the statistical, the ideal and the natural. The statistical definition focused on what was characteristic of the majority of people. The 'ideal' aspect may be 'statistically infrequent, or . . . not found at all in the population examined'. The tension – often the contradiction – between the statistical and ideal definitions of 'normality' are often papered over by the use of the natural definition, in which what was socially and culturally particular was considered biological and universal – that is, natural. Wrote Eysenck:

> Thus, we consider it normal for the male to be dominant and the female to be submissive; we consider heterosexual attraction normal, homosexual attraction abnormal. We would hold these views even though it could be shown that in some communities, among the ancient Greeks, say, homosexuality was statistically more frequent than heterosexuality, or that among some nations, say the ancient Egyptians, the women tended to be more aggressive and the males more submissive.

All this brought into sharper relief for Frank how his own small world had been shaped in various ways, from childhood onwards, through the Scouts and the Guides, in the way boys and girls at school had separate playgrounds, and how they were then policed by prefects and teachers. When Frank had wanted to do an art class, for instance, he was told he could not because that subject was reserved for girls. Eysenck's main point, which Frank absorbed, was that authority was often deployed to police the natural definition of 'normality', to 'be on the look-out for, and to condemn, reject, and punish, people who violate conventional values'.

Frank always had a book in his back pocket, so he could read whenever he had a few moments to spare. This was not in itself an affectation – although what was an affectation was that he always made sure the title was facing outwards, the cover on show. This sometimes backfired, as when a teacher confiscated his copy of *Uses and Abuses of Psychology*, deeming it unacceptable for a fifteen-year-old schoolboy – which only confirmed Eysenck's warning about figures in authority.

His growing understanding of gender roles and psychological categories informed Frank's short story 'Tch! Tch!', which is about how school socials were constructed as authorised places where boys and girls could interact in approved ways, but even here informal rules and social categories came into play.

The protagonist is anxious because he has started casually dating one of the girls at school, and so is now expected to take her to the dance and act in particular ways. 'He was nearly forced by circumstances to take his school-fostered girl friend to the dance.' What he fears is the inevitable situation following the dance, on the walk home, when he will be expected to kiss her, or at least to try to kiss her. His conditioning for this moment has come from talking with his friends and watching films.

> He knew what females were for but with the same attitude as he knew the uses of a telephone; he knew that there was such a thing as love but he also knew that there was such a thing as soap; he had always protested

a life of bachelorhood but he did this with the same thoughtlessness as he said 'goodmorning' to his parents at the breakfast table. Females were now in a new and painfully sharp perspective.

Frank Sr tried to influence his youngest son politically, by giving him copies of a new magazine, *The Free Spirit*, published by the recently formed Australian Committee for Cultural Freedom, the president of which was the former politician and recently retired Chief Justice of the High Court, Sir John Latham. The magazine was distributed to members of the Liberal Party in Australia. Although *The Free Spirit* carried some domestic content, it mainly comprised syndicated pieces from international magazines, such as *Encounter*, from the United Kingdom, and *Commentary*, from the United States. This exposed Frank to an eclectic mix of international writers and topics.

The first issue came out in August 1954, with an introduction by Latham. The opening line set the tone for the magazine's agenda: 'The conflict between freedom and authority cannot be settled or adjusted by the mechanical application of any absolute rule.' Although a person might support and promote certain religious or political principles and practices, Latham said, they must do so voluntarily. What violated freedom was when a person was compelled to do so.

For Frank Sr, giving his son this material to read might have had an unintended consequence, one that unwittingly inverted the Hicklin test in order to undermine the 'householder test'. Frank Sr read *The Free Spirit* as reinforcing the fight for freedom against communism, which he saw as the animating force behind Labor Party politics in Australia. Young Frank read the same arguments as reinforcing, in part, his own fight against parental and school authority, and the conformity of their social, political and religious doctrines. His parents might have chosen their positions and attitudes voluntarily, but these had been imposed upon Frank. Although his father had given *The Free Spirit* to Frank to counter the influence of the *Current Affairs Bulletin*, Frank used the ideas expressed in both magazines to sharpen his thinking against all forms of conformity, and to strike out on his own intellectual path.

Frank's religious faith, for example, had begun to wane during his time at Wollongong Tech, but it was not until he was at Nowra High that he began consciously overriding the habits of faith. He was unable to get out of going to church with his mother each Sunday, but he decided to stop saying his prayers each night in bed. He awoke the next morning relieved to find nothing had happened.

Rebellion against religious authority was a theme Frank explored in his story 'On Going to Church'. Formally, it was the most inventive of the stories Frank wrote at this time. The narrative wove together three perspectives of an otherwise ordinary event: going to church. The main through line is a third-person depiction of an outwardly obedient and polite adolescent who accompanies his mother to Sunday service. The second thread is spun by the minister's sermon, snippets of which are presented throughout, without context, and which punctuate the third perspective, which is the internal monologue of the adolescent, commenting on the sermon and on the other parishioners, contrasting their pious idealism with his growing awareness of a discordant social reality.

The boy's consciousness drifts in and out of other fragments of memory and sexual fantasy. He has a brief sexual fantasy about a middle-aged woman 'with exciting proportions'. But he is interrupted by a reminder of the outside world, suggestive of the influence of Frank's Cold War reading material: 'A jet aeroplane whistled above the church and he thought of the approaching war and the insecurity of the world. He wondered if it was worth while planning for the future.' Then his thoughts turn to memories of the previous night, his girlfriend, her perfume still on his coat, their 'sensual kisses and thrilling caresses'.

The story concludes with the narrator returning home with his mother. 'At home he changed his clothes, ate his breakfast and settled down with the Sunday papers opening them directly at the court reports for the latest sex crimes.'

At the end of the 1954 school year, Frank joined the editorial committee of his school magazine, *The Platypus*, as the sports editor. That edition contained a short story of his that drew together many of his nascent political and social concerns, particularly regarding his general fear of an approaching war. The story is called 'Is This Us?', and it tells of Johnny Australia, a schoolboy in his final year of high school, as he faces his future.

Johnny sits for his Leaving Certificate, and then finds out he has been successful enough to go into the field of machinery manufacturing and design. But before he can enter the design firm, war breaks out and the country's youth is mobilised. The story ends with Johnny answering the call for enlistment:

> A hate of the world burned in Johnny. Yes, it was once a beautiful world, but now it was a disgusting world, sordid, and full of injustice. He took his coat and went to enlist. The mountains looked dull and uninteresting, the sky a dirty blue; the town was buzzing with wide-eyed, panicky people; business had stopped; people gazed skywards, watching and wondering.

The story is overwrought and melodramatic, yet it reflects the pitch of paranoia that characterised the first decade of the Cold War. It was an atmosphere particularly heavy within the Moorhouse family, in which the domestic scene was often crushed between international politics and local community activities.

The high rhetoric of Frank's story was inspired by the history textbook which he was reading at school. *Modern Britain* (1950), by Denis Richards and J.W. Hunt, began with the eighteenth-century agrarian revolution in England, as a precursor to the industrial revolution, and finished with the end of World War II, the start of the Cold War, the threat of atomic war and the hopes of the United Nations.

In his story about Johnny Australia, Frank was exploring his own concerns ahead of his final year of schooling: the final exams for his

Leaving Certificate, and the pressure he was putting on himself to succeed. He wrote of Johnny in the story: 'his mind, like a record, repeated: "This is it, Johnny; this is it; this is failure or success in life!"' It was a moment of reckoning already confronting Frank's friend Peter Martin, who had completed his final exams, finished high school and was awaiting his results.

Over that summer break, Frank and Peter embarked upon a six-week bicycle tour. This was going to be Frank's own adventure, the equivalent of his brothers' canoeing down the Whanganui River. He and Peter had taken short bicycle trips before, but this time they planned a much longer venture: a 700-mile (more than 1100-kilometre) return trip to the Murrumbidgee Irrigation Area to pick fruit. Their bikes had four-speed chain gears, and generator-powered headlights and taillights. All their equipment – tent, ground sheet, change of clothes – was strapped onto steel carriers over their back wheels.

They departed on Tuesday, 14 December 1954. The plan was to ride the whole way, but on the morning of the second day they found an interstate truck driver who allowed them to hitch a ride. They travelled with him for twelve hours, until he left them at the junction of the Hume and Sturt highways. They rode to Wagga that night and camped at the local cricket ground. The next day, after only about 17 miles (about 27 kilometres), they were offered a lift in another truck.

Because of these truck rides – which Frank called 'hitch-biking' – they were two days ahead of schedule in reaching their destination. Even with that head start, they found fruit picking jobs difficult to secure. The apricot season was near its end, and the peaches were not going to be ready to pick until the end of summer.

In Leeton on 21 December, Frank celebrated his sixteenth birthday. On Christmas day they caught and ate wild duck, swam in the irrigation ditches and listened to bad Christmas music on the radio. By New Year's Eve they were in Forbes. Their campfire got away from them one night, the tent flap going up in flames. They stamped it out but Frank had lost a jumper and singlet. A hole had burned through his ground sheet.

At the Forbes Public Library, looking through the newspapers, Peter found out he had passed his exams. They cycled to Parkes, but by the time they reached Manildra they were both sick and sore, so they ended up catching a train to Katoomba. They descended into Sydney and spent the rest of their money at the cafes, before making their way back to Nowra over the remaining two days, arriving home on Saturday, 29 January.

At last Frank had his own real-life adventure he could write about.

The Free Spirit provided Frank with one of his first serious surveys of Australian literature. There was a series on Australian historical literature, discussing the novels of Marcus Clarke, Brian Penton and Eleanor Dark. It contained surveys of the 1890s, and the early era of *The Bulletin*, where fiction writing was described as being a legitimate form of social criticism. Henry Lawson and Joseph Furphy were cited as examples. 'I acknowledge no aristocracy except one of service and self-sacrifice . . .' Furphy's *Such Is Life* was quoted. Again: 'human equality is as self-evident as human variety'.

For Frank, the doors to this literary history were still open. These figures were not so distant in time from him in the 1950s: it was as though, looking back, he could still see their figures shimmering on the horizon.

Frank accessed informal sources of knowledge too. Clive Hamer, his English teacher, was writing a master's thesis on Australian literature. He did not teach Frank directly, but he did teach Wendy Halloway and Paul Coombes. They introduced Frank to Mr Hamer, and through him Frank learned about Australian literary journals such as *Southerly* and *Meanjin*. *Southerly* had begun in 1939, ostensibly as the organ for the Sydney Branch of the English Association. *Meanjin* began in 1940, originally as *Meanjin Papers*. While *Southerly* was culturally conservative, concerned with literary history, staffed and written largely by and for academics, *Meanjin* was centre-left politically, concerned with current and future literary trends and social movements, and published for a non-academic audience. Many contributors, including Clive Hamer, published in both journals.

Beatrice Davis, the book editor who had started at Angus & Robertson in 1937, launched an anthology of short fiction in 1942 called *Coast to Coast*, published annually until 1948, and biannually from then on. In 1944, she arranged for A&R to take on *Southerly*. While *Southerly* was initially given a firm institutional footing, *Meanjin* struggled, like so many literary magazines have. The founding editor, Clem Christesen, was twenty-eight years old when he started the journal, and throughout his long tenure *Meanjin* faced a constant financial struggle between printers, publishers and contributors.

Frank's English teacher, Eric Silk, encouraged Frank to read the literary pages of *The Sydney Morning Herald*, in particular the weekly column by Leon Gellert. Gellert was in his sixties, and had grown into the curmudgeonly persona he had adopted when he began writing for Fairfax during World War II.

It was in Gellert's columns that Frank read, possibly for the first time, about the Bloomsbury set, that clique of English writers, artists and intellectuals, including Virginia Woolf, E.M. Forster and John Maynard Keynes, who were associated with Katherine Mansfield and D.H. Lawrence. 'Not only did they serve the cause of art according to their convictions,' Gellert wrote, 'they also contributed, in their own way, to economics and international relations.'

While reading Gellert's weekly columns, Frank came across a series called 'Literary Australia', which showcased Australian writers. It began on Saturday, 23 April 1955, with number one, Banjo Paterson. Each piece included a photograph or painting associated with the writer under review, followed by a brief overview of their life and work, and an excerpt from one of their works. Frank cut these out and kept them on his writing desk at home, as a source of inspiration and motivation. If the series featured a writer he did not already know, he would order their books from the State Library.

This weekly series ran until January 1956, by which time Frank had left Nowra. It punctuated his final year of school with a weekly countdown to his leaving, and a regular reminder as to where he wanted to go. The final writer featured, number thirty-eight, was Vance Palmer.

Frank was drawn to the arguments against censorship in *The Free Spirit*. In the October 1954 issue, he read about various restrictions some Australian states were introducing to regulate publications, and the arbitrary ways in which they 'recognised literary or artistic merit'. The following March, John Latham wrote a statement regarding the Obscene Publications Bill, then before the federal parliament. 'Censorship is undesirable in principle,' Latham wrote, defending also, in context, writing about sex, horror and cruelty.

Gellert's weekly columns reinforced this argument. In one column, he detailed his brush with the censor, and how, as the literary editor of a major metropolitan broadsheet, he still had difficulty getting the necessary books for review. He outlined the history of literary censorship and some associated legal cases, including the recent case of James Joyce's *Ulysses* (1922) in the United States, and how that book was still banned in Australia. Gellert concluded that the 'Freedom to Read' should be added to all other freedoms worth fighting for.

Frank's first direct encounter with censorship – besides his Eysenck book being confiscated – happened in June 1955, when he founded, edited and published Nowra High's first 'noticeboard' newspaper, *The Students' Voice*. It was modelled, in part, on *Elouera*, from his days at Wollongong Tech. It was just two pages, with two columns on each page, typed and pinned to the school noticeboard. Frank introduced it as an 'organ of opinion' for the students. 'Later it is hoped that a separate edition will be produced for the girls,' he wrote in his first editorial.

Mr Armitage, the headmaster, provided Frank with a special message to be published in the first issue. But before he did, and upon reading the initial drafts of the newsletter, he told Frank he could not publish the word 'bull', used in its colloquial sense. Frank pushed back, using arguments he had learned from *The Free*

Spirit against censorship, but to no avail. The word 'bull' is not to be found in any issue of *The Students' Voice*.

The first issue of the newsletter contained mainly sports results. By the second, in July, Frank was able to have multiple copies printed and distributed. 'NEW SERIES' was added to the masthead, with Frank's editorial declaring: 'The "Voice" becomes louder.' The second issue contained further sporting news, but with 'the girls' included in the mix. By the third issue, the workload on Frank was too great. It was August and he had to study for his Leaving Certificate. In the fourth issue, the new editor noted: 'THANK YOU FRANK.'

Frank produced *The Students' Voice*, in part, as a training ground for his future career in journalism. But a more immediate reason was to spend more time with Wendy. They had their first official date on Saturday, 31 March, when the Roxy showed *Broken Arrow* (1950), a western film, starring James Stewart and Debra Paget. While Frank and Wendy sat together in the dark of the cinema, Mr Halloway waited outside, intending to take Wendy straight home afterwards.

Mr Halloway normally did not allow Wendy out on dates with boys, especially not before she was sixteen years old, but Frank had asked him personally for permission. Perhaps he was caught off guard by Frank's formality. Perhaps it was because Frank was the son of one of the leading families of the town – Mr Halloway held Frank Sr in high esteem. Either way, that one date was all he allowed.

Wendy's movements were highly proscribed by her parents. She had to be home from school by 4 pm each afternoon, so she could not linger in the milk bar with other students. When there were school socials, Mr Halloway drove Wendy there and waited outside to take her home afterwards. An Irish Catholic father of four daughters, Mr Halloway used the fear of God to instil in Wendy and her sisters a general suspicion about the intentions of men. He said men were only ever after 'one thing' – but he could never bring himself to say exactly what that was. He did not believe his daughters really needed a high-school education, and felt they should leave school at fifteen and get a job, in order to start building a nest egg before their inevitable marriage.

All that this instilled in Wendy was a pervasive state of anguish and confusion, particularly as she harboured personal ambitions. She had to convince her parents to allow her to complete high school. One of her teachers even intervened on her behalf. Somehow it worked, although she had to bear her father's heavy social restrictions. School activities provided a cover under which Wendy and Frank could see each other.

They were both in various school sporting teams, and the teams travelled together to nearby towns to compete with other schools. Being prefects also provided opportunities for them to socialise more freely. When Wendy joined the editorial committee of the school magazine, Frank requisitioned the magazine staff to help with the production of *The Students' Voice*. From the first issue, she was the point of contact for advertisements. She was Frank's editorial assistant, and it was her influence that enabled the integration of 'girls news' into subsequent issues of the newspaper.

Paul Coombes lived with his father, a single parent, in a rented house at Shoalhaven Head, north-east of Nowra, on the other side of the river. Paul called the place 'Poverty Point'. It was a depressed area, characterised by heavy drinking and violence, but Paul's father was generous and supportive. He worked hard at the paper mill in Bomaderry, and some weekends he held parties.

The front room of Paul's house had a Masonite floor, polished with hops, which was used as a dance floor. Frank would go to Paul's for these weekends, where they would be allowed to drink beer. On such evenings, drunk on beer and talking of Steinbeck, Poverty Point would become more like the fictional Cannery Row. Out here, serious drinking was accompanied by more serious talk, about politics, philosophy and economics, but also about girls and the nature of love and sex.

Frank wrote down his own ideas on the matter, 'Some Thoughts on Love', which addressed the problem of adolescent love and the social prohibition against having sex. Practically, this was to avoid unwanted pregnancies. Morally, it was a religious and social custom that 'a girl should keep her body for the man she marries'. Frank argued that this all went against the 'natural course of loving'. He knocked down each argument in turn: contraceptives can prevent unwanted pregnancies, and God doesn't exist. He thought the marriage question was still valid, though, but only if the onus of choice shifted from social convention to the girl herself and the inviolability of her consent. 'If a girl believes she should keep herself for the man she eventually decides to marry there is no question of her being right or wrong.'

The problem, as Frank saw it, was that adolescents became frustrated and conflicted between 'loyalty to the natural self and loyalty to parents as the guardians of Convention'. Betraying the first loyalty led to feelings of despair, as well as emotional conflict between the girl and the boy. Betraying the second led to guilt and general unhappiness. Either way, the conventional attitude always pressured the girl into making an untenable choice. 'Perhaps the fault is that Society has not bothered to force any moral obligation on the males of the community,' Frank concluded. 'The problem of yea or nay rests on the conscience of the girl.'

For a sixteen-year-old boy in Nowra in 1955, this was a somewhat enlightened position to adopt.

Frank began thinking of the thematic connections that existed between his short stories. During the final year of high school, he pulled many of his stories from the past two years together under the general heading 'This; the World of the Adolesense'. He grouped stories together in various categories – sports, religion, romance and social – but also paired the stories within each aspect across two separate parts, to indicate a development of these themes:

Part I
ASPECTS
(a) sporting 'The boy who tried'

(b) religious 'It hurts'
(c) Romantic 'Tch Tch'
(d) Social
    (i) problems of
    (ii) ambition of 'The boy who did his duty'
    (iii) fears of

Julius Caesar Act IIII

Part II

(a) sporting 'On a football match'
(b) religious 'On going to Church'
(c) Romantic 'On a milk bar'
(d) Social 'On a school social'

The reference to *Julius Caesar* remains a mystery. The act of Shakespeare's play to which he refers includes Antony's famous speech: 'Friends, Romans, countrymen, lend me your ears; I come to bury Caesar, not to praise him . . .'

The story 'On a Milk Bar' is a study of different characters coming together in a local milk bar. The sights and sounds of the milk bar itself become another character. Ted is the proprietor. There is a waitress. Two sailors and a 'redlipped good time girl' sit at a table together. At the centre of the scene is a group of four male youths, smartly dressed, unevenly shaved, with pimples on their faces: 'They glare of adolescence.' One of them wants to listen to a Western song on the jukebox, but he is ridiculed by the other three, who want to play something more 'modern'. While they sit and tell each other stories and lewd jokes, a middle-aged salesman, propped up at the counter, overhears them. The milk bar is described as a place where 'obligations and responsibilities are forgotten'. But it is only a momentary interlude: everybody slips out into the night again, back to their formal lives.

'On a School Social' develops the theme of 'Tch! Tch!'. It is about a school dance, but this story has a happier ending. Here the boy escorts the girl home after the social. The inevitable moment arrives. 'He was nervous and she was breathing heavily.' And then: 'Their lips met. When he opened his eyes the lights along the street were blotches of yellow on a sheet of blackness. He pulled her closer. To himself he muttered "Jesus Christ, what have I been missing."

In 1955, Frank sent application letters for journalism cadetships. He listed the following seven principles as guiding his decision to enter journalism, which also guided his approach to writing generally:

> Then the time came for me to make a decision as to the occupation I was going to enter and I chose Journalism. These are my reasons;—
> (1) Writing gives me the fullest satisfaction. The finishing of an original story imbues me with a feeling of contentment and achievement.
> (2) The desire to express my opinions and to have them noticed.
> (3) My aversion to prejudices and bigotry which compels me to try to destroy false notions and to always give the truth. Coupled with this is:
> (4) My wish to see the world a free and a just place not a world of propaganda, lies, censorship, and bias.
> (5) My interest in other people and in current affairs because I believe that only by being fully conscious of the world about us can we live and judge fairly.
> (6) To learn to be skilful and honest journalist.
> (7) To serve my fellow citizens.

Frank had a strict daily schedule for study, which started in the early morning, before school, when it was still dark outside. He also studied at night during the week. Although he still shared the sleepout with Arthur, his brother was usually out after work, with friends or with his fiancée, Rhonda. They were going to be married in October. So Frank often had the room to himself.

Their mother maintained a strict curfew of 11 pm. One night Arthur stayed out until well after that time, and so instead of coming through the front door, he climbed through the window of the sleepout. Frank was already in bed asleep. The commotion woke him, and, thinking it must be morning, he loped out of bed, and sat at his desk to study, bleary-eyed in the lamplight. Arthur steered Frank back to bed, covered him and turned out the lamp.

———

Frank had been writing sketches and essays about what it was like to be an adolescent. It was as if he wanted to pin down his own experiences before he moved on to the next phase of his life. Between October and November 1955, during his final exam period, Frank wrote three essays, effectively three iterations of the same theme: 'The World and Me', 'A Ramble in the Mind of an Adolescent', and 'Rambling in the Mind of an Adolescent (Part II)'. He conceded adolescents were inexperienced, half-educated, insensitive and emotional. But the adult world was no better. Regarding the social and political mistakes being made, the generational stakes seem to be one of adults simply 'passing the buck'. A characteristic of adulthood seemed to be a defeatist attitude and acquiescence to social conventions, with minds dulled and broken by boredom and worry.

Politically, the nub of these mistakes for Frank was the tension between economic security and personal freedom, which the adult world avoided by creating a false choice between them. Communism was an attempt at achieving economic security, but at the cost of individual freedom. And although the alternative preached individual freedom along with economic competition and insecurity, Frank noted that such individuals were not as free as they imagined. Individuals in the West were heavily regulated by two externally imposed disciplines instilled since childhood: 'to count money and to tell the time'. To these Frank added the repression of sex, the suppression of 'free true thought', starvation and lack of racial freedom – 'there should be no colour bar'.

'So this is where I stand,' Frank wrote. 'I believe that complete planning of an economy for the common benefit is possible but I cherish with my life the personal freedoms. Who am I to support?' Frank thought adults were handling the question so poorly that his generation would not even be allowed this choice. 'I will probably have this decided for me by a conscription notice,' he wrote.

Frank used these essays to outline his strategy for entering the adult world. He needed to be 'sensible, factual, logical, and tolerant'. His personal goal was to become an 'observer and a scholar'. He wanted to go to university in order to study subjects he felt would give him the intellectual grounding he required: psychology, economics and philosophy. But also English literature, 'which will enable me to express my views strikingly'. But most of all he wanted to accept the challenge the previous generations had surrendered, so as not to 'leave it to the next generation to puzzle out'.

But in the third essay Frank undermined his own resolve, deflating his own self-confidence. 'I have just realised one of the most typically human traits in myself which has caused Rambling in the Mind of an Adolescent is to be almost hyper-critical,' he noted. He berated himself for not submitting his essays and short stories to publications, realising this was because of a fear of rejection. He still carried the wound from *Australian Magazine*'s rejection in 1953. But he feared somebody else would publish the same ideas he had, and the 'praise and profit' would go elsewhere. He then criticised himself further for thinking in such self-interested terms: the very attitude his initial criticisms were levelled against. And so the hyper-critical loop continued.

It was against this background that Frank wrote about his use of alcohol as a crutch or social lubricant. Drinking in secret, or with close friends such as Paul Coombes, had become a way for Frank to relieve the pressures he placed upon himself, and to silence his internal monologue, especially when it became self-critical dialogue, splitting into a more general interior hubbub of worry, doubt and accusation.

> I have just fully realised that I have the power to escape ridicule and embarrassment in drunkedness. I hate having to argue for my rights or for my reputation. Now I will never have to argue for them; I will get drunk. Damn the world. I don't have to worry if you laugh at this essay. In fact I don't have to worry about anyone or anything.

Frank explored these themes in a short story called 'The Boy Who Wanted to Be Big', about an adolescent, nearing his final exams, who goes with a friend into a pub to drink, even though they are both underage. They are seen by two off-duty teachers. At school, they are called to the headmaster's office for a dressing-down. The boy's girlfriend is even less impressed, which puts the protagonist in a foul mood. At home, he says, 'To hell with study,' and starts to read a Steinbeck novel instead. The thought of suicide comes to him. He considers methods, a bullet or jumping from a great height. He then leaves the house, heading for the railway bridge.

> His brain turned against itself and reproduced the troubles and slights of the past till they glared and leapt like fires. He wondered what death would be like.
>
> He started to cross the street but stepped back to avoid a speeding car – but he stepped back to avoid a speeding car – but he stepped back to avoid a speeding car. The will to live was still there. It caused him to smile bitterly.
>
> With resignation he murmured 'Bloody adolescence' and wondered when he would grow up.

Frank wondered the same thing, too.

Wendy and Paul were on the school magazine committee in 1955. Frank was not on the committee, but as outgoing school captain he had to provide a joint statement, along with his co-captain, Helen Jordan, for the magazine. 'We decided to advocate Participation,' they wrote.

In the 'Literary Section' of the magazine – opposite a full-page advertisement for Moorhouse the Machinery Man Pty Ltd – was Frank's essay about his and Peter's cycling trip the previous summer.

This was followed by two short vignettes written by Wendy. One is called 'Terror by Night', about an eleven-year-old boy who is accidentally locked out of his home. While waiting for his parents to return from a party, he reads a comic book, *The Terrors of Mars*.

He gets so absorbed in the comic that when he hears a noise in the distance, coming closer, he becomes increasingly fearful – but it's only his pet dog.

The other story is more revealing. In the previous year's school magazine, Frank had written a piece titled 'Is This Us?', in which he asked questions about his future, his final school year and beyond. In 'The Sun Came Up', Wendy did the same. But as a young woman in 1950s regional Australia, her challenges were different to Frank's: she had other limitations and conventions with which to contend.

At that time, most young women could not have careers – at best they had temporary jobs, which they left when they were married, in order to keep house and raise a family. Most of the other girls in her class at this time aspired to become schoolteachers. Wendy wanted something else, but she was unsure what.

Her story was about a young woman who was grieving the death of her parents in a car accident. She wonders about her own future without them, and remembers her father's words: 'No matter what you do Linda, do it well.' She quickly finds her resolve: 'First she must have something to "do well", a career. "I've always wanted to know why things are; the reasons behind everything. I'll find the answers!"'

In the purgatory between final exams and results, Frank started writing a novel. Although he had spent the past two years writing short stories about adolescence, none of their stories or scenes appeared in the final draft of this longer work, although there are familiar themes. One section recalls Frank's argument against the role of prefects within the school. In the novel, the protagonist, Simon Egg, is such a prefect, 'one of the aristocrats of the school', albeit one who believes the prefect system to be 'a sham'. But Frank did not rework his old material, attempting instead to write more broadly about adolescent characters, while at the same time examining them from a distance and criticising their behaviour, if sympathetically.

He had completed the first chapter of this untitled manuscript by the time he left Nowra at the end of the year. The opening chapter introduces Simon Egg in his final year of high school, studying for his Leaving Certificate. At a Sunday church service he prays to God to help him pass the exams, succeed in getting into university and become a 'worthwhile economist'. He prays for guidance regarding his relationship with his girlfriend, Shane, to know if adolescents can truly be in love, and to resist physical temptations when they arise.

Frank's two years of hard work at school were reduced to a single sentence in *The Shoalhaven and Nowra News* in December 1955: 'FRANK MOORHOUSE, jun., son of Mr and Mrs F.O. Moorhouse, of Worrigee Street, has chosen journalism as a career, and has been accepted as a cadet on the "Daily Telegraph" in Sydney.' In reality, Frank had only been accepted as a copyboy, but the perilous compromise with journalism had begun.

Frank moved to Sydney to begin his apprenticeship, and so missed his high-school graduation. Wendy wrote to him afterwards that when Paul Coombes went up to receive a prize, he had a paperback sticking out of his back pocket – in imitation of, or perhaps homage to, Frank – with the cover facing outwards, the author's name in large type: PLATO.

Meanwhile, Frank was out of Nowra at last. He had finally begun his independent life.

4

'I Feel Like Some Other Species Looking at Humans'

Frank arrived in Sydney on the second weekend of December 1955, moving into a boarding house on Bartlett Street, Summer Hill. He started work as a copyboy at *The Daily Telegraph* on Monday, 12 December, on the 5 pm shift.

Pushing his way through the city streets, the bustling people, the traffic and the trams, Frank felt a little out of step – the country boy from Nowra. *The Daily Telegraph*'s office was on Castlereagh Street, the same street Frank's mother had walked down almost daily between the wars while working at Farmer's Department Store, and which still housed the offices of *The Bulletin* and, since 1887, Angus & Robertson. Frank later told Wendy he felt like Davey Crockett coming in from the wilderness.

On his first evening at work he was sent to the editorial section, where he met the chief of staff, Mr Dougherty. Frank was told to follow the other copyboys around, so he might learn the geography of the building and what a copyboy did.

In a letter to Wendy, Frank outlined his different tasks. The first was to sit in the office with all the other copyboys and wait until a buzzer went off. This indicated which journalist or cadet needed assistance. A copyboy then went to that department and did whatever job they were told to do. One of Frank's tasks on his first night was to take the messages coming off the telegraph machine from Melbourne to the 'cables' desk, where they would be distributed to journalists.

The second task of the copyboy was to deal with the subeditors ('the subs'). 'These gents sit on a "U" shaped table drinking tea and smoking,' he wrote. On the table were two baskets, NEW COPY and PRINTER. In the first basket went all the stories journalists had written, which then required subediting. When they were finished, they put the final copy into the PRINTER basket. Frank was to take the copy from the PRINTER basket, add the date and time, and then send the copy down to the printing room in the basement via pneumatic tube.

'That, honey, is what your boy friend does for £4 week,' he wrote to Wendy.

'You know what I would do if I were a copy boy,' Wendy replied. 'I'd most probably put all the stuff out of the "new copy" basket on to the "cables" desk and put the teletype machine down the suction-tube. Then I'd go drink some tea with the men at the U shaped table.'

A week later, Frank had his seventeenth birthday.

Frank continued to work on his novel about adolescence, and was progressing by about two pages each day. Some days he thought the work seemed 'excellent', but on other days it felt 'flat and dull'. He realised this feeling must be familiar to other writers, and was part of the writing process.

The narrative was structured across a week in the life of Simon Egg. The first chapter, completed in Nowra, was set on a Sunday. Chapters two and three took place the next day, Monday. Chapter two introduced Simon's family and the small, conventional strictures within which they operated. 'Routine was useful because it saved thinking – a painful activity for comatose minds,' Frank wrote. 'Simon felt disgusted for his families dull routine and swore never to submit to such a life.'

This attack on the conventions of his family is thrown into a different light, when, in the same chapter, Simon Egg considers the day and week ahead, implying the adolescent world is equally structured by routine and convention. This is reinforced in the third chapter, when everything Simon predicted plays out: the same routines, the same conversations, the same adolescent rituals. When Simon meets up with Shane and asks her if anything exciting happened to her over the weekend, he is met with a smile. 'She smiled at him because he asked the same question every Monday.'

On Wednesday, 18 January 1956, *The Daily Telegraph* held an internal examination for copyboys to be promoted to cadet journalists. 'My luck may be in,' Frank told Wendy. But he was not confident, especially as he had been working there for less than a month. He was the only one who had completed a Leaving Certificate, so he might have had a slight academic advantage over the other copyboys, but many of them had more experience on the job.

When the results came in, Frank was near the top of the list. Wendy said the result was not surprising, as everybody had confidence in Frank's ability – except Frank himself. As a cadet journalist, he was given a copy of *The Daily Telegraph*'s style guide and writing manual, compiled by the legendary Brian Penton. He joined the Australian Journalists' Association.

Frank's first day as a cadet journalist was on Monday, 30 January. He was assigned to a journalist, Peter Finn, who was on the beach beat. Frank made telephone calls to each of the Sydney beaches, to compile a list of figures – the number of rescues and drownings, the tidal levels, bluebottle sightings and so on – which Finn then wrote up into a story.

Frank still wanted to attend university. Throughout January he had been working his way through various subjects in preparation for his matriculation exams in February. He was studying broadly, including shorthand, psychology and philosophy, focusing on Plato and Marx. He found it hard to concentrate for too long on any one subject, so he studied each in short bursts, in heavy rotation. In a practice exam he had failed history, although he had scored highly in English. He dwelled more on the failure.

Frank's inability to concentrate was due in part to his already heavy workload at the newspaper, his novel writing and his constant letter-writing to Wendy and Paul. At work, he was usually on the night shift, so his sleep patterns had become erratic. He worked on weekends, his days off being Wednesdays and Thursdays, which he spent drinking, reading and writing.

By March, having passed the matriculation exams, Frank's workload became heavier still. Enrolled at the University of Sydney, Frank attended lectures every morning except Saturday and Sunday. Philosophy lectures at 10 am and English lectures at midday. On Wednesdays and Thursdays – technically, his 'weekend' – he had psychology lectures at 2 pm. He would then meet up with students from various courses, eating and talking in the Student Union cafe. Other nights he would be back at the *Telegraph*.

By this time Frank had all but abandoned his novel. He had probably only finished chapter four, set on the Monday night, when Simon takes Shane on a date to the cinema. Once more, the evening is dictated by descriptions of decorum and convention. When Simon meets Shane, for example, he compliments her: 'He told her that her dress looked beautiful because he had read the Women's Weekly Teenage Advice Page and it said that it was tactful to say something like that. Shane told him his tie looked well and Simon smiled because that was also on the Teenage Advice Page.' After the date, Simon reflects on the question of adolescent love and the question of sex.

For this section Frank reworked some of the general arguments he had made the previous year in his essay 'Some Thoughts on Love'. But he also went further, conceiving of a scheme in which adolescents could live together, alternately staying at each parents' home and, with wise use of contraception, exploring each other emotionally and sexually, to see if their romance could last. If not, they could end the arrangement amicably.

Frank found his first real news story while doing the routine beach rounds: a new species of jellyfish had invaded Sydney's beaches. It was bluish-pink, about four inches in length, similar in appearance to the bluebottle, but its sting was worse. His story made page nine of the country edition, and Frank was asked to do a follow-up.

For this he located a specimen of the jellyfish on Coogee Beach, and spent hours with a woman scientist at the Australian Museum testing the specimen. The story made page four of the final edition; he was 'getting closer to page 1', he told Wendy. The story was picked up by the Melbourne *Argus*, which was thrilling for Frank. But it also delivered him a sharp lesson in the realities of journalism. Frank was already aware of the creeping hyperbole journalists used to liven up their stories: a fellow cadet had used the figure '400' in a story, which the editors changed to '800' so as to be more dramatic. Frank had written, 'Many bathers had been stung by jellyfish,' but the editor of *The Argus* changed 'many' to 'hundreds'. When Frank tried to correct him, the editor dismissed his concerns, saying, 'You'll learn.'

Cadets at the time attended a lecture series given by renowned local or visiting journalists. The lectures themselves were – or so Frank surmised – designed to remind cadets of the high ideals of journalism, as a bulwark for their morale against the diurnal reality of the trade, which otherwise chipped away at their resolve. Many North American journalists had come to Australia for the Olympic Games in Melbourne that year. A visiting Canadian journalist gave a lecture on Canadian newspapers, which Frank found interesting. But in other lectures the pretence was often revealed when the lecturer went off script.

In mid-February, soon after Frank's jellyfish story broke, Bertram 'Don' Whitington – a well-known Australian journalist, and the father of Frank's fellow cadet journalist Mike Whitington – gave a lecture on the 'Qualities of a Reporter'. He spoke about some of the lengths journalists he knew had gone to in order to get a story. This included hiding in cupboards during private meetings, climbing onto the roofs of meeting rooms and getting politicians drunk. One reporter tried to get into a private convention by cutting the power to the building and entering the hall under the cover of the darkness and chaos that ensued. Frank reported these incidents to Wendy without much apparent enthusiasm.

But at times the idealism of youth could even rub off onto a jaded older journalist. When Frank's jellyfish story was published on page six of *The Argus* on 3 February, under the title 'A new "sting" in Sydney surf', he was gratified to see that the Melbourne paper had retained his initial wording, keeping 'many' in favour of 'hundreds'.

Wendy visited Sydney in February, and they went on what was probably their first real date since they had seen *Broken Arrow* at the Roxy two years earlier. It was on this date that Frank first told her he loved her. Wendy did not reciprocate, but she later told him she liked him more each time she saw him.

Later that month, when Wendy started back at school, she swore to herself that she would concentrate on her schoolwork and not think about Frank. In geometry class, when the textbooks were randomly assigned and the students were asked to write their names on the inside cover, Wendy discovered that the previous user of her copy was Frank Moorhouse. After a telephone conversation later that month, Wendy wrote: 'Frank, I know now that I love you . . . My feelings are now at the same level as yours and I don't know what we're going to do.' The letter made Frank 'weak with happiness'.

Frank and Paul Coombes had continued their discussion on books and ideas, sharing and recommending books to each other. This included *About Ourselves and Others* (1941), by William A. McRae, an early advocate of psychotherapy in Australia. McRae was an early clinician studying the effects of shell shock on Australia's returned soldiers. Frank had been reading *Sex and Society* (1955) by Kenneth Walker and Peter Fletcher, which included chapters on 'Sexual Morality before Marriage', 'The Homosexual' – which included a plea to decriminalise homosexuality – and 'Transvestism and Sado-Masochism' – which argued that men dressing and acting like women was far more common than was previously believed, and that the psychological reasons for doing so were not very different from 'every other citizen who changes his personality as often as he changes his clothes in order to keep up appearances as he moves from one environment to another in the course of a day'. Frank wrote excitedly to Wendy about the book. 'It is an enlightening book with some startling facts in it,' he said. 'As far as I am concerned it should be a school text book for fifth years or perhaps parts of it in earlier classes.'

Meanwhile, Paul was working on his own writing. He even had his first entree into the world of Australian literary magazines. Clive Hamer, who was friends with Clem Christesen, had passed along an essay Paul had written about adolescence. Christesen rejected the manuscript but invited Paul to send *Meanjin* any future work he may have. 'I thought it was a brush off,' Paul told Frank, 'but Hamer who has dealings with them (knows Editor) reckons it is good. He says that there are 3 gradings: 1. Sent back no note or anything; 2. Sent back encouraging slip (close to being published); 3. being published.'

Frank returned to his unfinished novel, perhaps motivated by Paul's submission to *Meanjin*. The next two chapters are set on Tuesday and Wednesday, respectively.

In chapter five, Simon goes to the staffroom during the lunch hour, to speak with his economics teachers. He wants to discuss an essay he has written and is seeking more feedback. He wants reassurance and encouragement that he was on track to become an economist. But Simon leaves feeling dejected.

In chapter six, Simon visits the Vocational Guidance Counsellor. There he is given a personal report compiled from a battery of intelligence and aptitude tests which the students have taken. When he reads the report, he finds it is filled with general praise for his abilities, his high intelligence and his clerical skill. The report concludes: 'Any clerical profession or own choice of Economics being suitable.' This is the encouragement he has longed for.

But his elation is short-lived: when Simon and his friends compare their reports, they find they are all formulaically written, uniformly full of the same praise, each promising success in whatever occupational field the boy has chosen.

This pushes Simon into depression. 'He shut his eyes. He repeated to himself you are a failure – you are a failure – you are a failure – you are a failure – why don't you wake up to yourself – why don't you wake up to yourself.' But then another part of him starts up: 'stop saying these things or you will go mad – you will have a break down – get control of yourself.' Now a third part of his mind kicks in, at once cynical and sarcastic: 'stop making yourself crazy – you're trying to bring on a nervous breakdown – you fool – you weakling – stop putting on an act – stop being adolescent.' Finally, Simon regains his composure – what he calls his 'single mindedness' – while passing a final judgement on himself: 'You hopeless bastard.'

These different modal voices within the character of Simon reflect in large part the hypercritical splitting of self Frank wrote about in his essays the previous year on the ramblings of his own adolescent mind.

Chapter seven returns to the domestic scene, describing Simon's father and older brother, who both work in the family timber mill. Simon is frustrated with his family, with the family business and with his not having a place within it. It is at this point that Simon – who began in the novel by praying for God's help amid the tribulations of his final year – starts questioning his faith. 'He felt very much alone in the world; he felt no external presence.'

This emptiness and lack of external support – from religion, from family, from school – leads Simon further into despair. He contemplates suicide. 'He knew he would not commit suicide because he was to scared of agony and injury although life seemed worse … All adolescents thought about committing suicide – it was another adolescent trait. Hell, why shouldn't adolescents think about suicide?' But here the catherine wheel of Simon's fractured internal monologue lists all the reasons for such despair, and then undermines them by judging them ill-conceived and adolescent – a thought that keeps the argument in perpetual circular motion.

'He clenched the iron frame of the bed and tried to stop thinking.'

Wendy's parents knew she was receiving letters from Frank, but they were not aware of the depth of their relationship. But by April – perhaps after seeing the regularity of correspondence, and the occasional telephone call – they were becoming suspicious. They urged Wendy not to fixate too soon on a single boy. In May, Wendy's father had a 'heart-to-heart talk' with her. 'He was very serious and he told me that I had all my life in front of me and that I was to get serious with no one boy,' she told Frank.

In April, during the school holidays, Wendy stayed with her older sister in Sydney. Frank's work friends finally got to meet her. They liked her immediately. Frank took Wendy on a harbour cruise, where they spoke freely about their dreams of a future together. Frank wanted to edit a country newspaper, and he wanted Wendy to work beside him, just as they had done on the student newsletter in high school.

'I love you so much Frank, and I want the dreams we dreamed in the showboat to come true,' Wendy wrote to him when she had returned to Nowra, 'but as the phrase says, "only time will tell".'

After Frank saw Wendy off at the train station, perhaps motivated by their future dreams, he went back to his boarding-house room, sat down and pushed himself to finish writing his novel – the final chapter. He had already completed chapter eight, a short piece in which, on the Friday at school, Simon and the boys decide to spend the weekend at the beach. Simon adds to the plan by suggesting he will get some alcohol for them to share, and they readily agree. Getting drunk is his idea of escape from the pressures of adolescence.

The final chapter ends with Simon and the boys at the beach on a Saturday night. They sit in a circle on the sand, around a fire, and pass around a bottle of sweet sherry. After the third bottle is killed, Simon finds his moment of inner peace, the novel's epiphany:

The world was mellow. It was impossible to think of the future or the past . . . Simon did not have a thought for intelligence. For once it was accepted that they were all equal – no one said it – no one thought about it – it was a self evident truth. No pains worried their minds or bodies. No responsibility expect to pass the bottle. The only job to do was to experience the drugging sweet wine.

The final line showed an awareness – on the part of the narrator, at least, if not the protagonist – that this moment of peace was temporary: 'Three boys on a beach had forgotten the world. But in the morning . . .?'

After typing 'THE END', Frank wrote to Wendy: 'I finished it and after rereading it I decided it was not presentable. It needs more body and the plot has to be strengthened. I will not send you a copy of the present form because I want you to read the perfect product only.' But at least the first draft was finished.

The complete manuscript has fifty-five typed pages, broken into nine chapters. It contains a preface, in which Frank's intentions are outlined in detail, reiterating much of what he had written in various essays and stories over the previous few years. 'This story was written by me, an adolescent,' it opens. 'It is therefore immature in both style and treatment.' The preface was signed: 'Frank Moorhouse Jnr.'

Although Frank was still only seventeen years old when he typed these words, he had already moved beyond the adolescent world of high school. And yet he had carried over into his new circumstances the character traits, habits, behaviours and dispositions which he had hoped to have outgrown. He was impatient to do so, but he had begun to suspect such aspects of character were going to be part of his adult world.

'My novel was a flop, honey,' he wrote to Wendy. 'I would like you to read anything I felt was worthwhile but this, I am afraid, is rubbish.'

In response, Wendy wrote with characteristic sobriety: 'Well I won't offer my condolences to you concerning your novel because I think disappointment is one part of writing a novel.'

Frank said he would need to spend another six months completing it, but that did not eventuate. He quietly shelved the project. What was significant in the letter Frank wrote Wendy in his initial excitement at having finished the draft was his first mention of marriage, albeit couched in a joke: "Fraid it won't finance our wedding honey, might have to use your wedding ring money to have it published.'

Frank kept his social worlds separate. Many at the *Telegraph* did not know Frank was doing full-time study at the University of Sydney, and vice versa. Frank persevered with his degree, although he was increasingly worried he had lost the habit for hard study. His favourite part was the research and essay writing component of each subject.

In June, the topic he had thrown himself into reading about was on the theme of hedonism. 'I'm getting all wrapped up in this damn topic,' he wrote to Wendy. Most of what he was reading took a dim view on hedonism, arguing that pleasure ought to be governed by morality, and not the other way around. But this led Frank to examine more closely the role of morality in society, and the idea that most people perform moral acts because they fear an external punishment – a loss of happiness, a removal of pleasure – and so their immediate motive is not to be moral, but only to avoid punishment. To what extent, therefore, can we say that such a person is moral?

Frank used his time at university to attend meetings of different left-wing political groups and clubs – such as the Labor Club and the Eureka Youth League – although he was noncommittal about joining any of them. Some of the gatherings were small and disorganised. At one meeting in June Frank was one of only four people who turned up. Other groups were more organised. One group, associated with the Communist Party – probably the Eureka Youth League – selected Frank to attend, as its representative, a weekend course in September on newspaper and bulletin production, including layout, design and printing. Frank did the course more out of an interest in publishing than out of any affinity with the Communist Party. Unbeknown to him at that time, such activities brought him to the attention of the Australian Security Intelligence Organisation (ASIO). His file records that he was 'a member of the Communist-dominated Sydney University Left Club'.

Meanwhile, with his cadet journalist friends Peter Bonner and Mike Whitington, Frank had decided to start a new magazine. They had settled on the name: *Trend*. It was to be a contemporary popular culture magazine. Frank put the business plan together. They were going to form a liability company called 'Young Australia Publications PTY Ltd', to avoid personal liability if the magazine were to face libel suits or fines for obscenity. That they were already thinking about such protection is an indication of the type of material they hoped to publish. It was to be a private company – modelled on Moorhouse the Machinery Man Pty Ltd – with twenty shares available, priced at £10 each. This would establish a board of directors, which would constitute the core collective of contributing writers and administrative staff.

They began looking for shareholders and contributors, and started writing copy for the magazine. By the end of June they had 12,000 words, but they had already run out of ideas, and had failed to rustle up the requisite shareholder support. 'It seems a pity after the amount of work we have put into it,' Frank told Wendy. 'Still we have a lifetime in which to start magazines.'

A third social world Frank maintained was his old life back in Nowra, which he visited frequently, on weekends, with Wendy being the anchor that kept him in touch with his family and schoolfriends. Frank, Paul and Wendy continued to read widely and discuss books. Frank was exploring American literature more systematically. He read John Dos Passos's *U.S.A.* trilogy (1937), which he recommended to Paul. He retrieved all of his John Steinbeck novels from Paul on one of his visits to Nowra, so he could re-read them more methodically. 'Beautiful characterisation and portrayal of life,' he told Wendy regarding Steinbeck.

In April, when Wendy was feeling down about Frank being so far away in Sydney, Clive Hamer tried to cheer her up by showing her and Paul a love poem called 'A Ballad on a Country Love', which he had written when he was first engaged to his wife. Writing to Frank about the poem, Paul called Hamer a 'courting wretched man in love', and he wrote a parody, called, 'The Elegy on a Country Athlete'. Wendy also wrote to Frank about the poem, but was more generous:

> Mr Hamer when he was engaged to his wife wrote a poem about his love for her. Thinking that I would appreciate and understand it he let me read it. It's a lovely thing and to heaven if it doesn't sound like us. Paul as soon as he read it commented on the fact.

In the end, Paul got caught up in the moment, admitting to Frank that his attempted parody 'reverted from satire to seriousness and now it is hard to understand'.

Clive Hamer was responsible for an obsession all three friends shared during the latter part of 1956. *The Family of Man* was a photographic exhibition first shown in New York City's Museum of Modern Art (MoMA) the previous year, before beginning a world tour. Although the exhibition would not come to Australia until 1959, Clive had given a copy of the book from the original exhibition to Wendy and Paul, and they in turn shared it with Frank. The book contained all 503 photographs – taken in sixty-eight countries – constituting the exhibition. 'It was conceived as a mirror of the universal elements and emotions in the everydayness of life,' said the curator of the exhibition, and director of MoMA, Edward Steichen, 'as a mirror of the essential oneness of mankind throughout the world'. The images moved through the stages of life, from birth to death, youth to old age, depicting family and community life, from various countries around the world.

Frank first referred to *The Family of Man* – as 'our' book – in a letter to Wendy in August 1956. Paul talked about it in a letter to Frank in October, arguing that the book showed how all people were one, all sharing the same emotions. In November, responding to something Wendy had previously said, Frank referred to the book as a way to describe his developing political sensibilities. 'I like your idea of "one big happy family",' he wrote. 'The book "The Family of Man" was an attempt to spread that idea. If family feeling (good feeling) could be spread world-wide than the problems of war would be solved.'

By December, Wendy had to intervene in order to preserve the book from becoming damaged through overhandling. 'I finally got the book "The Family of Man" covered with that clear plastic,' she told Frank. 'At least it will save the book from further damage – that is unless it lands in a mincing machine.'

Paul read Joseph Furphy's *Such Is Life* (1903), which he thought was a 'mighty' book. He compared Frank's sketches of Sydney life, from his letters, to Furphy's writing. He reminded Frank how Furphy kept a diary and, before he narrated an incident, would tell the reader on what date from his diary he was drawing on.

It was around that time that Frank began keeping his own private journal. It was perhaps in an effort to move beyond his abandoned novel of adolescence. 'Today I have decided to begin my journal,' he typed on the first page. 'I am aged 17 and 5 months. I think the journal will record what I call "seeings" which will provide material for future stories.' Above the word 'seeings', he wrote the word 'sightings'. He went on: 'The form will be prose but at odd times I may feel the urge to use free-prose. I want to train myself to "see" things.'

The first page described in some detail the experience of walking through Redfern, looking at the tenement buildings, studying the individual names on the houses, while thinking about D.H. Lawrence's *Kangaroo*. Frank focused, in particular, on how, even though there were no people about, he could see where the 'humanness' of the inhabitants over generations had shaped the built environment by their comings and goings, the shapes of their lives and the impressions they left behind.

This was the only entry in Frank's writing journal for 1956. Like the novel, it was abandoned.

Frank did, however, write more short stories, which he showed Wendy. And Wendy was very honest in her judgement. 'I am sorry that you did not like my writings,' Frank wrote. 'I will try and change something.'

Soon after, Wendy replied to another story: 'I really did enjoy your short story. There was only one thing I didn't like. The ending was right but somehow you made the boy superior to the poor girl . . . I like to make up my own ending to it, so I'm satisfied.'

Wendy was not the only person who did not think Frank's stories were working. He had followed Paul's lead and started submitting his work to literary journals, including *Meanjin*, but was rejected every time, and without much encouragement. 'I am pretty disheartened about my short story writing,' he confided to Wendy in August. 'I don't know what we will live on if my writing fails us.'

Wendy had to decide what she was going to do when she completed her Leaving Certificate. She had once suggested to Frank that she thought she could be a journalist too, but immediately dismissed the idea as being farfetched. 'Big laugh,' she wrote.

Frank did not think it impossible, and he was consistently supportive of the idea, encouraging Wendy to take the idea more seriously. He told her about Sue Smith, a second-year cadet he worked with, and Smith's example intrigued Wendy. 'Right now I admire any girl that takes up journalism and makes a success of it,' Wendy wrote to Frank. 'Perhaps she will turn out to be what I had high hopes of being. Well, anyways here's to her!'

One time, during the regular cadet lectures, the American journalist Robert Ruark took questions from the floor. One young woman asked if he thought a girl had a chance in journalism, and Ruark said yes. He went on to say – and Frank eagerly relayed all of this to Wendy – that girls were in some ways better than boys, especially in general reporting, because they could get stories from places men would get black eyes. Ruark said he had once worked under a woman editor.

When a scriptwriting cadetship came up at the ABC, and Frank urged Wendy to apply, she did. 'They won't want anyone from the country,' she said, 'especially a girl.' Once more, Frank encouraged her by telling her about a female cadet journalist he knew: 'Sex is a handicap but Lois demanded to be given an opportunity to prove that it wasn't. I am sure that you will receive the same opportunity. She is also a "country girl".'

Wendy did not get the ABC job.

Wendy wanted to move to Sydney. She had a sister there, but their father did not want Wendy living with her. So Wendy had to find other accommodation, but also find an entry-level job to cover her living costs. That prospect limited her options for further study, as the added costs and time required to study would diminish her capacity to support herself. It was a conspiracy of circumstance, narrowing some pathways but making others appear more appealing: marriage and family life, which would usually involve giving up the idea of further study or a professional career.

Paul Coombes, like Frank before him, had fewer social obstacles and more options from which to choose, as well as more confidence in his ability to make a decision. He planned to become a journalist. Frank and Paul were already talking about getting a flat together when Paul graduated from high school and moved to Sydney. Part of the reason they wanted to flat together was so they could share their expanding library of books.

When Frank started at *The Daily Telegraph* he had met a journalist, three years his senior, named Richard ('Dick') Hall. They shared some night shifts, and started drinking together. He introduced Frank to many Sydney pubs, and as they moved around he would point out the establishments Henry Lawson had patronised. Frank showed Richard a draft of one of his short stories, to which Richard's diplomatic response was: 'I won't say it is bad.'

In late August, Frank was reassigned to the court rounds. That meant moving to the day shift, which freed up his weekends for the first time that year, but it also put pressure on his university studies, affecting his attendance of weekday lectures. Reluctantly, he dropped out.

It was on the court beat that Frank met a D-grade journalist named David Gyger, who wrote for a competitor. David was an American who, like many others during this period, had come to Australia to attend the Olympic Games in Melbourne. But when he landed a job in Sydney, he decided to stay. He had a girlfriend in the United States, Janet, and the couple would send each other tape recordings in lieu of letters, a new technology that fascinated Frank. David and Frank shared an interest in literature and ideas, so they started meeting up for spaghetti lunches in between court cases, or else for drinks after work. At one of these lunches, Frank tried to argue against the proposition that international travel broadened the mind. His new American friend was sceptical.

Increasingly, Frank was coming to understand that human beings often acted according to motives they themselves did not fully grasp. This was reinforced for him on a daily basis in the Sydney courts. 'Central Court is a school in human behaviour,' he wrote to Wendy. 'Every conceivable form of behaviour is described in the court. I sit in the press box absorbing all this "life" and my dull mind is slowly warmed up to question after question about life. I feel like some other species looking at humans.' Frank was feeling tired and disconnected from life. Politically, Frank thought his capacity to participate in the world, and to affect social change, would be through his writing, his journalism and his fiction. But his lack of progress was edging him towards a state of futility and apathy. He wrote to Paul:

> I looked at the world and then myself and I realised the feeble influence one single unknown human has. I tell myself my task is to train my mind not necessarily to reform the world. As a writer I think the task is to describe life as it is. If the description is accurate the injustice will [be] brought to notice. The offering of solutions is difficult. I am wary of didactic writing. Gorky did not preach; he only described.

Frank and Wendy's relationship was predominantly epistolary. They had spent more time reading each other than they had spent sitting with one another in the same room. When they did see each other in person, it was only for brief periods, and they had little privacy.

In his essay 'Some Thoughts on Love', Frank had argued that too much pressure had been placed by society on women to regulate male desire. He suggested that more pressure perhaps needed to be placed on men to control themselves. But he was now finding that, in practice, this was harder than he had thought.

Matters were complicated somewhat by Frank's recent discovery – in an article he had read, and which he discussed with Wendy one night on the telephone – that women had sexual desires too, which could undermine their self-control. 'I thought the boy was the only weak one,' he wrote to her.

> You know that I have been depending on you to have the common sense or will power or whatever you want to call it. Now I see that I've been putting too much responsibility on you. But honestly I don't know what happens from now on. We will just have to support each other.

This realisation actually placed their relationship on a more equal footing, and led Frank and Wendy to communicate with each other more openly. Frank's self-restraint lasted until October, when he tried once more to persuade Wendy to consider, if not sex itself, then at least the consequences of avoiding sex, if only from the male perspective:

> I am debating whether I should tell you about 'the pain'. The pain is caused by unfulfilled stimulation. It is more an ache I think. Boy's nickname it 'Lovers Testicles'. It is not an unbearable ache – just uncomfortable. It only occurs occasionally after a particularly torrid burst e.g. Sunday afternoon.

Wendy's response was equally direct: 'It's only fair that males should suffer that "itty-bitty" pain because their life is heaven compared to the pain a woman suffers throughout her life, e.g. puberty and motherhood.'

The coordinates of love and sex, which had marked the discursive terrain of their relationship over the past several months, were soon joined by another reference point. Since abandoning his novel in April, Frank had started raising the topic of marriage – half-jokingly, but still, for all that, half-seriously. Wendy was more cautious than Frank. The only pull the idea of marriage held for her at this stage was as an escape from indecision. Marriage would foreclose her need to choose her own life course, so it was a temptation, but still it was one she wished to avoid for as long as possible.

For Wendy, the question of sex was accompanied by enormous anxiety and nervousness, due to the almost complete silence and lack of information regarding sex available to young women at the time. Matters came to a head one weekend in Nowra in early December 1956, when Frank and Wendy had a heated discussion. She was trying to get him to appreciate that, when it came to sex, women always had more to lose than men. Young couples at this time had no access to contraception, and generally felt terror at the prospect of pregnancy, particularly outside of wedlock. If they were discovered, Wendy said – or, worse, if she got pregnant – Frank might be labelled a 'monster', but she would be a 'tramp'. Later, reflecting on the argument, she spoke about them both 'being scarred by the battle marks of the fight between us and convention'. In the end, Frank accepted Wendy's position. They decided instead to develop the 'mental side' of their relationship, and ease up on the physical side.

During this period, Frank was finding succour in literature, in particular D.H. Lawrence's novel *Sons and Lovers* (1913). He found parallels between the novel and his relationship with Wendy. He would tell her about it over the telephone, and type out long excerpts to her in letters, together with his analysis of how they related to their situation – the problems of young love and convention, marriage and sex, and parental influence. He found the novel 'disturbing': he felt like a boy in a cinema shouting out to the good guy to look out behind him, as the bad guy creeps up.

I have become so absorbed in the characters of DH's book that I find myself telling the young lovers not to take so much notice of the mother. You see, the mother of the boy is abnormally domineering and cannot tolerate a girl taken her son from her . . . Mother love is one of the major themes.

After typing out one long excerpt about the characters Paul and Miriam, Frank stated: 'So you see we are not the only ones with the problem. This Paul had similar ideas to me – or I have similar ideas to him. And Miriam (the girl) had similar ideas to you.'

It was around this time Frank first met John Burrows.[1] They had their first sexual encounter one evening in December, after much drinking. There had been a mutual attraction between them since they had met socially, but it was only under the influence of alcohol that Frank allowed himself to give in to his homoerotic desire. Afterwards, he was stricken by guilt and disgust and repulsion, the sources of which he could not fully articulate. He distanced himself from John, but over the following week or so John made repeated overtures of conciliation: they were drunk, it was a one-off thing, it would not happen again. They tentatively mended their friendship, and continued socially as they had before the incident.

Frank had long harboured sexual fantasies about men, but had tried to suppress them. He had read about homosexuality over the years – in Eysenck, Kinsey and Freud, and more recently in *Sex and Society* – and had intellectually accepted that human beings had an inborn bisexuality, and that the prohibition against homosexuality was one of the hypocrisies of conventional morality. He understood this abstractly, but in practice it was a very different story.

---

[1] 'John Burrows' is a pseudonym for a man who would have a fifty-year sexual relationship with Frank. He is not a public figure, and their relationship was conducted in private. He agreed to speak with me about his relationship with Frank on condition of anonymity.

At work, he had sat in courtrooms and watched cases being built against hapless men charged with what society and the law considered 'obscene' offences. Between 1954 and 1957, for example, the number of arrests for the crime of homosexuality in New South Wales almost doubled, but reporting about them in the press was all but suppressed. At home, Frank had sat through monologues from his family about the dangers of homosexuality and communism. All these voices would clamour around him, contributing to the negative self-talk of his inner, competing and hypercritical monologues. It was an emotionally gruelling set of voices which said, 'Do you really think you are doing a wise thing?' whenever he deviated from the 'normal'.

He felt guilt about Wendy. He knew he could never tell her about any of this. All year he had been espousing to her what he called his 'Frankness and Sincerity Theory', which he had tried to install as the basis of their relationship. In April he had written to her: 'As you know it is my dream that one day (maybe 1000's of years hence) all humans will be open and frank, and that such words as blush, modesty, unspeakable, embarrassment will be unknown.' In October, he had told Wendy that, although he found it hard in some cases, he was trying to adapt himself to always being honest in his own relationships.

But Wendy was sceptical of the idea, not just as it related to the world in general, but even in their own capacity to be truly open and honest with one another. She perhaps thereby inadvertently provided Frank with a rationale for not telling her about his sexual encounter with John, or his underlying homoerotic desires. She had written to Frank in October:

About that idea of being open and frank. I'm not sure how I feel about. Every person in himself is a secret. No person knows another person perfectly. You might say you do but there are still hidden parts of that person. If you are to have openness you must first do away with all the secrets in humans themselves. Perhaps it would be good. I haven't really considered it. Though it would be good for me for I get embarrassed quite easily. I don't know whether we'd be happier on the whole to have no secrets. A secret shared is a bond between people, something that brings people closer together. If we did away with this we'd do away with a part of love. Frankness and openness can only be a part of people who understand and love each other e.g. in families. So superman, all you have to do is to make everyone into one big happy family, thus solving all problems of peace and frankness.

This had triggered Frank's response regarding *The Family of Man*. But in his secrecy about his encounter with John, Frank had proved Wendy right.

But he could not even tell her that.

In October 1956, Frank had been called up for his National Service medical exams. In January 1957, he started three months of National Service training at Ingleburn, near Campbelltown, south-west of Sydney. In a very real sense, this was the 'conscription notice' he feared one day receiving. It made the prospect of war, and his involvement in it, more acute.

Frank was in 7 Platoon, B Company, 13th National Service Training Battalion. He arrived on the first day with only his toothbrush, shaving gear and call-up form. Everything else he would need — from his uniform to his socks and underpants, from his pyjamas to his comb — was issued to him on arrival. He was assigned a bunk in a hut, along with other recruits.

In spite of Frank's stint in the Cadet Corps at school, his disdain for authority and convention, and his growing political radicalism, meant he was never going to embrace his 'nasho' experience. 'How can a socialist fit into a capitalist army?' he wrote during his first week. Frank was aware of how the training was supposed to break down individual resistance. In a handwritten diary he kept during this period, Frank wrote frequently about his desire to 'defend my own freedom', for 'independence and freedom', and how, even while following orders, he would maintain his inner freedom. He wrote how, in the middle of drills or when pressed into some group activity, he would say to himself, over and over, phrases such as

'They can never cage my mind' or 'The physical restriction will stimulate my mental movement'.

After the first couple of weeks, Frank began to find moments of enjoyment in some of the work. Perhaps it was just physical tiredness, but he found some relief from the pressures of his everyday life and worries, regarding Wendy and John and his job. There was also relief from drinking, as no alcohol was allowed on base.

Another saving grace he had not previously considered was that, as they were all conscripts rather than volunteers, there was a wide cross-section of the male community present. There was, for example, a conscientious objector, who would sneak away whenever possible to read Hemingway's *A Farewell to Arms* (1929), while Frank would sneak away to read Shakespeare. In spite of this, Frank was often melancholy. His mood, he told Wendy in a letter, was such that he wanted to do nothing but walk around with his hands in his pockets, kicking stones.

The first weekend in February, Frank had leave. As he had not been able to drink for the past few weeks, he got very drunk with some of his friends in Sydney. On Saturday, 2 February, after much drinking, Frank and John Burrows had their second sexual encounter. The details are forgotten, but they appear to have gone further than their previous encounter in December.

Early the following week, Frank wrote to John telling him he had considered breaking off their friendship completely, but he wanted to give John an opportunity to explain himself. John tried once more to repair their friendship, arguing that they had overcome the 'problem' once before and could do so again. He said what he was going through was 'hell unequivocably hell', and he hoped Frank was not going through the same. They spoke about their homosexual encounter in terms of it being a 'crime', 'self-punishment' and a 'sin', and otherwise skirted around what they referred to as the 'type of behaviour that shames us both'.

Frank threw himself back into his military training, appreciating the distraction of the daily routine. But pressure was growing inside him, and it needed to be released. That came the following Saturday night, one week after his second encounter with John. He was lying around the hut with his bunkmates, all of them bored and restless. Somebody suggested they raid the neighbouring hut. The idea spread and finally exploded into action. 'Fellas who had never raised their voices before were infected by the spirit,' Frank wrote afterwards. 'It was a type of release.' They raced into the next hut, hollering and swinging, and a fight ensued. Eventually, a lieutenant arrived and the fight stopped. They were marched to the Guard House and charged with having caused a disturbance, with damage to government property.

The following week, again on leave, Frank met with John, and after some initial embarrassment, they tried to act as normally as possible. They did not speak about their encounters, pretending nothing had happened, and afterwards Frank returned to camp. But matters were not settled – not for Frank, at least. He continued to brood, and finally sent John a letter, which John received as the 'worst shock of my life'. He read Frank's letter in 'horror'. Frank had decided to break off their friendship completely: their relationship was irreparable, and Frank could no longer 'tolerate' John's presence in his social circle.

John described Frank's letter back to him as being accusatory, of turning the situation 'into a monstrous and disgusting situation in which' Frank was acting as if he had been 'victimised' by John. In his defence, John tried to correct the record: they were both drunk, but they both knew what was going on and had both participated voluntarily. John conceded that Frank was clearly facing a 'real confusion', but he was 'running away' and 'retreating' from himself, as much as he was from John or the situation.

Buried in Frank's accusation was his unresolved trauma from his middle-school experience of sexual molestation. He had not told John about that adolescent experience, although he basically accused John of the same crime, so they were speaking and acting at cross-purposes. John had previous experience with men, and so in his initial encounters with Frank knew what he was doing and was comfortable with the situation. Frank may have known what he wanted, but he did not really know what he was doing. He did not have the same experience and self-awareness regarding his sexuality. His emotional and intellectual understanding had not caught up with his physical desires. On both occasions, Frank needed to be drunk in order to overcome his own sexual inertia.

Frank's reply to John no longer exists, but somehow they returned to some semblance of platonic friendship. It helped that Frank still had more than a month remaining at camp. Eventually, towards the end of his National Service, on his final leave, Frank spent a long, chaste evening with John, in which – for the first time, sober and in person – they spoke freely with one another, defining their moral ground. Frank admitted that on sexual matters he had difficulty with 'direct expression'. Afterwards, John wrote about their conversation, in which they rationalised their relationship, arguing for 'the lack of significance of any physical behaviour in itself – one can draw neither a positive nor a negative value judgement in the absolute'. John summarised their shared understanding:

> Any act becomes significant only insofar as we ourselves THINK it to be so – it is only good or bad as we ourselves visualize it to be the one or the other. And here is where society and conventional behaviour and all that sort of thing comes into the picture. For, though we may intellectually reach some logically well thought out solution to a puzzle, there still necessarily remains somewhere in us the conditioning we have continually received from society regarding such things as standards of moral conduct. It takes great strength and emotional fortitude to defy conventional morality at any time, and the inner conflict which often results from such defiance is tremendous. Witness the past three months.

It was, in many respects, the mirror of the argument Frank had put to Wendy the previous year.

Frank had by then moved from the boarding house on Bartlett Street to a flat in Kings Cross, on Darlinghurst Road, which he was sharing with Paul Coombes and David Gyger. In the flat, Frank, Paul and David had a photo gallery on the living room wall of their respective girlfriends: three of Wendy, two of Carol and one of Janet.

'I am becoming increasingly disillusioned with journalism,' Frank wrote to Wendy before moving into the flat. For her part, Wendy had settled on nursing as a career choice. One of her sponsors on her application for the hospital training course in Sydney was Purth Moorhouse.

After completing his National Service training, Frank returned to *The Daily Telegraph* on a shift from 2 pm to 11 pm. He told Wendy this would help with his 'attempted reformation', because working nights would stem his drinking. He had two nights off each week, one of which he planned to spend with Wendy – although she would not be in Sydney until May.

On his other night off, Frank and David were attending a 'Publications Typography' course at Technical College. Even when Frank was feeling disillusioned with journalism, he retained an interest in the technical side of publishing. He and David often talked about one day starting a newspaper together.

None of this curbed his drinking. On one night out, Frank was with a friend, Tony. They were talking about Hemingway and the need for life experiences in order to write. They persuaded one another to go to Kings Cross to experience visiting a prostitute. They went down a particular laneway and Frank paid a woman and went inside.

There were no lights on in the house, except for a lamp in the corner of a room, and in the dim light he could see a chair and a double bed. The woman made Frank sit in the chair, and he unzipped his trousers while she fetched a basin of water and roughly washed his penis. She then lay on the bed, pulled up her skirt and summoned him to her.

They attempted sex. After a while she said, 'Are you coming yet?' and when he did not reply, she said, 'Okay, get off, I can tell you're finished.' But he was not finished. He did not even really get started. Afterwards, as she showed him the door, Frank tried to make some human connection.

'How are the tough economic conditions affecting you?' he said.

'It don't worry me, love, I only do this while me husband is away,' she replied. 'Mind the step.'

Around this time, Frank told Wendy he was unhappy and depressed. He traced the cause to his drinking and his worries about their future together. 'I fear that unless I give up drinking and get down to some earnest work I will be shipwrecked,' he wrote. He blamed his drinking on the company that he kept, particularly his work colleagues. 'Living in Sydney and with a flat and many drinking friends my attitude and character I think have degenerated,' he wrote.

He could not be open with her about his encounter with the prostitute, or his recent experiences with John Burrows. And he could not talk about how the failed experience with the prostitute was probably a reaction to the situation with John, an effort to test his heterosexuality. So he blamed his drinking, because alcohol had lowered his inhibitions before each of these sexual encounters. 'It seems to me that drinking is demoralising,' he told Wendy. 'With a few beers under the belt I used to get a "couldn't care less" attitude and say "whats the use".'

Frank's guilt led him to try several times to break up with Wendy, but almost straightaway he would realise he needed her and they would reconcile. Often Wendy just ignored the break-up letter and pretended she had not received it, writing to him as if responding to a previous letter.

On one occasion, after sending one of his break-up letters, Frank drank heavily and tried jumping out of the window of the third-floor flat on Darlinghurst Road, but he was held back by David Gyger and another friend who was visiting that night, Steve Dunleavy. A crowd had gathered below and the police came, but they did not press charges.

Much of this malaise formed the background of an untitled short story Frank wrote during this period. The general form of the story is of a comedy, in which Thomas brings Kathy up to his flat to have sex for his first time, but he fails to perform and so sinks into a funk. The story ends with him overcoming his emotional difficulties, and they successfully consummate their young love.

Frank drew heavily on his recent experiences in the detail of the story. Thomas recalls visiting a prostitute during his National Service training. Frank's 'Theory of Frankness and Sincerity' is expressed through Thomas, and Wendy's sceptical response comes through in the words of Kathy.

When Thomas and Kathy try to have sex, Thomas physically cannot go through with it: '[H]is body was not now responding to her the way it should. He seemed numb around the waist. Fear.' Thomas construes this fear as being emotional and psychological, imagining the opprobrium of society – mother, father, ministers of religion, conventional ideas about women and sex – looking over his shoulder.

But there is a third character in the story, an ever-present centre around whom the young couple rotate, a man named Jimmy. It is Jimmy who has brought Thomas into his circle of friends and introduced him to Kathy. And, after his failed sexual encounter, it is Jimmy whom Thomas calls upon for assistance. Jimmy diagnoses Thomas's problem as 'functional impotence'.

The story of Thomas and Kathy is almost a satire on middle-class social conventions, and Frank used the split consciousness of Thomas and the ironic narrator to hold up these conventions to judgement. But it is Jimmy who complicates the narrative.

Several details point to Jimmy being based upon John Burrows. Thomas and Jimmy are never described as being anything other than friends, but an underlying homoeroticism is hinted at in the moments preceding his impotence. When Thomas and Kathy are first in bed together, a thought flashes through Thomas's mind that Kathy has previously been with other men, and he becomes at once excited and jealous: 'The idea of other men began to excite him and he didn't know why.' A few moments later: 'His body was in rebellion against him. His muscles ached. He wondered if he was normal. His mind was disarrayed.'

This story was, in many respects, a marked advance over Frank's earlier novel on adolescence, and he was finally beginning to write about the adult world in which he was living. He was becoming more deeply invested in the moral dilemmas that, as an adolescent, he had judged from the outside. His own certainties were beginning to break down, and he was using his writing to grind them down even more.

In some respects, this untitled story loosely parallels the triangle of characters in James Baldwin's 1956 novel *Giovanni's Room*, between the protagonist, David, struggling with his bisexuality, caught between his girlfriend, Hella, and the man he is involved with, Giovanni. It was a novel John Burrows had shared with Frank as a way to put their situation into perspective.

Wendy arrived in Sydney to begin her nursing training in May 1957. She moved into the Nurses' Home at the Royal Prince Alfred Hospital, in Camperdown. Her parents assumed this would mean Wendy would be under strict surveillance, but that was not the case. The Nurses' Home did have a 10.30 pm curfew, but for the first few months Wendy attended classes and workshops during the day, and afterwards would go to Frank's flat in Kings Cross. Often she cooked supper for Frank, Paul and David, before Frank escorted her back to beat the curfew.

Frank was again on the court beat, and so keeping regular hours, and he and Wendy fell into a comfortable domestic routine. Almost immediately this brought some stability into his life. And so, twelve months after first abandoning his writing journal, Frank made a fresh start. His first entry copied the entry he made a year earlier, but updated it: 'Today I have decided to write a journal. I am aged 18 years and 5 months. I think the journal will consist of what I call "significant incidents" which will provide material for future literary work.'

This time the journal was not abandoned after a single page, but extended over the next eight months to 280 typed pages. The journal became a daily discipline, regardless – or even in spite of – whatever else was going on in Frank's life. He would describe, mainly in 'free prose', seemingly banal events, overheard conversations or brief interactions – on the bus, on the tram, on the street – or else general thoughts about life and love, politics and literature. In each moment he would try to pinpoint some interesting aspect of human behaviour.

A recurring feature of the journal was Frank's observations of the dynamics between adults (usually parents, but not always) and children. Sometimes they reminded him of his own childhood experiences, and he used these moments to interpret his memories of his family. On one occasion, for example, he saw a small boy with a plaster on his leg, and it reminded Frank of his own 'grazes of boyhood' – but then he realised the child was not injured at all, but was only play-acting, and the mother was angry: 'you naughty boy / you deserve a belting for wasting mummy's sticking plaster'.

> and he thought
> perhaps unconsciously that by putting on a plaster
> he would receive the love-sympathy
> perhaps he was starved for mother love

Over the coming months, when Wendy had finished her initial training and was doing nursing shifts at the hospital, her encounters with Frank became more sporadic. Sometimes they met during the day for lunch in the park, or went to the cinema at night; on weekends they might attend parties together.

This lack of routine meant that, some nights during the week, Frank was able to slip back into old habits. Not long after, Frank and his friends went out drinking one night, roaming the streets. They tried to get into a stranger's party, and when ejected they starting throwing rocks at the house. They were arrested, charged for offensive behaviour and jailed overnight. In court, they were released on bond.

Frank managed to have the story suppressed in the newspapers, so his family in Nowra would not find out. He could not hide the incident from his bosses at work, however, and after being initially dismissed from his job, he made a personal plea to Frank Packer, who reluctantly allowed Frank to keep his job – but only after giving him a dressing-down and suspending him for a week.

In August, Frank was suddenly summoned to Nowra. Moorhouse the Machinery Man was in financial straits. There had been a drought and farmers were tightening their belts, choosing not to upgrade or purchase new agricultural equipment. The business had undergone an expansion over recent years, which, under the present economic circumstances, necessitated a sudden contraction. Workers were laid off. The advertising budget was cut in half. The family was unsettled.

Frank suspected he was going to be pressured to stay and help the business during this period, and before arriving in Nowra he rehearsed his arguments as to why he could not do so. But he was not prepared for what he found.

> an air of insecurity
> hangs around my old comfortable
> home
> and around the familiar cream
> workshop
> it hangs around
> like smoke on a calm day
> an uneasy
> frightening atmosphere

For Frank's whole life, his father had been the strong centre of the family and the business. Now he had succumbed to some private darkness, and could not rouse himself to work. He was lying around the house, losing himself in sleep. Purth was often teary, worrying about her husband because she had never seen him like this before. Not this bad, anyway.

The inherited dark humours Frank Sr had tried to stay one step ahead of, keeping them at bay with his work ethic and productivity, had finally caught up with him. At one point he was in tears, and he held Frank's arm and told him he could no longer find the answers to problems like he did when he was first building the business. Frank's brothers were butting heads; they had different personalities and different approaches to management. They had their own ideas about the direction the business should take – or should have taken – and in the pressure of the current situation it was easy to hold each other to blame.

In spite of Frank's complicated feelings towards his family, he had always considered them a secure and stable background in his life, even as he railed against them. His adolescent rebellions against the conservative, business-oriented way of life of his family had required their conventionality to be fixed and mundane. Now it was seemingly coming apart.

> i never considered
> that our family
> could ever
> be unhappy
> nor could i ever conceive
> that my father's business
> could be
> insecure

The suicide of Frank's grandfather, Frederick Moorhouse, was still a family secret at this stage, even from Frank's father. So Frank had no context for his own psychological struggles, let alone for those of his father, or how each reflected the other.

After a couple of days in his old home, Frank was preparing his escape. He had left his typewriter in Sydney and so he wrote his journal by hand, considering his experience with anxiety and depression.

> i have noticed
> that growing inside of me
> is a feeling
> a constant feeling
> which is aroused

when ever i
contact
anything unpleasant
it shys away
in pain
when anything unpleasant confronts it
it senses
unpleasant situations
like a bloodhound
sniffs the scent of an escape
and having sensed the situation
urges me away
it tells me to get away
to escape it
i think it is a dangerous feeling
because life seems to hold so much
which is not pleasant
and when this feeling cannot escape
from an unpleasant situation
it panics me
or fills me with despair
it bucks and rears in terror
pulls at my inside
like a frightened horse
at a leash
it tears me
i fall into depression
like being in a dark pit
with no idea
of how to climb its walls
it leads to defeat
and defeatist policy never wins

A couple of months later, when back in Sydney, Frank reported on a Rotary meeting for *The Daily Telegraph*. The speaker, a psychiatrist, informed the businessmen in attendance that they should support mental health services for their employees, and the presence of mental institutions in society more generally, because it would reduce absenteeism and inefficiencies in the workplace. It would, in the long term, save industry millions of dollars each year in lost productivity.

Frank confided his disagreement with this rationale in his journal:

> i thought that was not the right approach . . .
> and i thought that perhaps industry caused the mental illness
> and the idea was therefore a little illogical
> because if industry causes the mental illness
> curing them will mean changing industry
> probably shifting the emphasis from profits to human relation

This echoed what Frank had noted in Nowra back in August:

> it seems
> that there is one thing
> far stronger than the family
> and that is
> the business
> it shows that the family
> is somehow built on the business
> and it is shameful
> that so much importance
> should be placed
> on the making and spending
> of money

For the business was, in reality, built upon the family, their success as human beings, and not the other way around. And the tragedy of the situation in Nowra was that Frank's family could not in that moment recognise this for themselves.

Sometime before August, Frank and Wendy had begun having sex, despite their previous pledge to wait until they were married. Wendy had not learned much more about sex since the previous year – which was nothing. To find out more, she plucked up the courage to ask one of her biology teachers at the nursing college, but they were more embarrassed than she was and did not answer in any great detail.

In the end, amid the paucity of useful, factual information available to her, Wendy resorted to looking up words in the Penguin *Dictionary of Biology* (1954):

> PENIS. Organ associated with the duct from testis, used to introduce sperm from male to female.
> VAGINA. Duct of female mammal (excluding monotremes) connecting uteri with exterior via a short vestibule; receives penis of male during copulation.

And then, in the entry before a definition of Charles Darwin's theory of sexual selection, was the closest she could find to a definition of sexual intercourse:

> SEXUAL REPRODUCTION. Reproduction involving fusion of haploid nuclei, usually of gametes (q.v.).

In contrast, Frank had written in his journal about the experience of sharing his bed with Wendy, the warmth of it, the smell of sweat as a result of their love-making – but also of the sense of fear that, for him, accompanied the act. There was no mention of ducts or vestibules. Frank and Wendy were not using protection, as contraception was nearly impossible to acquire without a marriage certificate. And then, at the end of November Wendy told Frank she thought she was pregnant, a fusion of haploid nuclei.

On Wednesday, 27 November, Frank wrote in his journal: 'Wendy and I have a suspicion that she is pregnant. I was not angry nor was I fearful. I was surprised to find that I was calm, and slightly happy . . . I want a child . . . I resign myself to the fact quite happily.'

In response to this change in circumstance, Frank acted decisively. He realised he could not afford a child on a cadet journalist's salary in Sydney, so a work colleague arranged for Frank to take up the position of a D-grade journalist in Wagga, at *The Daily Advertiser*. That same week, Frank resigned from *The Daily Telegraph*.

Amid all this activity, Frank's underlying anxieties emerged. One night he was drinking at the flat with John Burrows. He had not told John about the pregnancy, or that he was looking for another job, or that he might be leaving Sydney – and him.

After finishing a bottle of wine, Frank went looking for his rifle. He loaded it and turned it on John. 'I am going to shoot you,' he said.

John forced a smile, but his eyes grew wide in fright. 'No, you won't,' he said. 'You aren't the kind that shoot people.'

'Dare me to shoot you,' Frank said. 'Go on.'

But John did not dare him. He talked Frank down and took the rifle away from him.

A week later, Wendy and Frank found out she was not pregnant after all. It was a false alarm. On Wednesday, 4 December, Frank wrote:

> she said she was a little relieved
> but sorry in another way
> because it would have meant marriage
> i felt relieved
> but not very sorry
> being a person who likes to decide when i am going to do things
> having been pushed around my circumstance
> quite a bit
> now i have a job in country
> which i applied for when we thought wendy was
> and it looks as if circumstance will push me into

Frank felt compelled to move to Wagga and take up his new position, especially as he had already resigned from his job in Sydney. Meanwhile, Wendy would remain in Sydney and complete her nursing training. Frank consoled himself that the new job was a promotion of sorts, even if it was in Wagga. It would also be an opportunity for him to ease up on his drinking, escape Sydney and concentrate more on his writing.

5

'Is This You, Moorhouse?'

When Frank was in Nowra that August, during his family's tribulations, he stayed in his old sleepout. On the first night, he sat at his old desk, just as he had done during his high-school years, the desk at which he'd taught himself to type, writing his first short stories and essays.

> is my writing
> worth the time
> and the concentration?
> have i a place
> in the world of writing?
> here i sit at my old school desk
> where i wrote many
> to-be-world-shattering short stories
> which lie in the folders
> marked
> 1954
> 1955
> carefully preserved to assist
> those who want
> my old work
> when i am famous

He thought that night about what he was trying to do in his writing, how he wanted to 'describe people as they are', to show the small details of their lives, which even they might otherwise miss or not be conscious of. In doing so, he wanted to show people that they could 'change the bad things they do and multiply the good things'. Through his writing, he wanted to lift the 'ordinary person' out of being simply 'a member of the majority' – the 'mob/group/public' – and allow each individual 'to feel recognised'.

> i want to recognise
> the 'person'
> i want to give recognition
> to give consciousness

And finally:

> by doing this
> i should entertain

In the month before Frank was summoned back to Nowra, Frank, Paul and David had vacated their Kings Cross flat. David Gyger would soon after return to the United States. Meanwhile, Frank and Paul had moved into a new flat in Bondi, along with a few other journalists.

Back in Bondi that October, after returning from Nowra, Frank wrote a new short story. The raw material for it can be found in Frank's journal, in snippets of encounters with a woman named Shirley, and in her relationship with one of those ubiquitous Americans in Sydney at the time. She was a waitress at the Pacific Hotel, underneath Frank's new flat. They first met in early August, when Frank started eating breakfast at the hotel. He noted in his journal that he was served by a pretty blonde waitress. By the end of September they had got to know each other well enough for Shirley to confide in Frank, as he noted in his journal:

> shirley told me her problems today
> she told me that she had fallen in love

> with an american sailor a year ago
> and he was arriving back in sydney next month
> she said he had asked her to live with him
> while he was on seven days leave
> shirley did not think this was right

The following month, following the American sailor's visit, Frank again wrote about Shirley:

> shirley wears a silver u.s. dollar
> around her neck on a chain
> and she carries a photo of her u.s. sailor boyfriend
> in her pocket
> i believe she loves america not the sailor
> i believe america is symbolised by the sailor
> love bites on neck proudly exhibited

The final entry concerning Shirley appeared a few weeks later, in early November.

> pretty shirley came to our flat
> with her rockan roll records
> and her latest problems
> pretty shirley put on her rockan roll
> and settle down on the bed
> with a sigh of relief
> (i think they are like a drug to her)
> she leaned over towards me and said
> 'i tried to commit suicide
> on saturday night
> i took sleeping pills
> and some poison'
> her big eyes and melancholy face drooped
> and pretty Shirley – waitress at the bondi pacific
> talked about suicide
> about the possible birth of her child by an u.s. sailor

> . . .
>
> pretty shirley – waitress at the bondi pacific
> is just as much
> a spokesman for life
> as i
> and she rates
> rockanroll as interesting
> and talkworthy
> as her life and death
> i think i may have been
> overestimating the value of life
> before

The story Frank wrote is set in a flat above the Pacific Hotel. The first-person narrator tells the story of an evening when he invited June, a waitress from the hotel, up to the flat for a drink, and she shows up with an armful of rock 'n' roll records. They listen to the records and she talks about her American sailor boyfriend, who is visiting next month and wants to live with her during that time.

Some of the dialogue is drawn from Frank's journal entries, at times almost verbatim. But what is more important, when comparing the completed story with the journal entries, is the suppression of Frank's own commentary about the situation, the rearranging of the chronology of Shirley's story to become June's story, and, in the process, the removal of certain details – such as the silver dollar on a chain around her neck, the photograph, the lovebites, her attempted suicide and her possible pregnancy – all of which could have been used in some heavy-handed way. Although these details are absent, their associated emotional charge remains, but in a more focused way, redirected towards a suggestion of sexual assault, condensed into a brief exchange.

> She turned from looking out the window and stared at me with a very serious face. She said, 'Could a man do anything to a woman while she was asleep without her knowing?'

I was a little startled by the frankness of the question. 'No, I don't think so,' I said. 'The woman would know unless she was dead drunk or drugged.'

The conversation stopped for a few seconds while June thought. She started to drum her fingers on my arm in time with the music beat.

In the final analysis, what is interesting about this story is just how different it is from the material on which it was based, and the degree to which it bears the marks of Frank's developing craftsmanship. His imagination was increasingly detached: this was the first story in which Frank shifted the focus away from a character based on his own perspective, the first-person narrator, and put the emphasis on another character. The narrator became an ironic observer of other characters' lives within a narrative form that contained them both.

A couple of months earlier, in September 1957, Frank tried to articulate in his journal how the act of writing made him feel:

i must express the inner excitement i feel
after i have written a short story
i get up and walk around and around
i look at things but do not see them
i touch things but do not feel them
i am frightened to read or touch
my story
as though i fear that it will dissolve
or read foolish
i lose all self consciousness
and a feeling replaces it
i am inclined to strut
i feel as though the story was a part of me
and after great pain and effort i have torn it
away
but my body does not feel any pain after its removal
only restless excitement and a type of joy
or just joy

> no particular type
> a gladness that the piece of me has been removed a pride in the place removed
> and a relieved happy feeling in my self
> for quite a long time after the writing of the story
> i am frightened to read it
> and do so with trepidation

Having completed 'The Young Girl and the American Sailor' in November, Frank put one typed copy in a folder with his other finished stories, then he typed out another copy, placed it in an envelope and submitted it to *Southerly* for consideration, which he then promptly forgot about.

Frank arrived in Wagga on Christmas Eve, moving into a room at the Pastoral Hotel. He stopped by the newsroom, where he met the editor, Eric Irwin, and the chief of staff, a woman named Alex Garner. By Boxing Day he had already hit a low point. 'I felt like quitting today,' he wrote in his journal.

But over the next week he wrote a few news stories and 'friendly-met' a few people. He worried about falling back on old habits. 'I've met two reporters and both are alcoholics,' he wrote to Wendy. 'Thought I could get away from drinking . . .' On 30 December, in the final entry of his writing journal before he abandoned it for good, he wrote:

> i realised today that i have been drinking
> to become accepted by the group
> i drank all night
> and did not collapse
> and the group recognised me
> and i am now invited to their parties
> and am treated as a friend
> and can joke about drinking sessions
> and hangovers

> but i did not enjoy the drinking so very much
> i had to drink to become accepted

The main difference between *The Daily Telegraph* in Sydney and a regional newspaper was that the journalists in Wagga were not in competition with each other to break stories. 'Everything that a reporter writes gets in the paper,' he told Wendy. 'It is glorious. The sub editor usually comes out to the reporters' room and begs for copy . . . If by any chance they get too much copy they hold it for the next day.'

The thrill of getting his first page one story quickly wore off when it became a weekly occurrence. Another difference between Frank's metropolitan and regional experience was that the small team of journalists in Wagga was given the opportunity to try their hand at different types of reporting. Frank embraced becoming the drama critic – just as he had for *Elouera* at Wollongong Tech. He borrowed books on theatre studies from the Wagga library, and asked Wendy to find books for him on drama criticism from Dymocks in Sydney.

Frank worked the evening shift. His daily schedule was to get up each morning by 8 am and have his breakfast in the hotel dining room. He would read the newspapers, attend to his correspondence and then work on some creative writing. After his first couple of weeks in Wagga, Frank began writing a novel based on his National Service experience. After lunch he would read until it was time to go to work. He borrowed Jean-Paul Sartre's novel *The Reprieve* (1947) from the local library, telling Wendy it came 'close to achieving an "overall" portrayal of life'. He followed this by reading *Iron in the Soul* (1950), the next book in Sartre's *The Roads to Freedom* trilogy. In reading these books while working on his own novel, Frank was thinking about war and peace, and pacifism and non-violence. 'Through my writing I can spread this idea,' he told Wendy. 'People have to refuse to fight.'

Very quickly the routine began to sap Frank's enthusiasm for journalism, and he started making mistakes, which his supervisors noticed. One time he left half the names off the caption accompanying a photograph, his only excuse being that he had drunk five beers beforehand. In order to regain his focus, Frank enrolled in two correspondence courses: a diploma of journalism through the University of Queensland, and an agricultural course through Sydney Technical College. He hoped the diploma would help him get promoted to C-grade, and that knowledge of agriculture would make him a better regional journalist.

He tried to give up drinking, and recounted to Wendy in his letters to her the number of days he had gone without a drink. He began to save money, managing to regularly save £5 of his £15 weekly salary. He even bought himself an easel and paints, and on his days off work he began painting landscapes, finally taking up the practice he had tried to enrol in while at high school. 'I am looking forward to painting because it is silent, peaceful and restful occupation,' he told Wendy. 'It gives me time to think and allows my boiling spirit to simmer down.'

Frank was still determined to marry Wendy. In January, he asked his parents for permission to do so. Such permission was required by law for anybody under the age of twenty-one. Frank's plan was to marry in February, but his father denied his request, reasoning that Frank and Wendy were too young and had no security. As always, Frank did not argue, instead swallowing his anger and disappointment.

Another obstacle was Wendy's nursing course. She still had three years to go, and she wanted to finish it. If they married, she would be forced to give it up. Frank suggested Wendy could transfer to Wagga, which had a training school for nurses, and they could lie about her marital status. 'No need to tell them you are married,' Frank suggested.

Perhaps the main obstacle to the possibility of marriage, though, was Wendy herself. She had only been in Sydney, away from her family, for less than a year. She was still finding her own way in the world, and now, with Frank in Wagga, she was exploring life independently for the first time. And she liked it. She was socialising with her nursing friends, and she was discovering many different people, including men, who were not journalists. Marriage had previously been a temptation for Wendy, because it meant shedding the burden of choosing her own life course. Now, as she was becoming more self-confident, that choice was less of a burden. She wanted to finish her nursing training, but that was also a good means of putting off marrying Frank.

Wendy had more immediate concerns. She had missed her period, and once again was frightened that she was pregnant. She was at the time working in the maternity section of the hospital. She watched and assisted in births, looking after the babies and mothers on the ward. She was also assigned to the segregation huts, where women who tried to self-administer abortions, or had sought out illegal abortions that had complications, were treated – kept away from the rest of the womens' ward.

This experience perhaps exacerbated her pregnancy fears – although this soon proved to be another false alarm – and she told Frank she had moments when she was uncertain about her love for him. Although this worried Frank, he was glad she felt she was able to be honest with him. Frank put Wendy's concerns down to her being alone in Sydney, and them being apart. 'I know how the city eats into a person's spirit,' he told her: 'the city made me mentally sick and some times I took my sickness out on you.'

In many respects, Wendy and Frank had switched roles over recent months. Previously, Wendy was writing from a small town to her boyfriend in the city, telling him to not drink so much. Now, Frank was writing from a small town to his girlfriend in the city, telling her the same. 'Be good don't drink too much,' he said, adding in parentheses: '(read Wendy's letters to Frank 1955).' To comfort her, Frank posted a gift he found in a shop window in Wagga. It was an ornament in the shape of a cat. He christened it Watchcat, and he told Wendy it was supposed to watch over her while she was in Sydney. On occasion, in his letters, Frank would ask after Watchcat.

Several friends from Sydney visited Frank in Wagga, but his new-found equilibrium was disrupted in February when John Burrows came and they resumed their sexual relationship. John would become a frequent presence in Wagga. It was not Sydney that had made Frank 'mentally sick', but the situation with John and Wendy: coming to terms with his mixed emotions relating to John, and his guilt at keeping the truth from Wendy.

This precipitated Frank's return to heavy and regular drinking.

In Wagga, Frank continued his National Service training. This included weekend bivouacs, held in the hills behind Kapooka Army Camp and, in April, a two-week training session at Holsworthy Military Camp.

On these camps, Frank and his platoon dug trenches, installed field telephones and carried out night patrols. They participated in mock battles, in which gelignite bombs and barbed-wire entanglements were deployed to create realistic warlike conditions. But the make-believe was difficult to maintain when, at the same time, they made use of flour bombs and carried light machine guns that did not fire live rounds and were, besides, 'not very light'. The nashos received lectures on jungle and mine warfare.

Cold War fears of the next hot war were also stoked in order to motivate the troops. But such talk only demotivated Frank further, and made him question the whole mentality of warfare. After his first bivouac, Frank was convinced training for war would not solve the problems of the world, and would probably go some way towards exacerbating them. What the world needed, Frank thought, was people training for peace.

The first step was for individuals to refuse to fight. Frank accepted that one person could not change things, but he refused to accept that things could not change if more than one person were to object. He started looking around for like-minded people and soon discovered Quakerism. He even went so far as to write to the Quakers in Sydney, to find out more information and to enquire about joining them. He shared their principles, but not the religious basis of those principles.

Frank no longer believed in a transcendental God, but during this period he began to think about a more impersonal force. He called this a 'Force of Goodness', which he argued was composed of tolerance, peace and 'human-to-human love', which was opposed to war and 'human-to-human violence'. Such a force, for example, animated *The Family of Man*.

Frank tied this belief not to religion but to politics, and to socialism in particular. 'This is the force which will establish true socialism on earth,' he wrote. The contradiction in Russian communism, he argued, was the use of violence to try to establish socialism – but this only undermined its legitimacy. 'Only Good can establish Good,' said Frank. His experience of National Service made Quakerism more appealing to him, particularly as a way to temper his understanding of a non-violent socialism.

These concerns guided Frank's reading during this period, and the drafting of his National Service novel. The books he borrowed from the Wagga library included Hemingway's *A Farewell to Arms* (1929), Turgenev's *Fathers and Sons* (1950), John Horne Burns' *A Cry of Children* (1951) and James T. Farrell's *The Road Between* (1949). 'Farrell is an American and has the modern American ideas of novel writing – short sentences, clever dialogue, sprinkled with sex, realism,' Frank wrote to Wendy. 'Farrell, John Horne Burns, and Hemingway write about the same basic things – bed, love-making, pregnancy and either birth, still-birth or abortion . . . John Paul Sartre also writes about the basics . . .'

But Frank told Wendy he was tiring of the basics. 'I want a restful description of a paddock of daffodils for a change.' He wanted to take six months off from journalism, to work on his novel. He wanted to write about the idea of peace.

Soon after his first bivouac, Frank and John Burrows, along with two locals, went to the Uranquinty Hotel, an illegal after-hours pub 9 miles (15 kilometres) from Wagga. That Sunday night was very rowdy, with drinking and carousing across all three floors of the pub, and spilling into the backyard. But what Frank liked most about it was that some of the men were passing around a guitar and singing western songs.

Frank had long been a fan of western music, as well as country and folk music. Wendy preferred rock 'n' roll, while Paul Coombes listened to jazz. But in Wagga, Frank was among the majority who disliked 'modern' music. Frank enjoyed going into pubs and hearing shearers take to the stage to sing songs like Gordon Parson's 'A Pub with No Beer' (1954), made famous recently by Slim Dusty, or else one of Frank's personal favourites, 'The Blackboard of My Heart' (1955), by Hank Thompson.

In Wagga, Frank bought his first three records of Australian bush ballads, including the soundtrack for the Australian folk musical *Under the Coolibah Tree* (1956), which Frank and Wendy had seen together in Sydney. He bought a copy of *Reedy River* (1953), written by the same composer as *Coolibah Tree*, Dick Diamond. *Reedy River* was a folk musical, based on the 1891 shearers' strike.

The opening song was 'The Ballad of 1891', composed in 1950; the words were written by Helen Palmer, daughter of Vance and Nettie Palmer, and the music by Doreen Bridges. Frank was drawn to tales of convicts and drovers and shearers, where 'each song contains a story of the early days of Australia'. This music provided a soundtrack to the early Australian short stories he had read and started collecting while living in Sydney, Henry Lawson, Steele Rudd and Barbara Baynton, and anthologies edited by A.G. Stephens and Nettie Palmer, among others. He later bought a copy of *Australian Folk Songs* (1958) by Burl Ives, when it was newly released.

Frank moved into a boarding house half a block from *The Daily Advertiser*'s office. It was convenient, but the retired old couple who ran it were constantly at each other's throats, and Frank was often dragged in to mediate. Finally, he found a house on the edge of town, on 7 acres of land, where he would live for the next eighteen months.

During the initial inspection, Frank joked to the landlady, 'I will run a few cows.'

She replied, seriously: 'That's all right.'

Frank had started his correspondence courses before moving into what he called 'The Farm'. His new daily routine involved getting up at 7 am, so he could study and cook breakfast, before doing his usual letter-writing, reading and work on his novel. In his journalism course, Frank learned about the history of Australian media and censorship, colonial governors jailing editors for libel, and the federal government censoring and shuttering newspapers – 'all very inspiring,' he told Wendy.

He was reading *A Guide to Australian Law for Journalists, Authors, Printers and Publishers* (1949), by Geoffrey Sawer. The book gave Frank his first outline of the structure of the Australian legal system. He learned that copyright protected original works, but that originality referred to *form* rather than *ideas*. Copyright was an asset, Sawer explained, 'dealt with as if it were a substantial piece of property', and could be transferred, bequeathed, mortgaged, licensed or sold. A comparison with his family's various patents would have been obvious.

The Sawer book had chapters on defamation, obscenity, blasphemy and sedition. This broadened what Frank had previously read in *The Free Spirit* and the *Current Affairs Bulletin*. A definition of obscenity, he learned, was at the court's discretion, but 'literary merit by itself is no defence'. The case cited was of the novel *Love Me Sailor* (1945), by Australian writer Robert Close. It was banned in 1946, precipitating three years of court cases. That first year, three Adelaide booksellers were prosecuted for distributing the book. In 1948, the book's publisher, Ted Harris, from Georgian House, and the author, Close, were convicted in Victoria for corrupting the morals of society, with Close being handcuffed and led from the court to begin a three-month prison sentence – although this was reduced to ten days on appeal. In 1950 the British import edition of the novel was banned.

For his agriculture course, Frank studied clearing, fencing and drainage, manures, weeds, as well as soil chemistry and the value of superphosphates. He figured that although only 18 per cent of the Australian population worked on farms, 100 per cent depended on them. Frank had long harboured fantasies based on Thoreau's individual socialism, and now, on 'The Farm', he was able to put them into practice. He made garden beds and built up the soil, planting cabbages. Later he grew onions and snow peas.

At work, Frank vacillated between enjoying the experience and variety of writing for a small-town newspaper and struggling to maintain his enthusiasm for writing yet another obituary, or covering yet another flower show or football match. 'But I gritted my teeth and sat at my typewriter determinedly repeating to myself "you wanted country experience you wanted country experience",' he wrote to Wendy. 'Christ am I getting it.'

One day in April, Frank was called into the editor's office. He thought he was in trouble for something. Irwin and Garner were both there, Garner holding up a copy of the literary journal *Southerly*.

She said, 'Is this you, Moorhouse?'

On the cover was written: 'Geoffrey Dutton, Francis Webb, Clive Hamer, Ray Mathews, Charles Higham, Nan McDonald, Bruce Beaver, Dal Stivens, and Frank Moorhouse.'

They shook Frank's hand, congratulating him on getting his first short story published, and he took the copy of *Southerly* back to his desk.

He opened the contents page and saw his name listed again. And then, to be certain, he turned to page 212. And there it was: 'The Young Girl and the American Sailor' by Frank Moorhouse. He was nineteen years old, and he was now a published author.

It was the story he had submitted the previous year. He had not received an acceptance letter, and did not know the story was going to be published. The issue – no. 4 of 1957 – had been delayed in publication, and took even longer to make its way to Wagga. Afterwards, to Wendy, Frank wrote:

> When I saw my name my head swelled a little but the important thing was a great happiness which spread through me as I realised what it meant to us. It is a sign that I can make money from writing other than journalism and that means more security for you and our children.

Wendy bought additional copies of the journal and posted them to Frank. He sent one to his parents in Nowra. 'I was wondering how Mum and Dad will like my short story,' he said to Wendy. 'I have a feeling they will be a little shocked. Guess they will be pleased too.'

But he was interrupted while writing his letter to Wendy, as he had to go outside to chase some sheep away from his cabbages.

One consequence of being a published fiction writer was that Frank's inconsistencies at work were excused as being part of his artistic temperament. His chief of staff, Alex Garner, even started lending Frank books, such as Dylan Thomas's play *Under Milk Wood* (1954). His publication in *Southerly* made Frank more determined to achieve another.

In May, Frank submitted a short story to *The Atlantic Monthly*, in the United States. The story was called 'The Affair with Andrea'. It was, in many respects, a character study of Alex Garner, although in the story she is named 'Andrea Gardener', introduced as 'the chief-of-staff of the daily on which we worked. I was the new reporter'. This first-person narrator is named Harry.

It is a study of an emerging social type, the modern woman, against a society resisting changing to accommodate such a person. Because Andrea sees in Harry somebody with whom she can speak freely about intellectual and literary matters, the staff begin a rumour that they are having an affair. Although Harry is irritated by the innuendo and aspersions placed upon his professional relationship with Andrea, he begins to accept the peer group assessment of her being possibly sexually open, because she is so modern.

So when, one evening, she asks him back to her place for coffee, he assumes he will be her next conquest. He has been told that 'coffee' is a euphemism, so he is disappointed when he arrives at her place to find she has, indeed, put on an actual pot of coffee. And that, instead of seducing him, she only wants to talk – 'about books, society, the "dreadfully dull" people next door, religion as the opium of the people (she was a confessed atheist which was one of the reasons for the sex-theory), politics and corruption, and the decline and fall of the trilogy'.

'The Affair with Andrea' was similar to 'The Young Girl and the American Sailor', but Frank now pushed the distance between the intentions of the two characters further apart. This creates a dual perspective in which, although Harry is unsympathetic to Andrea's situation, enough information is given that the reader can judge Harry for being self-centred, while also seeing that Andrea is lonely. She just wants somebody to talk to, somebody who will take her seriously as an intellectual equal. Frank allowed the reader to 'recognise' her as a person.

In May, Frank asked Wendy to send him copies of *Overland*, a left-wing literary magazine from Melbourne edited by Stephen Murray-Smith. It had started in 1954, but it was only in 1958 that Frank seems to have discovered it. Alex Garner probably suggested *Overland* to Frank. He was at the time working on a short story called 'Lonely Town', which he described to Wendy as being 'about a boy in a town where he is a stranger. He goes to a dance to try to find a girl to sleep with. He thinks that he is sexually frustrated but really he isn't. He is lonely.' Comparison with the story about 'Andrea Gardener' is obvious.

The previous six rejection slips Frank received from *Meanjin* had a subscription form pinned to them. Frank took the hint, subscribed and then submitted 'Lonely Town'. 'I want to crack *Meanjin* if it is the last thing I do,' he wrote to Wendy. 'It is about the best literary magazine in Australia.' But this story was also rejected. So he submitted another one. 'I am sending my story to *Meanjin*,' he told Wendy. 'I am determined to break them. It is becoming an obsession with me.'

Wendy, for her part, soothed Frank through his rejections, as she had done the previous year, and continued to read and constructively criticise drafts of his stories. At one point he said to her: 'I know you want to marry me only to be part of the romantic struggling existence of a writer. You'll be sorry.'

David Gyger had returned from the United States. He had inherited some money and wanted to start a regional newspaper. Frank and David had discussed the idea many times. It was one of the reasons they had done the Publications Typography course together the previous April.

But when David came to Wagga with his plan, Frank was initially dubious. He had finally settled into his role at the *Advertiser* and was doing his correspondence courses, with the hope of getting promoted to C-grade. This was all part of Frank's plan to achieve a level of security that would persuade his parents to give him permission to marry Wendy by the end of the year. There was no guarantee that David's newspaper would succeed, and Frank did not want to jeopardise his own plan.

David was undeterred. He hired David Stephenson ('Stepho'), a journalist David and Frank had worked with in Sydney. Initially, the four-page newspaper was going to call be called *The Wagga Express*. David Gyger discussed the project with the mayor, and threw a special banquet for potential advertisers at the best restaurant in town, Romano's. Speculation at the *Advertiser* grew about this competitor entering the field. Frank acted as if he did not know anything. Soon posters started appearing around the town, flagging a change of name: 'WATCH OUT FOR THE RIVERINA EXPRESS'.

'The Farm', too, had a change of name when David and Stepho moved in with Frank, and David installed a telephone and hot water. It was rechristened 'The Potato Patch'.

The Riverina Express had an initial circulation of a thousand, but towards the end of April it scooped the *Advertiser* in a spectacular manner when it managed to have an edition printed and on sale at the racecourse, including the result of the Wagga Gold Cup, about an hour after the race had been run. A team of thirty-five paperboys were on hand to sell the edition to the punters, which included a reduction in price from 3d to 1d. They sold three thousand copies on the day, and a further thousand before the end of the week.

Soon after this, Frank defected from the *Advertiser* to the *Express*. His first appearance was on 9 July, in an article about a steam box and massage clinic that had opened in town. 'This week I sat in a steam-box which reached about 120 degrees,' Frank wrote, 'and I liked it.' It was accompanied by a photograph of nineteen-year-old Frank, his head protruding from a large, body-sized steam box, towels being unceremoniously wedged around his neck, presumably to keep the steam trapped inside. The caption read: 'A Riverina Express reporter imprisoned in a hot-box starts to feel the heat.'

That same issue introduced a new column by John Penfold, 'The World Outside'. This regular column focused on international affairs, politics and economics. Penfold was a regional tutor for the Department of Tutorial Studies at the University of Sydney. He worked for the Workers' Educational Association, organising adult education classes across regional New South Wales.

John was an erudite man. He chain-smoked and was a heavy drinker. John became an enormous influence on Frank. At a time when Frank was increasingly concerning himself with political and economic questions, John urged Frank to think in an international context – and he gave Frank the intellectual resources to do so, supplying him with books, magazines and journals. But it was mainly through their ongoing conversation that John imparted to Frank that it did not really matter what the subject was one was pursuing, what mattered was 'the spirit of inquiry', and that every subject, if pursued far enough, invariably opened up and led back to every other subject, each coalescing around and informing the human experience.

But there were limits to Penfold's patience with Frank. One night Penfold refused to dine with Frank and David at Romano's because Frank was inappropriately attired. On another night at Romano's, with Frank this time appropriately attired, Penfold introduced him to the martini cocktail.

Working at *The Riverina Express* initially reinvigorated Frank's passion for journalism. They were working regular fifteen-hour days. There was camaraderie in working closely and living with a small, dedicated team. There was uninterrupted intellectual discourse, but also ongoing innovation on the more technical, business and strategic aspects of the enterprise.

Frank arranged and wrote the copy for an advertisement for the *Express* on local radio. He wrote, designed and typeset 'The Bulletin for Advertisers', a pamphlet to inspire confidence among advertisers and attract new clients. He developed a scheme to attract and motivate the paperboys, who each had their own route and territory, where they sold the paper door-to-door. Called 'A Bulletin for Newspaper Boys', it included tips on how to sell the paper, plus a points system, in ten-point increments, to encourage the boys to do well: every 120 points would earn a free cinema ticket. By the end of the following year, the *Express* would employ 256 paperboys.

But the *Express* team could not keep up this pace and pressure indefinitely, and soon cracks began to show. Stepho was in charge of securing advertising, for which, as a journalist, he quickly lost enthusiasm. And David, who was also better suited to journalism, was finding being responsible for the business side of the operation a constant struggle. And at 'The Potato Patch' the colleagues and housemates were quickly getting on each other's nerves. What Frank found most difficult about the extended working hours was that he did not have time to study or write fiction. He was also finding it hard to maintain regular contact with Wendy in Sydney.

At 'The Potato Patch' they had adopted a house kitten, named Nod. One evening, with Nod sitting in his lap, Frank wrote a long letter to Wendy, which transcribed an imagined conversation between Nod the cat and Frank, talking about Wendy.

> Nod thinks your letters show a great deal of love and said I was a very lucky boy. I agreed with him. 'I love her more than I can tell you, Nod,' I said.
>
> He said, 'Frank, old man, the way you sit in the armchair and stare into space for long periods indicate to me that you are thinking of Wendy and missing her. I have a fair idea how much you love her.'
>
> Nod said that he was glad that you did not see some of the glances I give to pretty Wagga girls.

But such light-hearted letters hid an undertow of uncertainty in Frank and Wendy's relationship, brought about in large part by the distance between them, and their less frequent correspondence since he started working at the *Express*. 'I feel a terrible fear that we are growing away from each other,' Frank wrote to Wendy. 'I think it may be caused by the long separation . . . I realise that we must soon come together again or we will jeopardise our life's happiness. Perhaps even three months will be too long. Darling I am frightened – for us.'

One outcome of working on all aspects of a newspaper was that it encouraged Frank in his long-held dream of running his own country newspaper with Wendy. 'I am eager to get a paper of my own,' he said. 'No not "of my own" but "our paper".' He harboured what he called a 'secret wish' that the *Express* would fail, so he would have an excuse to go back to Sydney and be with Wendy. By August he was addressing his letters to 'My Darling Wife Wendy'.

Meanwhile, back at 'the Patch', his garden beds failed, the onions did not come up and the cabbages all died. Frank was left to scythe away the weeds. 'I was stupid ever to leave Sydney,' he concluded.

―――――

On 23 August, the People's Republic of China started bombarding the Quemoy and Matsu islands in the Formosa (Taiwan) Strait, both to test the commitment of the United States in the area and to perpetuate Mao's communist revolution domestically. 'It isn't easy to evolve a Western policy,' John Penfold wrote in the *Express*. 'We don't want Western prestige damaged; still less do we want to be involved in a war over islands to which we have no right and for which we have no need.'

Frank's National Service obligations weighed heavy on him during such crises. It had been drilled into his thinking that the next international incident could precipitate the next world war, and he wondered if this might be that spark. Emotionally, such warmongering placed Frank back into his early, pre-conscious childhood, and the stultifying atmosphere in which he was born.

A Quaker who was passing through Wagga sought Frank out at work. Frank was happy to chat, but was initially wary of the man, even as he continued to admire the Quakers' principles. Frank had all but abandoned writing his National Service novel, although he wanted to get back to it. The story arc he had planned was that his protagonist, while in the National Service, becomes a Quaker and refuses to fight when war is declared.

In his next column, Penfold wrote again about Formosa and the temporary ceasefire. That weekend Frank had arranged to meet Wendy in Nowra, they travelled back to Sydney together. The following week, Penfold wrote a third time about the international situation, which had heated up once more: 'President Eisenhower has defined the American position, and despite the phrase that no American would be asked to fight "just for Quemoy", the position defined is one of fighting if necessary to defend the islands.'

Frank wrote to Wendy about Formosa, wondering what he would do if there was a war, and if he was called to fight. 'My conscience would not allow me to fight,' he told her. 'I would probably be gaoled as a conscientious objector and this would separate me from you.' Frank spent that weekend in Maroubra with Wendy. It was a rare treat for the couple to see each other two weekends in a row.

The tensions in the Formosa Strait were soon resolved, and a fragile peace restored. But Frank's mood lingered. There would always be a next time. That coming weekend was going to be the first Quaker service in Wagga. He decided he wanted to attend, and he tried to convince Wendy to meet him in Wagga for the third weekend in a row, so they could go to the service together. Frank explained how, although he did not believe in the religious basis of Quakerism, he did share with them a concept of prayer as a form of self-examination:

> We can sit quietly anywhere and examine harsh words we may have said or rash, cruel actions we may have taken and decide to change in the future. Prayer in my mind is this. It must of course lead to a more perfect sort of human. That should be the aim of every human.

This mirrors how Frank had, only the previous year in Nowra, described his approach to writing. He associated this concept of prayer with his own political ideals: 'My idea of God is this "socialist love".'

On Sunday, 28 September, Frank attended the Quaker service alone. During the period of silence, he had an epiphany. The very next day he wrote to Wendy's parents asking for permission to marry their daughter. He wrote also to his own parents. And then he wrote to Wendy. 'The battle has begun,' he said. He explained his epiphany to her: 'I went to the Quaker meeting on Sunday. That is where I decided to marry you. We had about an hour of "silence" I treated it as meditation – very deep thinking it was too. The atmosphere was wonderful and if ever I had divine assistance it was then.'

Wendy was annoyed Frank had not spoken with her before approaching her parents, although she consoled herself that they would probably refuse to give permission, as they had previously. And then, at the end of that week, Wendy received a brief note from her father.

> Dear Wendy,
>   Just a hurried note Darling to say that Frank wrote and asked if you could be married (Gee you lucky people). I said it will be OK so come home your next leave & we will discuss everything then,
>   All our love
>   Dad

That same day, Frank told Wendy he had received a letter from Wendy's parents giving their 'blessing and consent'.

Frank's parents only replied after they had arranged for Wendy's parents to come over one evening to their home to discuss the situation, and to assure them Wendy was not pregnant. Only then did they give their permission. It is not clear why Frank and Wendy's parents gave their permission on this occasion, when they had so firmly refused earlier that same year. Purth sent Wendy a card, welcoming her to the family and offering her some advice on approaching life with Frank: 'life is made up of many things – and isn't all what one is hoping for – but tolerance and understanding of each other will help'.

During their eight-week engagement, they hurriedly arranged the wedding, their week-long honeymoon in Kiama and their living arrangements back in Wagga.

Stepho had resigned from *The Daily Express*. His departure from 'The Potato Patch' made room for Wendy after the wedding. She was not happy about the prospect of sharing her first home with Frank's boss, but Frank and David tried to accommodate her concerns by building a wall through the house, effectively dividing it into two flats.

Meanwhile, in Sydney, Wendy's friends and sisters thought she was having the usual pre-wedding jitters. But it was more than that. Since the marriage announcement, she had felt trapped by the situation. She had given notice at college, which ended her eighteen-month nursing career. But also, since the engagement, she had met somebody else.

Wendy had been posted at a convalescent home in Parramatta, where she met a doctor from Fiji named Rampal, who was in his final year of training. Wendy and Rampal quickly fell for each other, but Wendy was engaged to Frank, while Rampal was also promised to somebody in Fiji, where he would return after completing his medical training. That their relationship was never fated to be only made the brief period they had together more significant.

There were a couple of periods during their engagement in which Frank did not hear from Wendy for long stretches, and when they did finally speak, he was curt to her over the telephone. She felt guilty, and Frank felt suspicious. The irony of the situation was Frank was still seeing John Burrows at the time; John would even be attending their wedding.

In the week before Frank's epiphany at the Quaker service, he had broached the topic of homosexuality with Wendy, albeit in passing. After the weekend they had spent together in Maroubra,

Frank hitchhiked back to Wagga, and one lift he got was from a Canadian man. 'He was very interesting but he was a blatant homosexual,' Frank wrote. Frank described how this man had made his intentions known, 'attacking' Frank's 'morals', which Frank resisted, adding in parenthesis: '(You had taken away my frustration – even if it had ever been as bad as to force me to homosexuality honey).'

It was a throwaway line, and Wendy could not have interpreted its deeper significance at the time. But it does suggest that only a few days before he finally agreed on marriage with Wendy (and their families), Frank still considered his sexual relationship with John to be, at least in part, the result of his heterosexual frustration. His expectation seems to have been that once he was married to Wendy, the physical side of his relationship with John would cease.

Frank and Wendy were married on 29 November 1958, at All Saints Church in Nowra. Wendy wore a ballerina-length gown of cream satin, styled on the Empire line, with a short fitted jacket. She wore a cap of orange blossoms and a short veil, and she carried a bouquet of white gardenias and orchids. Her former teacher Clive Hamer and his wife, Joan, were present, as was Aunt Sylvie Moorhouse, from New Zealand. David Gyger was Frank's best man. As a wedding gift, Frank Sr and Purth gave Frank and Wendy a cabin at Shoalhaven Heads, on a small parcel of land. This was to provide them with a secure foundation upon which to build a family home – and lure them back to Nowra.

After a reception at the Nowra RSL hall, Purth gave Wendy a more personal wedding gift, the book *Married Love* (1918) by Marie Stopes. The book was banned for a period between the wars, in large part because Stopes was an advocate for birth control. The gift was, in many ways, quite apt. Over the previous year, since her first pregnancy scare, Wendy had at least four more, due in part to insufficient physiological knowledge and an inadequate sexual understanding between Frank and herself.

It is unclear if Purth's gift had any deeper import or warning. After all, Stopes wrote the book after the dissolution of her own marriage with a man who had been unable to consummate their marriage and was probably homosexual. She was eventually successful in soliciting her divorce, but in making her case she had made a study of all the available material pertaining to sexuality, particularly its social, religious, psychological and, most importantly, physiological aspects, all of which became the basis for *Married Love*. 'In my own life, comparatively short and therefore lacking in experience though it be,' Stopes wrote, 'I have known both personally and vicariously so much anguish that might have been prevented by knowledge.'

Their honeymoon was at the Brighton Hotel in Kiama. Frank's oldest brother, Owen, drove the newlyweds to the hotel, although he had openly disapproved of the marriage, arguing they were too young. It made for an uncomfortable journey. Everybody else at the hotel was their parents' age or older. It was as if they were play-acting as grown-ups. A few weeks before the wedding, Wendy told Frank she calculated she would be expecting her period on the honeymoon. 'The one week in our lifetime when we don't want visitors and they come,' Frank replied, good-humouredly. But the hotel bed was large and they slept far apart from one another.

That week was the first time they had spent so much time alone together since they won a three-legged race in 1952.

Frank continued at *The Riverina Express* into 1959. The arrival of a new cylinder press at the local printery, which produced the newspaper, persuaded David Gyger to make the standard weekly paper eight pages in extent. This effectively doubled the workload, with twice as much news copy and advertising required to fill the additional pages. As the chief human interest and community reporter, Frank's role became busier still.

One of the stories Frank wrote about was Sheekey's Pty Ltd, a locally owned soft drink and ice manufacturer which had operated in the town since 1925. Frank detailed the process of collecting the reusable bottles, cleaning them and then refilling them with soda pop, made from carbonated water and flavoured syrup – all at the rate of 240 dozen bottles per hour.

It was probably during this period that Frank represented the newspaper at a gathering of the Young Liberals of Wagga Wagga, the sons and daughters of the local business and farming community who were involved in local politics. At the event, Frank met a Coca-Cola executive from Atlanta, Georgia. Frank argued with him about capitalism, US imperialism and socialism.

One of the topics Frank wrote frequently about in the *Express* was Australian folk music. The Wattle Recording Company, one of the main record labels specialising in Australian folk music, started sending Frank complimentary albums, which he reviewed. The expanded extent of the newspaper allowed him more opportunity to indulge his passion. He reviewed albums by The Bushwhackers and The Ramblers, as well as records like *Convicts and Currency Lads* (1957), with Australian songs performed by English performers Ewan MacColl and Peggy Seeger, and *Australian Folk Songs* (1958), by Burl Ives. Frank wondered why Australian folk was not more popular, and why people increasingly preferred more modern music imported from the United States. He surmised it was because radio stations were not giving Australian folk music a 'fair go'.

In his articles, Frank would explain the background to well-known folk songs. He described how this music tapped into Australia's oral culture, from a period when songs were not transcribed or lyrics written down, but were passed from performer to performer. He wrote about how this oral culture was associated with the early bush ballads, yarns and short stories – the nascent Australian literature. Henry Lawson's ballads, for example, had recently been recorded, orated by Leonard Thiele.

Frank argued that Australian folk music had contemporary relevance. When a shearers' strike in the district was threatened, Frank suggested 'The Ballad of 1891' from the *Reedy River* record 'could become very topical'. He noted how, on the day Slim Dusty's recording of 'A Pub with No Beer' was released in North America, the Canadian brewery workers went on strike for better conditions, ensuring the record became a success – and, riding on that popularity, the song drew attention to the strike and the workers' demands.

The most innovative argument Frank made for the validity of Australian folk music was filtered through his own internationalist political ideals. He argued that such music bore traces of the Australian migrant experience, the tunes coming from different countries of origin, but the words depicting early Australian realities: 'the hardships of droving, strikes, and the tragedy of the convict days'. The music of more recent arrivals, the so-called 'New Australians', could update this stock of migrant experiences, keeping the music vital.

Frank found reinforcement for this view when a visiting lecturer from the WEA spoke in Wagga on the topic 'International Understanding Through Music'. The speaker argued that Wagga should have a folk festival, which could be used to bring local migrant communities together. They would bring their own musical backgrounds, unique instruments and folk songs, which could be performed and shared, and at the same time they might engage with and adapt Australian folk music traditions as a way of learning about Australian cultural history. In the enthusiastic article Frank wrote about this lecture, he focused on the claim that 'music could be of very practical use in the achieving of world peace'.

It is in this context that Frank's interest in Australian folk music can be more broadly understood: part of his restless search for cultural forms that might incorporate and propagate his hopes for international peace and fellowship. It was a search very much guided during this period by the presence of John Penfold. When the *Express* doubled in size and required additional material, Penfold developed a new series, called 'What's Doing in the U.N.?', which reported on the diplomatic work of the United Nations. Penfold introduced Frank to the organising aspects of the WEA, and the importance of education as a means of affecting social and political change.

Due to his relentless workload, Frank had again abandoned his attempts at achieving a formal higher education credential.

He had suspended his correspondence courses in journalism and agriculture. This only compounded his earlier disappointment at dropping out of his philosophy and psychology degree. But Penfold salved Frank's disappointment by arguing that the WEA promoted education that was uncoupled from the limits of academic credentials, as a form of ongoing free inquiry.

The larger *Riverina Express* required longer working days and irregular hours at precisely the moment Wendy and Frank should have been spending more time together. But Frank's social life, which always involved alcohol and conversation, was an extension of his work life, with the boundaries between work and play becoming increasingly blurred. For Wendy, the challenge of this was compounded by having to share 'The Potato Patch' with David Gyger next door, although he was always very kind to her and tried to give her privacy. But work invariably intruded upon the domestic scene, with John Penfold and other hangers-on often congregating at the house to drink and talk long into the night.

As much as Frank liked John Penfold, Wendy disliked him – and for many of the same reasons. John's usual posture at their frequent gatherings would be leaning against a wall, resting on his haunches, arm draped across his knees, his other hand almost always holding a drink, his eyes half-closed to stop the cigarette smoke from blinding him as he held forth on a seemingly endless monologue. He rarely spoke to Wendy, or acknowledged her presence as anything but Frank's wife. His views on women were old-fashioned. The more Frank fell into John's orbit, the more Wendy felt excluded from it, and the more distant she felt from Frank. On these occasions, Wendy played the dutiful wife, providing refreshments and tidying up afterwards.

On the evenings when Frank stayed on at the pubs in town, it was to the exclusion of Wendy, who was left alone at the farmhouse. She would drink too, whether anybody was home or not. She did not particularly like Wagga, and it certainly did not compare with the busy life she had left behind in Sydney – along with her friends, her developing career and her independence.

Wendy did try to make the most of her situation. Frank and David brought her into *The Riverina Express*, giving her the opportunity to acquaint herself with different aspects of journalism. Later that year she got a job as a laboratory assistant at the local Agricultural Research Institute. One of her tasks, for which she had her photograph on the cover of *The Agricultural Gazette of New South Wales*, included assisting with research on cereal root rot fungus affecting wheat crops.

She was lonely, but she noticed Frank was also changing. The laughter and fun she had experienced with him when they were first together was becoming the exception, rather than the norm.

Frank was secretive regarding the changes he was going through. He was increasingly experimenting with cross-dressing. A year earlier, while living in the flat in Bondi, he had his first experience wearing women's underwear. In Wagga, after his marriage to Wendy, he had access to her wardrobe, and he would take advantage of her working to steal moments at home during the day, under the ruse of his journalistic rounds, to dress in her underwear and clothing. Such moments were followed by feelings of disgust and disappointment, and the shame of it began his withdrawal from her. Wendy recognised the distance between them, but did not know the cause.

Frank had a minor breakthrough when *Southerly* published his poem 'I Saw It from a Double-Decker Bus'. He continued submitting to *Meanjin*, and Clem Christesen continued rejecting his submissions. Frank also collected rejections from *The Atlantic Monthly* and *Overland*, but it was the repeated rejections from *Meanjin* that burned.

In February, Frank wrote an anonymous piece for the *Express* venting his frustration. Under the headline 'Meanjin Lends Hand to Wrong Writers', Frank attempted a high-handed argument that *Meanjin* was 'accepting the Commonwealth literary subsidy under false pretences', because it was 'supposed to exist to allow young writers to have their short stories, poems and essays published and thus exposed to criticism from other writers and critics', but it had over the past year published material from overseas writers. 'Getting into print is heartbreaking enough for the young Australian writer now without him having to watch space and attention in his own magazines go to overseas artists and writers,' Frank wrote. 'It is disheartening to see a magazine like *Meanjin* shirking its job of finding and helping Australian writers.' Frank included in his examples of 'overseas writers' an Australian-born writer who had long since departed for England, which he felt should be disqualifying.

But Frank's argument was not really with people from overseas being published in *Meanjin*. It was not even that other Australians were being published in *Meanjin*. It was that *he* was not getting published in the journal.

In June, Frank had learned of the inaugural Stanford Writing Scholarship, sponsored by the University of Melbourne. The purpose was to send an Australian writer under the age of thirty to the Writing Center at Stanford University, California, for one year. For his application, Frank had pulled together what he felt to be his best four short stories. This included his only published short story, 'The Young Girl and the American Sailor', as well as 'The Affair with Andrea'.

Another story he included was 'In Bed One Night'. In content and style this was closer to Frank's earlier work from high school, and it may have been written around the time he was working on his abandoned adolescent novel. It was written in a stream-of-consciousness style, about a boy living at home with his parents who is told to go to bed by his mother, and all the thoughts occupying his mind as he drifts off to sleep. Finally, he falls asleep without saying his prayers. 'I reckon nothing happens when you don't say your prayers . . .'

The remaining story, 'The Six Young Men', appears to be a reworked excerpt from his abandoned National Service novel. The story begins with the six men sharing a base hut. They talk about sex, and decide that on their next leave they will visit a prostitute. All except one, a quiet man named Charlie. The rest of the men – except the first-person narrator, who just witnesses the scene – accuse him, half-jokingly, half-seriously, of being a homosexual.

> 'What's wrong with you? You're a bloody homo are you?'
> 'I don't want to go to bed with a harlot.'
> 'You're a bloody queen – got no guts.'
> 'I tell you I just don't feel like it.'
> 'Come on, show you're a man.'

At which the narrator reflects: 'Here was someone dissenting: someone disputing the mightiness of the mob.'

When the night of leave comes, the five men go down to the Kings Cross red-light district, but only one of the men, Gordon, after many drinks, goes through with it. The rest get cold feet. They drink and talk, and their talking allows for each to save face. One of them brings up venereal disease, and the training videos they have watched at camp. Finally they meet up with Gordon, and return to camp.

Then, in a masterly narrative reversal, the characters slowly transfer their opprobrium, half-jokingly, half-seriously, away from Charlie and towards Gordon, mocking him for visiting a prostitute. The story ends with them all in their bunks, and with Gordon lying awake wondering if he has a venereal disease.

The Stanford application required three literary referees. Frank approached Kenneth Slessor, the editor at *Southerly*, and James McAuley, the editor at *Quadrant* – a conservative journal founded in 1956 as a successor to *The Free Spirit*. He also approached Clem Christesen at *Meanjin*. Frank sent each editor the four short stories and a copy of his application.

McAuley declined, as he felt he could not sponsor an application for an author whom he had not personally published. Christesen also declined, adding a note of explanation:

> I'm afraid I'll have to return the typescripts, with my feelings unchanged about the work you have sent to me ... It's all right to get it out of

your system, I suppose, but the way you have handled your 'subject' is, in my opinion, commonplace.

I will be only too happy to support your candidature when you begin writing with more penetration and sensitivity.

It is unknown what Slessor's response was, but in any case it was moot. Without the requisite referees, Frank was unable to apply for the scholarship.

The following year, after further rejections, Frank succeeded in having his second short story published. 'One Night in Bed' appeared in *Westerly*, a literary magazine from Western Australia, founded in 1956.

In December 1959, in an effort to cut operational costs, David Gyger purchased a set of printing presses from nearby Lockhart and had them transported to Wagga. This allowed the *Express* to print in-house, while also creating a new revenue stream: custom-printing letterheads, envelopes, invitations and business cards.

The only catch was that the previous owner of the printery also owned the local weekly newspaper, *The Lockhart Review*, and he would only sell the business and printing press together. So in order to cut the costs of producing one newspaper, David doubled the number of newspapers he operated. A publisher's statement explained that *The Lockhart Review* and *The Riverina Express* would maintain separate identities, with no duplication of content, and although they would both be printed in Wagga, the advertising and editorial offices would remain separate.

This meant David suddenly had an opening for a newspaper editor, and Frank quickly volunteered for the role. This was the chance he had long been waiting for. It was an idea kindled early during his romance with Wendy – to run a country newspaper, with her working by his side. It came at the right time, too: they could rekindle their relationship and start afresh together.

For Wendy, this meant she would finally be living alone with Frank, for the first time. At the same time, she was offered the opportunity to take on a responsible role in a new business. This was her chance to 'have something to "do well," a career'.

When Henry Lawson was twenty-one years old, he was already a published short-story writer, a journalist and a newspaper editor. Frank, who was already a published short-story writer and a journalist, took over the editorship of *The Lockhart Review* a little over a week past his twenty-first birthday.

In Lockhart, Wendy took control of the office and the advertising role, and soon after started doing local reporting. They resided first at the Commercial Hotel, which was near the newspaper office. Lockhart was much smaller than Wagga, closer to the size of Nowra, and the locals did not particularly like losing their printing business, or the fact that their local newspaper was being run by outsiders. They became more suspicious when they found out how young Frank and Wendy were, and alarmed when they discovered that they did not attend church of a Sunday.

The first edition of *The Lockhart Review* under its new management was published on Wednesday, 6 January 1960. When Frank and Wendy moved to Lockhart, David had bought them an automobile. Technically, it was for work purposes, because every Tuesday, after finalising the weekly newspaper, Frank had to drive the 50 miles (80 kilometres) to Wagga to have the paper printed, and then return with a thousand copies in the boot, ready to distribute them each Wednesday morning.

A Western musical show came to Lockhart a week or so after the first edition was published, which allowed Frank to voice his well-rehearsed arguments about Australian folk music. According to the laughter and applause from the audience at the show, which Frank and Wendy attended, everybody appeared to enjoy the show. 'But the terrible aspect to me is that the shows don't bother with Australian folk music and the audiences are satisfied with having American cowboy songs dished out by Australians imitating Americans,' he wrote. 'It seems that the closer to America the show is, the happier we are.' What most irritated Frank was that many of the great Australian folk songs had actually emerged from the district surrounding Lockhart, Wagga and the Riverina, but the locals did not care.

It was in his second editorial that Frank set the tone for his tenure at the *Review*. In nearby Urana, a court case was heard in a closed session. Two young men had been charged with carnal knowledge of several young girls. No other details were known. The general consensus in the district was that such a case should not be reported on. Frank disagreed.

In an editorial titled 'Face the Facts', Frank listed the reasons he had heard defending the closed session and the general press silence: the parents would suffer, the town would suffer, the public should be protected from such sordidness – '(newspapers should print more comics and less "disturbing" material)' – and 'the girls are usually to blame in these cases (which means tacitly that justice is not being done by arresting the young men)'. Convention and reputation would conflict with reality.

Although Frank agreed that the names of juveniles should not be published, he disagreed with everything else. The real suffering, Frank argued, came from 'whispering campaigns', from rumour and gossip, usually ill-informed or exaggerated. 'The value of fair newspaper reports of the case is that the rumours and wild stories are wiped out and replaced with facts – both for and against the defendant,' he wrote. Frank argued that a transparent press was a corollary of a fair justice system.

That said, Frank was firm on where the responsibility in such cases should lie: with the male perpetrator. 'In this specific type of case the parents of young children should know that some men evidently do not regard children [as] inviolable.' Frank's own experience, from his middle-school years, attested to this fact.

At the end of February, Frank's strong editorial stance began to get under the skin of the locals. Prince Andrew, Duke of York, was born on 19 February 1960, the third child of Queen Elizabeth II. In the next edition of *The Lockhart Review*, Frank suggested that most people were not that interested in the occasion, and he criticised the way the 'mass-circulation press' disproportionately presented the news, in an attempt to whip up public enthusiasm.

'They treated the birth in a similar way to the Melbourne Cup,' he wrote.

Frank listed some of the ways in which the baby prince was irrelevant to the lives of most Australians: they would never have anything in common; they would never have the same outlook, 'because of his sheltered upbringing'; they will never face the same problems; and he would live in relative luxury all of his life, 'without very much effect on us'. 'It must be remembered that the royal family today is hardly more than an ornament and serves little function in government. Perhaps its most important function is to keep before our eyes a standard of living which we should struggle to attain.'

Frank concluded: 'But, apart from all this, we happily congratulate the Queen on the birth of her child.'

The following week, Frank published some of the angry responses to his editorial, including:

> 'I'm sure all true Australians would be disappointed when they read your criticism. Only a foreigner would fail to understand our interest in the Royal birth.' (F.I. Davis)

> 'I personally consider the whole article in the worst possible taste.' (M. Potts)

There was an official complaint from the executive (signed by the president, secretary and treasurer) of the Lockhart Sub-branch of Returned Soldiers, Sailors, and Airmen's Imperial League of Australia, which concluded: 'Perhaps there were few outward signs of enthusiasm in Lockhart, but your article certainly acted like a bucket of cold water on the private joy and happiness of your readers.'

Frank even got into a fistfight over the matter with the newspaper's previous printer, an old man named Clarrie, who bailed Frank up out front of the newspaper offices at the time. Despite the backlash, Frank continued to publish all the letters and criticisms levelled against him. It was another couple of weeks before any reader wrote defending Frank's editorial position.

'Your statements were absolute fact. I agree the Queen and her family are far removed from our way of life . . . I hope that your spirits have not been dampened by the controversy this Editorial has apparently caused, and that you continue to write your "leader" in a fashion fitting any competent and fearless Editor.' (P.O. Mathews)

Although Frank used the *Review* to criticise the society in which he lived, he also campaigned for more constructive measures in the town. In May, for example, Frank joined a local committee organised to raise £500 to support World Refugee Year, to which he provided publicity.

A more sustained campaign in the newspaper advocated for a regional library to be established. The issue was drawn out for months, with frequent articles and editorials about it. But all to no avail, as the shire council abandoned the project, citing budget restrictions. One counsellor said the money would be better spent on roadworks. Another said: 'I would also have to be convinced that there will be a demand for books by the future generations.'

Perhaps the most important measure in which Frank was involved during his time in Lockhart was regarding the introduction of the WEA. He had drummed up enough interest that a course on the topic of Australian political parties commenced in April, in the upstairs lounge of the Commercial Hotel. This first meeting occurred on a cold, rainy night, during an electrical blackout, with the lecture and discussion being conducted by lantern light. Only eight souls braved the weather that first night, but this was followed by ten lectures, held fortnightly, with twelve people finally completing the course.

The lectures were presented by John Penfold, and were followed by a general discussion among the attendees. A portable library of selected books was made available to the participants. In early September, a public meeting was held to discuss further adult education classes in Lockhart, with a new series proposed to begin that same month, with five fortnightly lectures on foreign affairs.

Some of the township perceived the WEA as a communist front, and that these classes were being used to corrupt the locals. Frank already had a reputation as a godless anti-monarchist, so being a communist too was not much of a stretch. It did not help matters that Frank and Wendy were friendly with a local vegetable grower, a 'New Australian' and staunch communist, who would come to town each week to sell his produce. He would talk and argue with Frank and Wendy about politics, and probably about what he had read in the latest edition of *The Lockhart Review*.

When they arrived in Lockhart and stayed at the Commercial Hotel, it was the first time Frank and Wendy had lived alone together since their honeymoon at the Brighton Hotel in Kiama the previous year. They soon rented an old homestead on the outskirts of town. The property had chickens and mudholes, and they would often eat scrounged eggs, cooked in as many different ways as they could, as well as yabbies, which were not quite the same as the prawns from Nowra, but good enough, as they were free and money was tight. One time they found a baby opossum by the side of the road, beside its dead mother. They adopted it and nursed it back to health, but one day it escaped, and for the rest of their time in Lockhart they heard scratching and pattering sounds from the ceiling.

In December 1959, the film adaptation of Neville Shute's 1957 novel *On the Beach* had been released. Frank and Wendy drove to Urana to see the film. The possibility of a nuclear apocalypse weighed upon them both, and may have motivated them to drive to Canberra occasionally, to attend Quaker meetings. Although Frank's National Service obligations had been fulfilled, their concerns for world peace were as strong as ever, and their desire to make the world a better place was never far from their public actions.

Tramps sometimes came through Lockhart, for example, and Wendy and Frank helped them whenever they could with food, clothing or money. They were like the old-time swagmen from the songs and yarns Frank so loved, but mostly these men were World War II veterans who were broken and had no place in society. They wandered around the outback towns, never staying too long in any one place. One had placed a symbol on the door of *The Lockhart Review*'s offices, a message to the other tramps that meant 'friend inside'. As *The Bulletin* had written of Frank's journalistic forebear Charles Watson back in the 1880s, 'the weary tramp was never known to pass his office unassisted'.

Such altruistic motives did not always extend to treating themselves, and each other, with kindness. This time in Lockhart was the first Frank and Wendy had worked together for any extended period, and they quickly began to irritate one another. Frank was never comfortable with non-sexual intimacy, with general touching or hugging. Wendy was very much the opposite, needing such warmth. But during this period, Frank had withdrawn sexually from Wendy, which, at a time when she was becoming more sexually mature and self-confident, only widened the void between them. Wendy wanted to talk about their physical distance and her frustrations, but Frank refused to speak about the matter. Eventually, Wendy stopped raising the topic and tried to ignore the problem.

At first, when Frank drove to Wagga each week with the new edition of the newspaper, Wendy accompanied him. But after a while she stopped going. She would stay behind in Lockhart, where she had joined a local singing group called 'Charlie and the Girls'. Each Tuesday night, at the end of her hectic working week, she would meet the group to rehearse. This was her chance to assert her independence. At other times, in her loneliness, she drank alone. One night she drank a bottle of vodka mixed with pineapple juice, and was violently ill.

On the evening of Thursday, 5 May, Wendy and Frank were driving along the Milbrulong Road, about 9 miles (15 kilometres) outside Lockhart, when Frank lost control of the automobile and it overturned, throwing them clear from the wreck. Although they were not seriously injured, Wendy was admitted to Lockhart District Hospital, where she was treated for shock, and was only released from the hospital on Saturday. A short time later Frank developed nephritis, an inflammation of the kidneys that he suffered from for a few months, although he still managed to meet his weekly deadline with the newspaper, producing eight pages of copy and advertising each week. Both these events – the car accident and Frank's illness – occurred during the period when the first series of WEA lectures was run in Lockhart. The fortnightly appearance of John Penfold in town did not alleviate the strain on Wendy and Frank's marriage.

In September, around the time the second lecture series was commencing, a vacancy came up in Sydney for the position of Assistant Metropolitan Secretary of the WEA. Frank applied, and, with the support of Penfold, was successful in getting the role. Frank and Wendy's last edition of *The Lockhart Review* was published on Wednesday, 5 October. It was their fortieth weekly edition. They had a farewell dinner in Wagga on the night the final edition appeared, with the full team from *The Riverina Express*. By the end of that week, Wendy and Frank were back in Sydney.

In their final edition of the *Express*, Frank was interviewed at their rented homestead, with the opossum probably still hiding among the rafters. 'We are truly sorry to be leaving,' Frank was reported as saying. 'My wife and I will count our stay in the Lockhart district as one of the happiest in our experience.'

It was probably the first time in his role as a journalist Frank knowingly told a lie.

6

'There Are Those Who Kick, Those Who Get Kicked, and Those Who Kick Back'

In October 1960, Frank and Wendy moved into a flat in Surry Hills, in inner Sydney. Frank threw himself into his role at the WEA, organising lectures and classes. He used his contacts to find Wendy a job as reporter for *The Eastern Suburbs News*. She quickly developed her skills and confidence as a journalist. Away from Frank, she grew more personally independent. In November, Wendy spent her twenty-first birthday alone, queuing outside the Sydney Town Hall to secure a ticket for the final Sydney performance of Paul Robeson, the African American singer and political activist.

One of the few activities Frank and Wendy enjoyed together was musical theatre and Australian folk music. They attended shows at the New Theatre, which held a revival of the musical drama *Reedy River*. Through the New Theatre, Frank and Wendy became friends with many folk performers whose records they had listened to, and Frank had reviewed, over previous years. They became friends with Alan Scott, from The Bushwhackers, often drinking together and arguing about politics. Alan gave Wendy one of his tin whistles, on which she practised the tunes of her favourite folk songs. They also met George James, an amateur folk singer and professional journalist who had recently moved to Australia from England.

In early 1961, Frank, along with Richard Hall, Frank's journalist friend from *The Daily Telegraph*, and Jim Thorburn, who ran the Pocket Bookshop in King Street, organised what they called the Sydney Left Club. It was an attempt to create a forum for the non-communist, anti-communist Left, in an effort to reawaken socialism in Australia. They would meet in a Chinese restaurant in the city, sharing a meal, and would then turn the restaurant into a makeshift lecture hall – a kind of radical Rotary meeting. Attendance was usually between seventy and ninety people. Frank integrated his unpaid work with the Left Club into his paid educational work at the WEA, with the Left Club providing an outlet for his more activist tendencies.

Wendy's own political activism developed. She joined the editorial board of *Outlook*. The magazine was financially backed and editorially supported by Helen Palmer. Palmer had started *Outlook* in 1957, after she was expelled from the Australian Communist Party for circulating the 'Secret Speech' of Nikita Khrushchev, in which he denounced Stalin's crimes. Wendy was introduced to the *Outlook* crew through her involvement with the folk scene surrounding the New Theatre. There was some overlap with Frank's activities, as *Outlook* quickly became the unofficial organ for the Sydney Left Club, with many of the contributors and staff of the magazine – including Palmer – attending and speaking at the monthly lectures.

The purpose of the magazine was to create a more inclusive socialism in Australia. It published pieces criticising South African apartheid and the treatment of Indigenous Australians, and campaigned for nuclear disarmament. This latter topic was of particular interest to Wendy and Frank, especially since they had seen *On the Beach* in December 1959.

Wendy actively searched for topics and stories for the magazine. In her correspondence with Clive Hamer, Wendy asked him to alert her to any forms of 'country instituted socialism' he and Joan might experience in Orange, where they had recently moved.

During their first year back in Sydney, Frank was drawn into the nascent Film Study Group. It had formed under the auspices of the WEA, which encouraged members to inaugurate various clubs and societies to pursue niche interests not otherwise covered by the curriculum. The WEA could not supply funding, but they would provide meeting rooms and the use of equipment, as well as their internal membership lists for communication and promotional purposes.

Frank was the initial WEA liaison for the Film Study Group, arranging the room and chairs and organising the projectors and screens. The first meeting was held on 23 February 1961. Founding members included Michael Thornhill, a few years younger than Frank, and Ken Quinnell, only a year younger than Frank. They quickly became firm friends, and soon afterwards Frank started sitting in on the sessions. Another member was John Flaus, several years older than the rest of them, who already had a long involvement with film societies and film criticism.

The Film Study Group provided Frank with some respite from his political activism and organising work, while nurturing his artistic sensibilities. The attendees would watch a film and then hold a critical discussion. As with journalism, Frank was as interested in the technical and production processes of the film industry as he was with story and content. At first he sat back and listened to the more knowledgeable conversations happening around him, absorbing ideas others were sharing. Later, as he learned, he became more actively involved in the discussions, and more confident in his own criticisms.

Many members of the Film Study Society were also serious about producing their own films, especially Michael Thornhill. In 1956, Michael found work as an assistant film projectionist at a Hoyts cinema in Melbourne. There he met another young film buff named Russell Boyd. By 1959 Michael was back in Sydney, working as an assistant film cutter-splicer (editor) for the ABC, for their news and sports coverage. His own stubborn ambition to be a filmmaker matched Frank's determination to be a writer, even though the prospect of being a filmmaker in Australia in 1961 was only slightly more farfetched than becoming a professional fiction writer.

There were just twenty-four novels published in Australia in 1960, one more than the previous year. Although there were five collections of short stories published in 1959, none appeared in 1960. But since World War II there had been fewer than a dozen full-length feature films produced in Australia. Leaving aside the Commonwealth Film Unit, which made newsreels and documentaries, there was basically no film industry at all.

The contraceptive pill became available in Australian in January 1961. It promised broad social freedom, but had little direct impact on Wendy and Frank, the sexual side of their relationship remaining non-existent. They were still living together, but leading separate lives.

Through the Sydney Left Club, Frank met a woman named Bev. They had a brief but intense affair. Bev was thirty-four years old, Frank twenty-two. She was married and had young children. When Wendy learned of the affair, although she was hurt, she thought it might do Frank some good. She hoped he would sort out his sexual problems and then come back to her. But the situation only fuelled Frank's indecisiveness. He wanted to live with Bev but he did not want to leave Wendy.

Bev even suggested to Frank a living arrangement she had heard John Stuart Mill and Harriet Taylor had in the nineteenth century. Taylor was married with children, and she did not want to leave them, but she wanted to have a relationship with Mill. So they had a shared living arrangement, with a schedule and allotted responsibilities. 'So she got both,' Bev explained to Frank, 'living with husband and family and seeing Mill regularly; and the husband put up with this and even got to be quite friendly with Mill.'

But Bev's husband did not put up with it, and neither did Frank's wife. When he suggested the arrangement to Wendy, she decided to leave him, moving out of the Surry Hills flat. Only in Wendy's absence – and with Bev's husband ending her affair with

Frank – did Frank realise he only wanted to be with Wendy, but by then it was too late.

And so, by October 1961, twelve months after they moved back to Sydney, Wendy and Frank's marriage had ended. 'I think at this stage I am quite happy to be out of marriage as an institution,' Wendy wrote to Clive and Joan Hamer from her temporary lodgings in Randwick. She explained the situation succinctly, in her usual forthright manner:

> The main breakdown in the marriage was sexual. Both of us were completely unsatisfied – I have felt this way since last year in Lockhart but Frank wouldn't talk about it and to save what I thought was worth keeping, I ignored the problem and kept on hoping that things would work out.

She told the Hamers about Frank's relationship with Bev, and her own sense of relief when she finally decided to leave. Soon after, Wendy moved to Bathurst, working as a D-grade journalist for *The Bathurst Advocate*. In a letter to Frank, she said: 'I listened to you on the phone tonight and I realised the futility of our relationship. We've left each other's spheres – I don't know you anymore and obviously you don't know me.'

Around this time, Frank met a young woman named Sandra Grimes. She was seventeen years old, working part-time at the WEA library while studying at the University of Sydney. They struck up a casual friendship which quickly developed into a sexual relationship.

In Bathurst, Wendy contracted German measles, so she was forced to take leave from work. She was also forced to leave her hotel in case she infected other guests. With nowhere to go, she returned to Sydney, where she was met by her father, who brought her back to the family home in Nowra. When she had sufficiently recovered, but before she was ready to return to Bathurst, she visited the cabin at Shoalhaven Heads – the wedding gift from Frank Sr and Purth Moorhouse. There she discovered Frank in bed with Sandra.

Wendy returned to Bathurst. She moved into a boarding house and continued working as a journalist. She joined an amateur dramatics group and one night they had a read-through of Tennessee Williams' 1955 play *Cat on a Hot Tin Roof*. In reading the play, Wendy felt an uncanny affiliation with the character of Margaret, a sexually frustrated wife locked in a marriage with a withdrawn husband named Brick, mourning the death of his friend Skipper. In the play, Margaret suspects Brick and Skipper had a homosexual attraction.

Homosexuality had not been in Wendy's social frame of reference until she returned to Bathurst. She had an openly homosexual neighbour in her boarding house, with whom she became friends. She also became friends with a homosexual couple, both of whom were schoolteachers. Through the theatre she came into contact with less conventional people, and her social network quickly broadened.

Cat on a Hot Tin Roof provided Wendy with a lens through which she began to see her relationship with Frank in a new way, particularly regarding his sexuality. It raised questions and doubts for Wendy, but she could not articulate them at the time, quickly dismissing them instead. After all, Frank had had two affairs with women in the past year alone. Although Frank had not wanted a sexual relationship with Wendy, he seemed capable of having such a relationship with other women. The fault, Wendy erroneously concluded, lay with her alone. As she previously wrote to Frank: 'I am the reason for our marriage failure and I have full understanding of why you went to Bev and found love.'

Although Frank doubtless had a degree of emotional immaturity and male callousness – for all his bravado in fleeing convention, he could withdraw into it when it suited him – a major factor was his own unresolved sexual and gender confusions. He could not speak freely about these with Wendy, largely because he could not articulate them adequately to himself.

After eight months in Bathurst, Wendy returned to Sydney. Australia had a few months earlier sent its first troops to Vietnam. In early October 1962, during the Cuban missile crisis, she ran into

George James, the journalist and amateur folk singer. They had a brief affair, against the backdrop of war and potential nuclear catastrophe. In November, Wendy moved to Brisbane to take another journalism job, and a few months later George James contacted her and asked if he could move to Brisbane to be with her. She said yes.

Soon after, Wendy changed her name, slightly. 'It's Miss Moorhouse what you write to,' she said to the Hamers when giving them her new address in Queensland. 'I am creating the myth that Frank is my brother.'

In 1962, Frank achieved a personal milestone: he finally had a short story published in *Meanjin*.

'The Uniformed Stray', his third published short story, is set in a country town called Smallton and narrated by a nameless local journalist. The narrative develops a strategy Frank used successfully in both 'The Young Girl and the American Sailor' and 'The Affair with Andrea', in which the narrator is a character within the story but the emphasis is shifted to the study of another character, here a local policeman. Constable Casey is trying to maintain his authority and public standing in the community as a police officer, while also wanting the community to like and respect him as a fellow citizen. It is an adult version of Frank's school prefect stories.

Frank's relationship with Sandra Grimes had grown more serious, and by early 1962 they moved into a flat together in Surry Hills. Although Frank was twenty-three years old and Sandra just seventeen, she was the more socially confident and assertive of the couple – or, at least, the less self-conscious and shy.

Sandra had grown up in Sydney. Since the age of fourteen, she and her friends had entertained themselves by going into the city each weekend, wending their way through different social scenes, anywhere they could drink and dance. One of the scenes Sandra moved through was among an older group of people, associated with the University of Sydney, who occupied the Royal George Hotel in Sussex Street. She had moved out of home early, and by the time she was sixteen she had already lived briefly with a man in Paddington. The following year she became involved with Frank.

Sandra was a student at the University of Sydney, something Frank greatly admired, but which also intimidated him a little. Frank's lack of a degree was a source of frustration. In January 1962, the University of Queensland informed him that he could re-enrol and finish his diploma in journalism, but his workload and financial precariousness yet again forced him to let the opportunity slide. In July, he began a new correspondence course through the University of Queensland, in economics, but by August he had withdrawn once more. Such continued setbacks stung.

Although they were living together, Frank and Sandra led relatively independent social lives that only gradually converged. He was fully occupied with the WEA, where he had recently implemented an innovative strategy. The organisation's traditional mode of operation was to lure workers into the WEA building in the city to attend formal classes. But Frank's plan was to take the WEA to where the workers were, setting up makeshift classrooms on worksites and in office blocks, and making classes available before and after work hours, with less formal seminars during lunch breaks. He pushed for more non-vocational subjects to be available, such as philosophy, history, politics and literature. This increased public participation, and one of the unintended consequences of that was that more women – secretaries and office clerks – began attending classes that were previously populated mainly by male blue-collar workers.

Frank was also involved with the Left Club and the Film Study Group, as well as carving out time to read and write, which continued to be a central daily activity for him. Finally breaking into *Meanjin* had boosted his confidence, and he redoubled his writing efforts.

Sandra was taking classes at the university, studying and working part-time at the WEA library. She socialised with her friends at the Royal George, especially with her close friend Gillian Burnett, whom she had first met in 1960, when Gillian started seeing a man named Darcy Waters, one of the regulars at the Royal George.

Darcy's friend was Roelof Smilde, who since 1959 had been with Germaine Greer, who had arrived at the University of Sydney from Melbourne.

Early on, when Frank and Sandra shared a beer together, it was usually at the Trades Hall. Frank would sometimes accompany Sandra to the Newcastle Hotel, her preferred pub. Finally, sometime in 1962, Sandra took Frank to the Royal George, probably on a Thursday night, which was their busiest night, to meet the group.

Darcy Waters and Roelof Smilde were the Scylla and Charybdis of a social scene that was colloquially known as the Push, into which Frank had finally made his descent.

The Push traced its intellectual roots to the early thought of John Anderson, a Scottish-born Australian philosopher who had taken up a chair in philosophy at the University of Sydney in 1927, establishing the Freethought Society soon after. Darcy Waters joined the society after entering the university in 1946. By then, Anderson was becoming more conservative, more elitist and increasingly anti-communist. Such positions began to isolate him intellectually from his students, who had retained a closer allegiance to his earlier critical and pluralistic writings.

Various political issues saw Anderson and his own students on different sides of the argument, including the question of conscription during the Korean War, Prime Minister Menzies' Communist Party Dissolution Bill and the subsequent referendum. A quorum of Freethought Society members – including Darcy, who was the secretary at the time – had regrouped off-campus to form the rival Libertarian Society.

Roelof Smilde had migrated to Australia from Holland with his family. Previously a peripheral figure in the Freethought Society, he became more involved with the Libertarian Society. In October 1951, Jim Baker returned to Australia from Oxford University, where he undertook postgraduate work in philosophy. He had been involved in an earlier incarnation of the Freethought Society, but was overseas during the tumultuous period leading to its demise. Now he joined the Libertarian Society, bringing to it a more rigorous theoretical underpinning. In early 1952, they held their first meeting back on campus.

The Libertarian Society limped along for a few years, meeting sporadically until 1955, when other figures joined the group, including Les Hiatt, an anthropologist. By 1956 they were meeting weekly. In September 1957, a newsletter, called the *Libertarian*, was first published, but this was superseded just a month later by the *Broadsheet*, which became the central organ for the Libertarian Society. It published papers that had been presented at the weekly meetings and occasional essays, as well as book reviews and brief reports on incidents of authoritarianism in Australia, including an index of censored publications. In 1959, the society started meeting twice each week, on Monday nights at the Haymarket Club, off-campus, and on Thursdays at lunchtime on-campus in the Philosophy Room.

The momentum leading to the formation of the broader Push was social rather than intellectual. After Monday-night meetings, members of the society would go for drinks. The same group of drinkers started gathering on Thursday nights as well. Since 1955, the core group had met at various pubs, such as the Tudor Hotel or the Assembly, but from 1957 they had settled on the Royal George. Along the way they accumulated other drinkers and talkers, otherwise unaffiliated with the Libertarian Society.

It was no coincidence the society's momentum increased in 1955, when the 10 pm pub closing time came into effect. Since World War I, pubs had been forced to close at 6 pm. But decades of cultural habit ensured most working men, especially those of the older generation, still headed home at the dinner hour. This left the pubs free for a younger generation to move in. Although the number gathering at the Royal George each week was large, Frank was – through Sandra's close association with Gillian and Darcy – quickly received into the inner circle.

Frank attended Libertarian Society meetings as often as his workload allowed. He read all the back editions of the *Broadsheet*, which provided him with a potted history and context for the society. Typed on foolscap, in two columns, it was in design and layout very similar to *The Students' Voice*, which Frank had edited in high school. Frank discovered there was a rich vein of books and ideas he already shared with the libertarians, which included Freud and Marx, as well as the novels of John Dos Passos, Jean-Paul Sartre and D.H. Lawrence. Albert Camus was widely read in both the Sydney Left Club and the Libertarian Society too.

Frank had long held that individuals ought to be liberated from social convention, and he argued for free expression and against censorship in all its forms. This was the guiding principle of the libertarians. It was during this period that they all read a newly published landmark study by Peter Coleman, *Obscenity, Blasphemy, Sedition: Censorship in Australia* (1962). What the libertarians offered Frank was an opportunity to broaden his thinking, and to test his ideas in conversation and debate.

Frank was also introduced to new ideas. He encountered the work of Wilhelm Reich, who, in books such as *The Sexual Revolution* (1951) had taken Freud's theory of psychology to its logical endpoint: if sexual repression was the cause of many personal and social neuroses, then freedom of sexual desire could lead to the liberation of the individual, and, in turn, to the liberation of society. In *The Mass Psychology of Fascism* (1946), Reich argued the family unit was the 'reactionary germ cell' that, through parental repression of childhood sexual development, supported an authoritarian society, preparing children to grow into reactionary and conservative adults. Frank found this framework useful in helping him put his own childhood and family life into critical perspective, as he reflected more deeply on his own psychological and sexual development.

Frank had never supported Soviet communism or the uses of revolutionary violence to bring about social change. His preference was for some form of non-authoritarian socialism, but he had come to Sydney holding the view that the state, tempered by traditional national party politics, provided a framework within which social change could be effected. Through the immediate influence of the libertarians, Frank abandoned these beliefs and came to see the state and traditional politics as inherently corrupt. This led him to place more weight on non-state, non-traditional solutions to effect social change, requiring increased community organising and social engagement. However, this was not something the libertarians believed in or actively pursued.

Frank quickly realised that, as much as he agreed with the libertarians amid the social atmosphere of the pubs, there were deeper intellectual and practical differences eddying below the surface. They acknowledged the authoritarian aspects of social convention and censorship, but did little to confront these, and nothing really to push back against them, if only to slow their steady encroachment.

Religious conventions in Australian society still ensured that Sundays were free of gambling, hotels were shut and cinemas closed. The contraceptive pill had been available since early 1961, but after the first year less than 10 per cent of married women under the age of forty-five were using it, and it remained difficult for single or unmarried women to access. Abortions among the women of the Push were common, and involved a whip-round at the pub for the funds, with the woman travelling to Melbourne for the procedure.

Frank would have recalled Wendy's stories from her nursing days in 1958, working in the 'seg huts' where women who suffered complications due to poorly or partially performed abortions were kept in isolation. Frank was more acutely aware of the subtle, but no less damaging, psychological and emotional complications afflicting individuals due to the lack of sex education generally or the public acceptance of sexual diversity.

Frank had read books – such as *The Acquisitive Society* (1920), by R.H. Tawney, and *The Affluent Society* (1958), by John Kenneth Galbraith – which had tried to describe society as a whole according to one of its dominant characteristics. Frank had looked hard at Australian society in general, at the supposedly liberated people he was socialising with at the Royal George in particular, and at the broader social and professional milieu of Sydney. He tried to put his finger on what characterised the current moment, and how he could best describe it. He sat down one day in early 1963 to write about what he had decided to call the Gutless Society.

Frank was now working two jobs. He had full-time employment at the WEA, and he had recently become the editor of *The Australian Worker*. Prior to 1913, this newspaper had operated under the banner of *The Worker*, the newspaper Henry Lawson had edited. Lawson's appointment had been temporary, and Frank's role was too, running from August 1962 until January 1963. Both had hoped for a more permanent offer.

Frank was not in the role long enough to make any substantial changes, but he did introduce a book review section, where he mainly reviewed works of media theory, a growing interest of his at the time. Frank was well aware of the historical legacy of the newspaper, its support for workers and its advocacy for radical change. He worked from the same old rolltop desk previous editors had sat at, their notes and manuscripts still pigeonholed and filed away in its drawers. It was probably at this desk, among those ghosts, that Frank wrote 'The Gutless Society'.

It was published in the March 1963 issue of the *Broadsheet*, and filed under the heading 'CONTROVERSY'. The editorial statement remarked on how Frank's contribution was outside the norm: 'For the first time in a long while, we have received an unsolicited article – The Gutless Society – which, we hope, will stimulate a number of replies from libertarians and their drinking companions.'

Frank's collective term for the Push – 'the libertarians and their drinking companions' – was 'the dissenters', those who congregated at the Royal George and the Newcastle hotels, and who are 'inclined to whine when something inhumane or authoritarian happens'. Frank's thesis was that 'we are gutless because we aren't game to engage'. Such engagement was necessary, he argued, in order to influence the type of society in which they claimed to want to live. He offered two arguments supporting this position: self-preservation and obligation.

The first was a form of enlightened self-interest: 'We should protect ourselves by altering social conditions – let's widen the areas of freedom; establish new boundaries of social tolerance; acquaint wider sectors with suppressed ideas.' The argument of obligation was based on a 'straight forward' sense of 'helping to free those who aren't free and should be'. The dissenters were, intellectually and socially, already free enough to diagnose society generally as being restricted. So, as a commission of that freedom, they ought to expand its reach to include others who might be suffering from its lack.

These arguments contained fundamental criticisms of the Push. The self-preservation argument implied that their disengagement from society could lead to an erosion of the freedoms they currently enjoyed, with ever tighter social and legal restrictions being placed upon them. The obligation argument contained a more serious criticism: by not helping those who were not already free, even while theoretically committed to the idea of liberty, they were in practice supporting an anti-liberty position: 'being privileged and maintaining privilege, as it can be argued we are, is anti-freedom'.

Frank drew a clear distinction between their self-identity as free individuals opposed to convention and the reality of their situation, where they had simply replaced one set of conventions with another, and ones that reflected rather than opposed the broader culture they otherwise claimed to reject. Frank called the Push a clique. 'It's clique-fashion to whine about the social conditions – the sickness,' he wrote. 'It's the club-like engagement locked in its conventions and cushioned by its camaraderie.' And then perhaps the most heretical charge: they were conservative and reactionary. 'There is a type of conservatism or even reaction among dissenters,' Frank stated: 'A sort of "let things be" approach.'

Frank did not want to let things be. He wanted engagement geared towards change. What he meant by *engagement* was something different to straightforward *activism*. For Frank, an essential characteristic of engagement was reciprocity. He wanted to elicit a response: he wanted others to respond to him as much as he responded to them. There was a rhetorical aspect underpinning this form of engagement, requiring long-term strategy, method and technique.

'Talk doesn't convince in one evening,' he wrote. 'It is sometimes hard to detect change even over a long period. But I've seen it happen to myself and I've seen it happen to others. Ideas and arguments percolate and change the texture and point of our attitudes.'

His intuition was that people were not normally put in a position of defending or reasoning about beliefs they had acquired solely through habit and convention. By making people defend their ideas – not through attack, but through questioning – an opening might be created in which they could be exposed to alternative ideas, which they would then inadvertently circulate, even if they did so while arguing against them. 'Before they could keep the ideas hidden and quiet but the threat forces them to circulate the ideas.'

Frank had included himself in the criticisms he levelled at the Push – he used the words 'we' and 'us' and 'our'. When discussing the 'clique' nature of those who drank at their pubs, he extended his description to also include the Sydney Left Club. He addressed the limitations of the traditional model of the WEA. 'I'm talking about something more militant and radical than adult education as we know it,' he wrote. By making these self-criticisms, Frank exposed himself as thinking differently, as being independent and on a divergent course from his cohort. This was, for Frank, an act of self-recognition, lifting himself out of the group.

The self-critical elements of the paper – the personal significance of which would not have been known to his contemporaries at the time – touched upon the dilemmas of his own conventional childhood, and what he saw as his obligation to ensure that other children did not suffer from the same ignorance he felt he was raised under. 'Young people should be given access to the suppressed ideas and information of our society,' he stated. He criticised his own personal disposition, his shyness and embarrassment, which he felt resulted from those dilemmas of childhood:

> Of course we're not all suited to face-to-face combat of this type. Perhaps some are better employed at art work, writing, or poster pasting. But

shyness and embarrassment should not be mistaken for inability to talk with strangers about subjects of importance. Shyness and embarrassment are scars of a sick society.

One month before the publication of 'The Gutless Society', on a Thursday evening, on Castlereagh Road, Frank was kissing Sandra Grimes goodbye when they were accosted by a police officer ordering them to stop what they were doing, because it was offensive and against the law. Frank wrote a letter of complaint to the Commissioner of Police, requesting clarification regarding whether kissing or cuddling in public was considered offensive, and in what way it was illegal. He did not receive a reply.

Such incidents, minor as they were, reinforced Frank's belief in the need for engagement to push back against the claustrophobia of social convention. After all, if a police officer found offence in a heterosexual couple kissing on the street, how would they react to what was happening between men in some of the private camp clubs in Kings Cross? The police raids and court cases Frank had witnessed as a journalist answered that question, and only strengthened his resolve.

That same month, James Baldwin's novel *Another Country* (1962) was added to Australia's index of banned books. This occurred against the background of the more publicised ban of D.H. Lawrence's *Lady Chatterley's Lover*, which had been in place in Australia – and virtually everywhere else in the world – since its publication in 1928. The United States had lifted its ban in 1959, and an unexpurgated edition of the book was published there. The following year, Penguin, based in London, indicated it would follow suit, which meant the restored novel would become available in Australia. Proofs were submitted to the Literature Censorship Board in Australia in February 1960 and it recommended that publication be approved.

In England, Penguin was charged with obscenity, and there followed a much publicised six-day trial in October–November 1960. The publisher successfully defended its publication, the ban was lifted and the novel was finally published in the United Kingdom.

In Australia, the novel was returned to the Censorship Board for review and once more the recommendation was to approve publication. The case was then submitted directly to the prime minister, Robert Menzies, and the federal cabinet, and each member was given a copy of the unexpurgated US edition of the book. They decided it should remain banned in Australia.

The December 1960 issue of *Overland* was dedicated to the question of censorship and obscenity, focusing on the *Lady Chatterley's Lover* case and publishing excerpts from the trial in England.

In 1961, Penguin published C.H. Rolph's book *The Trial of Lady Chatterley: Regina v. Penguin Books Limited; the transcript of the trial*, which followed the court case and the reporting on the case. The book contained excerpts from the novel, including many of the contentious passages cited during the trial. It was immediately banned in Australia.

In the April 1963 issue of *Westerly*, Frank's fourth published story, 'Mrs Turtle's Building', appeared. It is a first-person narrative, with the character Bernard Teller describing the ebb and flow of social acceptance in a small, bounded community: an apartment building in Surry Hills.

The story draws upon, conflates and reimagines the final days of Frank's marriage to Wendy, his relationship with Bev and his moving into a new apartment with Sandra. Teller's marriage is coming apart and he is having an affair with another woman, also married. Soon after Teller's wife leaves, his mistress and her two children move in. The story is about how this sudden change – with its perceived impropriety – is met by the other tenants, especially Mrs Turtle, the landlady.

Frank had stayed in contact with Clive Hamer, who was at the time lecturing on current affairs at the University of Sydney. In April, Frank asked Clive if he would speak at the Sydney Left

Club, on the topic 'Political Commitment for a Dangerous World'. The lecture took place at the Boilermakers' Society on Castlereagh Street, at 8 pm on Friday, 31 May 1963.

In his letter to Clive, Frank explained what they were attempting at the Left Club: 'We hope to attract a fair number of politically uneasy, politically curious, young people who perhaps are a little cynical about what can be done by discussion and action of a political kind.' Referring to his recent *Broadsheet* essay, Frank stated: 'Some of the libertarians could possibly be there ridiculing the idea of political action.' Finally, he warned Clive, who was an avid supporter of the Australian Labor Party, there might be people in attendance who saw the ALP as a 'bureaucratic machine which squashes their ideas'.

In August, Frank sent out another round of letters to solicit speakers for the Left Club, on various topics: 'The CND (Campaign for Nuclear Disarmament) and the New Left in Britain', 'Existentialism and the Left' and 'The Citizen's Rights and the Police', among others. The topic of nuclear disarmament continued to be of particular interest to Frank during this period. His ASIO file places him at the 'Australian Committee for Nuclear Disarmament – National Conference of State C.N.D. Groups', held in Sydney on 28–29 December 1963. In October the following year he was at a meeting of the 'Writers Group of the Australian Congress for International Co-operation and Disarmament', which included Helen Palmer and Frank Hardy.

Before Clive's appearance at the Left Club in late May 1963, Sandra had broken up with Frank. He had moved out of their Surry Hills flat and into a place on Wharf Road, East Balmain. The break-up was sudden and Frank felt somewhat blindsided at the time. Afterwards, in an effort to regain his balance, he contacted John Burrows, and Wendy.

'Thank you for the most sincere letter I have had from you for a couple of years,' Wendy wrote back, 'you almost sound as though you've returned to your old self. It's unfortunate that it should happen only through a lot of heart pain but I'm glad that the old Frank has reappeared.' She asked if it would be possible to borrow

Frank's Australian folk records so she could copy them to cassette tape to take with her when she went overseas.

In his letter to John, Frank confided more about his current depression and suicidal ideation. John's reply arrived a few days after Wendy's:

> I can't think of much to say in reply to your depressing outburst. You once rubbished me for expressing similar thoughts. I cannot accept suicide as a solution to anything, but rather a conscious retreat from the problem . . . Naturally death comes at some stage to all of us, and then we will find out what's beyond the door, but it's only cheating to kill oneself in despair . . . I accept that you have had some severe blows to your stability, but I won't accept that life can possibly have become so meaningless to you that you must escape.

John signed off, saying: 'I look forward to being with you once again before long.'

Frank had been in regular correspondence with John since arriving in Sydney, meeting in person when they could. What Frank did not know at the time was that the incident precipitating Sandra's leaving him was that she had stumbled across Frank's private correspondence with John, and so had discovered, in great detail, the true nature of their relationship.

It was also in May 1963 that Frank presented a lecture at the Rationalist Society, advertised in the *Sydney Morning Bulletin* under the topic: 'Are the arts a responsibility of the Trade-unions?' The immediate point of reference for this talk was Frank's thinking about the writing and activities of Arnold Wesker.

In 1960, thirty-year-old British dramatist Arnold Wesker had given a talk in Oxford on the vagaries of life as an artist in modern society. The talk – titled 'O, Mother, is it worth it?' – was republished in *Overland* that same year. Wesker's central point was that trade unions and labour parties had done much to create a society in which economic disadvantages could be overcome.

But they forgot one thing – and this for me is the terrible crux of the problem and God knows how they missed it: They had to make efforts to convince the stultified worker that he was as entitled to a fair share of the nation's economic life as anyone – but what action was taken to convince the stultified worker that he was just as entitled to his share of the nation's cultural life?

Trade unions needed to be more involved in building the cultural infrastructure of society, from theatres to music festivals, to publishing houses and libraries, to support for artists and arts workers. Wesker's address was sent to the secretaries of the various trade unions in Britain. This led to the creation of Centre 42, a trade union–backed touring arts festival bringing art and culture to the industrial regions of England.

Frank had first read about Centre 42 in *Outlook*, which claimed Australia needed something similar. Now he responded through this lecture to the Rationalist Association on the relationship between the arts and the trade unions.

He took as his starting point a reference from another piece by Wesker, published in *Encounter* in March 1962, which referred to the 'incestuous circle' of many arts organisations. Frank adopted this notion to describe what he had previously called the 'clique-fashion' and 'clique-talk' of the Push, extending it here to describe various literary magazines and arts organisations in Australia. 'Literary journals (left or right), university theatre groups and Pete Seeger "at homes" remind me at times of playgrounds to keep cultural workers off the streets of actuality,' Frank said. Such activities had a role, he argued, but they were not an end in themselves.

Frank pointed out the conceptual shortcomings of Centre 42, while identifying similar areas of reform already operating in Australia. His main objection was that Centre 42 did not engage with educational reform in schools, which was where cultural stultification was first imposed on individuals. Frank drew upon Raymond Williams' recent book, *Communications* (1962), which surveyed the media communications systems currently operating in England and their effect on culture. Frank cited the 'loss of curiosity and poor critical attitude of so many children' noted by Williams. In Australia, Frank added, the generally negative habits regarding arts and culture was a 'learned attitude' and not a 'critical one', and one which could be equally unlearned through a process of cultural criticism and education.

Frank noted that the WEA was trying to live up to its ideal of working through trade unions to make education a mass movement. The previous year, he arranged a talk at the Left Club about culture and trade unions. The speaker, John Baker, organised folk music concerts, and produced the first record of Australian trade union songs, *Oh Pay Me* (1962). But Baker told the Left Club he found strong opposition in the labour movement to the notion that culture was part of their area of concern.

'Union leaders generally were interested in the bread but not in the roses,' Frank argued. 'They will use cultural activity as a propaganda device but even then they use it grudgingly.' Even when they used it grudgingly, they did so in a very narrow way. 'It is a good book if it favours equal rights for Aborigines: it is a good book if the hero is a waterside worker,' Frank said. 'There is a tendency to judge art only by its political and social attitudes and not by the combination of attitude and artistic method.'

Frank ended his talk on an optimistic note, stating there was currently 'a labor government in N.S.W. building an opera house'. But in the course of his talk, he pointed out a less overt activity he had noticed at the WEA, and wondered if it marked the beginning of a far more interesting and powerful social trend: the increased participation of women in adult education. 'If adult education has had any real inkling of success in recent years it has been with women who have become aware of their under privileged status and who are searching through education for a fuller life,' he noted. 'Much more work of a Centre 42 flavour could be done in this direction.'

A case in point was that of Rosemary Creswell, three years younger than Frank, who worked as an 'office girl' at a radio station while also taking classes at the WEA. She took a bridging course to gain admission into the University of Sydney to study literature. That process required her to complete the English 1 subject at university, to prove she could handle tertiary education. Not only did she complete the course, but she placed near the top of the class.

Rosemary and Frank became firm friends. She taught him the art of sneaking out for a long lunch. The trick was to leave your handbag under the desk, your jacket over the back of the chair and a cigarette burning in the ashtray. Then you sneak out. If your absence was noted, these props would indicate you must be close by.

One day in July, Frank picked up the latest copy of the *Broadsheet* and read its front-page headline: 'CHARLIE BROWN REPLIES TO MOORHOUSE'. It had taken four months and two issues before a reply to 'The Gutless Society' appeared.

Ian 'Charlie' Brown's paper, 'The Societyless Gut', opens with an imagined tableaux of Frank (dressed as Spartacus) at the Epping Hotel, trying to engage the locals, but whenever he speaks, the crowd calls for more beer. Finally, they throw him out. Charlie Brown, meanwhile, is present at this imagined scene, having snuck in through the back, and uses the ruckus as a diversion to steal their drinks and chat up their women.

'Let there always be Moorhouse to lead the avant garde, to die for us, to fight for us and have the proverbial whatnot shot at them for us,' he wrote. 'Freedom needs him in the forces, but it doesn't need me.'

What affronted Brown most was Frank could not just let things be. Freedom, Brown argued, could look after itself. Meanwhile: 'Libertarians, at least when I knew them, rarely got beyond talking about social issues. This was their most attractive feature and bespoke their intelligence.' One of the benefits of not going beyond the talking stage was that it meant a general consensus could be reached without 'the pleasant group being ripped apart by sectional strife'. Frank's proposed engagement threatened to tear the group apart. It meant placing one's individual freedom at risk, which Brown thought contradictory. 'I resent the restriction upon my freedom that serving time in a gaol necessarily involves.' Brown concluded: 'So I don't intend to take time off from my drinking, talking and fornicating in order to get myself abused in order to make someone else's world safe for them.'

In the September issue of the *Broadsheet*, Les Hiatt replied to Charlie Brown's paper, ostensibly defending the libertarian position from the caricature Brown presented. Initially, Hiatt did not contradict Frank's paper. He even skirted close to endorsing Frank's self-preservation argument when he said Brown 'runs the risk of defeating his own ends'. But where Brown's position was animated by the reactionary spirit of the Push, Hiatt retreated into the conservative position Frank had also criticised:

> Perhaps in speaking of a Libertarian movement I am living in the past: The group that once developed and communicated what is peculiar to Libertarianism – namely, its views – appears to have disintegrated, dispersed, and lost its identity within or on the fringes of a large and loose association known as the 'Push'.

Only in his conclusion did Hiatt directly engage with Frank's argument, although he mischaracterised it: 'External forces have not caused the decline, and for that reason widespread proselytising of the kind recommended by Mr Moorhouse . . . would be no remedy.'

Frank was not seeking a remedy to the internal decline of the libertarian movement, nor its dissolution into the broader Push, but to direct the unused energy of that decline, organising its individual members towards more socially engaged purposes. Frank wanted more. He had concluded his original paper with a paean to freedom:

> If we want to keep it and enlarge it we'll have to do more than waffle among ourselves. We'll have to have some fierce arguments, hold together some rough meetings and employ some patient tactics. The people who don't like us to have much freedom, or don't want social

change seem to win too many times. I think I know why: we are at the pub and aren't showing any guts.

Something about Frank's paper had hit a nerve. Its subsequent rebuttals by Charlie Brown and Les Hiatt had proved Frank's argument that even if ideas do not immediately persuade, the threat of them forces their opponents to keep them circulating.

On Wednesday, 16 October 1963, a symposium was organised by Jim Baker at the Royal George, with Frank, Brown and Hiatt participating. Although the Push had been drinking there since 1957, this was the first time it hosted an organised event, and it was a cause for considerable interest. It was not a formal affair, with a steady flow of alcohol lubricating the proceedings. The minutes for the evening were taken by somebody named Sweeney, and published in the November issue of the *Broadsheet* under the title 'Activism versus Oblomovism'.

This title referred to the nineteenth-century Russian novel *Oblomov*, by Ivan Goncharov, regarding a character who was superficial, lazy and indecisive. A subsequent essay by his contemporary, Nikolay Dobrolyubov, 'What Is Oblomovism?', argued that the novel was a satire on the aversion of nineteenth-century Russian intellectuals to advocate for social change. As a description of the position of Frank's opponents, Oblomovism was apt. But setting it in opposition to 'activism' meant that Frank's original and more subtle conception of *reciprocal engagement* was lost in the subsequent fray.

Frank spoke first. He was nervous but did not let it show. He was prepared. He had five pages of notes, titled 'Hiatt's Propositions', numbering twenty-six individual points. This was background for a fifteen-page draft speech, which included a point-by-point rebuttal of Brown's claims. The draft speech opened with the paragraph:

> It is all very well to write militant articles about having guts. But to come down here to the George among people who probably disagree with me to the point of nausea brought home to me that I was not

strongly endowed with guts myself. It seemed politically wiser to ring Jim Baker and say I was sick. But I realised it required more guts to pull out than to stay in.

These lines are crossed out on the typescript, so it is unclear if Frank spoke them on the night. Based upon this typescript and Sweeney's minutes, though, what is clear is that Frank argued against Brown's contention that freedom could look after itself without needing to be achieved or maintained. 'Withdrawal is in fact a form of political action,' Frank was reported to have said. 'It helps to encourage the idea that the present is appropriate and allows the consolidation of orthodoxy.' He accepted that there are moral and legal penalties awaiting those who fight for freedom, but said the return might be 'greater general tolerance', so it was worth the cost.

Towards the end of his speech, Frank cited Walter Lippmann's *The Public Philosophy* (1955), which argued that freedom of speech is safeguarded by an obligation to willingly subject that speech to criticism and debate. But people tended to seek out protections in order to avoid such obligations. Frank concluded:

> That is why I would argue for militant methods to break the protection of the established ideas. The protection is a cunning thing because it appears that we have wider freedom than we do but what we have is dissent confined to the George, the WEA, little magazines. The society generally protects itself and especially its young from many ideas and from debate. I would argue that this is a limitation on us . . . We lose because we lose some of the development which comes from engagement and if we're interested in ideas and talking about them we should have the fullest access to them – and this means for me the right to debate and the open flow of ideas and information throughout the society.

Charlie Brown spoke next, repeating many of the statements from his July paper, the main thrust of which he summed up by claiming that there was a straight line leading from activism to the gulags, as the Russian Revolution showed. His conclusion was summarised by Sweeney:

The two decisive objections to activist campaigns for free love or legal abortion are, first, that you are going to run into opposition from prevailing powers – the Churches and all political parties (including the C.P. which hates free love), and, secondly, that 90% of the people you talked to would not understand you anyway.

Les Hiatt revised his previous argument in terms of what he was now calling 'selective activism', opposed both to Brown's inactivism and to what he reframed as Frank's unselective, or absolute, activism. Selective activism referred to 'the sort of thing carried on by libertarians in having meetings, criticizing and so on, which, while neither oblomovism nor activism of the broad kind Moorhouse recommended, was a definite form of activism'. Hiatt's broad criticism was not directed so much at Frank's argument as at Brown's position. In repeating his distinction between the 'libertarians and the general bohemian "push"', Hiatt argued, according to Sweeney: 'The push, which lacked intellectual strength, appeared to have swamped the libertarians. What was needed was a revitalizing of the old libertarian hard core, who at their best illustrated what he meant by selective activism.'

Although Frank did not seem to have persuaded many of those present to his way of thinking, he did succeed in one of his fundamental aims, which was to initiate a debate, to have people respond to that debate and then to shift the debate into a more public forum. This was modelled on Frank's strategy at the WEA of holding classes in workplaces rather than in classrooms. As Sweeney noted regarding the symposium: 'Even hardened oblomovists were stirred into action and made up a good part of the audience of over 100.'

Frank was unpersuaded by Brown or Hiatt. In fact, in their exchanges, both in writing and at the symposium, they acted in ways that only reinforced Frank's view that the dissenters operated as 'cliques': Brown embodied the 'reactionary' position of the Push, and Hiatt the 'conservative' position of the libertarians.

There was a telling moment in the Royal George symposium when Frank nodded towards his strategy of achieving reciprocal engagement. His final comment on the night was summarised by Sweeney as 'Mannheim's view that engagement is a test of your theories'. This referred to an argument the Hungarian sociologist Karl Mannheim had developed in his study *Ideology and Utopia* (1936).

Mannheim's sociology of knowledge attempted to explain the link between ideas and action. Ideas emerge out of social engagement, rather than the other way around. They emerge from the dynamics of group practices, rather than from the minds of isolated individuals. As such, ideas were tested, in a sense, by the degree to which they were affected by (and, in turn, affect) the behaviour of individuals in particular social settings.

One limitation of this was that some ideas, born within certain social settings, would only remain valid within those settings. The true test of an idea was to see if it survived outside the group setting within which it was initially developed. This was the strategy of a particular type of intellectual – which Mannheim called, following Alfred Weber, the 'socially unattached intelligentsia' – who were able to manoeuvre within and between various self-contained and competing social groups, to critically evaluate and synthesise the best insights from each, so as to produce a pragmatic strategy for engaging with society as a whole.

This was an activity in which Frank was self-consciously engaged at the time, as he simultaneously participated in a variety of formal and informal groups – the WEA, the Film Study Group, the Sydney Left Club, the Libertarian Society, the Push – maintaining his position as a free-floating observer of these activities even as he participated. The creative problem Frank had set for himself was how, from this peripheral, unattached and orbiting position, he could best engage with society as a whole. He considered literary fiction, as a form of imaginative inquiry, as a way to negotiate critically between the ideas and positions emerging from each of the groups constituting society, while simultaneously communicating across all groups.

This way of understanding literature was another point of divergence between Frank and the libertarians. For the libertarians, art in general was considered intellectually soft and subordinate to the rigours of philosophic reason. When they did read novels, it was as an illustration of some philosophical argument, or as a model for some approved libertarian behaviour. For Frank, this attitude was anathema to the conditions of reading and writing literary fiction, which for him was less didactic. Frank held the literary imagination as being a legitimate form of inquiry in its own right, one used to explore the limitations of reason, and which provided a means for going beyond those limitations.

It was around this time that Frank found other individuals who also took literature seriously. In the middle of 1963, one night at Lorenzini's, a wine bar on lower Elizabeth Street, Frank was introduced to Don Anderson. A year younger than Frank, Don had only the day before arrived back in Sydney from a period in Tasmania.

When Frank was a cadet journalist at *The Daily Telegraph*, Don had been at Sydney Teachers' College, and when Frank was in Wagga and Lockhart, Don was working full-time as a high-school teacher, while also doing evening classes at the University of Sydney towards an English degree. The university did not provide evening classes for its honours degree, so in order to further his studies Don stopped teaching and enrolled in daytime classes. In financial debt, he was forced to give up study and take a job a friend had arranged for him in Tasmania, but that had not worked out. He returned to Sydney determined to find a job that would allow him to complete his studies.

Frank knew only too well the feeling of having one's ambitions for higher education blocked by financial circumstances, so he was sympathetic to Don's plight. It so happened that Frank was seeking an exit from the WEA, not because he disliked the job, but because he wanted to carve out more time for his writing.

If anything, Frank liked his job at the WEA too much. As well as paying him a regular wage, it provided him with a secure framework and discipline within which to live, and an environment that he found intellectually stimulating. He was beginning to shape the program around his own ideas, as a means of testing those ideas in practice. But it was taking up a great deal of his time and energy.

As he did not want any of his organisational experiments to collapse, part of his exit strategy involved finding a suitable replacement for himself at the WEA, to allow for a seamless transition. When Frank met Don that evening at Lorenzini's, he soon realised he had found that suitable replacement.

Frank still needed to support himself while he was writing. He applied for a fellowship from the Commonwealth Literary Fund, with Clive Hamer writing a letter of recommendation. He applied for the Stanford Writing Scholarship. But he was unsuccessful in both.

Nevertheless, in October, he tried to resign from his job at the WEA but the board discouraged him from doing so. They hit upon a compromise. Don Anderson took over Frank's position as assistant metropolitan secretary, but Frank was kept on for an additional three months to shadow him, to train him in the role. This arrangement cemented Frank and Don's friendship, as many of Frank's informal training sessions with Don occurred at the Newcastle Hotel.

Frank learned much from Don's approach to teaching literature. One of the first courses Don put together for the WEA in 1964, for example, was on *listening* to literature on vinyl records – poetry, theatre soliloquies, stories – which returned literature to its oral roots. This was something Frank, with his interest in Australian folk and oral storytelling traditions, very much appreciated.

The WEA was flexible enough to allow Don to resume his honours degree in early 1964. Through this involvement with the English department at the University of Sydney, Don and Frank's private literature symposium expanded to include other figures from the department. Stephen Knight had finished his degree at the university in 1962 and joined the English department in 1963. Two years younger than Frank, he focused on medieval English literature, myth and folklore.

In the coming years, Stephen and Don would teach and then supervise Rosemary Creswell. Rosemary had been awarded a bursary for mature-age students to pay her way, but there was a catch: the English 1 course she had completed would not count towards her final degree, so she had to sit the course again. She did, again placing near the top of the class. Over the coming years, Rosemary became close friends with Frank, Don and Stephen, drinking with them at the Newcastle Hotel.

Another joining the English department in 1963 was Michael Wilding, who had arrived from England in order to take up a position as assistant lecturer. Frank and Michael were very different. Four years younger than Frank, Michael was from a working-class English background. While Frank's university ambitions had been thwarted, Michael had not only graduated from Oxford with first-class honours, but he had done so on a scholarship. What they had in common was a desire to write fiction.

Michael had not yet published any stories, while Frank had published four – and that interested Michael greatly, but also made him feel competitive towards Frank. What interested Frank was that Michael had started publishing literary criticism, and Frank was interested in ways to develop Australia's critical culture. They forged a friendship based on their shared literary ambitions, discussing where and how to get published, and how to carve out a literary reputation within Australia.

Frank's decision to leave the WEA to focus on his own writing paid off when, in early 1964, he had two more stories published, one in the autumn issue of *Overland* and the other in the March issue of *Westerly*.

The *Overland* story was called 'Spider Town'. It follows the brief career of a new editor at a regional newspaper, who with his wife is eventually forced out by the backhanded tactics of the reactionary and conservative townsfolk. The title comes from the closing scene, when the couple finally decide to leave: 'Around he felt the town lie like a huge spider and he felt as if he was standing in the soft texture of its body.'

'Spider Town' was linked to Frank's previous story 'The Uniformed Stray', both being set in the fictional town of Smallton. Both are narrated from the perspective of a journalist, but where in 'The Uniformed Stray' the journalist is unnamed, in 'Spider Town' he is introduced as Dennis Stevens. Both stories share the character Constable Casey. In a sense, this builds upon an idea Frank had toyed with in high school, when he started grouping together short stories with similar characters, locations and themes.

Frank played with this idea in his *Westerly* story, 'The Respectable Deviant', which was related to Frank's previous *Westerly* story, 'Mrs Turtle's Building', featuring the main character from that story, Bernard Teller. Here Teller is introduced as a young schoolteacher, accompanying his much older headmaster, Johnson, to a parents' and citizens' meeting. After the meeting, only a few stragglers remain, leaving Teller and Johnson alone with Mrs Turner, Mrs Cambridge and Mr and Mrs Ericson, drinking sherry and becoming unfiltered in their conversation. Mrs Ericson says she has read Seaforth Mackenzie's novel *The Refuge*, '"and according to it teaching doesn't appear to be straight-forward" and she giggled at her daring. Teller gave her a direct look of dislike.'

There is a factual confusion here, whether Frank intended it or not. The Australian novelist Kenneth Seaforth Mackenzie had a novel published in 1954 called *The Refuge*. But he had an earlier novel published called *The Young Desire It* (1937). In Frank's story, Mrs Ericson is referring to an inappropriate relationship between a boy pupil and male teacher, which appears in *The Young Desire It*, not in *The Refuge*.

> 'A terribly fine book,' the Head said, 'very fine description of the close relationship which can develop between boy and teacher.'
>
> 'As a matter of fact I've had a similar experience,' he said drinking his sherry, 'of course I've never really talked about it.'
>
> Teller stopped drinking and looked amazed as his mind clambered back to the conversation.

Johnson gives a potted history about how, when he was a first-year teacher, he fell for one of his students, 'a beautiful boy'. Throughout, it is the narrative role of the character Teller to moderate the reader's growing discomfort, as Johnson's story unfolds. At one point, Johnson states:

> 'I was just married and my wife and I were still sexually unadjusted. I remember thinking that I was probably homosexual and that I couldn't have a satisfactory relationship with women. I was thinking of leaving her and going to live with the other odd-ones out at Kings Cross.'

Mrs Ericson replies: 'Of course the psychologists say we are all partly homosexual but some of us can control it or something, don't they?'

At which: 'Jesus, Teller thought, where do we go next?'

Finally, Mr Ericson asks if Johnson slept with the boy, and Johnson tells them he did not – he resisted the temptation, and soon after the boy moved away from the school – 'and I think that saved us', he concluded.

The biographical fragments that mark the starting points for these stories are clear. 'Spider Town' drew heavily on Frank's short tenure as editor of *The Lockhart Review*. It made reference to his controversial editorials – on the royal birth and the magistrate's closed court in the sexual assault case – and even mentioned the local communist fruit seller. Frank also drew on his awareness – which had perhaps become more acute since – of Wendy's feelings of isolation during that period. 'She was physically innocent but yet there were yearnings which she had denied. To live she needed more than the love of a husband.'

'The Respectable Deviant', meanwhile, drew on Frank's own middle-school molestation – this being the first time he had written from this experience – as well as on his own 'sexually maladjusted' marriage and subsequent relationships with women. But he conflated these experiences and placed them at a distance from the narrator, as if to blunt their edges.

Following the text of 'Spider Town' in *Overland* that autumn was an advertisement for a new magazine, billed as a 'lively satirical monthly'. It was called *Oz*. It had launched the previous year – on April Fool's Day in 1963 – one month after Frank's essay 'The Gutless Society' was published in the *Broadsheet*.

The first issue of *Oz* carried an interview with an abortionist and an article about chastity belts, which led to it being prosecuted for obscenity and the editors fined. In February 1964, the cartoonist Martin Sharp was charged with obscenity for two cartoons, one in *Oz* and the other in the University of Sydney student newspaper, *Tharunka*. The *Oz* case spurred Morris West, president of the Australian Society of Authors (ASA), to enter the censorship debate, arguing publicly that policemen and magistrates were ill-equipped to pass judgement on obscenity or literary merit.

The ASA had only been in existence since June the previous year. When the Australian writer Dal Stivens had lived in England following the war, he had been a member of the Society for Authors. As an expatriate, he understood the unjust conditions Australian writers operated under – especially in comparison with their counterparts in England – and so in 1962, after returning to Australia, he arranged a meeting in Sydney to discuss the formation of an organisation to advocate for the professional interests of Australian writers. Members from the Fellowship of Australian Writers attended. But, although invited, no delegates from the Australian Journalists' Association showed. This reflected the dismissive attitude the AJA had in the 1930s, when Vance Palmer had tried and failed to advocate for freelance contributor rates of pay for newspapers and periodicals, only to be blocked by the AJA, protecting its own professional members.

The meeting Stivens organised took place on 24 October 1962. *The Bulletin*'s coverage indicated how little the rights of authors were taken seriously by the broader community. 'Under faded portraits of Henry Lawson and Joseph Furphy,' they stated, 'representatives from Sydney writers' groups listened to speeches on the subject of how badly off writers are.' The ASA officially launched on 26 June 1963. At the end of its first twelve months, it had 266 members – including the editors of *Oz*. Stivens was the founding president, but became vice-president in 1964 when Morris West took the main job.

Stivens had always been concerned with censorship. He had a unique perspective on the practice, having worked for the Department of Information and Censorship during the war. In 1964, the customs minister said in a television interview that a temporary exemption might be given for serious scholars and literary figures to access certain books on the banned list, if they could supply proof of merit and intent. Stivens sought permission to import *Lady Chatterley's Lover* and *Lolita*, arguing that he needed the books to further his literary practice. He had by then published two novels and five collections of stories.

Stivens went to the customs office and filled in the necessary paperwork. A few weeks later, a customs officer visited Stivens at home to corroborate his credentials. Stivens even had to show the officer the cupboard, complete with lock and key, in which the books would be kept secure. Finally, with his claim approved, he was permitted to order the books from overseas, but under one final condition: he had to surrender the books to the customs department after six months.

When the *Oz* obscenity case occurred, the ASA contributed £25 to the editors' defence fund, and individual members were urged to make additional donations.

Frank had published an essay in the June 1964 issue of *Oz*. As a consequence of his *Broadsheet* essay the previous year, culminating in the October symposium at the Royal George, he was asked to speak on the same topic at a session of the recently formed Humanist Society. Although this lecture and Frank's subsequent essay in *Oz* were also titled 'The Gutless Society', they were entirely different from his original piece, focusing on some ideas from the previous essay and building stronger arguments around them. Frank broadened the scope of his criticism to include not just his own generation but the previous generation as well.

'There are those who kick, those who get kicked, and those who kick back,' Frank opened. 'I suppose that all people kick back at some time, but some people kick back more than others.'

Frank examined the younger generation's adoption of traditional activism. They deployed demonstrations and protests as a spectacle to draw attention to an issue, but usually without any larger strategy. He called this an 'expression of impatience', albeit 'justified impatience'. But it short-circuited the development of any longer-term strategy. Frank associated this with 'functional impotence', which he saw as analogous to sexual impotence: 'the desire that something should be done without the instrument or the ability to do it, and as is often the case with functional impotence, the loss of faith that something can be done'.

Frank's corrective was to establish a committee system or meeting structure. The committee was wiser than any one individual, had more information available to it and could coordinate information more effectively. Most younger activists, however, rejected such systems. Frank countered that 'the rejection of the committee system is a rejection of a huge superstructure of ideas and methods. Embodied in the rejection is the wish to have one's own way without interference and to possess ideas without criticism.'

Shifting his focus to the previous generation, Frank diagnosed his elders with suffering from what he called 'organisational birth-control', which he defined as:

> . . . a tendency for the older generations to look for salvation through giving birth to a new organisation, or a new journal. Interestingly it seems to be the reverse of functional impatience. When the older generation sees a problem or has a disagreement it tends to see a new committee or a new organisation.

That is, they see such a system as an end in itself.

To illustrate this, Frank criticised his audience and hosts by asking why they had recently formed the Humanist Society, when the Rationalist Association already served the same function.

Two or more organisations pushing effectively the same cause would not improve the quality or outcome of that cause, but would simply displace the energy of a large number of people away from those ends, towards unnecessarily replicating administrative burdens, budgets and inciting petty rivalries between such organisations.

Frank diagnosed the older generations with what he called the 'wise young man panacea', which he defined as falsely looking for hope in recruiting young people to the cause.

> Older people think they have found an 'out'. They say the hope for the future lies with the young people. They have convinced themselves that the young people somehow have new wisdoms and new answers. But, unfortunately, the young are usually ill-equipped by their very age for many important forms of human endeavour. Lack of knowledge and experience is the common characteristic of the young. The attempt by the older generations to get out of their responsibilities and activity by leaving it to 'the young people' is dangerous.

This only fed into the 'functional impatience' of the younger generation.

The general solution Frank proposed was for the generations to work together: to unite the energy and tactics of the young with the experience and organisational skills of the old, from within a committee system that was self-consciously a means to some social end. Frank concluded with a reprisal of his view about the gutlessness of the current and previous generations, linked to the prevalence of censorship and repression: 'But if young people continue to grow up ignorant and misled in a sexually-sick society it will be partly because their parents and others they trusted practiced in their sex life a censorship and suppression similar in every way to that of the society around them.'

In 1961, soon after Frank had returned to Sydney, 39-year-old Donald Horne became editor of *The Bulletin*. One of his first editorial decisions was to remove the long-standing motto, 'Australia for the White Man', from the masthead. He was only in the role for two years, but it allowed him to reflect more critically about Australia.

The book that emerged from those reflections, *The Lucky Country*, was published in November 1964, and was arguably the most trenchant work of Australian cultural and political criticism of the 1960s. Its basic arguments were remarkably consistent with the arguments Frank outlined in his series on 'The Gutless Society'. Both writers were looking at the same Australian society, but from different ends of the telescope. Horne provided the broader account, taking the nation at large as his subject, and then bringing the focus down to its intellectual elites and various subcultures. Frank, in turn, started with his criticism of a particular Sydney subculture, and then, in his second paper, gestured towards the nation at large, past and present. The two were writing separately, without reference to one another, and so provide independent support for each other's work.

In the final pages of *The Lucky Country*, Horne outlined the general intellectual mode characteristic of Sydney: 'its acceptance of the inadequacies of life, political indifference and a sense of scepticism and gaiety'. He traced this back to John Anderson and the University of Sydney, with the contemporary iteration – Horne considers the Push from the outside, but without naming them – being characterised by 'an avoidance of "illusion" and "confusion", a destructive analysis of practically everything and the consolation of feeling oneself one of the elect'.

The line that would become synonymous with Horne's book – 'Australia is a lucky country run mainly by second-rate people who share its luck' – comes from his conclusion. The argument leading to that conclusion was that those who ran the country were 'exhausted', that there was 'little of the sophisticated political discourse that can refresh politicians', and that 'there are few channels for intellectual breakthrough'. For Horne, responsibility for this rested with the intellectuals themselves. This was where his central point coincided with Frank's argument regarding the link between intellectual inquiry and practical action. 'Australia has not got a mind,' Horne wrote. 'Intellectual life exists but it is still fugitive. Emergent and uncomfortable, it has no established relation to practical life.'

Horne reflected three of Frank's central arguments against the Push, which Horne saw as generalising across all Australian intellectuals and writers. Frank's first point was that they were reactionary: 'Almost all Australian writers – whatever their politics – are reactionaries whose attitude to the massive diversities of suburban life is to ignore it or condemn it rather than discover what it is.' The second point was that they were conservative: 'An intellectual community may be the force by which a new vision is conducted into general attitudes. Or it may be an insulating medium, of the conservative kind that may stifle intelligence, even making it look foolish or wilful.' Finally, Frank argued that those who were intellectually and socially free enough to diagnose society generally as being restricted were obliged, as a commission of that freedom, to expand its reach to include others who might suffer from its lack.

Horne echoed this view:

> Australians are often accused of being indifferent to freedom, of being submissive and potentially authoritarian; this seems a harsh judgement to make on the ordinary people. If the criticism is to be made it should be directed against the intellectuals; they are the ones who are normally expected to fight the forward battles of freedom.

Although Horne was sceptical of an intellectual breakthrough happening in Australia, he did see some glimmer of hope in a possible cultural breakthrough:

> In literature and some of the arts in Australia there has been all the confusions of a breakthrough. The old certainties have gone and the changes are in such contradiction and of such comparative violence that contemporary detailed evaluations are worth very little. In these, committed critics often give a bleak picture; they are confused and sometimes made angry by the sudden variety.

Once more, this reflected Frank's experience. He had long argued that literary criticism in Australia needed to be reinvigorated, in order to support and nurture a new literary culture, to act as midwife to the next cultural breakthrough. There was a practical edge to this, because Frank understood that a vibrant critical culture was required in order for his own writing to improve and to find an audience, and for him to eke out a living from his writing.

Although he had, since he first started writing, shown his stories to friends, he knew their judgements were limited and biased, and it was necessary to subject his work to independent critical assessment. He had learned much from the process of submitting his stories to literary quarterlies, as much from having his stories rejected as he did from having them accepted and professionally edited. This did not mean Frank automatically accepted the assessments he received, for good or ill. But it did mean that he was forced to think more self-critically about his literary decisions, his chosen techniques and his themes, and about how and why they assumed certain narrative forms. He used such feedback to refine and recalibrate his internal literary compass.

Finally, Horne shared with Frank – and with a number of other figures at this stage, including the ASA – the view that the main obstacle to permitting both a cultural and intellectual breakthrough in Australia was the nation's cowering beneath one of the most pervasive censorship regimes in the world. In *The Lucky Country*, Horne repeated many of the widely known arguments against the arbitrary and uneven exercising of censorship in Australia, from the customs department seizing any and all incoming suspicious material, to various federal and state government decisions, and vice squads in each state intervening and pulling books and magazines as they saw fit, intimidating and controlling publishers, booksellers and printers.

'Throughout the century,' Horne wrote, 'where other democracies have censored badly Australia has censored worse.'

7

'I Am More Confused Now'

Frank developed a creative strategy during the mid-1960s where he would write a loose trilogy of short stories, based around the same character but with each story remaining discrete. By considering the same character in a different situation, or interacting with different characters, Frank was better able to define that character, to recognise them more clearly as a fictional individual. Already with pairs of stories, such as 'The Uniformed Stray' and 'Spider Town', or 'Mrs Turtle's Building' and 'The Respectable Deviant', there had been a crossover of characters with the same name, but the inconsistencies between these stories suggest such similarities were an afterthought. Now Frank began consciously creating more consistent, definite characters, considering them in separate story contexts, so the stories generated further resonances.

The first trilogy of stories he wrote was around a character named Thomas Wake. There is a draft story, 'The Short Misery of Thomas Wake', which was a revision of a previous untitled story. That story followed a character, Thomas, who through a close friend, Jimmy, meets a girl, Kathy, with whom he begins a relationship. He briefly suffers from sexual impotence, which – in the literal and metaphoric climax of the story – he resolves. In revising that earlier story, Frank wrote two more stories, 'Walking Out' and 'What Can You Say?'.

The latter goes back to the point when Thomas first meets Jimmy, and explores how Jimmy changed Thomas's narrow views about life and sex. The former goes back further, to describe how Thomas, one day in his early twenties, fed up with his conventional upbringing, walked out of the family home for good.

This initial trilogy formed the basis of a proposed collection Frank envisaged at the time, built around a series of three-story cycles. Frank described this, with somewhat awkward phrasing, as a 'book of short stories dealing with the development of Thomas Wake a young man of conventional upbringing who becomes increasing dissent to society'. A handwritten amendment to this typescript notes the underlying theme: 'freedom of thought and its pain'. Frank lists nine stories, noting that three were already written: the Thomas Wake stories. Another three stories were based on Kathy, including one on her 'infidelity'. Another three stories are listed as 'national service': Frank was probably planning to recycle material from his abandoned novel. The third story in this trio is described simply as 'homosexual adventure'.

In July 1964, Frank won first prize in the Banjo Paterson Literary Competition for 'Walking Out'. He won £50 worth of books from Angus & Robertson. The judges' report stated:

> The author of 'Walking Out' has uncovered the deep spiritual uneasiness of a young man of 22 who resolves to make a decided move towards independence and integrity.
>
> His dilemma is presented with controlled intensity that is completely convincing and in an idiom that, while it is almost brutally frank, perfectly exposes the mind of the type of character portrayed.

Coincidentally, the head judge, and probably the person who wrote this report, was Clive Hamer. The submissions were blind, however, and Clive did not know Frank was the author until after the decision was finalised. Later, they corresponded about the story and how to get it published.

'Walking Out' was written in the first person, in the character of Thomas. It echoes J.D. Salinger's *Catcher in the Rye* (1951), but where Holden Caulfield saw 'phoniness' in the world around him, Thomas Wake saw a more Australian form of 'bullshit', in which he included himself. 'And then even when I did know I was bullshitting it didn't stop me from being false,' Thomas soliloquises. 'I knew the letters at work were bullshit but it didn't stop me writing them. I was a bullshit-artist and I knew it.'

Regarding the threat of censorship, Frank said he would not omit the word 'bullshit', because he had consciously chosen the repetition and rhythm punctuating the prose. He admitted he was concerned about the use of obscenity in the story, the swearing and the sexual description, not because it transgressed any moral or conventional modes of taste, but for a more fundamental, literary reason: 'Can you communicate if you offend?'

Clive's response to Frank was supportive, but considered:

> You frequently cannot communicate if you offend but sometimes a shock is a pre-requisite to communication. You must first remove old prejudices, before you can communicate any new message. This is the basis of brain washing and religious conversion (see Sargent: *Battle for the Mind*, and Tillich: *Shaking the Foundations*), but it is also, in a milder form, a necessary part of any teaching process. The risk in the shock technique is that you will go too far, or that you will defeat your end altogether by setting up complete resistance, but the risk has to be taken.

Clive drew a personal line at explicit sexual description: 'This seems to me to be the one area where you are wrong (and also many modern young people and writers.) Some, like D.H. Lawrence and Dean Moriarty (*On the Road*) seem to think that there are no human ills that orgasm cannot cure. They're wrong.'

This caveat aside, Clive ended on a positive, if not a possibly backhanded, note: 'I agree that the term "bullshit" is important to your story. It is not merely indispensable, but might be called the motif.'

Frank's concern recalled his argument from 'The Gutless Society', particularly the speech he gave at the Royal George, which cited Walter Lippmann on the obligations underpinning freedom of speech. The section of *The Public Philosophy* Frank cited makes a distinction between liberty and licence. 'If there is a dividing line between liberty and license,' Lippmann wrote, 'it is where freedom of speech is no longer respected as a procedure of the truth and becomes the unrestricted right to exploit the ignorance, and to incite the passions, of the people.'

This distinction informed Frank's question to Clive Hamer. Frank used liberty as a procedure, a means to an end, and not as an end in itself, not as a right or a licence. Precisely because such freedom is not an inviolable right, it must be practised, and the conditions for it continually recreated and vigilantly maintained. This distinction marked the fundamental difference between Frank and the Libertarians of the Push, as they deployed freedom as licence – as an end in itself.

Frank submitted 'Walking Out' to *Southerly* but it was rejected. Clive suggested *Meanjin* or *Overland*. Clive had already shown the story to part-time WEA lecturer Norman Talbot, who had just been appointed literary editor of *The Australian Highway*. Clive thought the story would be a good fit for the WEA's quarterly journal. He withdrew the story when he learned Frank had been appointed to *The Australian Highway* as managing editor. 'With all due respect to the editor of Highway I think the story deserves a better launching pad than that,' Clive later wrote to Frank, 'and I think it's a pity to carry on the practice . . . of a magazine publishing the editor's own work.'

'Walking Out' was eventually published in *Westerly*, in the fourth issue of 1964. When Frank finally received his copy of the magazine, his excitement quickly ebbed when he found they had censored the story without informing him. The indispensable 'bullshitting' and 'bullshit' was shortened to 'bull', which shattered the rhythm of the prose, to the point it was at times ungrammatical: 'And then even when I did know I was bull it didn't stop me from being false. I knew the letters at work were bull but it didn't stop me writing them. I was a bull-artist and I knew it . . .'

The new editorial team of *The Australian Highway* was announced in the August 1964 issue, with Frank at the helm, Norman Talbot as the new literary editor and Ken Quinnell, from the Film Study Group, as 'typographic advisor'. Ken helped Frank modernise the design and layout of the magazine. Frank's aim was to turn the staid adult education quarterly into a literary and culture magazine, albeit grounded in the WEA's ethos of education as an agent for social change. This was an attempt to put into practice Frank's argument for a closer relationship between the arts and trade unionism, as well as the need to provide independent criticism of Australia's literary culture.

Frank's first issue was published in December 1964, with an editorial titled 'Where Do You Stand?', which urged readers to consider their position on adult education. He offered a loose taxonomy of the different ways people approached the WEA. The *monastic* approach was for people who 'see the WEA as a monastery of intellectual activity in a non-intellectual community. In this monastery they can pursue their studies quietly and with the minimum of disturbance.' The *elitist* approach tended to agree with the *monastic* approach, to the extent that the WEA was for a minority who wanted to pursue their studies unharrassed. However: 'The elitist also feels that an enlightened community is important for the preservation of basic freedoms, including the freedom to study . . . the student has a responsibility to "leaven" the community, that the studious minority has a responsibility of providing intellectual leadership in the community.'

The approach of the *mass educator*, by contrast, considered the WEA as an 'educational vanguard' which 'has the responsibility of creating a critical and informed community and they see the intellectual quality of the community as directly affecting their life as a student . . . They also hold the view that social prejudices against education have to be broken and certain social habits attacked.'

Although Frank saw the merit – and the temptation – in all three approaches, his position at this stage leaned towards the mass educator, and it was to this end that he shaped the editorial policy of *The Australian Highway*.

Frank continued to read broadly in sociology and psychology, and to test these ideas against his own observations of urban Sydney life. In February 1965, he had a brief essay published in *Oz*, based upon these reflections, called 'Just Another Unhappy Joke'. Frank considered the psychological impact of living in a modern city, in which an individual is overwhelmed daily by 'thousands of visual impressions', resulting in a 'dulling' of the senses, a protective measure against the sensory overload. To gain the attention of such an individual, it is 'only the startling which will register in memory or cause an itch of curiosity'. And so an escalation of competing stimuli proceeds, to dull and startle an individual in turn.

The result of all of this was an increase in *anomie*, a term Frank took from Émile Durkheim's sociological study *Suicide* (1952). 'He used it,' Frank wrote, 'to describe the condition which arises when people lose their beliefs or are bewildered by competing beliefs.' He cites Durkheim as saying that such people feel 'alone, isolated, in a hostile, unmanageable environment' following 'a restless movement, a planless self-development, an aim of living which has no criterion of value and in which happiness lies always in the future'.

Frank posited two ways of overcoming *anomie*, each equally destructive. The first was directed inward, resulting in suicide or other self-destructive behaviours, per Durkheim's study. The other was directed outward, in subordinating oneself to accepting social and political arrangements leading to authoritarian or totalitarian outcomes, on both the political Right or Left. Such external arrangements, Frank argued, 'can create a feeling of oneness, [and] give a feeling of identification and meaning which frees people of anomie'. Frank drew on Christian Bay's book *The Structure of Freedom* (1958) to support his case. Bay argued there was a correlation between, as Frank paraphrased it, 'the growth of freedom and the growth of anomie'. Bay's argument, which Frank held up as the core paradox of the current moment, was that 'people will have to accept a degree of anomie if they want wide freedom'.

Frank found this paradox expressed in the contemporary use of the word *village* in various contexts, pointing in two opposite directions. Kings Cross, for example, was considered a 'village', but there were also 'shopping villages' appearing on the suburban landscape. Frank considered both uses of the word. First, the positive use: 'Village has the non-anomic associations such as small, quiet, traditional, and neighbourly. A village can be pictured as a place where everyone is known and where certain norms of behaviour are accepted.' Second, the bastardisation of the term: 'Commercial *villages* in a big city are then perhaps just another of the sad illusions, one of the incongruities of our city life. But perhaps we are now adjusted to living a paradoxical life and the idea of a "city of villages" will sink into our subconscious mind with the other contradictions, illusions, and insanities to be, paradoxically' – and this stands as the conclusion of Frank's brief essay – 'just another unhappy joke our society had on us'.

Frank's next *Highway* editorial, 'Of Ova Seize', appeared in the autumn 1965 issue, arguing against the popular claim that overseas travel ('ova seize', in the vernacular) broadened the mind. It was a variation of an argument he had first tested over spaghetti lunches with David Gyger in 1956, and had probably refined in the years since, as, one after the other, people associated with the Push – including Germaine Greer, Clive James and Robert Hughes – left Australia. They were the more recent examples from a long history of Australian expatriates – such as Ethel Florence 'Henry Handel' Richardson and Christina Stead. 'The problem generally was summed up by George Orwell,' Frank wrote, citing Orwell's 1940 essay 'Inside the Whale', 'when he said that the penalty for leaving your native land was "transferring of your roots into shallower soil".'

At twenty-six years old, Frank had not yet ventured outside Australia, although his parents and older brothers were frequent international travellers, due to work or, in the case of his parents,

Rotary. Frank had recently received a letter from his father informing him they were going overseas to attend the Rotary International Convention in St Louis, Missouri. 'These Conferences are really the last word in organisation,' Frank Sr wrote, 'and they certainly do not miss any tricks when it comes to getting the story over.'

The feature essay in the autumn issue of *Highway* was by Don Anderson, writing on James Baldwin's novel *Another Country* (1962). He argued that it was 'a profoundly moral novel: it diagnoses with clinical thoroughness personal and sexual and social ills which permeate our civilisation and debilitate many of us'. At the time Anderson wrote his essay, Baldwin's novel was still banned in Australia. As an academic, he had arranged for a special dispensation to access the book. That year, the Literature Censorship Board finally lifted its restriction on the book, three years after its initial publication.

This coincided with the lifting of the nearly forty-year ban on *Lady Chatterley's Lover*. Alec Sheppard, a bookseller, and Leon Fink, an entrepreneur, with support from the NSW Council for Civil Liberties, established a publishing company in Australia. They secured the rights to Rolph's *The Trial of Lady Chatterley*, which they smuggled into the country in eight separate parts. They found a willing printer, and in April 1965 they printed and distributed 1000 copies across Australia. This act forced the lifting of the ban from Rolph's book in May 1965. By July, Lawrence's 1928 novel was finally allowed to be published in Australia.

By the middle of 1965, Frank had begun seeing a psychotherapist in Sydney. His most immediate concern was his break-up with Sandra Grimes, twelve months earlier, the aftereffects which he claimed to be still suffering. A more general reason for seeking professional help was *anomie*, with freedom and its pain.

In June 1963, after Sandra had broken off with Frank the first time, he briefly saw a woman named Susan. Much of their two-month relationship involved her listening to Frank talk about Sandra and his post-mortem of their relationship. When Sandra reappeared,

Frank quickly got back together with her, hurting Susan in the process. Their correspondence is interesting because of an insight in one of Susan's letters: 'The whole premise of this letter is that it is possible for people to behave differently if they are reached before their patterns become too set.' Frank took this to mean 'if I don't agree with your interpretation I haven't been reached'. And yet, in saying this, he proved her point, which was that Frank approached emotional and personal matters with a rhetoric of rationality and impersonality. It was as if he were examining himself, the other person and their shared situation from an outside perspective. He interpreted Susan's reaction to their parting, for example, as being 'anti-intellectual', when, in the circumstances, hurt feelings were only natural.

When Frank and Sandra had got back together in late 1963, Frank attempted to amend, rather than fully disrupt, his previous pattern of behaviour, but in ways that meant he depended even more upon such rational models for his emotional survival. He even diagnosed the source of their previous problems as being the absence of such an impersonal model.

In one typescript, Frank outlined a four-stage plan for the recovery of their relationship, 'based heavily on postulations made by Sandra'. Liberation from social convention had led to a vertiginous freedom, from which they needed to pull back while at the same time avoiding a retreat into mundane convention. 'The relationship has to be constantly reaffirmed and especially at times of delicate situations,' he wrote. They needed to 'develop procedures', by which Frank meant replacing social convention with personal rituals and symbols. 'I still feel that certain parts of the central relationship must be preserved and protected. It is perhaps a case of symbols and rituals. Symbols and rituals which mark the faith and strength of the relationship. These can be anything – Saturday mornings together – but they should be realised.'

One proposed model was to distinguish between their 'central' relationship with each other and their 'peripheral' relationships with other people. Simone de Beauvoir's memoir *The Prime of Life* appeared in an English translation in 1962. She recounted her relationship with Jean-Paul Sartre as being an '*essential* love', while their other sexual relationships were considered '*contingent* love affairs'. This had been a source of inspiration, or at least a justification, for the model of open relationships among some members of the Push. Frank admitted he may previously have been 'too dogmatic' in insisting on the priority of the central relationship, and said at times secondary relationships should take precedence. 'I had not realised this,' he wrote. 'I think this was one of the most serious errors I made.' It was a dogmatism born of vulnerability. 'My emotions were given too heavy a burst of insecurity.'

Frank introduced this topic of peripheral sexual relationships as a procedure to cope with his impotence. 'The terrible and destructive nature of the feeling of loss of sexual confidence,' he wrote. 'Probably of a fairly personal nature.' He cited Bertrand Russell and Wilhelm Reich as supporting the proposal that sexual attraction declined when the 'newness' of a relationship wore off, and that such attraction would ebb and flow in an open relationship with the beneficial presence of external sexual encounters. 'I now realise that this curve operated with Wendy and me during even the best parts of the relationship,' he wrote. 'And there is no doubt that my affair with Bev . . . refreshed our sexual life in the way that Russell observed.'

Here Frank was misremembering that his relationship with Bev occurred during the final period of his marriage with Wendy, and in fact had hastened its demise. Such peripheral relations did not refresh their sexual life. What Frank omitted entirely from this discussion was that his main peripheral relationship throughout his marriage was with John Burrows, and that he had hoped his marriage would help him overcome his homosexual desires and obviate the need for his relationship with John altogether.

In a typescript note to himself, probably written in mid-1965, during the period in which he had begun seeing a psychotherapist, he tried to outline his experience of bisexuality. 'I find it difficult if not impossible to talk clearly and honestly about my sexual feelings,' he wrote. 'I firstly am sexually attracted by men and women.' His sexual attractions may be associated with gender identity, with sexual relationships with women being 'important for my ego for my status as a person', while 'with a man I am free of the status in fact the opposite is needed and privately and personally I am interested only for enjoyment not for ego'.

Twelve months before he entered therapy, Frank had ended the second version of 'The Gutless Society' with a note on what he referred to as 'furtive radicals'. They resided mainly among the older generation – here he might have been thinking about John Burrows – but his description of this social type was very much applicable to Frank himself. In the coda to his lecture he therefore ended on a note of self-criticism:

> There seems to be a large minority engaged in the exploration of sexual relationships outside of the conventions. But the interesting point is that this exploration and its results are being concealed by many of these people. Where this concealment occurs among people who are concerned with freedom of action, freedom of information, and the creation of an open society, then they can be criticised. But I want to be gentle in my criticism because I realise that there are immense personal problems in becoming a sexual radical. The obvious case of extreme difficulty is the homosexual. If he behaves openly he will be persecuted and gaoled.

This was the closest Frank came in his public discourse at this stage to acknowledging the paradox between his commitment to being open and honest – the 'desperate need of openness about sex' – and his understanding of the practical difficulties for some members of society in doing so: 'Otherwise freedom-loving and courageous people take extreme precautions to conceal their views on sexual relationships and how they live sexually.' Frank was bordering on confession, and probably providing a more accurate explanation for why, twelve months later, he would be seeking out therapy: 'Somehow we have first to forge in our sexual relationships the confidence which will allow us to talk openly and freely about our problems and experience. The personal problems arising from sexual honesty are tormenting.' Frank's relationship with Sandra finally ended around the time Frank presented this paper to the Humanist Society. The failure of that relationship was not a 'failure of procedure', but an understandable, non-intellectual, tormenting absence of 'sexual honesty'.

One of the discussion papers Frank had written for Sandra during the early part of 1964 ended with a note in parentheses: '(there is an appendix on "Honesty" to come)'. In his drafts for this piece on honesty, Frank wrote: 'The matter of honesty is one I haven't thought through. It amazed me that Jill, Harries, Penfold, Dodd and Hamilton in discussing human relationship said that honesty was not only impossible but unwise. I argued against this.'

This was a topic he had thought through quite thoroughly in the past, but had since conveniently forgotten. His 'Frankness and Sincerity Theory' was first proposed to Wendy in 1956 as the basis of their relationship. And yet, in 1964, Frank felt he had not quite thought the question through. His amazement at his friends arguing against the possibility of radical honesty belies the fact that this incredulity was precisely Wendy's position when Frank first proposed his theory to her all those years before.

Frank did not even really believe it himself, as he wrote in his journal on 28 January 1962, soon after leaving his marriage, and soon before first moving in with Sandra:

> the truth –
> well yes
> no one tells the truth
> all at once . . .
> you get at it bit by bit . . .
> but even then
> our life long training in concealment
> and deceit
> works a little . . .

Frank had proposed his 'Frankness and Sincerity Theory' to Wendy only a month or two before he had begun his furtive and ongoing relationship with John Burrows. Wendy did not know about the nature of Frank's relationship with John. But by the time Frank was trying to salvage his relationship with Sandra in 1964, Sandra did know about the nature of Frank's relationship with John, and it was the reason she had initially broken it off with Frank. He did not know Sandra had discovered his correspondence with John, and so did not understand how hollow his aspirations for radical honesty must have sounded.

Once more, this was all baked into the pattern with which Frank approached his relationships, as a self-protective measure. Frank was able to be honest with John, at least regarding his confusions and anxieties, but John did not know about Frank's cross-dressing.

Another person Frank managed to speak with 'clearly and honestly' about his 'sexual feelings' and proclivities during this period was a woman named Norma Crinion. She was eight years older than Frank, politically radical, with a fiercely independent spirit. They had a brief affair but, finding themselves sexually incompatible, they became lifelong friends. Norma suffered from bouts of depression, and it may have been this shared experience that encouraged Frank to open up to her about other parts of his personality. She responded by chaperoning him to the Purple Onion club in Kensington, which had drag acts, femmes miming to records. The Purple Onion had opened in 1962, a year after the Jewel Box and Les Girls had opened in Kings Cross.

Norma probably knew Frank was seeing a psychotherapist in mid-1965, and might even have encouraged it. Frank told few people about it at the time; he was becoming adept at keeping aspects of his life and relationships compartmentalised.

As Frank's relationship with Sandra began very soon after he and Wendy separated, he had not given himself any time to process the demise of his marriage. The same problems that undermined his marriage were carried over into his new relationship, and the more recent reverberations he had been feeling could well have been aftershocks. But beneath each of these was his childhood, his family and his adolescent experiences: the material security but emotional insecurity that characterised his upbringing; his predisposition to depression and anxiety; his middle-school molestation, developing same-sex attractions and furtive cross-dressing, which abutted the narrow conventions of the day. Frank had dealt with none of these adequately before he started his relationships with Wendy and then John, but they exerted a strong undertow in both, which together set the pattern for each relationship that followed.

Full-time employment and regular, organised public engagement had always offered Frank a structure within which he could organise his life. They provided him with an outward focus and a sense of relief from the pressures of his personal life, his relationship dilemmas and his psychological anxieties. Since the age of seventeen, Frank had worked full-time, sometimes at more than one job, while also pursuing his writing. But in 1964, Frank had for the first time consciously reduced his paid employment in order to put his writing at the centre of his daily activities.

One aspect of not having full-time employment to which Frank struggled to adapt was managing his finances. He had always been relatively unconcerned about money, which was easy when he had a regular income. He would borrow money from friends and had always been able to repay it quickly when his next pay came in. In turn, he was generous in lending money to friends. The few short stories he had published did not pay much. He had taken the part-time job at *The Australian Highway* largely to supplement his savings and cover some of his living expenses, but it was only a quarterly journal and the salary did not stretch far. So he found it increasingly difficult to adapt the lifestyle he had come to enjoy in Sydney to his new austerity. By March 1965 he was receiving regular notices about overdrawn bank drafts and unpaid accounts from David Jones, where he bought gourmet foodstuffs on credit.

The effect of this on Frank was more than financial. The loss of an external structure and regular schedule led to the disorganisation of Frank's life, allowing the pressures of his relationship dilemmas, and his psychological anxieties, to come to the foreground. Frank did not keep any direct notes regarding his psychotherapy sessions, but his concerns were carried over into his reading and professional writing during this same period. He dedicated an editorial in the winter 1965 issue of *The Australian Highway* to his reading of the psychoanalyst Erich Fromm. *The Art of Loving* (1961) outlined the need for 'educated love' – built upon the practices of concentration, discipline, patience, concern, faith and objectivity – as opposed to narrow, romantic love. Frank argued such an 'educated love' opened up a 'fearful chasm', caused by the awareness 'that knowledge is infinite', that a person can never fully understand anything:

> ... that the human mind is deceitful (rationalising, distorting, and concealing) and that true intellectual objectivity has to guard constantly against the personality and its insecurities and fears. Personal status, irrational loyalty to a set of ideas or a way of behaving (as in, say, political parties) and the need for personal identification through opinion (as in the role of the rebel) can seriously interfere with intellectual objectivity. Likewise these things can damage love.

This argument builds upon, and helps address, Frank's earlier analysis of *anomie*. But here Frank located its source, following Fromm, in the failures of parental and social authority. Frank attributed the rarity of educated love to a 'breakdown of guidance mechanisms in society', and added: 'Complaints of poor quality sex lives can likewise be attributed.' He goes on: 'In our society books on sex (and by association, the books on emotional problems) are often banned, the subjects are distorted or taboo in most families, the priests and the elders are either ignorant, quiet, or hostilely insincere about their own lives.'

Frank concluded that society was only then, in the mid-1960s, finding a new form of guidance, born through crisis, from psychoanalysts and mental health professionals. The persistence of these concerns in Frank's thinking over time is shown by an unpublished letter to the editor he wrote to *The Sydney Morning Herald* nearly two years earlier, in September 1963. He concluded his letter: 'Sensible, sympathetic guidance for young people in their sexual relationships (married or unmarried) is difficult for people who are already suffering, as adults, from a sexually-sick upbringing. But we are not so sick that we cannot sometimes rise above it to be rational.'

There is here a glimpse of why Frank placed so much stock in putting his relationships in an impersonal, objective framework. Such rationality was, for him, an indication he had risen above, or at least could hold at bay, the effects of his 'sexually-sick upbringing'. But at the same time, it held him back from fully committing to a relationship with another person.

During this period, the only stability in Frank's life was his writing. He would write first thing each morning, for at least four hours. He would write at least a thousand new words each day, but often more. He would then redraft previous stories. He was in the habit of doing at least five typed drafts of each story, annotating and correcting each typescript by hand, then retyping the whole story anew. He would rotate what he was working on between each draft, so he was always working on several stories at once, each at different stages of completion. His strategy of working on a loose trilogy of stories, based around a particular character or theme, only reinforced the efficacy of this process.

By 1965, the stories Frank was writing satisfied him, and he thought they were an advance on his earlier work. But they were increasingly being rejected by mainstream literary quarterlies, mainly due to censorship or obscenity concerns. Instead of changing the stories, Frank began seeking out alternative outlets for publication.

Pluralist was a short-lived journal produced by people associated with the Libertarian Society. In May 1965, it published the shortest story Frank had yet written, called 'Nish', a third-person character study of a middle-class, middle-aged grotesque. In the winter issue of *Highway*, Stephen Knight reviewed *Pluralist*, stating:

> Frank Moorhouse's 'Nish' is a different matter. This very short tautly written piece seems the best he has written yet. In his most recent

stories he has been exploring with growing confidence those fringes of the mind where madness and violence lie, and Nish's brand of secret, hot, destructiveness is created with disturbing sensual power. Moorhouse has had quite a lot of trouble with censors lately: if they really knew how to protect our pure Australian society they would leave his so-called obscenity alone and try to stop him writing so well about the violent and anarchical lunacy that is just below the surface of human behaviour . . .

Soon after, in *Red and Black*, another short-lived journal, but with more of an anarchist bent, another of Frank's Thomas Wake stories was published, 'What Can You Say?'. One day Thomas finds Jimmy at home, depressed and resignedly suicidal. He has taken a number of sedatives.

> I asked him what was wrong.
> He looked nowhere and said, 'futility.'

One interesting features of this story – and one of the creative consequences of Frank's working on stories in a series or loose trilogy – was how his previous stories became a background against which he was able to inquire more deeply into various aspects of his characters and their emotional lives. The previous stories sometimes became redundant as a result, and Frank would abandon them. In this case, a previous story, 'The Short Misery of Thomas Wake', itself a revision of an earlier story, was condensed into a single paragraph around which the story 'What Can You Say?' could hang. Here was how the whole of the first story appears in miniature in the latter story (with 'Kathy' becoming 'Wesley'):

> The first girl I became interested in was named Wesley. She was beaut. But I was a dismal failure with her in bed. I felt as if I was a dead loss as far as sex was concerned. I thought I must be queer. It was about two weeks before I could make love to her properly. Jimmy made me read a few psychological books about it. I think I would have gone off my head if he hadn't been around to explain it.

Another consequence was that characters from one series could migrate into another series. In the August issue of *Squire*, a men's magazine, Frank had 'Bryan's Story' published, which includes Wesley from 'What Can You Say?'.

In August 1965 Frank applied once more for a fellowship from the Commonwealth Literary Fund, and once more his application was unsuccessful. At the same time, he embarked on a project to establish a weekly community newspaper for inner-city Sydney bohemians. Frank was the managing editor, and the associate editor was Ken Quinnell. Ken was still working with Frank on *The Australian Highway*, but his main job was with a commercial book publisher. Frank had recently published a piece in *Highway* by David Gyger, about the life and death of *The Riverina Express*. David had closed his regional newspapers and was working at the recently launched *Australian* newspaper in Canberra. He still owned the printing plant in Wagga, and Frank's plan was to co-opt it for his publishing venture in Sydney.

The newspaper Frank and Ken conceived was called *City Voices*, modelled on the New York alternative newspaper *The Village Voice*, founded in Greenwich Village in 1955. In the prospectus, Frank compared the cultural significance of Paddington, Kings Cross and Balmain, to its American counterpart: 'in New York it is symbolised by Greenwich Village with its intellectual activity, its creative activity, its small societies, its learned societies, its organisations of dissent, its nonconformity, and its own social habits'.

The underlying idea for the newspaper went back to Frank's 1956 plan for a culture journal called *Trend*. The business model for *City Voices* was basically the same: a private company with ten partners, each owning an equal number of shares. For *City Voices*, these partners included Frank and Ken, but also Sandra Grimes and David Gyger. Another partner, and the secretary for *City Voices*, was Norma Crinion. Her first task was to set up a post office box.

The original contract had Frank working full-time for the first twelve weeks, at £20 per week, and Ken working part-time at £10 per week. The first edition of *City Voices* was published on 17 September, but the newspaper lasted only five weeks, folding on 15 October.

In the post-mortem Frank wrote for the partners, he outlined some of the problems it had faced. The main problem was Frank's capacity to fulfil several roles that had been collapsed into the managing editor's role, including soliciting advertising as well as general administration. On the editorial side, he found it difficult to manage the freelance contributors, who were mainly academics not experienced with weekly publishing schedules, tight word limits and hard deadlines. Another difficulty was that Frank was not always in Sydney during this period. He had recently left Balmain and moved into a cabin in Bundeena, a village south of Sydney, on a beach near a national park. It was a thirty-minute ferry ride from Bundeena to Cronulla.

The short run of *City Voices* belies the scale of its ambition, and this was perhaps its fatal flaw. The newspaper was to be the vanguard for the broader agenda of City Voices Publishing, which was to include magazines and books. Its strategy was to invite other 'little magazines' – presumably Frank was thinking of publications such as *The Pluralist*, *Red and Black* and *Balcony*, but possibly also more established literary magazines – to publish under the colophon of City Voices Publishing, while retaining financial, editorial, artistic and typographic independence. The benefit of operating under a collective umbrella was going to be discounts in printing costs – all to be done at David Gyger's printery in Wagga – as well as shared office facilities and other operational services, including distribution channels and mailing lists.

A surviving remnant of *City Voices* was that Frank took over the PO box Norma Crinion had opened as its administrative address. Frank initially shared the box with Murray Sime, who was two years younger than Frank and studying law at the University of Sydney. He was a frequent drinker at the various pubs and parties at the time, and had become Frank's firm friend and ally. Frank would use this PO box for the next forty years.

Frank had a story published in the October 1965 issue of *Australian Letters*. 'Dead' refers back to his 1963 story 'Mrs Turtle's Building', except 'Mrs Turtle' became 'Mrs Curry'. A story called 'Apples and Babies' was published in the December issue of *Squire*. The protagonist's younger sister, Sue-Anne, appears in the background of 'Bryan's Story' as a woman with whom Bryan once had a long-term relationship.

Living at Bundeena was not good for *City Voices*, but it proved to be valuable for Frank's own writing. The publication of these stories in *Australian Letters* and *Squire* marked the start of a particularly productive period of writing. Frank's idea of approaching each story as part of a loose trilogy was abandoned, but the underlying method remained, with one story suggesting two or more others, each moving in unexpected directions, surprising even Frank himself. It was as if his method of writing contained its own internal compulsion.

January 1966 began with Frank having another story published in *Squire*. 'Honey-comb Is My Favourite Sweet' is another of Frank's studies in contrasts, between a small country town upbringing and the city life of an adult bohemian. The story traces how the unnamed first-person narrator is charged and fined for being a pornographer, his work as a journalist having pushed him into the magazine market, and from there to working with 'girlie' magazines – such as *Squire*. The narrator worries what will happen tomorrow, 'after the court hearing and the afternoon papers are printed', and what they will think of him back in his home town. 'But I probably won't know because I can never go back there now.'

Frank also had a story published in the February 1966 issue of *The Bridge*, a relatively new publication from the Australian Jewish Quarterly Foundation. In 'The Falling of the Star', Frank returned to themes drawn from his time in Wagga in the late 1950s, but also drawing on his recent experience publishing *City Voices*.

The story is about a third-year cadet journalist working on a small-town newspaper called the *Recorder*. A new weekly newspaper opens, called the *Star*, operated by a man named Darcy, disparagingly called a 'mad idealist'. Staunchly independent, Darcy played a losing game, stuck between attracting and maintaining his advertising revenue while also holding the town's powerful figures to account through his reporting. Attracted by the idealism of this new paper, the narrator leaves the *Recorder* to join the *Star*. But when the paper begins haemorrhaging advertisers, Darcy compromises his ideals and joins the Chamber of Commerce. He claims this will not change the policy of the paper, but the cadet sees it as the beginning of the end. 'It's the aristocratic embrace,' he tells Darcy, shortly before resigning and leaving journalism altogether.

Michael Wilding and Stephen Knight co-edited the autumn issue of *Balcony*, and included Frank's story 'Dry Munching'. It was, in part, a story about the attempt to cross the generational and cultural divide, a question raised in his second 'Gutless Society' essay. Frank was writing and publishing more during this period, and he was reading more too – although his reading was being curtailed by the state.

In November the previous year, the customs department had seized a copy of J.P. Donleavy's novel *The Ginger Man* (1955), which Frank had ordered from overseas. Frank was summoned to discuss the matter. Earlier, in April 1965, Frank had applied for an exemption to have the novel imported. 'As a professional writer I feel that it is important to study developments in writing overseas,' he wrote in justification. 'Donleavy is considered to be an important writer.' Frank also cited his memberships of both the Australian Society of Authors and the Australian Journalists' Association. In February 1966 – after the book had been seized – Frank's application was belatedly approved and he was given the book – but only on condition the book was returned to customs at the end of six months.

The Film Study Group had been holding screenings and discussions since 1961. By 1966, it had launched an accompanying publication, *SCJ: The Sydney Cinema Journal*, produced by Ken Quinnell and Michael Thornhill. The latter had become a broadsheet film critic, working variously for *The Sydney Morning Herald* and *The Australian*. The first issue of the *SCJ* appeared in autumn, and included an essay by Frank titled 'Sing a Song of Sex', an examination of Richard Lester's films *A Hard Day's Night* (1964) and *Help!* (1965), which starred The Beatles.

Frank's essay opened: 'When the entertainment industry takes a pop singer and makes him a film star it combines the two most potent images in popular culture.' He traced this amalgam of music star and film star back to Al Jolson in *The Jazz Singer* (1927), through various screen cameos of Louis Armstrong, playing himself, as well as a litany of fictional characters played by Bing Crosby, Frank Sinatra and Elvis Presley. The Beatles were different, though. 'Sexually, the Beatles are "cool",' Frank wrote, by which he meant they had eschewed the mannerisms and gestures of the post-war male performing artist. Elvis Presley had curled his lip and gyrated his hips, but the four Beatles smiled and bobbed their heads, shaking their longish hair. They, too, exuded sexuality, but of a different sort.

Although most performers understood they had to create an 'emotional-sexual link' with their audiences, Frank argued, The Beatles saw more keenly that this link was mostly directed at the 'pre-conscious sexuality of girls between 10-14 years old, and not an overt, adult sexuality'. This involved imitating the girls, reflecting their own image back to themselves. Frank cited Dr Joyce Brothers: 'The Beatles display a few mannerisms which almost seem a shade on the feminine side . . . Girls in very early adolescence still in truth find "soft" or "girlish" characteristics more attractive than rigidly masculine ones.' Frank also cited Leslie A. Fielder, from the Fall 1965 issue of *Partisan Review*, to support his claim that The Beatles' sexual style represented a shift in the concept of masculinity, as 'symptomatic of a larger retreat from masculine aggressiveness to female allure'. Fielder argued that this style, 'though the invention of homosexuals, is now the possession of basically heterosexual males as well, a strategy in their campaign to establish a new relationship not only with women but with their own masculinity'.

Frank believed Richard Lester's films were preoccupied with questions of authority and restraint, and with positioning The Beatles as demonstrating an anti-authoritarian manner, albeit in a new key.

> The traditional anti-authoritarian feels that he lives in a hostile world which is trying to crush him. His attitudes tend to be those of the victim and he often places himself in this relationship to society . . . The new style is detached. It doesn't openly oppose and it avoids situations and attitudes which make for the feeling of victimisation. You live as if you're 'on top'. You reach a harmony with your environment by feeling superior to it and detached from it (the old style is being in *conflict* with it).

The world projected by such films, Frank concluded, was a 'fantasy world', into which one may 'venture a little way' while 'sharing a little of the romantic anti-authoritarianism'.

Frank himself shared something with this new style of anti-authoritarianism. Ever since his 1956 university research into the topic of hedonism, he had been trying in various ways to reconcile the pursuit of pleasure with some moral order. In his *SCJ* essay, he said: 'You live hedonistically and you preserve the romantic element of anti-authoritarianism – the freedom of impulse, spontaneity, irrationality – against regulation and restriction.' The blurring of gender roles and the shift in the conception of masculinity was appealing to Frank. And the limitations of the old, masculine, conflict-style anti-authoritarianism required a new cultural strategy.

The winter issue of *SCJ* – which included essays by Stephen Knight, Sylvia Lawson and John Flaus – included another essay by Frank, titled 'Teaching the Masses their Media', in which he examined the limitations of submitting popular culture to academic study, and what could be lost. This was a policy he traced back to a 1960 National Union of Teachers conference in Britain, titled 'Popular Culture and Personal Responsibility'. Frank quoted the stated objective of this policy: 'a determined effort must be made to counteract the debasement of standards which result from the misuse of press, radio, cinema and television: the deliberate exploitation of violence and sex; and the calculated appeal to self interest'. Cultural critics emerging in 1960s Britain, including Raymond Williams and Stuart Hall, had acknowledged the influence of that National Union of Teachers conference on their subsequent work. 'The core of their argument,' Frank stated, 'seems to be that the children enjoy popular culture more than the school curriculum and that the two are in conflict.' For Frank, this attitude was born of a 'sense of exclusion which popular culture creates in intellectuals', which had led them to react in various modes, both frustrated and angry – which Frank translated, in turn, as 'ridicule-it', 'control-it' or 'teach-it'. 'The conference's answer was *teach-it*,' Frank concluded. 'Grimly and moralistically.'

Nicholas Tucker's *Understanding the Mass Media* (1966) was the latest offering from this field, and was the subject of Frank's essay. The book was written as a tool for teachers to put popular culture on the school curriculum. Frank opposed this step, arguing that popular culture should not be taught in schools precisely because of its informal role in young people's lives. 'Perhaps for children it is a respite from a world of demanding relationships and participating activity – a part of their world which is informal and unsupervised,' he wrote. Frank suggested the non-intellectual aspect of popular culture was precisely its point, and why it was uniquely important. But intellectuals like Tucker treated this central concern of popular culture – 'the fantasy, the myth, the wish-fulfilment, the escape and vicarious living' – as if it were a point of failure. Frank concluded that Tucker's 'conception of "reality" is the expectations and experience of the majority laced with his morality – health, sobriety, work, and tolerance – a set of values remote from the complex, brutal, confused nature of much of life'.

Frank's two *SCJ* essays examined the same idea but from two different perspectives. When he argued that the 'line between reality and fantasy is generally self-establishing', he meant it could not be laid down in advance by some institutional authority, but must be achieved and maintained through informal individual experience, and in testing one against the other. Likewise, films such as those featuring The Beatles created a 'fantasy world' intentionally kept separate from 'the complex, brutal, confused nature of much of life'. But it was only against such a reality that the 'fantasy world' of popular culture could exist – not as a replacement or denial of that reality, but as a source of temporary relief, a place in which to safely explore and test imaginative possibilities.

Tucker criticised people's adulation of film stars, especially their supposed off-screen sex lives – as well as popular culture figures such as The Beatles – but Frank argued that the basis for such adulation was not linked to 'reality' at all, but to a knowing sense of 'unreality'. 'Tucker ignores the possibility that this vicarious-sexuality is a transition from painful puberty to real relationships,' he wrote. 'In adults it can be an entertaining alternate sexuality.'

One qualification to this argument, not appearing in the published version but taken from Frank's notes, stated: '[I]f your fantasys are leading you dangerously close to translation of them into reality and they are illegal or involve social or personal sanctions emotionally or practically then perhaps you should see a psychiatrist or talk to someone who may be able to assist you.'

In mid-1966, Frank started a relationship with Jenny Roberts. He was twenty-seven years old at the time, she was twenty-five. She had an infant son, Thomas. Originally from Sydney, she had graduated from the University of Sydney in 1962, but soon after had married John Roberts, a medical student, and moved to Canberra. Jenny's marriage had broken down by 1966, when their son was eighteen months old. She had moved back to Sydney and found work as a research assistant in the School of Political Science at the University of New South Wales.

Jenny met Frank at the Newcastle Hotel and they got together almost immediately. She had a place in Paddington at the time, and when Frank was in Sydney for the night, he usually stayed with her and Thomas. During this initial period, Jenny contracted meningitis and was hospitalised for six weeks. In July, while she recovered, Jenny and Thomas stayed with Frank in Bundeena. It was the honeymoon period of their relationship. She enjoyed the quiet of Bundeena, the soft light inside the cabin, insulated against the cold, the bricks and paper on the walls. Her family had a bush hut in Yerrinbool, where they had holidays when she was a child, and Frank's cabin brought back fond memories. They would bathe Thomas together and put him to bed, then share an evening meal, wine and bed. Bundeena became a refuge for Jenny.

For Frank, it was a rare moment of domesticity, which revived in him what he had sought with Wendy during their marriage. He wanted Jenny and Thomas to move in with him more permanently, but Jenny did not feel she could. She was in the middle of divorce proceedings, with the threat of a child custody battle in the air, and she was frightened for herself and Thomas. In the end, she did not move in with Frank, but Frank and Jenny were together, on and off, for the next year.

Meanwhile, Frank continued to write and publish at a prodigious rate, albeit in largely unknown publications. *Diafan 4* touted itself as 'a magazine for original fiction'. Its first issue was published in July 1966 – but that would also be its last. Frank had two stories included, back to back: 'A Story About How Things Aren't Right' and 'Nish's Sour Desire'. The first story explored a similar theme to 'Apples and Babies': personal exhaustion from living the bohemian lifestyle. 'Nish's Sour Desire' is the second instalment in a trilogy based on the thoroughly unlikable Mr Nish.

Frank also had a story in the August 1966 issue of *Squire*. 'Anderson, How Can There Be a Baby and No Crying?' was the second published short story Frank had written from the perspective of a woman character, albeit in the third person. She reflects on her former husband, Anderson Fith, and their time together. The story explores male self-deception and how a decision made within a relationship – especially when made by the man, as was often the case – has ramifications for how the woman recalibrates her behaviour to accommodate it, and how suppression of the woman's own desires generates further rips in the fabric of the relationship.

The theme echoes that of an earlier story, 'Bryan's Story', but with the perspective flipped from the man's to the woman's. Eventually, Frank would revise the earlier story to make the parallels more overt, and it became 'Anderson's Story'.

Harold Holt became prime minister in January 1966. In March, he tripled Australia's commitment of troops to Vietnam, including conscripts and national servicemen. In October, Lyndon B. Johnson visited Australia on a three-day tour, the first US president to do so. His public appearances attracted television and newspaper coverage, as well as protesters with placards – 'TRY LBJ FOR WAR CRIMES', 'GO AWAY, LBJ' – and chants of, 'Hey, Hey, LBJ, How many kids did you kill today?' In Sydney, Johnson's motorcade was disrupted when protesters lay down in front of the president's car.

One of the people who had tried to prostrate themselves on the road was Gillian Burnett. She had attended the demonstration with Sandra Grimes, who yelled so much she was hoarse for the next few days. That night they watched the television coverage to try to catch a glimpse of themselves, and the next day they scanned the photographs in the newspaper. Jenny Roberts had been present too, but her experience was less exhilarating. She had to be admitted to hospital briefly for treatment, the experience having overwhelmed her.

Frank was conspicuously absent from the demonstration. He had recently started working part-time as a journalist for the ABC, and at the time of the president's visit was in Boorowa, 180 miles (approximately 300 kilometres) south-west of Sydney. He read about the protests in the newspaper, and in a letter from Sandra in which she described in great detail the excitement, the anticipation and the moment when the motorcade drove past. Frank was very much opposed to the war in Vietnam, and especially to the sending of national servicemen. He had a more ambivalent attitude towards the protest movement, and towards demonstrations more generally as a tool for effecting social change.

This was not a position he had arrived at quickly. Frank had been following the student demonstrations at the University of California, Berkeley, since he first heard about them in late 1964. He was especially interested in how they became the model for similar protests across Australia the following year, including teach-ins, candlelight vigils, marches, concerts and strikes. In July 1965, at an event at the Australian National University, in Canberra, Morris West from the Australian Society of Authors spoke out against the war. This moment lent credibility to the anti-war movement for middle-class, middle-aged Australia. Frank followed these developments as best as he could, reading the nearly 600-page documentary source book and commentary *The Berkeley Student Revolt* (1965), edited by Seymour Martin Lipset and Sheldon S. Wolin.

But he did so from a somewhat removed perspective. Much of the movement and its activities emerged from university campuses, and Frank was not a student. He was by this stage nearly twenty-nine, and had long felt alienated from university life. He had also spent much of the past two years living outside of Sydney. By the time of Johnson's visit to Australia, Frank had been working as a journalist, off and on, for ten years. He had been observing the development of the protest movement from this professional perspective, keenly aware of how it was being shaped and manipulated by the media. Politically, he interpreted these events against what he had written in 1963–64 in the two versions of 'The Gutless Society', in which he had made an initial examination of the shortcomings of much social and political activism, while at the same time accepting the need for such action.

Frank wrote briefly about Berkeley in his final editorial for *Highway*, in the spring of 1966, before leaving for a full-time position at the ABC. His readings and notes on Berkeley were so extensive they spilled over into a separate essay he published in *Broadsheet* in November 1966. This was followed in December by a paper on the more general topic of political demonstrations, which he presented at a Libertarian Society conference soon after.

This paper was then revised and published in 1967 in the journal *Noise*.

In his *Broadsheet* essay, 'The Importance of the Word "Berkeley"', Frank examined the Free Speech Movement (FSM). He found its members' arguments to be 'curiously conservative', supporting existing American institutions and the role of the federal government in vouchsafing their civil rights, and calling on the university to provide a student government, which the FSM, via its student political party wing, SLATE, manoeuvred to dominate. In this sense, Frank argued, they 'did not want a dispersal of power as much as a transferral of power – to them'. And yet the FSM redeployed the rhetoric of Marx's notion of alienation, applied to the labour of being a student within the 'knowledge factory' of the modern university. So the FSM also harboured revolutionary aims: to wrench the university away from its subordination to government and private capitalist demands, and to reorient it towards society in a more revolutionary manner.

Within this, Frank suspected, resided an 'internal contradiction'. The FSM argued that the subordination of the university to capitalism resulted in a loss of independence, which undermined the core purpose of the university: to be an educational institution and a site of free enquiry. Pressing the university into the service of any revolution would simply exchange one form of subordination for another. 'This too must mean a surrender of independence,' Frank argued, noting that this was already happening within the changing attitudes of the students: 'The student activists criticised the lack of commitment among students and argued that it was their duty. They confused the categories of student and political activist. They were operating on the theory that performance in one category can be transferred as credit to another category.' In becoming activists, they forfeited the role of student, and so undermined the purpose of the university.

Despite Frank's criticisms, the main reason he had given so much consideration to the events at Berkeley was because he felt they 'seized important issues': their grievances were not local but resonated within universities around the world, and that resonance was what gave the word 'Berkeley' its importance. Frank cited the work of Paul Goodman, who was also critical of the movement, while remaining sympathetic to its aims and legitimate grievances. Frank wrote:

> Goodman in the book *Patterns of Anarchy* lists these requirements for the pursuit of knowledge and for the preservation and creation of critical independence: a small face to face community of scholars; the creation of a personal learning relationship between student and teacher; the existence of an 'academic guild' composed not only of professional teachers but of what he calls 'veterans' – writers, artists, editors, etc., whose allegiance is to learning.

Among Frank's papers and research notes on the topic of Berkeley, there is a seven-page typed report on how the WEA was already a model for the type of institution most closely matching Goodman's criteria. The WEA, Frank argued, was thus a legitimate alternative to the modern university.

The Libertarian Society held its annual conference in mid-December at Minto, south-east of Sydney. It included a forum on the Vietnam War, with Owen Harries and Roelof Smilde speaking. Frank's paper was on the topic of 'Demonstrations and Civil Disobedience', although its revised form was published in *Noise* in 1967 under the title 'The Nature of Demonstrations'. Frank opened by referring back to 'The Gutless Society', and how his thinking had since developed. 'I once thought that direct political action would create a freer society,' he said.

> I am more confused now. I am less certain about the way a society changes and consequently less certain about the relation between direct political action and change. And I am certainly doubtful about the positive relationship between direct political action and intellectual life – there may in fact be a negative relationship. While still being committed to self preservation, my own free development, the sharing of ideas, and the defence of my allies, I feel that there are other ways better for going about these things.

The framework of Frank's examination of the nature of demonstrations derived from his deep reading of mass media and communications theory, as well as of the sociology and psychology of attitude formation. The general problem, which this research threw into stark relief for Frank, was that most direct action, as currently performed, was counterproductive.

> It seems that people read and accept material from journals and TV and radio which endorses their opinions and attitudes; that people adopt those views and attitudes which secure them in their position, and raise their status, in the groups in which they find themselves; that change when it occurs is more horizontal than vertical (that is, from interchange between people at the same level rather than through leadership from above); that information and opinion from 'outside' is not received rationally, in the formal sense, but eccentrically – deflected, reflected, distorted, adapted, and reinterpreted; and that the unintended consequence of a communication is sometimes greater than the intended consequence.

Although Frank said at the outset of his lecture that 'I feel that there are other ways better for going about these things', he did not state what these might be. There is some indication, from his lecture notes and subsequent actions, that he was at the time considering a more personal way of going about things, and this had something to do with writing, with the political life of being a writer – which interacted with society in a more horizontal rather than vertical manner – and with literary fiction, in particular, which was a less rational, less formal means of communication, and so more attuned to the imaginative basis of society and the conditions of cultural change.

Summer's Tales was an annual anthology of short stories from Australia and New Zealand that began in 1964. Frank's short story 'Futility and Other Animals' was in its third and final edition, in 1966. The story draws, in part, from the emotional climate of

Frank's period in Bundeena with Jenny and Thomas, but also looks back to previous relationships. The underlying narrative structure echoes J.D. Salinger's 1948 *New Yorker* story 'A Perfect Day for Bananafish'.

This was the second story Frank had written that touched upon the theme of suicide, the first being a Thomas Wake story in which Jimmy is suicidal, giving 'futility' as his reason. This echoes one of the final letters Wendy sent Frank at the time of their break-up, and her description of 'the futility of our relationship'. A response came in 'Futility and Other Animals': 'Futility was a wild animal all right, and the gun was a way of scaring it. It could be a way of killing it for all time. Perhaps it was best when used only to frighten the animal away.'

In late 1966, Michael Wilding was to return to England. Before leaving Australia, he and his wife, Margaret, visited Bundeena to see Frank. It is not clear if there had been some miscommunication or if they had decided to risk visiting unannounced (Frank did not have a telephone at Bundeena), but that same day Frank was in Sydney. A young woman named Judy was staying in the cabin at the time, and she entertained the couple for the day. They had lunch and went to the beach for a swim. Michael saw Frank's writing desk, his typewriter, his notes and his folders of stories in various stages of drafting. He furtively read some of Frank's manuscripts, and begrudgingly noted that Frank was maturing as a writer.

Frank had published five short stories in 1965. One year on, Frank had another seven stories published. He had a number of folders with drafts of new stories in various stages of completion. Around the time of Michael's visit, Frank noted in his journal the first mention of a possible book of stories:

> Collection of Stories
> sick – confused – brave
> a collection (series) of stories in an continuous environment

The idea for the collection was in many respects an evolution of his 1963 conception of a book of stories based around the figure of Thomas Wake. This new collection had discarded much of the material that was more or less autobiographical. In the more recent stories, the characters were diversifying and becoming more independently fictional. This revised structure came as a response to the various rejections Frank had been receiving from book publishers, who were requesting a novel rather than a short-story collection. Over the previous two years there had been forty-nine novels published in Australia, but only eleven collections of short stories, most of them written by established novelists. In November 1966, in response to one such rejection, Frank offered this compromise:

> What I have done though is re work some of the stories to bring them . . . all into linked-relationship so that the volume becomes more what you felt it to be – a continuous story of an environment or a sub society – a fairly continuous narrative with no real central character. Characters appear in stories sometimes as the main characters and sometimes as minor references. Actually the idea of a series of stories describing an environment with intertwined characters interests me greatly.

Frank did not live in Bundeena much longer after that. He had grown tired of not having enough money, and he was increasingly accruing debt, his savings long since gone. For the past two years, at least, he was living on two-thirds of the national minimum wage. He had truncated his psychotherapy after eighteen months because of lack of funds. So in December 1966, while unsuccessfully getting his proposed book published, he applied for and secured a full-time position at the ABC.

He started his new job a few days before his twenty-eighth birthday.

In January 1967, Frank had a story published in *Oz*. 'O.K., O.K.' is a vignette satirising a white, male university student, who gets on a city bus and finds all the seats taken except for one next to a young Aboriginal woman. He sits beside her.

The story shifts between a third-person description of external events and the young man's first-person internal monologue as he orients his behaviour and thought, not so much in relation to the person beside him as an individual, but towards his own projections of gender and race, which he imposes upon her. These thoughts and behaviours are filtered through his progressive, modern ideals. He is, for example, a member of 'Student Action for Aborigines' (SAFA), which he feels obliges him, and authorises him, to strike up a conversation: 'If I don't talk with her my membership of SAFA means nothing. I'd be nothing more than an armchair do-gooder.' He worries momentarily she may think he is trying to pick her up. But he thinks speaking with her would be 'good practice' for the Freedom Ride in September. Finally, when she alights from the bus, he follows her and tries to strike up a conversation. But her response is definitive: 'Piss off.'

In the coda to the story, the young man's progressive ideals collapse and he momentarily admits the truth to himself: 'OK, OK, so I did want to screw her.' But even in his hypocrisy, he finds a foothold that allows him to maintain his righteous superiority: 'He sensed the pleasure of self-criticism.'

Frank had another story published that January, once more in *Squire*. The story, 'A Barmaid, a Prostitute, a Landlady', is a study of loneliness and para-social relationships, those one-sided human interactions usually associated with commercial transactions. Tom lives in a boarding house run by Mrs Thompson. He works hard all week in an office job and his only social life is two ritual weekly encounters. Every Tuesday night, Tom goes to the same pub, and buys drinks from the same barmaid, Sara. Every Wednesday afternoon, he leaves work early and goes to a brothel, but he prefers to see a different girl each time, if possible, because he suffers from premature ejaculation and is embarrassed to see the same woman twice.

She lay on the bed.

He sat beside her.
"Well, love?" she said.
He smiled.

"Here, I'll get you started," she said.

Then, it was over.

"Slow to start, quick to finish," she said.

"Yes," he said.

One Tuesday night, he tries to make a deeper human connection with Sara, but she brushes him off, politely but laughingly. When he visits the brothel he gets the same woman as last week, but she does not remember him. He tries to persuade her to share a meal with him after she finishes work, but she refuses. Desperate for human warmth, when he returns home he makes an ill-considered pass at his landlady, but she rebuffs and remonstrates him. 'He stood collapsed in his heart.'

It is perhaps the least titillating and most depressing story ever to appear in a men's magazine, certainly in *Squire*. But one man in Melbourne thought otherwise, and he happened to be a senior constable of the Vice Squad.

On 2 February 1967, at a newsstand in the Myer Centre, Melbourne, Senior Constable Eric Horne noticed a number of boys, whom he presumed to be between the ages of thirteen and seventeen, browsing a copy of *Squire*. He bought a copy of the magazine and immediately turned to what he considered to be an offensive 'article' called 'A Barmaid, a Prostitute, a Landlady' by Frank Moorhouse, which described a man having sex with a prostitute. In later news and court reports, the senior constable kept using the term 'article' instead of 'short story'. He possibly mistook it for a work of non-fiction. The magazine contained photographs of topless female models, which he also judged obscene.

The Melbourne Vice Squad seized the remaining copies of the January edition of *Squire* from the newsstand and charged the eighteen-year-old counter girl, as well as the management of the Myer Centre, with selling obscene material. But before the subsequent court case, the defence persuaded the prosecutor to drop the charges against the counter girl, to spare her further 'indignity'. The prosecution was supported by the Victorian deputy premier, Arthur Rylah, a notorious censorship crusader.

During the court proceedings, the defence asked Senior Constable Horne if after reading the magazine he felt corrupted, which precipitated the following exchange:

> SC Horne: 'What do you mean?'
> Defence: 'Were you inclined to go out and commit sexual offences?'
> SC Horne: 'No.'
> Defence: 'Do you find anything obscene about the female breast per se?'
> SC Horne: 'What do you mean "per se"?'

First Constable Clarence Thompson then took the stand and corroborated Senior Constable Horne's testimony. The defence talked about how personally unrewarding visiting prostitutes could be, and Constable Thompson said he would not know, as he had never visited a prostitute.

> Defence: 'The theme of the story is that it is an unrewarding experience.'
> FC Thompson: 'I hadn't looked at the story that way.'

The defence then called two psychiatrists and three academics from English departments to testify as to the psychological effect and the literary merit of Frank's story. Frank had always wanted independent, critical feedback for his work. And here he had his chance, although perhaps not in the circumstances he had imagined. This was the first time since the *Angry Penguins* obscenity trial of 1944 that literary critics and psychiatrists had been called to defend a literary work in Australia in court.

At that earlier trial, Dr Reginald Ellery had testified that the poetry of Ern Malley would not unduly excite the average reader sexually. For the psychiatrists at the *Squire* trial, the issue was likewise whether or not such publications could cause sexual deviancy. The prosecutor claimed the former, but the defence and the psychiatrists claimed the latter. One of the psychiatrists, Dr Bartholomew, even said a sexually deviant person could fetishise any object. This was a point the second psychiatrist corroborated, adding he knew of the case of a man who became sexually excited by the act of eating bananas.

The prosecutor was uncomfortable throughout the whole proceedings, to the point he was unable to speak directly about the matter at hand.

> Prosecutor: 'Do you find the nudes in the magazine provocative?'
> Dr Bartholomew: 'Yes.'
> Prosecutor: 'Do you agree that they are displayed to their best advantage?'
> Dr Bartholomew: 'No, not to their best advantage.'
> Prosecutor: 'Do you agree that the photographs show the obvious and then make the obvious more obvious?'
> Dr Bartholomew: 'I don't understand.'

The three academics argued that Frank's story had literary merit, that it was showing how sex without love was a hollow affair, and that the character in the story was portrayed as a lonely figure. John McLaren, from the Secondary Teachers' College, Parkville, said: 'It is an honest story.' Dennis Douglas, from Monash University, said the story dealt with universal themes, adding: 'It is written from a serious and mature point of view.' When Stephen Knight, from the University of Sydney, said the story had 'high literary merit', the prosecutor asked: 'As high as Shakespeare?'

> Knight: 'No, I'd say that Shakespeare had extremely high literary merit.'
> Prosecutor: 'Higher literary value than "The Changeling"?'

The prosecutor was referring to a Ray Bradbury story published in the same edition of *Squire* as Frank's story. But, perhaps because the previous question was about Shakespeare, Stephen Knight thought the prosecutor was asking about the seventeenth-century Jacobean tragedy *The Changeling*, by Thomas Middleton and William Rowley. That play was first performed in 1622, and first published in 1652, a generation after Shakespeare's death, and is a very different work. This led to general confusion through the remainder of Knight's testimony, as he and the prosecutor spoke at cross-purposes.

In the end, and despite the best efforts of the defence, the magistrate found the Myer Centre guilty of selling obscene material, and ordered all copies of the magazine destroyed. Magistrate Duggan, in his judgment, said: 'Having regard to the contents of the magazine, I find it is obscene because it unduly emphasises matters of sex in a manner which offends against the standards of the community.'

For Frank, this was much worse than when his use of the word 'bullshit' was censored by the editors of *Westerly*.

8

'Writes Short Stories and Does Not Intend to Write a Conventional Novel'

Television began in Australia the same year Frank became a cadet journalist. In a professional capacity, however, Frank had only more recently become involved in the new medium. At the ABC, he was at times reporting in front of a camera. In a letter home, Frank admitted to feeling very nervous in front of the television camera. His father's advice was to forget the camera and the microphone and pretend they were not present. But for Frank, the presence of these technologies, and the thought of their implications, were the very things he could not ignore – that was what made him anxious.

Ever since Frank was thirteen, when he penned an essay on the history of writing and printing, he had come to associate the art of writing with the craft of various underlying technologies. In a sense, he transposed his family's interest in agricultural manufacturing to the manufacturing of printed works, the development of dairy farming in the Shoalhaven with the invention of the Greek alphabet, the Gutenberg press, and their impact on the modern world. As an adolescent, reading his father's library of Herbert Casson books – which included histories of communications technology and transport, such as *Horse, Truck and Tractor* (1913) and *The History of the Telephone* (1910) – Frank learned to always consider the otherwise hidden, material ground which made certain cultural figures possible. Frank's subsequent development as a writer was inseparable from this keen awareness of the physical infrastructure, material form and technological processes of printing and publishing that made particular works of literature possible.

This had become a professional concern when he started working as a journalist, and pursued extracurricular study in typography and layout design, which he then put into practice with small-town newspapers. Frank understood the need to balance advertising and journalistic integrity and independence, which underpinned his thinking on the economics of writing. At the same time, Frank developed an interest in psychology and sociology, focusing particularly on attitude formation and the persuasive power of advertising and mass media generally. He read books such as Vance Packard's *The Hidden Persuaders* (1957), on advertising and psychological manipulation, and Raymond Williams' *Communication*, on the impact of media communications technology on social relations. By the late 1960s, he was lecturing on media theory and communications at the WEA, his various course reading lists having between twenty-five and forty books on communications and media theory, alongside histories of television, newspapers and publishing.

Prominent on all these lists was the work of the Canadian media theorist Marshall McLuhan. McLuhan was influenced by a Canadian economist, Harold Innis, whose work in the 1930s and 1940s was on the fur trade and cod fisheries in Canada. Innis was interested in how those industries developed a transportation infrastructure – his initial research in the 1920s was on the railway in Canada – which doubled as an early communications network. When Innis turned his attention to the paper and pulp industry, he became interested in the manufacturing of newspapers, which led him to spend the remainder of his life studying the history and impact of changing media and communications technologies on cultural forms throughout history, from ancient times to the present. This later work attracted McLuhan in the 1940s.

From Innis, McLuhan popularised the idea that the nation-state was itself conditioned by the development of communications technology. 'Socially, the typographic extension of man brought in nationalism, industrialism, mass markets, and universal literacy and education,' McLuhan wrote. 'For print presented an image of repeatable precision that inspired totally new forms of extending social energies.'

In the Australian context, this meant that the development of newspapers and printing technology in the colonial era, networked together via the railroad and telegraphic lines, created the conditions for the growth of industry, of education and of a centralised, federal government. According to McLuhan, 'Political unification of populations by means of vernacular and language groupings was unthinkable before printing turned each vernacular into an extensive mass media.' This explained the significance of *The Bulletin* and Angus & Robertson in the 1890s, and the vernacular literature emerging from this period, underpinning a potential cultural nationalism, which figures such as Vance and Nettie Palmer tried to revive.

It was McLuhan's second and third books that brought him renown in Australia. Both *The Gutenberg Galaxy* (1962) and *Understanding Media* (1964) were published during the period in which Frank had returned to Sydney. Although Frank's first explicit references to McLuhan do not appear until 1967, there are traces of his ideas in Frank's writing and notes as early as February 1965, when he wrote about how living in a modern city affected individuals, overwhelmed by the ubiquity of electrical media. This led Frank into a discussion on Durkheim's notion of *anomie* and the contradictory usages of the word 'village'. Meanwhile, in *The Gutenberg Galaxy*, McLuhan discussed the paradoxical situation of individuals in the mid-twentieth century living, through their media, in a 'global village', the outcome of 'a fragmentation which terminated, thought Durkheim, in the *anomie* of the nineteenth century.'

The influence of McLuhan on Frank's thinking cannot be overestimated, but it is also difficult to fully assess because many of the underlying ideas and ways of seeing the world, made famous by McLuhan, had been dormant in Frank's mind since adolescence. It was these interests that had attracted Frank to McLuhan's books in the first place. But when he did become familiar with McLuhan's ideas in the mid-1960s, they provided a framework that organised many of the variegated currents of thought that had become important to Frank over the previous years – of writing as a technology, of publishing as manufacturing, and of the economic, psychological and sociological processes of persuasion, attitude formation and cultural production – while at the same time providing Frank with a vocabulary to clarify and pursue his own critical thinking.

The 1967 *Squire* obscenity trial motivated Frank to consider more deeply the role of 'girlie' magazines in Australia. Since 1965, he had published short stories in such outlets. In *Dissent*, a radical journal, Frank pulled his thoughts together in the essay 'Girls Galore'. Frank's examination was limited to his own research and speculations, because one of the main books on the subject, *Smut Peddlers* (1960), by James Kilpatrick, was currently banned in Australia.

Frank opened the essay with an idea from *Understanding Media*: that the photographic image is a 'brothel-without-walls'. 'McLuhan suggests,' Frank writes, 'that the photograph is a technological extension of our fantasies (photographs are bad when they are too real) – photographs are expected to be better than reality.' Nowhere is this more the case, Frank argued, than in the rise of 'girlie, jerk-off, or pin-up magazines – the magazine containing photographs of nude or partially nude women – sold for sexual entertainment'. From this, Frank was able to focus not simply on the content of men's magazines, but on the medium of the magazine itself, and therefore could suggest a more dynamic interplay between such publications within the broader culture. He would have been unable to do so had he focused on a simple, and more traditional, content-analysis.

In the *Squire* trial, the defence had argued that a person's intentions in reading a publication may be at odds with the intention of the publication itself. Intentions are not singular, but multiple, and so are difficult to police or judge. In his essay, Frank cited Gillian Freeman, who suggested that lesbians probably read 'girlie' magazines intended for men, just as bodybuilding magazines were used by homosexuals. There were at the time four 'nudist' magazines published in Australia, Frank noted, with a circulation far beyond the number of practising nudists. He speculated that they were purchased for sexual titillation rather than to celebrate the nudist lifestyle. Due to a legal loophole regarding restrictions on 'modelling' versus 'life portraits', nudist magazines were able to include 'photographs of pubescent and adolescent girls and young boys'. Frank implied that this loophole allowed paedophiles to purchase what for them was pornographic material. Meanwhile, a magazine like *Squire*, containing a short story about loneliness, sexual inadequacy and the empty experience of visiting a prostitute, was charged, tried and convicted as being obscene.

Frank argued there was a dynamic and mutually reinforcing relationship between legal censorship, sexual taboos and pornography: enforcing taboos encouraged their transgression, which in turn fuelled demand for more erotica. 'Almost certainly a relationship existed between censorship taboos and the potency of some erotic material and some magazines gain attraction because they live on the border of the forbidden,' he wrote. Even in the absence of censorship or taboos, some form of erotica would still exist. Erotica was related to self-education and natural sexual development, from which Frank concluded that censorship on matters of sex leads to a distortion in the development of the adolescent and adult personality.

Frank considered men's magazines as part of the history of changing gender roles in Australia, an ongoing renegotiation between men and women. Between the wars, media institutions, concerned with public affairs, began as exclusively male affairs: 'men speaking to men about the affairs of men'. Women's magazines, such as *The Australian Women's Weekly*, emerged on the peripheries, to address domestic matters. But quite quickly such publications moved to the centre, facilitating a reconfiguration of gender roles, with women beginning to occupy a less peripheral position regarding public affairs. 'Today most newspaper and magazines are either bi-sexual or neuter and aim to be "family" publications,' Frank argued.

It was only as a response to this new configuration, Frank stated, that men's magazines emerged on the peripheries: 'The new male magazines are likewise indicators of a changing male role or perhaps of uncertainty about it resulting from the changes of femininity.' The current women's liberation movement brought a new style of magazine – such as *Nova* or *Queen* – which were symbiotically related to, and a counter-reaction to, men's magazines that otherwise responded nostalgically, defensively or aggressively to new social and gender realities. Frank saw this as a necessary phase in the process of a renegotiation between the sexes. Censorship and taboos surrounding pornography were part of a larger effort to maintain social control, to contain and slow down this reconfiguration of gender roles in society.

Frank's argument in 'Girls Galore', as well as his continued publishing in men's magazines, belied his deeper ambivalence towards these questions. His relationship with such magazines became more paradoxical when, later that year, he became an editorial adviser to a new 'girlie' magazine, *Chance*. His profile described him as being 'well known as the biggest libertine in the Libertarian movement . . . More handsome than Norman Mailer and never carries a knife.' He was praised for his role in the *Squire* case, for which he was now a martyr for pornography against censorship. His growing public persona was hyper-masculine and successfully heterosexual. And yet all his stories in men's magazines dealt with themes of sexual and emotional inadequacy, including a story written from the perspective of a woman – all of which ran counter to the purpose of such magazines, which, as Frank argued, catered to the fantasy of heterosexual masculinity. Frank's stories consistently questioned and undermined that fantasy.

One class of magazine Frank omitted from his essay were publications on the topic of transvestism, which he was furtively reading during this period – in particular, a small publication called *Transvestia*. But even here certain social restrictions were maintained. *Transvestia*'s stated aim was to cater for 'the needs of heterosexual persons who have become aware of their "other side" and seek to express it'. It did not cater to 'homosexuality, bondage, domination or fetishism. These are left to others to develop. They are no part of the areas of interest of this magazine.' Even in the underground press, it seemed, Frank could not find a place allowing for the full expression of his character.

Frank had another story published in *Squire* in February that year. 'Some Sort of Mistake' brings back the character Anderson Fith. The theme recalled Frank's unpublished 1958 story 'The Affair with Andrea', as both stories concern a lonely but liberated woman who simply wants somebody to talk with, somebody to take them seriously as an intellectual equal, and who will not simply treat them as a sexual object. Once more, it ran against what one might expect in a 'girlie' magazine.

Since Frank first met Michael Wilding, they had engaged in an ongoing conversation about fiction and the business of writing. When Michael returned to England in 1967 and accepted a job in the English department at the University of Birmingham, they continued their conversation via mail.

'What the hell is one doing writing stories anyway?' Michael wrote to Frank in February. '6 years of rejections.' Since 1965, Michael had had two stories published in *London Magazine*, and a third story published in the Australian anthology *Coast to Coast*. When they first met, Frank had already published four stories, and he had since published fourteen more. Although Michael did not like Frank's earlier stories, he was envious of his published output. For his part, Frank was envious that Michael had had two stories published internationally, something he had not yet achieved, despite submitting to American and English magazines for close to a decade. *Coast to Coast*, which Frank saw as a necessary step to being accepted into the Australian literary establishment, had also repeatedly rejected his stories.

In his first letter, Michael said: 'Last wed I wrote a story about Bundeena. It's brilliant: will send you carbon copy when I do final draft.' In August, Michael finally finished the story, posting a copy to Frank. 'I'm dedicating it to you,' he wrote.

The untitled story was about a one-sided rivalry between two writers, Graham and Joe. Joe lives with his girlfriend, Margot, in a stone cabin outside the city. He has written a dozen stories in two months, while Graham has not managed that in two years. Joe is preparing a collection of stories for a book. One day Graham visits Joe, but Joe is not home. Margot is, and she persuades Graham to stay. Their conversation is about Joe, about Margot's relationship with Joe and about Joe's writing habits. There is sexual tension between Graham and Margot, but Graham is distracted by Joe's writing desk, his typewriter and folders of story drafts.

The attraction between Graham and Margot provides sexual metaphors which – in a parody of *Lady Chatterley's Lover* – are transposed to Graham's reading of Joe's stories. He opens the folders 'as bees force open the petals of flowers', the stories are 'unclothed', his fingers gently turning pages 'as if he were prising oysters open'. Graham notices how Joe's writing has developed, matured. 'But it was Joe's new control that he was cursing, the bitch of assurance that was in Joe.' Graham looks for fault lines. 'But the old flatness was still there. He could find traces of it, of the old over-explicitness, the clumsiness: gold among the dross, the silt, the rubble. It gave him a sense of comfortable familiarity, an ease.'

At the beginning, Graham and Margot take care with the pages, so as not to alert Joe to their being disturbed. But by the end they have become less careful, their fingers greasing the pages, wine stains appearing. Finally, they turn to a story in the typewriter, accidentally tearing the page as they pull it from the carriage. 'Between them they completed the rape of the stories.'

After receiving a carbon copy of Michael's story, Frank replied immediately. 'Your story and your letter have turned me from wanting to go home to write to wanting to go and get immediately drunk,' he typed. 'The story. Shit it's all too much. It brought back to me the Bundeena times.' The character of Joe, his physical description, his behaviour, was clearly modelled on Frank, and the Bundeena setting, his writing life and his girlfriend at the time, Judy, were also recognisable. Glimpsing himself in somebody else's story forced Frank to expound his own approach to writing fiction:

I can't assess the story. It trapped me into doing what I berate acquaintances and friends for doing to my stories – attempting to make autobiographical analysis. I don't think – except in rare cases – it can be done. The autobiographical percentage is usually insignificant – or superficial – used for convenience . . .

Frank's judgement was jammed: he was caught between reading the story as a writer and a reader of fiction, and seeing it as a refracted shard of somebody else's memories of him processed into fiction.

Frank tried to tease from the story what was real and what was fiction, but also what was Michael's perception of him, and what was Judy's:

But I wanted to know how much of it is your image of me and how much of it was Judy's actual words to you. Disturbing. Dreadfully disturbing. I don't of course want to know. I'll leave it as it is – a short story. Of course if you were here I'd get drunk with you and cross question you – I'd probably force you down on the floor with a knife at your throat until you told me what was fiction and what was fact.

In his letter, Frank tried talking about other things, but he kept coming back to Michael's story: 'For christsake did you really rubbish my stories behind my back and do they all have all those faults "gold among the dross" for godsake? It seems a well shaped story. But I can't tell.'

In replying to Frank's letter, and in an effort to assuage him, Michael outlined the background to the story. He said he had gone to Bundeena one time, but with Margaret, so although Judy was there, the sexual aspect was fabricated. Judy showed Michael one of Frank's manuscripts, but that was all. Michael had once run into Judy in Sydney, after she and Frank had broken up, and she told him Frank had at one time 'had a disaster, saw psychoanalyst, had treatment, wrote about it, started again'.

As for Frank's stories:

Well, the stories. I did read through some of your stories there, careful *not* to smudge, grease or deface them. They were good, which upset me.

Dross etc? Well – I never thought highly of your earlier Overland (Spider Town) & Westerly (school teacher Lib broadsheet) stories – and I was looking for what I felt, still feel (though I've not reread them) were 'social realist' limitations: your new stuff is much richer in language. This anyway is my personal judgement based on preferences based on how I write (or think I write) myself. My feelings of curiosity, jealousy, envy, hostility – well they were all true enough – though perhaps not in the same proportions. Honestly, Frank, I don't know! But the story is meant to 'place' (to use a critical term I dislike) the writer's inadequacies, fears, hostilities – we're meant to see him critically – as well as Joe. He *isn't* idealized. The narrator's envy of that is partly suspicion and questioning; what envy he has is meant to be possibly naïve . . . The story's point, of course, is the way the narrator & girl betray Joe by pretending *not* to (by not screwing) – yet betray him worse. (It's my fetish about MSS – though I don't now hold it, & let people see what I'm working on, now).

In Frank's earlier letter, he pointed out that he had his own Bundeena story – 'Futility and Other Animals' – adding, 'I'll probably work over that cabin and its place in my life as a "setting" for various stories.'

Frank was living in a single room on Bayswater Road in Kings Cross. He shared toilet and bathroom facilities with other residents. Lacking a kitchenette, he ate at nearby cafes or brought takeaway back to his room. He made telephone calls, and took meetings, at a cafe in a nearby bowling alley. Otherwise, he worked at his desk each day, electric coffee pot plugged in nearby. He had settled into a daily routine, working for three to four hours first thing each morning. Sometimes, when he was feeling unsociable – which was often – he would work at night. He wrote a thousand new words each day as a minimum, then worked on drafts of other stories in various stages of completion, rotating through the roles of creator and editor/reviser.

He thought his earlier stories were trying, in too short a space, to say, as he wrote to Michael Wilding, 'everything about the Human Condition, like a ballad or a sweet folk song'. He started writing longer stories. 'I hope it indicates greater complexity. I hope it means more fully developed characters.' He began writing outside the restrictions of magazines – especially word limits – with a view towards the greater possibilities of book publishing.

Frank enjoyed discussing reading and writing, and the business of writing and publishing, but he was usually less forthcoming about his own writing, outside the bare mechanics of his routine. He certainly avoided discussing what a particular story might *mean* or be *about*. This was Frank protecting what he called his 'unexamined creativity'. Self-analysis risked making his work 'too cerebral', he believed, too 'cold'. He explained to Michael: 'I sometimes become sweaty and fearful when I cease being the hot creator (say in the first draft) and in a later stage of the same work become the cold editor-reviser. I wonder what sort of damage the editor reviser is doing to the work.'

There were other reasons Frank did not discuss his approach to writing. When Michael once asked rhetorically in one of his letters, '[H]ow can you make the decision to be a serious writer[?]', Frank explained in detail, over several pages of correspondence, how he considered that question, in all of its ramifications, while carefully avoiding a definitive answer. He latched onto the qualifying term 'serious', to distinguish their form of writing literary fiction from the 'hundreds of levels of writing' that existed – such as radio talks, advertising copy and pulp fiction – not because he thought literary fiction was some elevated form of writing, but because it was a more ambiguous level of writing, one lacking in general, predetermined principles. Other levels of writing had general principles that could be learned, and some degree of competence and success achieved. Writers could make a living from any of these, especially if they applied themselves diligently to their craft. 'But we have taken on the level which is impossible – to a large degree – impossible to judge at early stages,' Frank wrote.

This ambiguity forced Frank to avoid calling himself a serious writer: 'It's too close to saying "I am an artist",' he explained. 'The word artist should be applied by others never by oneself. Serious writer is a bit like that.' A more modest and pragmatic self-description, Frank suggested, would be to say one was committed to the 'occupation of writing'. The question of seriousness or success was for others to decide.

Frank unpacked this question further. It was not, for example, simply a matter of application. 'One could sit all fucking life time writing and never be a serious writer.' There were no internal criteria.

> Do we know *in ourselves*? Is there an intuitive sense which tells us we are wasting our time or that we are writing crap or that we are deluding ourselves with the conceit of being 'a writer'? Some days I could cry – and do – because I am wracked with uncertainty about what I am writing and its value – I get these dreadful anxieties . . . But on other days, and thank god I suppose most days, I feel that I am doing good work which gratifies me in the way nothing else does, and not only that, but I get the feeling that I am *growing* as a writer. There are inbetween days when it is fairly unyielding work, when it is a struggle to keep at it.

Unable to judge the quality of his writing, especially when he was in the middle of a story, Frank had a policy of always finishing a story, regardless of whether he would seek publication. He could always decide not to submit, but the discipline came from finishing, not publishing.

This was because 'publication is not the test either'. There were no external criteria.

> Objective judgement of literature. We know this is a shaky field. Writers just can't take the advice of Eng Lit Lecturers, or newspaper critics, or friends, or magazine editors, or other writers, in making the decision of a) whether to write and b) whether to give up c) or what to write . . . There is no one you can turn to who can solve the problem conclusively.

The absence of external criteria was why Frank found it difficult to judge the work of other writers, especially if he knew them personally.

I was telling a prose workshop which I'm a guest at that writers have extreme difficulty in maintaining objectivity towards the work of other writers. They either hysterically attack; excessively praise either because of their intimate affection for the writer or because they want to damn by overstatement; or they 'give a pass' out of a sense of craft masonry or self protection (not wanting to put the other writer on the offensive).

And yet in spite of this ambiguity, or perhaps because of it, Frank still sought praise for his efforts, if only to encourage him to keep going.

Christ I sometimes yearn for some sort of praise – some sort of favourable reaction – some sort of response which shows you are being read with interest. God almighty the idea of someone reading my stuff without prompting often strikes me as marvellous. That someone just reads my stuff because they are interested in the stuff, and don't have to talk to me about it.

Ultimately, Michael's question – '[H]ow can you make the decision to be a serious writer[?]' – was, for Frank, moot. This was a path Frank had started, single-mindedly, since childhood. It had long passed the point of choice. A more pointed question was: could he stop trying to be a serious writer?

As Frank observed, Michael had his academic career, as well as literary criticism, and he was successful at both. This provided economic security, which enabled him to write fiction. Frank did not have a university education or a career that provided such security. He harboured doubts about his ability to be a journalist. The question of whether to pursue fiction writing remained open for Michael because he had options, but for Frank it was not difficult. Writing fiction was all he had.

In 1968, in another letter to Michael, Frank intimated a deeper reason: writing had become a matter of faith.

Sometimes I find myself clinging, blindly, to my writing as the one permanent 'value' or activity worth continuing even though I sometimes am beset by doubts about my own ability and the place of literature – 'the crisis of literature'. Do you know? The sort of religious commitment I suppose – one doesn't really know if there is a God and one doesn't really know whether what one is writing is of value.

This was the first time in more than a decade, in any of his correspondence or journals or notes, that Frank mentioned religion. Writing had always been of central importance to him, but over this time, as the vestiges of his adolescent religiosity and its ideological substitutes were abandoned, writing became both a daily practice and a ritual. 'I become guilty if I don't write,' he told Michael. 'I feel uneasy if I'm drinking and haven't written that day . . . Real Calvinism.'

And yet, as with any act of faith, writing for Frank contained large doses of uncertainty and self-doubt: a view of paradise and a risk of heading in the opposite direction. As he wrote to Michael about the literary path they were both on: 'It's all so much hell.'

Frank came to an acute awareness of this doubt and uncertainty through his engagement with McLuhan. 'Marshall McLuhan (groan) frightens me,' he wrote to Michael. 'That's why I'm preoccupied. If we have only literature left as a stable factor – morality politics and other values under tremendous question – McLuhan gets at us more – writers as blacksmiths of this century.' Frank was referring to McLuhan's notion of obsolescence, which described how a change in media environment could render the previously dominant media obsolete. The way industrialism historically replaced blacksmithing, for example, so too, more recent changes in communications media risked obsolescing the prior dominance of writers and print culture. 'No,' Frank continued:

> McLuhan is saying more that our status as those best able to delve for meaning is under question. Our special status as those best able to extract insight. But we've always done this for a minority – at least at the first stage of communication – those who read – perhaps we then go to those who talk about us – and the filtering of parts of what people have distilled. But one of the things I meant to say to you earlier in

letters was this finally disturbing element of our lives – the questioning of the written word and printed word. So, we're disturbed both in our personality and in our world.

It was under such auguries as this that Frank continued to write literary fiction.

By August 1967, Frank had been seeing Jenny Roberts for more than a year, off and on. Their honeymoon period had long ended, and the reality of creating a stable life for each other, and for Thomas, became more acute. Frank had moved back to Balmain, where he rented a place on Church Street. His life now was more hectic than at Bundeena the year before, and continued to be economically unstable. Previously, when Frank and Jenny had tried to make it work together, Frank had 'fouled up', due to emotional insecurities and personal neuroses. Jenny had her own emotional insecurities, and in the end the incompatibility of their individual anxieties and personal difficulties made it impossible for each to provide the support the other required.

In June, Frank wrote to Jenny about how he was going through a 'hopeless period' and had 'paranoid anxieties' about what she was doing, and with whom she was doing it. A week later, his paranoia was confirmed when he found out she was seeing somebody else. Part of the reason they had separated after Bundeena was because she needed to appear 'reputable' in order to gain custody of Thomas following her divorce. Frank was jealous and hurt, but he still wanted to see her.

Sometime in July or August 1967, Jenny was admitted to a psychiatric facility. Thomas sometimes stayed with Jenny in the facility, and sometimes with Jenny's mother. She came out on weekends, and she and Thomas would sometimes stay with Frank in Balmain, but they could not make it work together.

Frank wrote to Michael in August saying he and Jenny were 'cautiously reaching toward each other', but only a week later they parted for good: 'I broke up with Jenny – Jenny became more stricken with anxiety – it became paranoid intolerable, violent, hysterical, Thomas was suffering.'

Frank had long found it difficult to keep his own anxieties in check, but increasingly the practice and discipline of his writing had given him some semblance of balance. His relationship with Jenny made him realise how delicate that balance was to sustain. 'But for the first time in my life I saw a real conflict between my writing and a situation where I was going to have to make decisions which were difficult and painful,' he told Michael. He chose writing.

In the August 1967 issue of *The Australian Highway*, Frank dedicated an essay to the subject of McLuhan's thought. 'Something about Marshall McLuhan' described the Canadian theorist's central insight: that technology is an extension of the human body. Frank listed examples, appending one of his own: 'the wheel is an extension of the feet – clothing is an extension of the skin – tools are extensions of our hands – and, presumably, plumbing is an extension of our alimentary canals'.

Just as the spoken word was an extension of our thinking, Frank continued, print technology increased the reach of our thinking – in distance, quantity, repeatability and durability. In the process, what was internal to each of us individually became externalised and shared socially. Each new development in technology, each new mode of extending the human body into the world, fundamentally changed the shape and tenor of society. For McLuhan, people before the 1960s had already extended their minds and bodies in various ways, but what the latest innovations in electric media – especially television and early computers – were doing was effectively bypassing that process and directly extending the human 'nervous system' into the world.

It was no wonder Frank became anxious when standing in front of the ABC television camera, microphone in hand.

The consequences of this for society included the formation of a 'world tribal village', which was where, as Frank put it, 'just about everything is known and felt when it happens'. But McLuhan's work pointed to a more concerning possibility for the young writer. He predicted a 'post literate' society, where, as Frank explained:

> ... presumably reading and writing will be more a minority activity than it is even now. Where the fact that Johnny can't read will not be important ... Presumably most people will become almost continually hooked up electrically to the rest of the world – both visually and aurally – as some people and their transistors appear to be now. The post-literate society would be oral and visual. A return to the 'depth tangle of complex emotions' found in pre-literate tribes.

This possibility concerned Frank, not just as a writer, but as an advocate for adult education. 'Most people who pursue adult education are typographical,' Frank wrote. 'Most people in the society at large are not – they are iconic.' This realisation marked the deep background to Frank's notion – presented in his correspondence with Michael Wilding – of the 'crisis of literature', when the place of literature in society is radically undermined by the changing structure of that society.

The same month his *Highway* essay on McLuhan was published, Frank wrote to Michael in England about Michael's car, left in Frank's care the previous year. The car was a Javelin, an American-made 'muscle car', converted in Australia to right-hand drive. Frank had not bonded with the car, as he explained to Michael: 'McLuhan says that the body of the car is an extension of one's skin and I don't feel comfortable in the skin.'

Significantly, it was in this letter that Frank first introduced his notion of the 'discontinuous narrative' form.

Frank described for Michael how he had brought together a number of his short stories into a book-length manuscript, and said his collection was 'now called a "discontinuous narrative" by me ... in a way the stories are all interlinked – common characters [and] environment – often [the] same incident from different points of view.' The previous year, in the notebook entry in which the collection was first mentioned, Frank referred to it as a '(series) of stories in a continuous environment'. Now he clarified this point, contrasting this 'continuous environment' with the individual but linked stories that emerged from this background, and which constituted in the foreground a 'discontinuous narrative'.

Frank's understanding and use of 'discontinuity' can be traced to his engagement with McLuhan's work. In *The Gutenberg Galaxy*, McLuhan associated 'discontinuity' with non-literate modes of discourse, in which experience was more simultaneous and less linear. In a section titled 'The new time sense of typographic man is cinematic and sequential and pictorial', McLuhan argued that 'discontinuity' was inseparable from 'a feeling of self-alienation', of *anomie*. In *Understanding Media*, he expanded these conceptions of 'discontinuity' to be characteristic of oral culture, the undermining of a fixed point of view associated with typographic culture, and the development of a more iconic, 'tribal' perspective.

McLuhan argued that newspapers were 'discontinuous' in their use of a 'mosaic' form, which held together the 'variety and incongruity of ordinary life'. Frank had long been drawn to the novels of John Dos Passos, particularly in the way he used newspaper techniques to construct an episodic narrative structure in his fiction. This had already inspired Frank to incorporate his own experience as a journalist into his approach to fiction. McLuhan focused on Dos Passos's literary technique, arguing it prefigured his own description of the mosaic form of modern newspapers. McLuhan referred to 'the principle of discontinuity as a means of enriching artistic effect'. Moreover, 'it is hard to see how anyone who set himself to rendering the diverse existence of multitudes of people could dispense with the technique of discontinuous landscapes. In fact, until the technique of discontinuous juxtaposition was brought into play it was not even possible to entertain such an ambition.'

It was just such a rendering of diverse characters in a 'continuous environment' that Frank had set out to portray in his proposed 'discontinuous narrative' form.

McLuhan's generation was purely typographic. The generation coming up under Frank, which McLuhan focused on, was largely iconic. But coming from the generation in between, Frank was more of a hybrid, somewhere between typographic and iconic. Frank's personal focus was on writing and the typographic culture, but he felt somewhat excluded from that world. And yet the more he dealt with such typographic people, the more he realised how ill-suited they were in coping with contemporary (iconic) reality. 'For typographic man the way of measuring the value of someone is by counting his vocabulary,' Frank wrote in his McLuhan essay, 'while ignoring his own crippled inability to respond to a variety of stimuli.'

This criticism transposed and expanded Frank's 'Gutless Society' argument. Frank had always been aware of the changing technological landscape through which he was living, and the shift in social and political configurations accompanying it. In recent years that awareness had become more acute. He had early on started using literary fiction as a form of imaginative enquiry, as a means of engaging more fully with the complexity of his social worlds. Increasingly, he was beginning to consider how the medium of literary fiction might be used to incorporate social changes and reflect them critically back to society.

Frank was considering how to incorporate the iconic into the typographic, to confront directly the 'crisis of literature' as a form of literature – and the form he proposed was the 'discontinuous narrative'.

In September 1967, 'The Crying Pain' was published in *Squire*. It follows Jerri and Marshall, after their separation, and the back-and-forth analysis of their marriage through their letters to each other. But in their correspondence Marshall meets Jerri's bitterness and spite with generosity and support, which only infuriates her more. Finally, after twelve months apart, he comes back into her life, wanting reconciliation, a new beginning. And then, after a month back together, he suddenly breaks it off. This comes as such a shock to Jerri that at first she thinks Marshall is joking, but then the hidden strategy from his initial correspondence becomes clear to her: he kept himself lovable so that he kept her open to him as a possibility, a future option, which he could then betray, so as to punish her. 'He had hid the bastard in him. But she had seen the bastard now.'

Later that year, Frank achieved a personal milestone. 'The Dirty Girl' was his first story published overseas, in the UK magazine *Stand*. It was similar in theme to 'O.K., O.K.', but the execution was pushed to a more absurd conclusion. An unnamed male protagonist, under thirty years of age and with a background in the army, begins work in a library, where he falls into a war of social attrition with a thirty-year-old librarian named Edna, who has worked there for the past ten years. In that time she has turned the staff kitchen into her own fiefdom, paying little heed to cleanliness and hygiene. He is neurotic and 'hypersensitive to breaches of hygiene', which undermines his progressive, modern ideals, exposing his underlying sexism and – when he learns that she is Lebanese – his racial prejudices. The story then follows Edna's escalating transgressions against hygiene, some perceived, some real, and the protagonist's descent into further neuroses and irrationality.

'This afternoon I read your STAND story,' Michael Wilding wrote from England, 'and laughed uproariously. It is incredibly funny – it really is good – in some ways one of your best.'

The stories 'O.K., O.K.' and 'The Dirty Girl' were satires on the hypocrisy and fragility of a white male ego confronted by a changing social dynamic. But they were still one-sided, centred on the male protagonist. A similar theme informed 'A Story of Nature', published in the summer issue of *Balcony* in 1968. But this new story was less satirical, making its point with more subtlety and seriousness, and with a woman as the central figure.

This story was the first in a trilogy mapping the progression of Cindy. A few months earlier, in the July edition of *Westerly*, the third instalment of this trilogy had been published. 'Her Mother's Visit' considers Cindy, six years after the first story. At the heart of the story is a dialogue, both imagined and real, between three generations of women, tracking the effects of social change. Cindy is caught in the middle, between her mother on one side, from whom she harbours habits and hang-ups from her upbringing, and her unborn daughter on the other side, whom Cindy hopes will be born into a world in which she will be free of such habits and hang-ups.

This was the first time in three years a literary magazine had published one of Frank's stories. He had had four previous stories in *Westerly*, but *Overland* and *Meanjin* had only published one story each – and the *Meanjin* story was back in 1962. Frank had continued to submit stories to these journals, and they had continued to reject them, due to the themes, form and language Frank explored. Frank's main avenue for publication therefore remained small, usually one-off political magazines, or else mass-market men's magazines such as *Squire* and *Chance*.

'Jack de Lissa pays for serious fiction,' Frank wrote in 'Girls Galore', regarding the publisher of *Squire*, 'which is rare in Australia and is one of the few editors (including the literary magazine editors) who is willing to fight against distributors and others for extended freedom for his writers.'

The middle instalment of 'The Story of Nature' trilogy failed to find a publisher at all. Frank wrote to Michael Wilding about its rejection by Clem Christesen at *Meanjin*:

> Christesen rejected my Second Story Of Nature with the comment that I was now ready to write a novel. If one more magazine editor tells me to write a novel I'll sue them. It's making me entrenched about the short story. I'm determined to show them that the short story is not an exercise for the writing of novels. The stupid shits.

Later that year, when Frank failed yet again to receive a fellowship from the Commonwealth Literary Fund, or scholarships from either the New South Wales government or Stanford University, he wrote to Michael: 'I feel alienated from the establishment of aust lit.'

Sandra Grimes bought a house on Ewenton Street, Balmain, in the mid-1960s. It was divided in two flatettes, and Frank rented one to use as an office. Their previous relationship now settled into one of landlord and tenant.

Meanwhile, Frank shared a house with Mike Thornhill in Balmain. Those who had frequented downtown pubs in the early part of the decade, as well as Sydney newcomers, were drawn to Balmain for its cheap rent. A new group there – artists, filmmakers, writers and journalists – slowly began to evolve a distinct identity. Their meeting place was the Forth & Clyde Hotel. One newcomer was twenty-year-old Wendy Bacon, recently arrived from Melbourne. At the Forth & Clyde one evening she met Frank and Mike, and soon after she started going out with Mike.

In April 1967, the American poet and critic Kenneth Rexroth visited Australia and attended a party in Woollahra. The younger Australians mingled awkwardly with the 61-year-old, who had written about and was loosely associated with the Beat Generation. For Frank, the experience showed how lacking in variation the Sydney scene had become. The conformity and habit of it all chafed.

Since his Bundeena period, Frank had become more interested in fine eating, particularly the ritualistic aspects of it. Don Anderson was accompanying Frank on this journey of discovery. 'I'm enjoying eating and wine more than ever and my social life is more that sort of social life,' Frank told Michael. 'Some of the push seem to share my interest too – a new concern with gracious living. We're holding a formal banquet next month – ten courses black tie – and *not* as a send up. It's hard to believe but it shows you we're growing.'

The banquet did not go over as planned. It was held at Mike Thornhill's aunt's house in Woollahra one Saturday night in August 1967. There were about twenty people at the formal dinner, sitting around a long, grand dining room table. The ten courses included a whole cooked goose and a great deal of alcohol, which quickly turned the evening into a much less formal affair. At one point Sandra sat on a glass, and had to be taken out to have the shards removed from her backside. Darcy and Gillian were there too. They met Wendy Bacon that night, and within a few months Wendy would leave Mike and start going out with Darcy. Gillian then started going out with Frank.

The banquet ended with the group peeling off in ones and twos to explore the house, to pass out or have sex – or all three. In the early hours of the morning, Frank remained alone at the table, amid the plates and food scraps, the empty bottles and the wine stains, living graciously to the end.

At twenty-eight years of age, Frank was beginning to feel physically corrupted by his lifestyle. He began the 5BX physical training regimen, 'to stem the degeneration a little'. Developed by the Royal Canadian Air Force in the 1950s, and repackaged for the public in 1961, '5BX' stood for 'Five Basic Exercises': stretches, sit-ups, back extensions, push-ups and running. Frank incorporated these into his daily routine.

He wanted change, but he was anxious about doing something to effect it. 'My only weak aspiration is going to go to New York where the push is bigger,' he confided to Michael, 'and more varied.' Frank had brought up going overseas before. 'Even if the neuroses are the same the backdrop will be different,' he wrote to Michael. 'Could give the agony a different flavour.' But he was anxious about the prospect of travel:

> I have an ambivalence about going overseas. I feel an obligation to go – as an educative and writing experience – but emotionally it scares me – I need a circle of friends and wider circle of acquaintances (I think). I will probably force myself, scholarship or not, to go to USA next year. I'm fascinated as I've told you, with the Americas.

By the end of 1968, Frank realised he had been going through a period of 'cultural neglect'. He worried this would affect his writing, as he explained to Michael:

> Have felt inadequate culturally. I realise how much now I've been investing in time and resources in drinking, fucking, and going down

through the whirlpool of the terrible dynamic of our group. I've been *thinking* but it has been too undirected and underfed. I'm intellectually undernourished. I think my writing may be too.

In February 1968, Frank and Mike Thornhill worked together on a short film script called 'What Can You Say?'. It was adapted from Frank's stories 'Walking Out', 'What Can You Say?' and 'Lou Shouted "Fly"'. The script was never finished, but it indicated a nascent collaboration between Frank and Mike. Frank's interest in film had developed over several years through the Film Study Group, but his more recent professional interest was also due to his dwelling on the 'crisis of literature' and his thinking about communications theory. He felt, in part, the need to transpose his typographic ideas into a more iconic medium.

In March, Frank began a part-time job lecturing for the WEA. His first ten-week course was called 'Meet the Editors', a cultural history of Australia's magazine culture, including men's and women's magazines (drawing on 'Girls Galore'), the little (literary and political) magazines, and teenage publications. This included a meet-and-greet with an editor from the types of magazines they had discussed.

Michael Wilding's Bundeena story was published that same month in *Southerly*. When Frank read the earlier, untitled draft, he suggested: 'I'd probably call it "Joseph's Absence". The emotional presence of Joe for them both [the characters Graham and Margot], the *power* of him was excellently created.' It was published as 'Joe's Absence'.

For Michael, this marked a turning point for his writing, in both style and theme. A few months after Frank first mentioned he was working on a collection of stories for a possible book, Michael wrote that he, too, was putting together a collection. He was working on a novel about the Push, motivated by 'nostalgia', but he found the traditional novel form too constraining. 'And of course this is where I am lost, since I've no shape, no form, no structure with which to make sense of Sydney.'

Frank suggested Michael adopt the form of interlinked stories to write about the Push, even as Frank distanced himself, in his own writing, from the Push. 'Why don't you do the PUSH as a interlinked volume,' he wrote. 'I suppose in a way I have but I don't see it as the PUSH.'

Michael echoed Frank's notion of 'discontinuity', arguing that the episodic form 'seems the form best suited for a) the discontinuity of our experience b) its temporariness, its lack of sustained plan or pattern.' Six months later, in July 1968, Michael was still working over this material: 'I'm writing my push discontinuous narrative (to plagiarise your phrase) and I've been consulting your stories, letters, letters from others, to try to remind myself of the push notation; the way people think, express themselves; what they select for mention.'

Michael was less nostalgic about Sydney as a literary hub: 'But who is left? If you're staying maybe we can form a nucleus of some writing. I liked Sydney … but I am worried about writing in a vacuum. I feel (don't you?) the need to know other people writing around me.'

Frank concurred, citing what he referred to as 'The Australian Trap. The small puddle.' Frank wanted to publish overseas, but for the past decade his stories had been consistently rejected by *The New Yorker*, *The Atlantic Monthly* and *Esquire*, among others. 'I have to go overseas too,' he wrote. 'I have to go to the States.'

What largely held back Australia's literary and critical culture was censorship, Frank believed, and what he called a 'proliferation of censors' at each level of publication. *Westerly* had recently edited one of Frank's stories, removing a masturbation reference without consulting Frank. *Pluralist*, supposedly a libertarian journal, had changed the word 'fuck' to '???' – otherwise the printer refused to print it. The distributor of *Squire* forced cuts in one of Frank's stories, and its printer complained about another. 'So in these cases you have printers, editors, distributors, and binders all exercising their dirty little moralism,' he told Michael. 'It also placed editing in the hands of people other than the editor.' Censorship was more than government policy. Since the colonial period, it had created habits and cultural reflexes in its citizens, pushing them to act in censorious ways.

Michael too had experienced such censorship. The crucial line in 'Joe's Absence' was, in *Southerly*, rendered nonsensical, perhaps by the typesetter or printer. The line 'Between them they completed the rape of the stories' was printed as 'Between them they completed the rap of the stories'.

Frank became involved in an effort to push back against censorship. He worked with a small group of writers, libertarians and anarchists – including Don Anderson, Wendy Bacon, Gillian Burnett, Norma Crinion, Sandra Grimes, Ken Quinnell, and Michael Thornhill – on a newspaper called *Uphill*. Inspired by Alec Sheppard and Leon Fink's publishing *The Trial of Lady Chatterley*, which forced the lifting of the bans on that book and on Lawrence's novel, *Uphill* planned on being totally free, unrestricted by censorship, convention or taste. They raised money towards it and started writing copy, but no printer would risk taking on the project and *Uphill* was abandoned.

In 1969 a compromised version of the newspaper appeared, for a single issue, before folding. By then, Frank was no longer involved.

In July 1968, Frank signed a contract with Gareth Powell & Associates to publish his first book of stories, *Futility and Other Animals*. One of the 'Associates' was Richard Walsh, formerly of *Oz*. Gareth Powell had an ambition to establish a magazine and publishing empire. A shareholder in the international men's magazines *King* and *Penthouse*, it was Powell who had started the Australian magazine *Chance*, bringing Frank on as an editorial adviser. When Gareth had emigrated from England in 1967, he read Frank's fiction in *Squire* and became – as Frank described it to Michael – 'terribly, and flatteringly, excited about it'. In *The Australian*, discussing *Chance*, Powell said: 'I've got a short story by Frank Moorhouse which is the best thing I've ever read . . .'

That story, 'No Birds Were Flying', was published in the December 1967 issue. It is a first-person narrative about Miss

Louise Henderson, a middle-class young woman, on the day she resigned from yet another office job – where the chief clerk was Mr Nish, who 'literally perved all day'. Sitting in the pub that day, she bumps into her friend Marylou, who was having a 'sickie' from her job. They concoct a half-serious, half-joking plan to start a 'call girl racket', the logistics of which they discuss at length. But Louise is simply postponing the responsibility of adulthood.

To all appearances, Gareth had the resources to back up his publishing ambitions. He treated Frank to lavish meals, cultivating Frank's penchant for fine dining. He bought several of Frank's stories for future issues of *Chance*, but payment was not forthcoming – except for $10 when Frank said he was broke. In August 1967, Gareth said he wanted to publish Frank's first book, which was what motivated Frank to float his notion of a 'discontinuous narrative'.

It was another twelve months before the deal was finally secured and an advance paid. But a few months later, by the end of 1968, Frank and Gareth's relationship had cooled. As a member of the Australian Society of Authors, Frank had his contract looked at, and was told it was 'unreasonable and unequitable'. One of the first items on the ASA agenda when they formed in 1963 was to push against the regime behind the colonial editions which, across various iterations, was still the dominant structure within which publishing occurred in Australia. This regime perpetuated itself through habit and silence, by publishers and booksellers, who benefitted most from not changing how authors were remunerated.

Frank was paid a $400 advance but offered only a 5 per cent royalty. He had negotiated that he would accept this rate, but only if Powell published the book without concession to obscenity or indecency laws.

Frank confided to Michael Wilding that he now hoped 'it falls through', because he did not like *Chance* or the organisation. Frank was also unsatisfied with the material. 'A little depressing that it's being published so long after writing,' he told Michael, '[and] some stories no longer reflect my style or interest or direction.' In an effort to revive the project, Frank was writing a cycle of stories on a homosexual theme, which he wanted included in the collection. As late as November 1968, he was working on a story called 'The Train Will Arrive Shortly'. The book was supposed to be published that December.

In October 1968, Frank drafted a talk for ABC Radio titled 'Popular Culture and Writing'. It was an attempt to respond to the 'crisis of literature', exploring how literary culture could relate to popular culture by incorporating the iconic into the typographic. Popular culture had become more prominent due to a shift in balance between work and recreation: there were more people who were working less, with more affluence and leisure. This was compounded by an 'international communications network', leading to more contact between national world cultures, resulting in 'a remarkably rich and intense popular culture'. Frank argued that this gave 'western countries an almost constant carnival or festive mood and appearance'.

Frank's central concern was how popular culture affected literary writing. He noted two tendencies: those who felt alienated by popular culture, opposed it or adopted postures of standing outside of it, and those who were more engaged with it, who immersed themselves within popular culture in order to understand it and to adapt their writing to it, but critically. Frank was drawn to the latter group, citing as an exemplar the fiction of Donald Barthelme.

In a February 1967 edition of *The New Yorker*, Frank read Barthelme's novella *Snow White* and, as he reported to Michael, he 'went wild with enthusiasm'. In September 1968, Frank bought Barthelme's latest story collection, *Unspeakable Practices, Unnatural Acts*. 'He's also acutely preoccupied with chaos both indirectly and through his structuring of material,' he wrote to Michael about Barthelme. 'More than say Salinger or Nabokov he's able to exploit the physical environment of urban domestic America (and other societies which are heavily influenced) the objects, the furniture, the art, architecture.'

Frank transposed this idea into his draft ABC talk, highlighting the impact of popular culture on Barthelme's language: 'A fascination with the nomenclature of the popular culture world, the brand names, the slang terms, the names of pop groups, styles, and the artefacts and materials.' In a handwritten marginal note, Frank added: 'Words which before would have been avoided for craft or moralistic reasons.' Frank's enthusiasm for this new form of writing was predicated on his dissatisfaction with his own past stories, especially those in his forthcoming book. But he was already working on new stories, his next book beginning to take shape. His enthusiasm with Barthelme was driving that new writing.

Around this time, on Sunday, 10 November, the Second Annual Balmain Reading of Poetry and Prose, organised by Frank and Ken Quinnell, was held in a boatshed on Wharf Road. The inaugural event, the Great Annual General Balmain Fireside Reading of Prose & Poetry, slated for 6 August 1967, had been postponed because of rain. Now, fifteen months later, the follow-up event occurred. People brought their own alcohol, cushions to sit on and food for 'The Table'. Poets read their own work, while others read from their favourite poets, such as Sylvia Plath and Chairil Anwar. And there were the prose writers, such as Frank. 'Short stories go over very well with verse,' he explained to Michael. 'People welcome the prose after a stream of verse.'

Frank thrived in this environment. He read a new story, 'The American Poet's Visit', a satire based upon the Push party the previous year attended by Kenneth Rexroth. Frank was always nervous before reading publicly, but alcohol helped steady him. Such oral readings served a pragmatic purpose, too. They enabled writers to bypass print censorship. They could air material they could not otherwise get published.

The spoken-word aspect of such events referenced Frank's understanding of the oral ground of literature. He enjoyed the immediacy of the audience's response to his writing. He watched how they reacted to the story as he read it aloud, each line or turn of phrase, and later he would redraft the story, or work on a new story, with these reactions in mind. In this way, an oral register entered into his writing process. The experience allowed him, for that moment, to find some relief from self, and to be relaxed in the company of others. He experienced afresh the feeling accompanying his classroom reading of Lawson's 'The Loaded Dog' back in 1948, and rediscovered the spark of literature that had led him to want to be a writer in the first place.

What Frank was doing, in his engagement with Barthelme and popular culture, and in his Balmain readings, was to find new ways of getting beyond the tired conventions of literary culture, and to engage more closely in his own fiction writing with the tenors of popular culture – to resist, but in an effort at establishing a reciprocal engagement. His essay on the French New Wave film director Jean-Luc Godard, published in the summer issue of *The Sydney Cinema Journal*, continued this engagement. A few months earlier, Frank had seen Godard's noir science-fiction film *Alphaville* (1965), at a WEA summer school run by Don Anderson. The previous year he had written to Jenny Roberts about how he had been to the cinema – twice – to see Godard's *Bande à part* (1964), even though he had seen it before:

> I've become a devotee of Godard – but I mean a real devotee. I've started a file on him. I'd like very much to write something about him. I feel I understand his style and attitude and I feel affinity with it. I'd be pleased if I was working in the same stance – I think to a degree I am. (I'd never tell Mike or Ken *that*.)

His *SCJ* essay, '*Alphaville* and Irony', examined the film in terms of its depiction of an ironic attitude, which Frank described as being one 'of the ways of dealing with the world – of dissolving guilt, remorse, recrimination, regret, and inadequacy'. Frank distinguished between ironic detachment and ironic involvement. The former – echoing Frank's earlier criticism of the Push – was 'where the person has as little to do with human endeavour as possible and leads a life of pure observation'. The latter – which reflected more closely his own position – was 'where the person participates in human endeavour but as both an observer and game player'.

This was Mannheim's 'socially unattached intelligentsia'. Frank's outline of Godard could be read as self-description:

> Ironic involvement is a description of a relationship to activity. It may in fact, queerly enough, have some of the outward manifestations or appearances of commitment but the relationship beneath the behaviour is radically and fundamentally different. Contained in the ironic attitude is an almost constant awareness of the briefness and insignificance of life, the absence of sacredness, the futility of effort, the paradoxical, the hypercritical, the betrayals, the pretensions, the deceit, the self-deceit, the mutual exploitation and the cruel and bewildering nature of the human condition.

Alphaville depicted this sense of ironic involvement within a technocratic society, devoid of art and poetry, with a diminishing vocabulary, and with no sense of the past or the future, just a constantly present, mediated moment. The film depicted the endpoint of Frank's 'crisis of literature', a print culture displaced by an iconic culture, individuals deskilled in how to make sense of an increasingly complicated and intrusive technology. Frank cited a central line from the film: 'There are times when reality becomes too complex for Oral Communication.' He concluded: 'A fairly constant preoccupation of Godard's is the utter inadequacy and absurdity of much human communication.'

The title of the WEA summer school was 'Connoisseurs of Chaos: Violence in Modern Fiction'. Frank later discussed how the violence in the film is a response to the inadequacy of human communication. 'Godard is concerned with violence,' Frank wrote. 'Perhaps it is because violence can be both an expression of failure of communication and *a form* of communication.' Frank considered the metaphor of the gun in modern culture, with reference to Lemmy, the protagonist of *Alphaville*:

> Guns, with which Goddard has a preoccupation, are 'persuaders'. They are used in gangster and Western films when people won't listen to 'Reason'. They are a way of expressing rage, fear, and censure. But the

revolver, as a symbol of our time, – the Nazi's luger, the secret agent's Browning automatic, the gangster's Smith & Wesson, and the cowboy's Colt 45 – are also encrusted with the eternal mystique of the 'Weapon'. Lemmy says that his revolver is his own weapon against fate.

This was an idea and a metaphor Frank had used in his story 'Futility and Other Animals'.

The paper Frank presented at the WEA summer school that year was on Doris Lessing's 1962 novel *The Golden Notebook*, which he used as a point of entry into a broader discussion about the reconfiguration of gender roles in society, and the 'sexual and emotional chaos' resulting from this process. The novel depicted a woman seeking independence and personal freedom, but failing to achieve a degree of harmony with herself and her own personality. 'A frustrating anguish of neurosis,' Frank called it. It was an example of what he elsewhere described as *anomie*.

This was Frank's first public statement about the growing influence of feminism, the general aims of which he supported, although he questioned the underlying oppositional binary upon which it was popularly based. '[Y]ou cannot change the role of women without changing the role of men,' he said. 'The changes which have come about in the role of women have tended to be seen in isolation as though men were capable of easy adaptation emotionally to a new type of woman.' Frank complicated this by putting the conventional gender binary into a broader context, where its imbalances were shaped largely by conditions external to gender itself – by the economic, technological and media configurations of society.

In this broader context, what Frank took from feminism was the realisation that men, too, were neurotically trying to find a degree of harmony with their own personalities within this period of social change. He cited John Clellon Holmes, the American Beat writer, who said men 'suffer from the same anxieties insecurities and identity crises that were thought of in the past as peculiarly female problems'. To which Frank added: 'We want to get in on the act too.' In opposition to this, he noted figures such as Norman Mailer, representing

'Masculism or Our Side', as being the more reactionary type of male, incapable of accommodating themselves to the new social order. Frank saw girlie magazines, as he had discussed the previous year, as a symptom of the unease felt among men since the 1950s, and as an attempt to reassert what they felt had been lost.

Frank identified three groups of individuals in contemporary society: those who are satisfied with their role in society, those who are not satisfied with their role but attempt a compromise with conventions, and, finally, those who are not satisfied and are incapable or unwilling to attempt a compromise, and so suffer for it. Here he referenced bohemians: 'These people tend to form a sizable sub culture with different often radically different mores from those of the standard.' At the same time, he suggested that this third position was perhaps not one chosen freely – despite their own post-hoc rationalisations – but was rather forced on such individuals, who were otherwise 'psychoanalytically ill equip to pursue and achieve the standard values'.

Frank associated himself with this third group: his description was a veiled self-description. He argued that its members found it difficult to be sexually monogamous, had difficulties with their parents, did not want to become parents, and did not value economic security. Such people became, among other things – and here Frank cited hobos, nuns and travelling salesmen – 'dedicated artists' or 'WEA lecturers (the marriage break down among adult educationists is remarkably higher)'.

In a sense, Frank was working through his recent break-up with Jenny Roberts, which was grounded in patterns of behaviours he carried over from previous relationships.

> A neurotic has feelings of unworthiness which come from their rejection as children, i.e. that they think they are unworthy of love as their childhood proves. When someone does fall in love with them they find this attractive at first – as a thing they seek but come to reject it because they unconsciously conclude the person is either lying, or a fool because they cannot see how unworthy and despicable the neurotic feels he or she is.

Such neurosis manifested itself as 'paranoia, compulsion, obsession, guilt, and self denigration'. He even gestured towards his decision to pursue his own writing in lieu of a permanent relationship with Jenny: 'But full dedication to a single purpose leaves little time for working or marriage and raising children and often is counter to economic security which is perhaps required for the first two standard values.'

Frank's debut book, *Futility and Other Animals*, was published in February 1969. The book contained twenty-four stories, collected in three parts: Confusion, Sickness and Bravery. This was the structure Frank had proposed in 1966. Fifteen of the stories had been published in various literary or men's magazines. The earliest story was 'Walking Out', from *Westerly* in 1964. All the previously published stories were restored to their uncensored condition. They had also been revised, to cohere more closely with the discontinuous narrative form.

'This Is the Part Called Confusion' contains three previously unpublished stories, 'The Story of the Knife', 'Across the Plains, Over the Mountains, and Down to the Sea' and 'Rambling Boy'. 'This Is the Part Called Sickness' includes the Nish trilogy, and two previously unpublished stories, 'Bread, Sugar and Milk' and 'I Am a Very Clean Person'.

The final part of the book – '. . . The Part Called Bravery' – includes the title story, alongside four previously unpublished stories. This includes a trilogy of stories concerning a homosexual man named Bernard. One of these, 'The Train Will Shortly Arrive', has Bernard return to his regional home town, where he recalls childhood and adolescent scenes of sexual awakening and experimentation – many consensual, some not – against the oppression of conventions and inhibitions. This includes a description of the first time Bernard was molested, from which the boy wanted to 'run run run away from the embarrassment and guilt which swirled way down under the desire and excitement'.

This was the second time Frank had fictionalised his own middle-school molestation – the first being 'The Respectable Deviant', not included in this book – but it was the first time he wrote about it from the point of view of a boy. It was a fictionalised account, and as such should not be taken as a direct representation of actual events. But it does suggest an ongoing reworking of the memory into Frank's adult life.

The book ends with the second and third instalments of the 'Story of Nature' series; the first instalment, introducing Cindy, appeared in the first part of the book. Of the three parts, only 'The Second Story of Nature' was previously unpublished.

The resonances of the individual stories are enhanced by the discontinuous narrative form. An author's note explains this framing:

> These are interlinked stories and although the narrative is discontinuous – there is no single plot – the environment and the characters are continuous. In some ways, the people in the stories are a tribe – a modern, urban tribe – which does not fully recognise itself as a tribe. Some of the people are central members of the tribe while others are hermits who live on the fringe. The shared environment is both internal – anxieties, pleasures, and confusions – and external – the houses, streets, hotels, and experiences.

This was Frank's first public statement regarding the discontinuous narrative form. In introducing Frank, the biographical note makes some bold claims: 'Writes short stories and does not intend to write a conventional novel. At present completing another discontinuous narrative called *The Americans, Baby*. Is opposed to all censorship.'

The publication of *The Trial of Lady Chatterley* in 1964 forced changes to Australia's censorship regime. In 1965, the states co-operated on a new regime, limiting the powers of customs and the police and creating more uniformity across all states. The National Literature Board of Review launched in January 1968, replacing the Literature Censorship Board and the Appeal Board.

The release of *Futility and Other Animals* was delayed by several months because of protracted negotiations between Frank and his publisher over the contents, concerns over censorship and the financial costs this might incur. Frank had restored censored swearwords and sexual references, and previously unpublished stories describing homosexual characters were included despite homosexuality being illegal in Australia at that time. The new Board of Review had already been in place for twelve months, but Gareth Powell was waiting to get a sense of how it operated.

When *Futility* was published, it was promoted as a test case. The question of censorship framed the reception of Frank's book. When *The Sun* reported on it in June 1969, noting that the board had not taken any action in the five months since its publication, Frank was quoted as saying 'the gate is wide open'. He said books still banned in Australia needed to be reassessed. Frank pointed out that although his book contained elements which might offend some readers, this was not his intent. 'I don't want to offend anyone,' he said. The reporter described Frank as 'surprisingly – rather a shy man'.

The first review, by Brian Kiernan in *The Australian*, in July 1969, reinforced *The Sun*'s framing of the book: 'The publishers of *Futility and Other Animals* anticipate it will provide the first test by an Australian book of the new federal book censorship system.' Kiernan referred to the collection's 'continuous use of four-letter words'.

In *The Bulletin* in July 1969, Nancy Keesing also focused on this language. 'Like not blowing one's nose between one's fingers there are certain social conventions which become habitual to almost everyone,' she wrote. 'The suiting of one's choice of profane and/ or obscene language to time, place, and company, is one of these conventions which, despite 20th-century alterations in manners, still prevails.' She found the use of 'four-letter words' in *Futility* to be 'unendurably boring and as meaningless'.

In October, Peter Cowan went further in *Westerly*, judging the book as if its sole purpose was to challenge censorship. 'From the publisher's statement,' Cowan concluded, 'the book seems intended as a challenge to the censor. While the whole sorry shambles of censorship in Australia needs every challenge we can provide, a book conceived in this way may suffer more than the censor.' Once more, the focus was on the swearwords: 'The four letter words, the shock situations, lose their impact from sheer overwork . . . The four letter syndrome is too easy. A story cannot be given tension or point by introducing a run of four letter words.'

Standards of taste had changed little since colonial times – it was as if these reviewers would have preferred the colonial dash, 'D——', *The Bulletin*'s 'blanky' or Furphy's '(adj.)'.

Several years earlier, John Burrows suggested to Frank that censorship undermined the appreciation of literary quality: 'The worst thing about reading a banned book, I reckon, is that you're inevitably looking for the juicy bits and why it was banned rather than regarding it as a work of art.' Framing *Futility* as a challenge to the censors ensured that any literary merit the book had would be a secondary concern. This was particularly deleterious for a book trying to introduce a new literary form – the discontinuous narrative – and that thus required new critical standards, not the forced application of the old standards for short-story collections or novels.

Kiernan was not convinced by the structure of the book, stating that the 'experimental form does not make the collection a unity'. Where he read the book as an uneven collection of independent stories, lacking unity, Cowan read it as a failed novel. Considering the book as wholly interdependent, Cowan found that the individual stories 'lack depth' and that 'we seem to be offered no insight', as if the book was positing, and failing to deliver, a singular, overarching meaning. 'We tend to move fast over the surface,' he wrote.

Keesing ignored the question of form altogether. Once she got passed the obscenity, she was taken aback by an obsession with the contraceptive pill. 'The Pill raises implications,' she wrote, 'that I had never thought of and makes this, for me, a surprising book.' Born in 1923, Keesing was from the generation prior to Frank's. Before the contraceptive pill, she stated, sex was associated with overwhelming terror and guilt, but the prevalence of the pill replaced that form of guilt with a new form of guilt, based on choice. 'Since I put away my invaluable Dr. Spock I doubt I've read quite so much about babies between one set of covers,' she wrote. 'Unexpected indeed.'

Regarding content, Kiernan explicitly identified the 'modern urban tribe' of the book as being the Push. This was something Frank wanted to avoid, not just because it was not entirely true – many of the raw experiences inspiring some stories had occurred before or away from Frank's interactions with the Push – but also because relying on such external references undermined the literary imagination, the transformation of experience into art. Such criticism reduced literary fiction to reportage.

Cowan, despite his criticisms, pointed out that Frank's 'real talent is obvious'. Kiernan concluded similarly: 'There is more promise than achievement in this book, but the promise is of something of real interest coming out of his future explorations.'

A long review essay appeared in *Southerly* in September, which better grasped the literary ambitions of *Futility and Other Animals*. This essay did not assume that the purpose of the book was to challenge censorship:

> Moorhouse isn't writing as an outsider looking in, he is not trying to titillate the reader with relaying four-letter words and shocking doings. Those are present, certainly but are not presented in the shock and censure manner of the bourgeois intruder . . . It is a world setting up its own values, its own ethic.

The essay situated *Futility* within existing Australian literary traditions, but only to emphasise Frank's working against these traditions, carving out a unique literary space. The two dominant groups of writing in Australia then were stories set in the outback and in suburban settings. 'Frank Moorhouse is independent of either of these groups. His concern is with inner city living, with the lives of those existing almost totally within an urban environment.'

Yet the review did not collapse fiction into reportage by referencing the Push. The characters could be located in any urban Australian setting, not necessarily or uniquely Sydney. Besides, the stories were not even focused on large group or movement dynamics. They were 'essentially human interactions in small groups of twos or threes in bare sets'. Such interactions took place on the peripheries of an urban tribe, rather than squarely within any such tribe. 'There may be a tribe around them, but it isn't portrayed as such in the book. And some of the people, particularly the homosexuals, seem not to belong at all closely to the tribal scene, but to have made glancing contact with it from their other orbits.'

The subtlety of Frank's writing – where the art was to 'conceal the art' – was set against the dominant trend in Australian fiction at the time, bent towards the baroque: 'This is not a style likely to gain recognition quickly in Australia, where the mannered rhythms of White, or the rich emotions and ornamentations of Porter or Keneally are the fashion.'

This review essay was written by Michael Wilding. Regardless of his earlier argument against the 'jolly mateship' of the literary scene in Australia, his close friendship with Frank over the years meant he knew better than most whether or not Frank had achieved what he was trying to do. Their friendship and professional rivalry was based on brutal honesty with each other about their work. In this essay, for example, Michael pointed out that the middle section – 'This Is the Part Called Sickness' – did not work, especially the Nish stories, which allowed little room for sympathy. He thought the other stories in this section leaned too much towards the stereotypical.

Michael was more familiar with the discontinuous narrative form, and so was better equipped to approach it critically. Against the view that the individual stories lacked conventional unity and closure, Michael stated: 'The success of Moorhouse's stories comes from their lack of such explicitness, from their assembling by hint, association, by a careful cumulative process.' And against the view that the narrative as a whole lacked continuity, Michael stated: 'Plotting for a bohemian milieu is a severe problem . . .

In societies liberated from the social norms, the plots for depicting social normalcy are irrelevant.'

Michael concluded by suggesting the broad intent of Frank's project:

> Behind all these stories lies the ethic of being true to oneself, breaking with delusions and deceits: the occasional three- and four-letter words, the occasionally aberrant activities, are all in the service of this quest for the honest way, are presented to us not to shock, but to ask for a new, truer, fairer way of life. His characters would probably arraign him for it, but the impulse behind their writer is that of the moralist.

9

'The Stories Aren't Dirty Enough'

Mike Thornhill attended the Second Annual Balmain Reading of Poetry and Prose in November 1968, where he heard Frank read 'The American Poet's Visit'. A couple of days later, he started thinking about making a short film based on Frank's story. Mike was working then as a freelance film and sound editor, and teaching a course on film at the University of New South Wales. Several larger film projects of his had recently stalled, so he decided to make a short film. He did not want to make an art film, which was fashionable at the time, but rather a straightforward narrative. Frank's story seemed a good fit.

Frank was intentionally uninvolved in the project. He justified his decision by citing the auteur theory of film, by which the director had the right to do what they wanted with the source material: to consider the original work as a starting point only, and to take it in any direction they wished. The script Frank and Mike had worked on together that February had been abandoned, as Frank had become uncomfortable returning to a work that was ostensibly already complete. He had found reworking the material and transposing it from one medium to another difficult, and it made him anxious. He was in no hurry to repeat that experience.

Mike teamed up instead with Ken Quinnell, and in December – around the time 'The American Poet's Visit' was published in *Southerly* – they wrote a script, using about two-thirds of the dialogue from the original story and adding the rest themselves, consistent with Frank's style and intent, which was to create a satire of the Push. As Mike said the following year, when interviewed about the film by *Masque* magazine: 'The story was a gentle social satire. Rexroth is seen as an aging political activist, the locals as armchair philosophers who espouse permanent protest rather than reformism.'

Mike was always peripheral to the Push. He did not consider himself a member, and so was not as invested in mythologising the movement as some others were. When Frank was asked about the film in an interview with *The Australian*, he said: 'There is satire, not directed at the American poet, but at our behaviour, the Australian behaviour. The story is self mocking.'

The twenty-minute film was shot over two weekends in January 1969. The editing and soundtrack were completed in four days in May. Mike calculated that a professional short film would cost $4000 to $5000, but they produced *The American Poet's Visit*, auspiced through *The Sydney Cinema Journal*, for only $900. The film was shot in black and white, not for aesthetic reasons but because it was cheaper to develop, required less lighting equipment and meant that less time was spent on establishing the shots on set. Russell Boyd was the cinematographer.

The set itself was a single room, but the cast was large and at times unwieldy, not being professional actors. There were five leads, five supports and about forty extras – the partygoers. Most of the people in the film were the same people who had attended the original Push party in 1967, including Roelof Smilde, Darcy Waters, Sandra Grimes and Sandra Levy. It was John Flaus's first time acting. John Rybak played Kenneth Rexroth, because he was the only American on hand.

The extras grew bored on set and drank too much. Parts of the film were ad-libbed conversations which Mike caught on camera, later editing them into the final cut. But when it came to the script, he pushed the actors to follow their lines. He was accused of being a tyrant and a dictator.

One interaction during the first weekend of shooting set the tone for the whole shoot. Albie Thoms, an underground filmmaker who had been at the original party, was cast as an underground filmmaker. During his scene, he asked Mike: 'What's my motivation?' When relaying the incident a few months later, Mike said: 'Not knowing anything about psychological realism, I wasn't, I'm afraid, of much assistance.' Actors basically playing themselves, re-enacting a party they had attended, and yet not knowing their own motivations was precisely the lack of self-consciousness Frank's story was satirising. But Thoms did not appreciate this, complaining on set, as Mike later relayed in his interview, that it 'wasn't cool to put your own scene down, man'.

The broader target for the satire of 'The American Poet's Visit' was Australia's relationship with the United States, which Frank saw as being based on forms of mimicry. In December 1968, he delivered a paper at the Student Power Conference on the topic 'Mimicry in Australian Politics'. It was a companion piece to his 1966 paper, 'Demonstrations and Civil Disobedience'.

The notion that Australia was a mimic culture had long occupied Frank's thinking. In *The Lucky Country*, Donald Horne criticised Australians for not originating ideas on their own, but simply copying them from other countries. Horne associated this with 'a limited view of the possible' in the Australian character, adding:

> [B]ut if something new is demonstrated as being possible – and this demonstration often takes place in a more innovatory country overseas – then they accept it. Good-oh. The Yanks can do it. We'll have a go at it too. What they find it difficult to do is to imagine the new for themselves.

Frank accepted this analysis, but saw it as a baseline only. He drew upon his own practice and understanding of creativity to add a more positive interpretation of mimicry, and a new line of criticism. For him, the starting point of any creative act involved some degree of imitation, and it was only from within this initial act of mimicry that a point of difference or originality could be achieved. Frank noted the 'novice artist's imitation of the style of a master as a way to personal originality or at least competence'. So Frank did not consider mimicry as indicating a lack of imagination per se, but rather as an inadequate or foreclosed use of the imagination, one that fails to go beyond imitation and into difference, from copy to originality and, finally, self-competence.

Frank's new line of criticism was that Australians rarely took this second step, and so failed to achieve self-competence:

> The mimicing of overseas cultural ferment helps classify our sort of culture but also contains the contradictions that there is an ever-increasing loss, diminution of the distinction between *foreign* and *local*. Our mimicry does distinguish our culture while at the same time making it superficially more difficult to recognise.

Frank's positive, critical interpretation of mimicry was, for him, a process of recognising what was uniquely Australian, what he paradoxically called the 'Australian synthesis'. 'Australia is heavily a mimic culture,' Frank wrote. 'We are unique only in the special blend of external influences which we create – the Australian synthesis.'

Frank's main focus was with the 'Americanisation of the Left protest groups'. Superficially, this was expressed through personal ornaments – lapel badges, pendants, long hair, 'message tee-shirts', and posters (Dylan, Che Guevara and so on), all of which were copied from American culture. Another area of concern was the importation of American folk and protest music. Such music was 'totally unrelated both in surface reality and in spirit to Australian conditions', Frank argued. 'Our racial situation, our industrial conditions, and our political style could not be related to the songs imported from the States.' Here he was repeating arguments he had made in the late 1950s, and ideas expressed by John Baker in a

1963 lecture at the Sydney Left Club, regarding the marginalisation of Australian folk music.

Such mimicry went deeper, and informed political ideas and actions, often disregarding local contexts. Frank drew upon a recently published book by Wolfgang Wickler, *Mimicry in Plants and Animals* (1968), which argued that mimicry occurred in nature, among animals and insects, as a strategy for survival, for protection, 'to fool predatory third parties'. Australian political cultures, particularly dissenting ones, initially required such protection, Frank argued, as Australia had a smaller, more dispersed population. So they mimicked American forms of protest in order to overcome 'isolation and impotence', to overcome being numerically small and ineffectual in Australia, to build morale and to feel they were part of something larger, something international. 'In so far as mimicry of overseas movements is dramatic – that is, an acting of these movements rather than a response to actual conditions – mimicry is perhaps a way of learning, of going through a phase of development, growth play,' he wrote. But although initially valuable, such mimicry, if its development stalled at this initial stage, risked remaining blind to actual local conditions and soliciting inadequate political responses.

The central example in Frank's notes on political mimicry and its limitations concerned Aboriginal affairs. Frank Hardy's recent book *The Unlucky Australians* (1968) documented the events of 1966 involving Aboriginal stockmen at the Northern Territory cattle station Wave Hill, and the subsequent march, led by Vincent Lingiari, to Wattie Creek, to reclaim traditional Gurindji land. In a Left publication, ostensibly reviewing this book, Frank cited the reviewer's conclusion: 'Black power is at long last becoming a real issue in Australian politics and it is convenient to consider it in the context of student power.'

Frank saw this as attempting to shoehorn a traditional labour dispute, combined with a new awareness of Australian Aboriginal land rights, into the language of American civil rights. 'The article, together with other articles in this and other left publications strained to use the vocabulary of black power and student power,'

Frank wrote. It therefore missed what was unique to the local context – Australian Aboriginal land rights – and it limited the effectiveness of that vocabulary to fully understand or further this local cause in any meaningful way.

To support this contention, Frank cited an article he had commissioned as editor of *The Australian Highway* in 1965: 'A White Man's Blindness', by John Powles. The author had been vice president of the Student Action for Aborigines. Frank recalled Powles' experience of white Australian students becoming aware of racial discrimination through hearing about the discrimination of African Americans in the United States. They adopted tactics of protest from the American model, in order to demonstrate at US embassies in Australia, in solidarity with the cause for American civil rights. But, as Powles stated: 'From the US came a reply: "Thanks for your support but what about the Australian Aborigines?"' Only then did Australian students begin the Student Action for Aborigines. Even then, one of the first actions they performed was the Freedom Ride in February 1965, a bus tour of regional New South Wales towns, in an effort to draw national and international media attention to racial inequality in Australia and the poor living conditions of Aboriginal people. This was, as Frank noted, in imitation of the 1961 Freedom Ride in the United States, an act of mimicry with diminishing returns.

What was blocking Australia from taking the next step, Frank argued, from mimicry to self-competence, were the Australian political movements and local media mutually reinforcing each other, which foreclosed the political will and imagination of each. Local protest movements performed actions that were proven overseas to have gained media attention. When they gained the attention of local media, this reinforced the strategy of mimicry. But what these movements misunderstood was that they were gaining the media attention for very different reasons than their overseas models. The Australian media, Frank argued, was itself operating under the conditions of a mimic culture: Australian journalists and editors simply saw what was considered 'news' overseas, then sought out the same or similar stories in the Australian context.

And Australian protestors were only too happy to comply. A symbiotic relationship was thus created, one providing the performance, the other providing the script, regardless of either's purchase on local reality.

Against this, Frank argued for the next step to be taken, towards a 'Grand Synthesis', which he defined as a 'creative and original blend of European-American-Asian influences' – and he gestured also towards the unique influence of Australian Aboriginal culture – in the formation of what could be a unique 'Australian synthesis'.

In November 1968, Frank had given notice to the ABC of his intention to resign. He had been planning this for six months. Even as he was putting the finishing touches on his first book – which he did right up until his resignation – he was already thinking of his next. 'Interestingly,' he had written to Michael Wilding in July, 'I have discerned three main preoccupations in my stories over the last year – firstly, a concern with various characters I've created, secondly, a fascination with contraception!!! And thirdly, a fascination with American-Australian relationships. The other development is a switch to humour. One or some of these lines will be the basis for a new book.' A month later, to demonstrate his new direction, he sent Michael a draft of a long story, called 'Five Incidents', comprising vignettes about various characters, not quite young, coping with ageing, sex and the augurs of death.

When Frank finally left the ABC, he told Michael he was doing so 'with a certain elation and a certain sense of doom'. The latter was his 'inevitable poverty without employment prospects'. 'But the elation comes from the idea of being free from the routine of journalism, and an unstable excitement about my new book "The Americans, baby" – a discontinuous narrative with strong political preoccupations.' This was the first time he mentioned a title for his new project.

In resigning from the ABC, Frank wanted to open himself up to possibilities and unpredictable experiences. He planned on living on $46 per week and to write for one year. His last day at the

ABC was on Friday, 17 January 1969 – soon after Mike Thornhill wrapped up shooting *The American Poet's Visit*, and shortly before Frank's first book was published. Full-time employment had always provided Frank with an external structure to regulate his life, and distract him from his inner dilemmas. Five years earlier, when he resigned from the WEA, it took six months before a personal crisis necessitated eighteen months' psychotherapy. This time, it took Frank less than a month before, in February 1969, he felt compelled to write to his previous therapist, pleading: 'I seem to be having a number of personal crises which suggest that I resume psychotherapy.'

This was, in part, brought on by the publication of *Futility and Other Animals*, and the public collision, both real and imagined, of various social worlds Frank had previously kept compartmentalised. In particular, all the anxieties regarding his family came to the surface, pulling him towards them and repelling him at the same time. The first letters he wrote home are no longer extant. His father's replies do exist and indicate that Frank made his parents fully aware of his psychological distress. In March, Frank Sr replied:

> Yes my dear – we are fully aware of your unhappiness over the past years . . . wishing we could do something to help – we are here – your own loved ones waiting – & believe you me Owen & Arthur are concerned also – perhaps if you could talk things over with us – an outlet is what is needed, not bottle it up – we are certainly willing to listen and help – glad you are having help – never lose faith – have something to hang on to – and remember as I have said before – we need you as much as you need us.

By April, Frank's condition had worsened. His father wrote to him, saying he had wept 'tears of anguish' thinking about Frank's situation: 'We have lived through the same problems perhaps,' he wrote.

> Mum and I certainly have heavy hearts and feel we have failed you somehow in our lives. We feel that you do not experience the joy of

coming home . . . I fear sometimes that you are too much like me. I have been through periods of dreadful depression and have come to be very careful that these periods do not warp my thinking. Having a home to come to often helps and we want you always to feel that you can come home.

In June, Frank explicitly stated he was not going to return to Nowra ever again. 'Our apartness is a complicated emotional problem which cannot I feel altogether be resolved although there is no suggestion on my part of talking in terms of blame or responsibility,' he wrote to his parents. 'The problem is somewhere in my personality and the unchangeable events of my childhood.' And then, the break:

> The resumption of closer ties with you and the families of Owen and Arthur is probably difficult if not impossible. Partly because of the widely varying views of life and ways of life, and partly because of the embarrassment a 'wayward' son in a country town could be. I hope though we can remain in communication . . . Psychologically it is partly because I live, unconsciously, in great fear of you – and Owen. It is a deep and painful fear, and although not conscious most of the time, is difficult to dialogue.

Much of this was initiated by the publication of *Futility and Other Animals*, and the anticipation of the media reporting surrounding it. Frank feared his parents were being exposed to parts of his life he had otherwise kept from them. He admitted the strange paths he had followed in his life might seem in conflict with the paths taken by his parents and brothers. As if defending himself to some invisible tribunal, he laid out in his letters home his professional résumé, his reputation as a short-story writer, his work as a journalist, his role at the WEA and his contribution to 'the intellectual life of Sydney'. 'Nor is it basically a life far from your ideals,' he stated. 'My concern for education comes from you, although I interpreted it slightly differently, my respect for inquiry comes from you, and the values you taught me.'

Regarding his book, Frank conceded that it might seem on the surface to be obscene, but that it was the product of 'sound craftsman ship' and 'honest attempts at exploration of the human personality'. Frank wrote:

> I hope the book apart from giving pleasure to those who read my type of fiction, will also liberate or help liberate some people from guilt and distress over sexual matters. I suffered from sexual ignorance and a fear of sex however I fully realise how difficult if not impossible it would have been for you to help me on this matter not only because of your own personal reticence, but also because as an adolescent it became so difficult for us to communicate.

A week later, Frank received a letter from his mother. She avoided mentioning his assumed break from the family, and instead, as his father had done, offered only unconditional support. 'You are our son and always will be – your life is yours to live as you wish . . . I hope and pray you will be given peace of mind – when you have this you will have happiness,' she wrote.

Two days after writing his final letter to his parents, Frank contacted his psychotherapist. In February, this therapist had referred Frank to a colleague, but Frank had never heard from that man. Only in June did Frank contact his therapist again, telling him the referral never eventuated. 'I left it a few weeks and then wrote a letter to him asking if there'd been some confusion about appointments and the arrangements,' he explained. 'He didn't answer. Because of a degree of demoralisation on my part I let it slide.' Frank requested the referral be chased up or he be given a referral to another therapist, but to no avail.

For five months Frank had needed professional care, but none was forthcoming. During that period, and in that emotional state, he severed ties with his family, causing much needless distress to them, but most of all to himself.

In February 1969, Frank had a new story published in the magazine *Man*. 'The Supersonic Coward' was a riff on the idea that if a technology is pushed far enough, its purpose and effect will eventually flip into its opposite. Or, as the narrator states early in the story: 'The very machines which were the means for extending the power of man's limbs also tore them from him.'

Chris is not only scared of flying, but is obsessed with the notion that an airplane will fall out of the sky, crash on him and kill him. These fears are played out in the story, first at work – when his boss wants him to fly to Melbourne for a conference, but Chris prefers to take the train – and then at home – when his wife becomes increasingly concerned that he is risking his standing at work by refusing to fly. Chris is accused, in short, of being a coward – a supersonic coward – for not keeping pace with advances in technology and speed, for not conforming to the culture they have precipitated and for being too eccentric in his personal views.

Meanwhile, the reviews of *Futility and Other Animals* had only exacerbated Frank's distress and self-imposed estrangement from his family. His only solace was in writing, working on material for his next book. A few months later, in the June edition of *Chance*, he had another new story published. 'The Coca Cola Kid' introduced the character Becker, an American who was an executive for the Coca-Cola Company and was stationed in regional Australia. In the story, Coca-Cola stands, by synecdoche, for American imperialism, international capitalism and the Americanisation of Australian (mimic) culture more generally. It was the first in a series of six stories Frank wrote in early 1969 based around Becker.

The story draws on Frank's experiences in Wagga, where he met a Coca-Cola executive at a Young Liberals social event, and his reporting on Sheekey's, the locally owned soft drink and ice manufacturer that had operated in the town since 1925. He was writing at this time under the influence of Barthelme, who had, Frank felt, a 'fascination with the nomenclature of the popular culture world, the brand names'. In Frank's story, the popular cultural effect of the Coca-Cola brand is levelled against the more local manufacturers, who reside outside of such popular culture. Incidentally, a year before Frank started working on his Coca Cola Kid stories, the Nowra Cordial & Ice Works, with which he had grown up, drinking their aerated soft drinks as a child, had burned to the ground, ending the era of locally produced cordials and soft drinks.

Frank had finished other stories, some of which he showed Don Anderson. In July, Don took the carbon-copy typescript of those stories on his WEA regional tour. He was accompanied by Stephen Knight, who was also reading *Futility and Other Animals*. Stephen wrote to Frank from the road. 'I think I find the homosexual-oriented stories the most arresting,' he said, referring to *Futility*, 'perhaps because stories of that sort that I've read before tend to have a rather shrill note of propaganda about them, whereas you seem to have objectified the whole thing very well.' But it was the new draft stories, which Don had shown Stephen, that most interested him. 'The Coca Cola Kid' bothered him at first reading, but the second time through he liked it more. He found one of the other Becker stories to be more immediately arresting.

'Becker and the Boys' follows the Coca Cola Kid's recruiting of an Australian band to perform a jingle for a local commercial. He feels he has been professionally pushed to one side, exiled to Australia. He takes tranquilisers to calm his nerves, and finds Australian culture utterly boring – even at parties with transvestites. There are dark themes in the story, but the narration is pitched to a more comic tone. Stephen found this aspect of Frank's new material refreshing, and a distinct break from the stories in *Futility*.

Another example of this, which Stephen and Don read on the road, was a draft story called 'The Girl Who Met Simone de Beauvoir in Paris'. It is a satire on male insecurity in the face of the growing influence of feminism in Australia. Another story in Don and Stephen's cache of typescript drafts was 'The Revolutionary Kidney Punch', referencing the 1966 visit of President Johnson to Australia and the protests in Sydney. In this story, Frank brought together his theme of Australia as a mimic culture – in this case, he focused on the disjuncture between American folk songs performed in an Australian political context – and his arguments against the efficacy of political demonstrations.

'I think if you're planning to use these stories in another book,' Stephen wrote to Frank, 'then you'll get a good coherence among them.' He added a wry word of encouragement: 'If you feel there's no point in writing, recall that your stories cheered me up one Friday in Wagga and made Anderson late for his dinner, and if that doesn't make the Nobel prize look small what does?' Then Stephen turned back to the *Squire* case, at which he had testified in in Frank's defence: 'Having typed you this report I am now ready to reconsider Det. Sgt Whitehead's inquiry about your position vis a vis Shakespeare.'

Since Frank left the ABC, his annual income had dropped from $5700 the previous year to $1500 in 1969. His savings had not stretched as far as he had hoped, so he needed additional work. From April to May of that year, he taught his weekly Editors and Writers course at the WEA. He received a $2000 grant from the New South Wales government to work on his second book.

He also applied to the Commonwealth Literary Fund, proposing that he travel to Vietnam for up to two months to interview soldiers, 'absorbing something of the situation'. He explicitly stated he did not want to go as a journalist, but to 'go essentially as a *fiction writer*. I want to absorb and fictionalise, not report.' This would be background for his project The Americans, Baby, which was about the 'American-Australian relationship – not in a political sense but with the atmosphere of cultural change which comes from it'. He also wanted to examine 'Australian-Asian relations'. But his application was rejected, with the CLF stating that it was 'outside the scope of the Fund's activities' for Frank to travel to Vietnam during a war.

That year the Australian Society of Authors surveyed its 846 members, and the results provide some context to Frank's position within his cohort. Forty-three per cent claimed that writing was their 'only or principal source of income'. Frank was among the 24 per cent who published short stories in newspapers or magazines, the 34 per cent who did freelance journalism and the

15 per cent who did public lectures. Although 64 per cent of writers were male and 35 per cent were female – similar to the ratio among American writers at the time – the figure was more evenly split for those writing fiction, which accounted for 39 per cent of the total. The rest, mainly male writers, wrote non-fiction. Frank was among the 23 per cent who had published both nationally and internationally, the majority publishing only in Australia. He was among the 12 per cent who were under thirty-five years of age, with 65 per cent of respondents being over forty-five years old. In the aggregate, Frank was very much in a minority position, even within the small Australian writing community.

Frank took a close interest in the ASA's survey, and he considered seriously its proposed recommendations for the improvement of the writer's lot. One was for some form of public lending rights (PLR), to reimburse authors whose books were held in libraries and made freely available. This was a problem Vance Palmer had noted in the 1930s. The ASA had submitted a proposal for a PLR scheme to the Attorney-General and the Sydney Chief Librarians' Committee, but it was rejected. Since 1964, the ASA had a subcommittee lobbying for an expansion of the Commonwealth Literary Fund, both in scope and funding, and it continued to do so each year. In 1967, it managed to secure increased funding for literary journals. The CLF funded six full-time fellowships, which the ASA lobbied to be increased to provide a living wage for the duration of the fellowship. Another area of focus for the ASA was trying to get freelance writers, and the publications using freelance writers – newspapers, magazines, radio, television – to re-examine their rates of pay and ensure they were equitable.

In short, by 1969 Australian writers were still seeking a just reward for their literary work, consistent with the use and value made of that work by the public and educational institutions. They needed more money in order to write in the first place. Little had changed since the days of Marcus Clarke or Henry Lawson.

Twelve months earlier, when he resigned from the ABC, Frank told Michael Wilding he planned to write a long essay on the cultural function of newspapers. The result was a 9000-word report published under the title 'Now Here Is the News . . .' in the *Current Affairs Bulletin* in November 1969.

Frank had been reading the *CAB* regularly for half his life. It was the publication he read throughout high school – to prepare himself for his planned career as a journalist, to expand his general knowledge and to keep abreast of current events. So it was fitting that, nearly fifteen years later, Frank would write this critical evaluation of the news media in Australia for the *CAB*, drawing on his experience in the industry, his research and lecturing on the sociology of the media, and his views on the formation of social attitudes, through ever-changing communications technologies. The report was described by the *CAB* as Frank's farewell to journalism, ending his perilous compromise – he was 'a young Australian writer turned from journalism'.

Frank's initial target was what he called 'journalistic mystique': the capacity of 'news sense', of assuming to know what was and what was not considered news, while also adopting a posture of objectivity, of fair hearing, or the empirical interpretation of the bare facts. Frank argued that this was simply cover for an unexamined, subjective and institutionally self-reinforcing criteria. Cadet journalists were inculcated by their subeditorial staff towards adopting this unexamined criteria, and so on, up the chain, and hardened into certain habits of mind. 'News values tend thus to be self-perpetuating within an organisation,' Frank argued. These values remained unexpressed, though, and so were rarely examined self-consciously or self-critically. In this, journalists typically adopted a 'guardian' position, defending a particular set of orthodox values, positions and sentiments: the status quo. In the Australian political landscape, this meant journalists 'naturally never reach beyond those reflected in the orthodox political parties'.

Another target was, in maintaining this status quo, the lazy journalistic assumption that national associations or peak bodies represented whole classes of people, as though the population were constituted of homogenous blocks. This practice was related to the time pressures on journalists, on the one hand, and to the growing complexity of the society they covered, on the other, which forced them to approach the same, official sources for comment, which they knew would be readily available. In this way, newspapers created the impression that all doctors held only one view, as stated by the Australian Medical Association; or that all ex-servicemen shared the same attitudes and opinions as told by the Returned & Services League (RSL). 'Seeking the plurality is a difficult task and a confusing one,' Frank argued, 'pressures of news dissemination and the human desire for an orderly set of information work against it.' This desire underpinned the rise of public relations as an industry, Frank noted, with 'news release' and 'press kits' ready to assist time-pressured journalists with prefabricated and simplified stories. In this new equation, the public relations man ceased to be an intermediary, becoming the source itself. They blocked journalists from finding their own stories, and from evaluating and corroborating alternative sources.

A final topic Frank addressed was the question of 'the masses'. Coincidentally, while Frank was preparing this *CAB* report, his 1966 *SCJ* essay, 'Teaching the Masses Their Media', was republished by *Screen Education* in the United Kingdom and *Kino* in New Zealand. That essay was concerned with the mass media generally, and with popular culture in particular, while in his *CAB* report Frank looked at the link between the masses, their media and the news.

Frank argued that the traditional model of journalism – with its postures of objectivity, impartiality, fair hearing and accuracy – was predicated upon a process of *informing* an individual reader, a 'model of the rational-democratic man'. This assumed a one-way view of communication. But Frank drew upon recent sociological research which suggested such a model was wrong. Individuals were group-based, modifying information depending on the values of the group of which they were members, and which they wished to protect. On this model, less individualistic and less rational people were 'fixed in their ways', 'do not like unpleasant ideas' and would only 'hear what they want to hear', according to the values of their group. Psychologically, they were motivated by compliance – seeking reward and avoiding punishment – and they identified with organisations or figures of authority that represented the group faithfully. In this, the one-way view of communication was flawed, with a more accurate depiction being a two-way tension between media and audience.

Frank noted a shift in the subjects of media, with public figures increasingly being crowded out by journalists seeking out private citizens for comment. Talkback radio, on-the-street interviews, write-in programs, camera crews going inside people's houses, game shows based on personal relationships: more and more ordinary people were becoming consumed by the news instead of simply consuming the news. '[M]ass media has meant that not only do more people *read* or *view* news,' Frank observed, 'but that more people are *reported* as news.' But in doing so, they are being reported on not as individuals, but as representatives of a particular group or type of person, within which their individuality was otherwise subsumed.

In concluding, Frank quoted Marshall McLuhan on newspapers being read 'in order to plunge, to involve yourself in the communal bathtub. Nobody reads a newspaper intelligently or critically. That's not what it is for. It's there for a communal sense of sharing something, for splashing around in.' Frank corroborated this by citing a report by Hugh Mackay, an Australian communications theorist, which argued that people used the media, firstly, to occupy their time, as content to pepper their daily conversations, and secondly, as part of a search for self-identity, an expression of their personalities: 'in the simplest possible terms the viewers' response to the mass media is really their response to themselves; they are using the media only to make clear to themselves what kind of people they are and what beliefs, opinions and attitudes they hold'.

A subtext to Frank's analysis of the news reflected his circumstances growing up in Nowra, and his early experiences of the role of local media, particularly *The Shoalhaven News*. This included his family's ongoing engagement with the press, both for business purposes – advertising and advertorials for Moorhouse the Machinery Man – and for their social concerns – Rotary, the CWA, the Red Cross, the Girl Guides and Boy Scouts, peak bodies and civic organisations with their regular 'news releases' and dedicated columns. Frank's experience of his childhood was often mediated through these outlets: he read community stories, the social pages, reports of his brothers' adventures and his own misadventures. Now, in 1969, especially with *Futility and Other Animals* coming out, Frank's name was once more appearing in the news media – not as a by-lined reporter but as the subject being reported on – and Frank's family's experience of him was being mediated through the press.

Frank did not go to Nowra for Christmas that year, but he had resumed communications with his family. In December, after his thirty-first birthday, Frank even contacted Owen, then forty-one years old. Frank said he had been thinking about the distance between them. 'Of course it comes from a long way back and is related to my problems as a child with mum and dad,' Frank wrote, 'and almost certainly with you (what the psychiatrists I guess would call sibling rivalry).' For his part, Frank regretted the distance, suggesting it was due, in part, to the 'compulsion of personality' and his own 'difficult development'. Frank also suggested it was due to Owen's 'ideas' – meaning his political views and general outlook – which differed greatly from Frank's.

Owen's reply came in the New Year, saying it was 'true we could hardly be classed as regular correspondents but nevertheless a bond exists'. He agreed they lived in different worlds, Frank in the literary world, Owen in the world of business and manufacturing. 'No doubt our age gap accounts for some of this gap and coupled with a single purposed desire to individually succeed in our fields probably makes us "rugged individualists",' Owen wrote.

But Owen's interpretation of their distance contradicted Frank's. Frank thought their distance was due to them being so different, but Owen suggested it was because they were similar:

Certainly no animosity exists from my side and I have never considered the possibility of any from yours – just an awareness of your devotion [to what] you were and are doing which is understood more by me than perhaps anybody else as it consumes your every quiet moment to dream anew ample to whatever the job is in hand and the rest of the world slips by along with time.

Frank was still drawn to the South Coast region, even if he avoided Nowra. Since his personal crisis, and in the absence of psychiatric help, Frank attempted his own makeshift regimen to regain his mental equilibrium. He threw himself into his work, but frequently took time off to drive inland or along the coast, revisiting his old regional haunts. He started spearfishing, though 'unsuccessfully'. He was drawn to small-town life, wanting to escape from the bustle of the city. He had cultivated a sense of community in Balmain, but that lacked distance and landscapes. Around this time, he travelled to Yass to interview the editor of the local newspaper, and he felt a strong sentimental and nostalgic kick for the life he could have had: in a small town, working at a local newspaper, in a domestic marriage. 'But jesus,' he wrote soon after in a letter, 'I just sat there in his sun verandah and yearned for it.'

As part of his regimen, Frank returned to various adolescent pursuits and interests. He started painting again, which he had not done since he was in Wagga in 1958. With the initial cheque from the sale of *Futility* he bought himself a Winchester lever-action rifle, like he had seen in cowboy movies when he was a kid, and took up target shooting.

Shooting, spearfishing and painting were all solo pursuits for Frank, and he did not want an audience. These practices were ends in themselves, and not some means towards bettering or selling himself. 'It's the first time I've been able to break my father's iron training that everything one did had to relate to either business or self-promotion,' he observed.

The cache of stories Don Anderson and Stephen Knight read on the road in mid-1969 included 'The Coca Cola Kid', since published in *Chance*, and 'Becker and the Boys', which remained unpublished. Since then, Frank had written four more stories about Becker.

'Becker on the Moon' contrasts life in an American city with the Australian outback. Becker meets Terri and her father, 'Rotarian T. George McDowell', in another story, 'The St Louis Rotary Convention 1923, Recalled'. As Becker is to Coca-Cola, so McDowell is to technology: he refers to himself as a 'technological missionary'. In another story, 'Soft Drink and the Distribution of Soft Drink', Becker, attending a seminar sponsored by Coca-Cola, downplays the negative associations of Coca-Cola with American imperialism and bad teeth, while Terri, amid this conservative, business crowd, defends the need for women's liberation.

The final story in the cycle, 'Jesus Said to Watch for 28 Signs', sees Becker fired from his job at Coca-Cola. Later that night, drunk, he shows up at Terri's place, where he drops acid for the first time. He considers the twenty-eight signs he should have noticed and acted upon, referring back to events from the other stories in the series that have led to this moment. With this, Frank completed his six-story cycle, a discontinuous narrative regarding the Coca Cola Kid.

In June 1969, the American novel *Portnoy's Complaint* (1969), by Philip Roth, was banned in Australia. Later that year, at the University of New South Wales, the Kensington Libertarians, including Wendy Bacon, pushed for the abolition of the Student University Council. Their opponents argued that this would result in the cutting of essential student services, such as the student newspaper, *Tharunka*. Not backing down, Wendy decided to prove it was possible to publish an independent student newspaper.

Thor-out was hastily put together over two weekends by Wendy and a handful of libertarian and anarchist students, assisted by some of the figures behind *Uphill*, including Frank. It was financed and published by Roelof Smilde. A key component of the publication was its use of offset printing, a relatively new technological innovation that allowed publishers to print in-house, bypassing professional printers altogether. The publisher kept control over production and so could avoid censorship. 'Offset printing means the shifting of emphasis for intellectual and imaginative writers, from the traditional quarterly, to the faster, cheaper offset publication – usually a tabloid,' Frank later wrote. 'It accelerates the movement of ideas [and] de-sanctifies imaginative writing.'

The success of *Thor-out* resulted in Wendy Bacon, Alan Rees and Val Hodgson being elected in early 1970 as editors of *Tharunka*. The Student University Council, which they had once tried to abolish, now provided them with a small budget, office space and on-campus facilities. The new editors encouraged contributors from outside the university to refashion the publication into a general newspaper for Sydney intellectuals. One compromise they endured was the use of professional printers.

The third edition of *Tharunka*, in March 1970, contained the forty-nine couplets of a bawdy folk poem titled 'The Ballad of Eskimo Nell'. Its opening salvo:

When a man grows old and his balls grow cold and the end of his nob turns blue.

When it's bent in the middle like a one-string fiddle, he can tell a yarn or two.

So find me a seat and stand me a drink and a tale to you I'll tell,
Of Dead-Eye Dick and Mexico Pete and the gentle Eskimo Nell.

The Office of Student Publications, on seeing the proofs, sought legal advice, which counselled that it would be prosecuted if it published the ballad. The editors were instructed not to publish. Meanwhile, the printer had independently decided not to proceed, not just because of 'Eskimo Nell' but because of other content as well, which it arbitrarily deemed obscene. Hemmed in on two sides, yet unperturbed, the editors secured another printer and the edition was published.

On the day of publication, an on-campus meeting was called for the editors to explain their actions. Two thousand people appeared, overwhelmingly supporting the publication. It was condemned in the mainstream press and by the state government, which only fuelled awareness and interest of the newspaper, especially off-campus, and its circulation rose from 13,000 to 17,000 copies sold.

There was a palpable sense of liberation in seeing such a sexually explicit – and, for some, obscene – poem in print, beyond the mere content of the ballad. The editing, writing and publishing of *Tharunka* was largely done by young women. A decade earlier, in libertarian circles, the *Broadsheet* was an entirely male affair. Women were allowed to type each edition, but were not invited to write for it – Germaine Greer was a notable, and one-time, exception. But in 1970 Greer published *The Female Eunuch* and Kate Millet published *Sexual Politics*. Second-wave feminism was on the rise. 'Eskimo Nell' was already widely known by men in its oral form – in male-only enclaves such as dressing rooms, sporting clubs and so on – but here it had been brought into the public arena, exposing male juvenilities and, as it was mainly men in authority who were rushing to condemn its publication, hypocrisies.

For Frank, an added layer of interest in seeing an oral work appear in print was its illustration of how different mediums created different cultural effects. This was tapping into the *Bulletin* tradition of the 1890s, which brought the vernacular into the mass media, but *Tharunka* was disrupting conventions rather than establishing them. Its success in reaching a broad audience off-campus proved to Frank that it was possible to achieve what he and others had tried to do with previous publications, such as *City Voices* and *Uphill*.

This gave Frank an idea, and so in April, in the very next issue of *Tharunka*, he included an eight-page supplement of fiction, made up of pieces not published elsewhere due to censorship concerns. This was Frank's iteration of A.G. Stephens' Red Page. The literary supplement published work from twelve authors, including Thomas Keneally, A.D. Hope, Thomas Shapcott and Michael Wilding.

Two pieces that were called out by the media and government for particular censure were an excerpt from Frank Hardy's unpublished 'The Outcasts of Foolgarah' and a new short story by Frank called 'Letters to Twiggy'.

Frank's story followed the one-sided correspondence of a male fan of the British model and actor Twiggy. This anonymous fan was of the same lineage as Nish, the grotesque from Frank's first book. But the underlying theme of this story played on Frank's 1966 *SCJ* essays on popular culture. Frank had argued there that people's adulation of film stars and their sex lives was not linked to 'reality' but to a knowing sense of 'unreality'. In 'Letters to Twiggy', Frank satirised such para-social relationships between fans and celebrities, showing the negative consequences when the distinction between reality and unreality is lost.

Frank's introduction to this literary supplement positioned him within the broader *Tharunka* project, and he articulated his views on the role of fiction within the larger project of liberation from censorship: 'The censoring of the obscene and erotic is part of the political suppression of all counter-cultures – of alternatives to the State and the "Australian way of life."' Or, as he put it, more succinctly: 'ESKIMO NELLS everywhere have to be liberated.'

In the June edition of *Tharunka*, the editors printed a poem titled 'Cunt is a Christian Word', taken from an American underground newspaper, *Horseshit*. Frank saw the poem as dealing with the 'crippling nature of virginity', but the authorities saw it as simply obscene. The editors, the Director of Student Publications and the printer, Rotary Offset Pty Ltd, were all issued summonses.

That same month, the federal Liberal government's Minister for Customs, Don Chipp, spoke out in parliament against Australia's current censorship regime, on the principle that it constrained individual liberty. At the same time he introduced a classification system for films in Australia that would allow for their greater distribution, while also providing individuals with a way to regulate their own viewing.

In August, the *Tharunka* case was heard at the Central Court of Sydney. The printer pleaded guilty, accepted a $200 fine and gave an assurance that it would never work with *Tharunka* again. The other defendants were less cooperative. A man in a gorilla suit, led by a trainer, accompanied Wendy Bacon and three other women, each of them wearing a nun's habit with a slogan emblazoned across it: 'Cunt Is a Christian Word', 'A Dry Cunt Is a Safe Cunt', 'I Am a Mother Fucking Christian Cunt', while Wendy's habit read 'I Have Been Fucked by God's Steel Prick'. They had the offending poem printed on leaflets, which they distributed to passers-by from the courthouse steps. Wendy refused to remove the habit before entering the premises and so was charged with a further count of obscenity.

It became untenable to publish *Tharunka* under the auspices of the university, so a new newspaper, produced off-campus, was created. In September 1970, *Thorunka* was born, channelling the original, independent *Thor-out*. Some of the staff of *Tharunka* continued to produce the 'official' student newspaper while working on *Thorunka*, but others – including Bacon – left to work solely on the new project.

In August 1969, Penguin had decided to defy the national ban on *Portnoy's Complaint*, and by September 75,000 copies had been printed and distributed across Australia. The Angus & Robertson chain of bookshops – the retail arm of the Angus & Robertson publishing company – stocked the novel, as did many independent bookshops and sex shops. This kicked off a series of prosecutions and trials across five states, against both the publisher and the booksellers. The fight against literary censorship in Australia had finally gone mainstream.

Soon after *Futility and Other Animals* was released, Frank and Gareth Powell parted ways. Powell, whose central concern was magazine publishing, thought Frank needed a publisher better able to provide the necessary distribution and marketing for books – and so did Frank.

In January 1970, Frank submitted his six Becker stories – referred to as 'The Coca Cola Kid narratives' – to the University of Queensland Press. 'It would be a slim volume,' he wrote to the editor, estimating they comprised about 20,000 words. Frank was impatient to have a new book released as quickly as possible. He anticipated difficulties in getting the manuscript published in Queensland, however, because of censorship issues. The new vice-chancellor, Zelman Cowen, was under pressure regarding anti–Vietnam War protests on-campus.

Frank sent the manuscript to Giles Gordon, an editor at the Gollancz publishing house in London. This time he referred to the cycle of six stories as 'The Americans, Baby'. By March, Gordon had rejected the manuscript. He considered the individual stories 'brilliant', but felt that they did not hang together coherently. Once more, Frank met with resistance over the discontinuous narrative form, with the standards of the novel – a clear narrative arc leading to a satisfying dénouement – being imposed upon it instead. 'For all the interlocking developed through the book,' Gordon wrote, 'it doesn't *seem* as planned as it is obviously intended to be because it doesn't seem to get anywhere ultimately.' Gordon wanted the Australian/American relationship to be explored more deeply. In the end, Frank advised Gordon to pass the manuscript on to his new agent in England, Anthony Sheil & Associates.

That same month, 'Becker and the Moon' was published in *Southerly*, and 'The Coca Cola Kid' won the 1970 Henry Lawson Short Story Prize.

By 1969 there were frequent protests and clashes with the police over the Vietnam War. Frank's friend Murray Sime was arrested and beaten for his role in organising one of the protests. For a week over April and May 1970, the Students for a Democratic Society (SDS) held an anti-draft 'be-in' at the University of Sydney. This included a 'teach-in', led by Don Anderson, Stephen Knight, David Malouf, Michael Wilding and Dennis Altman. There was a screening of Michael Thornhill's film *The American Poet's Visit*. Frank joined A.D. Hope, Dal Stivens, Frank Hardy, Nancy Keesing and Michael Wilding in reading their work.

Frank read a new story at the event, 'Dell Goes into Politics', which was published the following year in the anti-war anthology *We Took Their Orders and Are Dead*, edited by Michael Wilding, David Malouf, Shirley Cass and Ros Cheney. Frank won the 1970 State of Victoria Short Story Award for the story. Ironically, the prize cheque for $250 was presented to Frank by Arthur Rylah, the censorship crusader who had previously supported the Victorian obscenity prosecution of Frank's story 'A Barmaid, a Prostitute, a Landlady' in *Squire*.

Melbourne's *The Age* newspaper usually printed the winning story, but it baulked, citing obscenity concerns. *The Sunday Review* in Melbourne decided to publish it, but wanted offensive lines removed. Frank reluctantly agreed, needing the money, but the story was ultimately pulled.

Don Anderson invited Frank to read some stories to his WEA class and talk about the creative process behind each. Frank was apprehensive. He had read his stories to groups before, but this was not the Balmain Reading of Poetry and Prose or an anti-draft teach-in. Considering the tenor of the times, Frank assumed that 60 to 70 per cent of the general public would find his work offensive. The WEA class was perhaps an unrepresentative sample, occupying a space between the general public and Frank's subculture. He thought they might be more open-minded, as they had self-selected to undergo adult education, studying literature.

Frank was also uncomfortable about explaining his creative process, something he rarely did. The event reminded him of the Rotary talks called 'My Job', where members spoke about their work. He worried that speaking about his creative process would give too much away. 'By doing this I face the danger of a magician who explains his trick – of losing the illusion (as well as being in breach of conjurer's ethics),' he explained, 'but some magicians can do this as well as the trick and shape the exposure of the trick into part of the performance – it probably then becomes a trick within a trick anyhow – an illusion within an illusion.'

The three stories Frank read were 'Dell Goes into Politics', 'The Coca Cola Kid' and 'Anti-Bureaucratisation & the Apparatchiki'. He introduced 'Dell Goes into Politics' by saying it was 'what some Australian magistrates might call obscene or indecent', adding: 'if anyone thinks they will be offended I'd prefer they left before or after the story not during – it puts me off.' There were three walkouts.

Although he was shaken, Frank read the story and explained that it was based on a classic theme of returning home and finding you cannot revisit the idyll of childhood or recapture the comfort of the past. Frank admitted this was a recurring theme in his writing, having based five stories by then on what had been for him the first hard lesson he learned in life. It was through writing and rewriting, Frank explained, that elements of a story or character revealed themselves to him.

> I began writing the story from the recurrence of the 'home going' idea and I knew from what I had written early about – she had to go home – it was not until the final draft that I realised that 'of course' Dell is pregnant – Dell herself concealed that fact even from me – as well as from herself – one of the facts she would not admit until forced. She hid until the story was nearly finished.

This was the process, whereby Frank would come to recognise his characters as individuals, as if independent from himself.

Reading 'The Coca Cola Kid', Frank told the background story about his meeting a Coca-Cola executive in Wagga. Frank made an important admission regarding the interplay between experience and fiction, and the distorting effect the process of writing was beginning to have on his memory. 'I don't know if I had that sort of contact with Becker the Coca Cola salesman' as depicted in the story, he said.

> One of the losses the short story writer suffers . . . is that he loses the incidents of his life – he loses the accurate memory of how it actually happened once he uses however loosely a mood or an incident or

a character – the created incident, mood or character is not simply confused by the fiction it is in fact replaced by the fiction.

This was something Frank first mentioned to Michael Wilding in 1967, when Frank read a draft of 'Joe's Absence':

> The worse thing is of course that the stories distort your memory. By incorporating one incident and processing it into fiction I find it impossible to remember how that incident occurred in reality. I have difficulty in remembering now what incidents occurred in my life and what occurred in stories. Am I going mad? Is it some mental disease? Personality disturbance?

After the class, Frank had eighteen face-to-face responses to his readings, plus six responses reported to him via Don Anderson. Only nine were positive. The remaining fifteen were on a negative spectrum from 'unpalatable' to 'offensive' to 'distressing'. That did not include the three people who walked out. Frank wrote a ten-page document titled 'Reactions Following the Reading of a Short Story to an Adult Education Class' – correcting it afterwards to 'an Obscene Short Story'. 'In my case,' Frank noted, 'my head was banged against the deficiency in my understanding of my own society – I had inaccurately estimated the acceptance of sexuality in literature and the extent of liberation from inhibition and sexual fear.'

Analysing the negative responses, Frank found various lines of justification: the stories were sensational and intended to shock; they were not original but relied on the 'fashionable use of four letter words and sexual descriptions'; sexuality was not a legitimate area for fiction writing ('it belongs in the private lives of the bedroom not in the pages of a book'); the works immorally exploited autobiographical material ('perhaps callously, if insensitively') in the guise of fiction; it was in 'bad taste' to use 'the audience as a test group say to provide material for yet another onslaught on sexual normality'; and, finally, Frank was 'sexually obsessed and the stories were simply manifestation of a morbidity'.

The experience shook Frank's confidence. He admitted 'it would be nice to be sure enough to dismiss all the negative reaction as being motivation by sexual repressed personality', but he knew that would be a feint. It acutely reminded him that the 'response is vastly uneven' when a work enters the public sphere. He drew a comparison with the news, in which reading the newspaper 'is not guaranteed as an "unoffensive" pleasant experience'. A similar horizon of expectation operated in the classroom. Education required an 'open sensibility' in order to 'absorb' or 'stretch' one's intellectual attention: 'education can be absorbing and explosive and quickening, but it can be agitating, and one can be frustrated by failure of communication and conflict'. Frank was concerned that 'social convention' was merging with 'educational demands', when they should be kept separate. Such a convergence would result in an 'activity masquerading as education', leading away from free intellectual enquiry and towards 'endorsement, confirmation and consolation and amusement'. This was not something Frank was interested in, nor what he thought the WEA – or tertiary education generally – ought to be aligned with.

Frank was still wrestling with the question he had asked Clive Hamer in 1964: 'Can you communicate if you offend?' And Frank's intention was, as always, to communicate.

Mike and Frank started a production company together, calling it Thornhill & Moorhouse (T&M) Films. Their first project was a thirteen-part television series called 'The Americans, Baby'. In May 1970, they began shooting the pilot episode, based on Frank's story 'The Girl from the Family of Man'. Frank had written the script, but he found the process difficult, for the same reasons he had declined to write the previous script for 'The American Poet's Visit'. Working closely with Mike on the script was an interesting and intense experience. With Mike's encouragement and guidance, Frank slowly overcame his anxieties about the scriptwriting process.

After Frank wrote a first draft on his own, he would rework it in collaboration with Mike. They would go through the script line by line, scene by scene, with Mike telling Frank what would not work cinematically. Mike would not suggest specific changes, leaving Frank to come up with alternatives to test against Mike's cinematic imagination. They would work together in a room for days at a time, Frank on the typewriter, Mike reading over pages and pacing around. On set, Frank was also involved. He pushed the dolly, worked the clapper board and brought sandwiches for the cast and crew.

The July edition of *Westerly* published 'The Girl from the Family of Man', which drew on Frank's obsession with *The Family of Man* photographic exhibition. That same month, *The Bulletin* published 'The Machine Gun', which followed Turvey, 'a revolutionary poet', and his newly acquired Bren gun. The story considered whether the gun was a 'political metaphor' or a 'political reality'. Frank was continuing his examination of the image and reality of firearms, as a technology and a cultural icon, which he began in his 1968 essay on Godard's *Alphaville*.

'The Machine Gun' is punctuated by several italicised paragraphs, unattributed excerpts from Che Guevara's *Bolivian Diary* (1968) lifted from the magazine *Ramparts*. The contrast between these narratives points to the difference between actual revolutionary action and the urban Australian mimicry of such action. This was Frank's first publication in *The Bulletin*, after several years of rejection, but it was not an auspicious introduction. Frank's text was altered without his permission. A reference to masturbation was omitted and a reference to 'a fuck' was changed to 'a woman'. It is unknown if these changes came from the copy-editor or the printer.

Donald Horne had once more taken over the editorship of *The Bulletin*. He had been following Frank's career, and after reading *Futility* he asked Frank to submit a short story. Learning of Frank's journalistic background, he invited Frank to become a regular writer for the magazine, producing what Frank called 'workmanlike piece[s] of journalism' of around 1000 words, for which he was paid $50 per week. It was understood that this was a retainer of sorts. Frank was paid whether he submitted copy or not, Horne making it clear that Frank should use this opportunity to work on his fiction. Frank began referring to Horne as his patron.

The first piece Frank wrote as staff writer for *The Bulletin* was a review of Hal Porter's collection of short stories *Mr Butterfly and Other Tales of New Japan* (1970). Frank rarely wrote reviews of other writers' fiction, but he used this opportunity to implicitly distinguish between the traditional Australian short story, represented by Porter, from the generation prior to Frank's, and the modern Australian short story, represented by Frank's own generation, himself included.

The stories displayed Porter's 'solid craftsmanship', but over half of each narrative was given over to descriptive detail: what characters looked like, the decor and settings in which they acted. What was missing was any emphasis on relationship or mood. 'When he leaves detail and moves to generalisation,' Frank wrote, 'he runs (and suffers) the risk of all generalisations – their tendency to split apart with exceptions and the unreliability of one person's data.' Characters became types, and were not recognised as individuals. And Porter's own fixed judgements of those types were brought to the foreground. 'His machinery of events is locked together by a moral frame,' Frank wrote, 'and he is not inhibited about expressing author distaste for morals, decor, behaviour or style.' Forcing such moralism over the stories constrained the narratives from exhibiting their unique vitality. 'He doesn't like his characters – which is not to imply that he should.' But by framing each story according to his personal judgement, Porter limited its possibilities. Ultimately, Frank claimed, Porter did not trust his audience: 'he shields the reader'.

Only knowing readers of Frank's own stories – very few of which were available in mainstream publications – would immediately see that he was in the process of overturning the literary conventions he outlined in this review: relationship and mood over detailed static description, individual characters over generalised types, and a questioning of conventional moral frameworks over the enforcement of such frameworks. Most of all, there was a greater trust and responsibility being afforded to the reader.

Finally, Frank said of Porter's collection, '[t]he stories aren't dirty enough'.

Since leaving the ABC, Frank had burned through his savings. He had quickly gone into debt with friends and with financial institutions. This was largely permissible in the bohemian subculture he lived in, the general argument being that they were living against capitalism, or working the system to their advantage. Frank referred to a 'policy of piracy', by which he would do whatever he could to get by, so long as he could put his writing ahead of everything else.

Behind this bravado, though, Frank found being in debt distressing. He suffered constant guilt, which he put down to his 'middle class conscience'. The constant concern with debt collectors and bounced cheques, the juggling of accounts, servicing old debt from one financial institution with new debt from another – it all contributed to his anxieties and, ultimately, put his writing at risk. Donald Horne's patronage had come as a lifeline.

It was in this context that Frank became involved in Australia's nascent film industry. In mid-1970, Frank was approached by the Commonwealth Film Unit with an offer for him to research and write an original film treatment. He was drawn to the opportunity of writing an original screenplay, one not based upon the adaptation of an existing short story. But most of all he needed the money, and the Film Unit offered him three months' funding, from July through September 1970.

This opportunity allowed Frank to bring together two areas of growing interest: psychoanalytic and psychiatric theories and the broader cultural resonance of the Vietnam War. The initial idea for his treatment was to describe the life of a 'professional nonconformist'. Frank began spending more time at the medical library at the University of Sydney and at the State Library of

New South Wales, combing through medical journals from the 1950s and 1960s. He looked at obituaries, finding individuals who had died during that period and who seemed unconventional for the times. He worked backwards through various medical journals and archives, tracing the arc of these people's careers in Australia. He then amalgamated them into a single fictional character.

The central figure he found was Reginald Spencer Ellery, the psychiatrist and author, who had died in 1955. Ellery worked to introduce the ideas of Freud into Australia during the 1930s and 1940s, when such ideas were still professionally controversial. Frank read two books by Ellery, his posthumously published autobiography, *The Cow Jumped Over the Moon* (1956), and his earlier work *Psychiatric Aspects of Modern Warfare* (1945). Ellery was socially affiliated with Max Harris and the Angry Penguins, even giving evidence on behalf of Harris at his obscenity trial in 1944.

Ellery's ideas and prose style immediately interested Frank. His book on modern warfare opens: 'Man is a maladjusted animal, living in an artificial way, with his head in the sky and his feet in the slime. Subservient to his emotions, he sometimes changes his position and puts his head in the slime also. This is characteristically human behaviour.' As Ellery stated in the preface to this book:

> War has not yet come to be generally accepted as a form of certifiable lunacy; and lunatics themselves never engage in it. That it should be the lunacy of sane men is civilization's tragedy. Lunatics for the most part are harmless; but the same cannot always be said of sane men. Sanity is a relative term. It may be merely a mask – and war but a masquerade.

Ellery concluded that efforts to overcome the 'larger lunacy' of war needed to be political, and ambitiously so.

In September, Frank started working on an outline, taking Ellery's life and career as a loose plot structure. Frank amalgamated other figures, such William A. McRae, the psychologist whose work Frank had first read in 1956. He drew on McRae's clinical work on the effects of 'shell shock' and 'battle fatigue' on Australia's returned soldiers, or what the psychiatric literature of the early and mid-twentieth century called 'war neurosis': the psychological effect of war on soldiers. Frank called his treatment 'The Great Warriors'.

In a letter to his UK literary agent, Gillon Aitken, Frank explained his choice of protagonist and subject: 'The shell shocked veteran tells you more about war than the person with surface normality.' And in a statement prescient of Australia's returned soldiers from Vietnam: '[T]he way the society reacts to those who don't make it tells you a lot about the society.' But Frank was clear that the social and political import of any work should not dominate the literary and human-scale aspects of the narrative.

> As I've said, I'm scared to death of talking in abstractions about history and national character ... But as you know the story and the picture are the masters – it's suicide to try to make them tell a history lesson or illustrate a preconception. It's got to be about small 'm' man not capital 'M' Man.

Even so, to suggest such a protagonist and subject in 1970, at the height of Australia's involvement in Vietnam, together with an overtly anti-war message, proved a difficult sell. In October, the Film Unit returned the treatment, rejecting the basic premise of the film: 'I was hoping we would reveal a central character who was very much the accepted good solid Australian,' Frank was informed.

The project was shelved, but Frank was able to spin the grant money out a little longer, supporting him as he worked on his next book.

10

'But the Important Thing I Want You to Know Is That I'm Trying to Be an Honest Craftsman'

Frank's second report in *Current Affairs Bulletin* was published in October 1970. In his first report, he had criticised the broad news media ecology of Australia. That provided a general context for this new report, which focused on a particular media institution: the ABC. The previous *CAB* report was only implicitly autobiographical; this was more explicitly so. The Australian Broadcasting Commission's radio service had begun only six years before Frank was born, and so when he outlined what he titled 'The ABC's Search for Identity', it invariably paralleled his own search for identity, his analysis being, in part, a form of self-analysis.

The ABC was, for most Australians, as for Frank, the 'first mass-media experience' a person had, providing their 'first formal cultural experiences'. The radio provided programming for every age group, and so would accompany an individual through the various stages of their life, from childhood (*Kindergarten of the Air* or, later, *The Argonauts*), through adolescence (*The World We Live In*, or various 'commercial serials, hill-billy music and hit parades') and into adulthood (*ABC News*). 'This writer', Frank said, 'completed the cycle' and became an ABC journalist, 'writing and editing the sort of news bulletins he had grown up on'. The broader institutional analysis required Frank to 'work through almost 30 years of experience with the ABC, thick with sentiment':

> So to write a *CAB* you have to forget your Argonauts' oath (whatever it was) and the oath you take as a journalist (about the Queen and the Official Secrets Act) and forget that your mates work in it or run it (or if they don't they will), and try to forget that you will almost certainly be looking for a job there tomorrow. And you have to rid yourself of the uncritical allegiance from childhood – when the ABC was the main coherent, authoritative noise in the background of your growing up.

Against this background, Frank identified, and moved quickly through, the various stages in the ABC's development, from its initial cultural mission, the tension between highbrow and middlebrow tastes, the need to inform and shape Australian culture versus the need to entertain and provide escape from it. Frank considered the transition from radio to television, the competition between the public broadcaster and commercial television, as well as the cultural competition between the ABC's initial mission of preserving British values with its later shift towards accommodating more cosmopolitan tastes. Arguing that the ABC had become more pluralistic during the 1960s, Frank cited an on-air interview with Brendan Behan's biographer, which openly discussed 'Behan's bi-sexuality, saying that he was not a raving queen or bent, but that if there wasn't a woman around he'd take a man'.

Frank paid close attention to the ABC's relationship with government, particularly regarding censorship. He outlined how, before World War II, this was based on servility and self-censorship, which during the war shifted more to externally imposed forms of censorship, with 'government representatives selecting and rejecting copy'. Frank argued that such censorship had not ceased, but had simply become more diffuse and institutionalised. He identified nine layers of censorship that still pervaded the broadcaster. These ranged from formal censorship – relating to legislation, obscenity and defamation laws – through to more informal censorship – based upon internal workplace culture, with senior staff avoiding 'offence', or simply 'keeping out of trouble' – through to middle and lower-level staff making assumptions about policy and independently acting upon them. All of these practices were kept hidden behind what, in his previous *CAB* report, Frank had called the 'journalistic mystique', obfuscated by a posture of objectivity.

Frank introduced an argument regarding an 'unwritten contract between the consumer and producer of mass media', grounded in the idea of *expectation*:

> A consumer wants to know in advance, in brief detail, what the programme is about, its *genre*, and its level, so that the consumer is in a position to make a choice. It is difficult to see the justification for confronting people with material which offends their personal or moral feelings. Those who want to engage in social and self-exploration should not attempt to impose their interests on others by ambush. This writer would call this 'violation of expectation' and it is the source of some demands for censorship.

This argument may seem strange coming from a writer who only months earlier had published 'Letters to Twiggy'. But this was a consistent line of thinking going back to Frank's question about balancing communication and offence. During the publicity for *Futility and Other Animals*, Frank repeatedly stated that his intention was not to offend, even though he recognised that some might consider the nature of some of his material offensive. For Frank, narrative fiction carried with it the *expectation* it would enquire into, and question, the cultural norms of a society. The 'unwritten contract' cut both ways, with certain *expectations* also being placed upon the reader.

Added to this was the question of context. In his *CAB* report, Frank referred to the expectations of mass media, of the national broadcaster. Writing for the alternative or underground press – outlets such as *Thorunka* – involved different expectations, precisely because the intended audience was different. *The Bulletin* involved different expectations again, but for the same reasons.

At the conclusion of his report, considering the future, Frank wondered how the public broadcaster could assert an identity in a pluralistic society, one far more heterodox than the society within which it had been formed – a society that included audiences for both *The Bulletin* and *Thorunka*:

> Culturally, Australia is moving toward an encounter – possibly of some social magnitude – between those who want less anxiety and uncertainty, less change in the moral and social structure, and those who want, say, total freedom of communication, informal restructuring of social relations and institutions, and less majority imposition of tastes and values.

The meetings at *Thorunka* sometimes had up to thirty people in attendance, with the editorial and administrative staff, writers and reporters, artists and illustrators and various hangers-on all having a say about the direction of the newspaper. Frank had not been involved in such a bustling newsroom since his cadet journalist days in the late 1950s. He later argued that this period marked a distinct shift among the libertarians, from '*advocating freedom of communication* to *freely communicating*'. This is what Frank had been arguing for since 1963. It was achieved mainly by a generational shift, with the old-guard libertarians quietly losing (or ceding) authority to a younger generation, even as they continued to be a presence. This new energy had come from outside the group, from the student protest movements and the women's liberation movement, albeit filtered through old libertarian notions.

The first edition of *Thorunka* was published in September 1970. It included Germaine Greer's essay 'The Politics of Female Sexuality', which argued for women to become more familiar with their own genitals. The second edition, published in October 1970 – the same month as Frank's *CAB* report on the ABC – included the first instalment of Frank's semi-regular column 'Around the Laundromats', signed F.M. and W.P.A., signifying Frank and Ward, his pet cat. The columns described Frank and his cat discussing current affairs while Frank washes his clothes at a laundromat.

The imaginary dialogue between Frank and Ward recalled the letters Frank wrote to Wendy Halloway in the late 1950s, when he was in Wagga and she was in Sydney. These included dialogues between Frank and Nod, who acted as Frank's alter ego. Unlike Nod, Ward was a very sweary cat, and more offensive:

> Ward . . . pointed at some unisex underwear on a trolley, 'It's certainly going to be the Poofters Decade,' Ward observed, without much enthusiasm.
>
> 'I don't think you should, in all good conscience, use the word "Poofter", Ward,' I said, firmly, 'but it's true that there's more bi-sexuality around – a good thing.'
>
> 'Animals have always swung both ways,' Ward remarked.

The second production from T&M Films was *The Machine Gun*, based on Frank's story of the same name. Frank wrote the script, having learned from his previous experience working closely with Mike. This particular story lent itself more readily to film, as it involved more cinematic techniques in its original version, such as flashbacks and a newsreel. There was a five-day shoot in January 1971. Later that year, the twenty-minute film was entered into, and shown at, the Benson & Hedges Awards for Australian Short Films, although it did not win. The awards catalogue noted: 'The symbol of the machine gun is constantly contrasted with the unreality of the revolutionary thinking of the hero and the stability of his environment – and yet?'

The unit manager on the film was Sandra Levy. She was, at that stage, nearly finished her degree at the University of Sydney, where she was studying for a BA in English literature and a diploma in education. She was later offered a traineeship at the ABC, where she specialised in script editing and producing. It was around this time that Sandra and Frank started going out.

On 4 February 1971, Wendy Bacon fronted court on an obscenity charge from the previous August, for wearing the nun's habit. The previous November, Wendy had been charged yet again, along with John Cox, for selling copies of *Thorunka* in pubs at Manly. They sold a copy to an undercover policeman. By the time of her court appearance that February, the *Thorunka* set had accrued forty-one charges. Frank sat in on the trial each day, writing one of his earliest pieces for *The Bulletin*. Wendy represented herself but refused to enter a plea or provide any information about herself.

'I appear because there are penalties which force me to,' she told the court. 'I am fundamentally opposed to this court system and for that reason I did not enter a plea.' She argued that entering a plea would be an admission that she *could* be guilty of 'obscenity', and 'to be found guilty of obscenity is to have committed no crime'. She called upon Plato's dialogue between Socrates and Euthyphro, to argue the relative nature of the concept of obscenity: is a publication obscene because the average man objects to it? Or does the average man object to it because it is obscene? Frank cited Judge Levine's response: 'The comments of Socrates are not relevant to New South Wales Law.'

Wendy was found guilty, but the judge refused to sentence her until he had more adequate information about her identity and background, which she refused to provide. She was therefore remanded for eight days, before final sentencing. She wrote a report from prison and was afterwards interviewed about her experience, which only brought more public attention to the case.

When the Australian Society of Authors wished to publish an article on the case in their in-house journal, the printer refused to set the type because it included the words for which Bacon had been charged with obscenity. The ASA management committee had to decide whether to censor the article and print it, replace the article entirely or find another printer (at great financial cost) and try to get the uncensored article published in full. Under the circumstances, and having a limited budget, they reluctantly chose to replace the article.

Following Bacon's trial, *Thorunka* changed its masthead to *Thor*. One of the first pieces it published was Wendy's report from prison. In a special edition on sex, Frank published an essay called 'The Myth of the Male Orgasm', his response to the 1970 pamphlet by American radical feminist Anne Koedt titled *The Myth of the Vaginal Orgasm*.

Koedt argued against the narrow psychoanalytic definition of female sexuality, which placed the source of the female orgasm in the vagina, with a satisfying sexual experience being possible only through heterosexual intercourse – penetration by an erect penis. A corollary of this narrow definition was the suggestion that unsatisfying sexual experiences were a sign of frigidity or neuroses in women, which required psychoanalytic treatment to overcome. Koedt argued that this supported the ongoing oppression of women as fragile creatures requiring psychological treatment to achieve normalcy.

Wrote Frank:

> Anne Koedt, in her pamphlet *Myth of the Vaginal Orgasm*, argues that men created this myth to deny the sexuality of women and the personality of women, and to establish male dominance by making the penis central to the sexual act and crucial for women's pleasure. (This is about the only part of the pamphlet I agree with. The rest seemed distorted by male hostility and hysteria.)

He argued that Koedt's 'myth has a rebound'. In short, the 'male hostility and hysteria' he noted with regards to the feminist position had its counterpart in a form of female hostility and hysteria found in men.

> The negation of female sexuality and the female as person psychologically rebounds on the male and deprives him of full sexuality. Paradoxically,

some men have to feel superior to the female and central to the act before they can function sexually at all. This permits simple functioning but denies the relationship the dynamic of full and joint participation and the male consequently loses the possibility of orgasm (but gains the consolation of ejaculation).

It was to escape this fateful double bind Frank was arguing for in 'The Myth of the Male Orgasm', not to dismiss Koedt's work, but to supplement its argument.

Frank wanted to decentre the penis from the sexual process. He argued that the central conceit of the ideology of male supremacy – the erect penis and the conflation of ejaculation with male orgasm – was, in practice, fundamentally flawed. He drew on Wilhelm Reich's distinction between ejaculation and orgasm. Ejaculation was often unaccompanied by pleasure. 'Maybe there is a minor discharge of tension, too, with ejaculation,' Frank wrote, 'but never total enough to be confused with orgasm.' And orgasm did not necessarily require an erect penis or ejaculation in order to be experienced. Frank transposed this distinction on to one between *'visible virility'* (ejaculation) and *'invisible virility* (orgasm, known only to self)'. The sources of *'visible virility'* are asexual in nature, constituted by masculine culture and geared towards dodging or avoiding the sexual question of *'invisible virility'* – which, in turn, undergirds male hostility towards women and the desire to dominate them.

'Virility is an amalgamation of asexual physical qualities,' Frank argued, 'stamina, endurance, strength, prowess in combat, all transferred across into sexual performance.' This leads to an emphasis on external quantitative measures, rather than internal qualitative experiences. 'Quantitative measurements are the usual way that men score their fucking and I think that generally this is the way men are thinking when they talk about it,' Frank wrote. 'These measurements are related to male ideology.' One such measure was an emphasis on stamina, rather than pleasure.

Other quantitative measurements are common too – number of women in a period of time, the length of time that a fuck took, the length of the penis, and the number of climaxes that the woman had during the fuck. The last one has odd implications. It also has a compensatory function for the orgasmically impotent male.

The anxiety lurking behind all this was the fear of impotence, of not achieving or maintaining an erection, let alone being able to achieve ejaculation. It was an anxiety compounded by the lack of communication *within* male culture regarding sexual matters, other than as a joke or as a posture of external virility. 'Taboos on sexual discussion and information has left any self-perceptive male with the "maybe-it-is-only-me" anxiety,' Frank wrote.

And it was this, Frank argued, which must be included in the broader cultural discussion – between men and women, between men and men, and between women and women – in order to adequately address the problem of transition, and the modifying of the personalities of both men and women, in order for society to move past traditional patriarchal structures. Fear and dominance were related, and in order to address the latter (as patriarchy), one must first address the former. Only then could 'full orgasm', for both men and women, be achieved.

> The conditions that permit full orgasm would seem to be: the absence of intersexual hostility or threat (is this possible in a male-dominated society or even in a transitional sub-culture?); low inhibition or absence of inhibition (can we jettison social conditioning by intellectual awareness?); and the capacity for surrender to pleasure.

The concerns Frank expressed in this essay were very much those he was confronting in his personal life, from his early relationship with Wendy Halloway up to and including his present relationships with various women. In writing this essay – and although he still partially hid behind a rational framework, speaking in generalities – Frank had come a long way from a decade earlier, when, during the collapse of his marriage to Wendy, the main breakdown of which was sexual, Frank had refused to talk about the issue.

The publication of 'The Myth of the Male Orgasm' was significant because it included Frank's first public admission of having had homosexual encounters, albeit in a publication with a particular and limited readership. 'I've had full orgasm in homosexual relationships (and also bad fucks),' he wrote. 'I've had full orgasmic experiences a few times which have made me weep through the intensity of their release – and also, probably, because of their rareness.'

After the essay was published, Frank wrote an appendix, which remained unpublished. In 'Afterthoughts on the Orgasm', he reflected on the essay, clarifying some points and revising others, but he added an additional argument that he was not yet prepared to make publicly, even to his own subcultural group, but which he was personally confronting. This regarded the question of gender identity. In order to overcome the inhibitions and sexual 'un-awareness' which blocked full orgasm, Frank argued for the liberation of 'male femininity' – a corollary to women liberating their 'masculinity', which he saw as being part of the feminist project. Frank qualified this as meaning 'using both masculinity and femininity as socially conditioned personality and behaviour patterns – not as parts of the immutable human condition'. He argued that such gender traits coexisted in every person. 'Although one strand may be dominant,' he wrote, 'the balance shifts from mood to mood, stage of life, relationship to relationship and that these various shifts and facets in our sexual personalities can be brought into erotic play.'

Frank had not seen Wendy since she left Australia with George James in the early 1960s. In England, for professional reasons, she adopted George's surname, although she was still legally married to Frank.

When Frank's first book was published, he put a copy in an unaddressed envelope, writing only 'Wendy' on it, but he never posted it. For her part, Wendy had followed Frank's career through her father, who often chatted with Frank's parents around town in Nowra. More recently, Wendy's father had posted her newspaper clippings about Frank's writing.

Still, it was with some trepidation that Wendy wrote Frank a letter in March 1971. 'It's a bit hard breaking the ice with words, after all these years,' she wrote. She was working as deputy features editor of *Women's Own* magazine in England, and she was in contact with a publisher who was on the lookout for Australian writers. She had heard Frank was trying to shop around his next book, and she offered to help him place it in England.

Her letter came as a surprise to Frank, but also caused him concern. 'My ex-wife wrote me,' he told Michael Wilding. 'It's the first letter from her for seven years. Naturally I'm suspicious.' Before replying, Frank made a series of notes to process his mixed feelings.

In his reply to Wendy, he was more cautious. He said he was 'stunned and delighted' to receive her letter, and he thought of her often, especially when travelling along the coast, which was full of memories and associations of their time together. He had bought a copy of *Women's Own* and he said he found it difficult to see Wendy working for that type of magazine, but he understood it was a job. Later, he would tell her she was 'a "natural" for journalism. You were almost from the beginning a better journalist than I.' He said his fiction writing and working for the underground press had started to cause some public pushback. 'My work is going further in a direction which makes it almost illegal in Australia and certainly,' he wrote, 'quite a few stories are not publishable.' He included with the letter his long-held copy of *Futility and Other Animals*.

Wendy replied, letting her guard down more. She and George had separated, she told Frank, and she was raising their two children on her own. It was difficult because in England a wife still needed her husband's signature on forms. And yet she sounded more independent and self-confident. This encouraged Frank to drop his own defences, so in their correspondence over the next few months they were able to achieve some semblance of the frankness and sincerity previously missing from their relationship.

Frank admitted that, with time and psychoanalysis, he had come to realise he had a 'pretty cold childhood', which led to his difficulties maintaining stable relationships with women. 'Looking back it seems that I needed to breakout and go on some sort of emotional-sexual journey which at least a conventional marriage could not have accommodated (no – not any marriage).' Frank told Wendy she remained a constant in his dreams, as a symbol of adolescent trauma perhaps, but also as herself, with more positive associations. 'I've always found this incredible – that you remained in my dreams like that,' he later wrote to her. 'It's psychologically fascinating.'

Wendy read Frank's letter with amazement. It liberated her from her years of guilt about their marriage, as she explained in her reply:

> When I wrote the first letter to you, I didn't think I had a hidden motive but when you replied in such friendly terms, I realised that I did, I needed to know whether you disliked me as much as I thought you did. I was truly unprepared for the fact that you still feel affection for me . . .
>
> I was very impressed by the lack of cynicism and the depth of charm in your letters. In many ways you are a stranger to me because we both must have changed so much but your letters brought back memories of you at 18, but a you with a much more rational outlook and a you with much more confidence.

Their correspondence had proven cathartic for both Frank and Wendy. They had each been carrying guilt over the breakdown of their marriage. Frank acknowledged 'the pig ignorance I had about sexual or emotional things and the failure or loss of communication between us'. Outside of psychoanalysis, Frank argued that the rise of feminism had helped him: 'The women's liberation problem for men is to learn how to live with a "real" person (without being corny).'

Coincidentally, Frank had been planning a trip to England that year, but he had postponed it until early 1972. In November

1971, after days of hesitation, Frank finally called Wendy on the telephone, to speak with her for the first time in a decade. They discussed his upcoming visit to England, and whether they could meet. Afterwards, he wrote to her about the call: 'We can still be intimidated by technological sophistication.'

Soon after Wendy first contacted Frank, he wrote a piece for *The Bulletin* about attending the International Rotary Convention with his parents in Sydney. Among 12,000 attendees from all over the world, Frank tried to delineate the general personality of the typical Rotarian, the idealistic business entrepreneur. He was trying to come to an understanding of his own father, and by extension himself and his own upbringing.

'Paul Harris said he founded Rotary in 1905 because he was lonely,' Frank wrote.

> Maybe loneliness is the key to Rotary. A businessman as employer is isolated from his employees by a relationship which had inherent tensions. He is also wary of his fellow business competitor. Finally, he had the loneliness of the competitive personality, the high-achiever, who has little time for socialising. Rotary is fellowship that doesn't waste time.

Frank argued Rotary was a form of 'ritualised fellowship', as 'a form of "male bonding" woven from customs, practices, codes, procedures, and a constitution which are tightly held to through the Rotary world'. He drew attention to their use of language, in particular the 'inverted maxim': 'Look for every opportunity in every difficulty rather than the difficulty in every opportunity', or else 'The man who tries and fails is better than the man who never tries at anything and succeeds'.

After the article came out, Frank's father wrote to say how much he liked it, and he felt the observations regarding Rotary were accurate. He reported that Frank's mother had been selected as 'Citizen of the Year' by their local Rotary club.

What Frank had left out of the article was an incident from the convention that offered an insight not just into his father, but into his mother, and perhaps also into their relationship. Rotary had chartered hundreds of buses to supplement public and private transport during the convention. At one point Frank and his father were squeezed into the back of a bus otherwise filled with American and Korean Rotarians. There was much confusion as to where they were, where they were going and how they would know when they got there. Then, from up the front of the bus, a voice cut through the hubbub, commanding everybody to 'please be quiet' – which they obediently did. It was Frank's mother. She took control of the situation and explained the route they were travelling, providing a running commentary on where they were in the city. Frank had cringed with embarrassment at the back of the bus, while his father beamed with pride.

In 1970, when Frank's parents were in England, he wrote to them about his idea for 'The Technological History of the South Coast', a retelling of his own prehistory, through the lens of tracing the advances in technology and the dairy industry: the cream separators and the milking machines, the telegraph and the local newspapers, the moving picture shows and cinemas, ice factories, soft drink manufacturing, radio and telephones – and the Moorhouse Dairy Boiler. This would build upon Frank's research in media communications, regarding how such communications technology created the cultural conditions for the growth of industry and education, a vernacular literature and a national culture.

Frank Sr applauded the idea. In England, he and Purth bought Frank a tape recorder. The following year, a few months after the Rotary article appeared in *The Bulletin*, Frank visited Nowra and used the tape recorder to record interviews with his father, about life on the South Coast in the late 1920s and the 1930s. It was a history he was filtering through his notion of the personality type of an idealistic business entrepreneur, to outline what he confided in a letter to Wendy was a work 'about electricity and mechanisation and about salesmen as the capitalist educators and spreaders of information'.

He was planning to write two books on this topic, one non-fiction and one fiction.

In early 1971, Frank had been approached by John Abernathy, of Angus & Robertson, asking if he had a manuscript they could read. Frank sent them 'The Americans, Baby', but for the first time he included stories he was saving for another project on male–female relations, adding these to the six Coca Cola Kid narratives, as well as other stories on American–Australian relations. This made the manuscript more ambitious in scope than when he had shown it to publishers the previous year. This may have been a provocation, because he indicated to Wendy that he was not particularly interested in publishing with Angus & Robertson. 'Naturally it will be a last resort,' he told her.

Although Angus & Robertson was an historically significant publishing house, it had not aged well. Since the war it survived on occasional support from the Commonwealth Literary Fund and various subsidies. When Frank Packer bought *The Bulletin* in the early 1960s – and made Donald Horne the editor – he also attempted to take over Angus & Robertson. He failed, but the internal turmoil from that event, and the fault lines within the organisation this exposed, never quite receded.

In 1970, Gordon Barton took over Angus & Robertson, in an effort to stabilise its operations and drag it into the modern world. What they did not know at the time was that the following year, as a consequence of the *Trade Practices Act 1971*, the price maintenance agreement between UK publishers and Australian booksellers – the latest accretion upon a colonial remnant of the British Empire – was rendered null and void. This effectively ended the publishing regime started in 1843, the most visible component of which was the sale of colonial editions. This opened Australia to the international market, which in practice meant UK publishers were in competition with US publishers to sell their books in the Australian market. The publishing of Australian content for an Australian audience continued to be disadvantaged.

In was against this background that John Abernathy informed Frank in September 1971 that there had been some disagreement among the editorial committee regarding his manuscript. Most liked some stories and disliked others, but for each person these were different. 'And the only common ground we have is that we think the collection as a whole is uneven,' Frank was told, 'and that it could stand compression: in my own view, you do seem to be making the same or similar points more often than you need to.' Abernathy wanted Frank to remove what stories he could, and then resubmit the manuscript.

What Abernathy did not tell Frank was that Beatrice Davis, the legendary book editor, did not like Frank's fiction at all. At sixty-two years old, she had been at the publisher for nearly half her life. She did not like the new literary turn, and was very much opposed to Angus & Robertson publishing Frank's book.

Frank waited three weeks before he replied:

> Naturally, it goes almost without saying, that I see the book as a unity. I certainly know which stories I consider key and which I consider fragments which support or elaborate or embroider the key stories. I suppose the fragments and minor stories are perhaps the ones which could be left out.

On 3 November, Angus & Robertson offered Frank a contract for *The Americans, Baby*, with a $500 advance against a 10 per cent royalty rate on the first 3500 copies. 'We're still discussing cuts,' Abernathy wrote at the time, 'but except for one or two stories our suggestions seem to cancel each other out.'

Frank accepted the contract, but he had an important stipulation: 'One special condition I'd like is that the book not be advertised or called a "collection of short stories" but either the genre left unclassified or that it be called something like a "discontinuous narrative".' He signed the contract on 11 November 1971.

Two weeks later, *The Australian* ran an article announcing the contract and forthcoming book. The article played up Frank's bohemian credentials, his association with *Thorunka* and the Push, and the fight against censorship. He was photographed in his Ewenton Street, Balmain, office, with his bare feet up on the desk, typewriter in his lap, sporting a ten-gallon Akubra hat. *The Americans, Baby* was slated to be published in April 1972.

Sandra Levy witnessed Frank's signing the contract for Angus & Robertson. It was during this period he started living with Sandra in her cottage in Balmain. He still kept his Ewenton Street office, where he would write most days. His moving in with Sandra was a gradual process, with him staying over one night a week, then two nights a week and so on. The other nights he mainly slept at Ewenton Street. He eventually found himself staying most of each week at Sandra's house, yet still considered the arrangement temporary, even as the relationship progressed from months to years spent together.

Frank tried to ensure they did not settle into a complacent domesticity. In his correspondence with Wendy, he argued that his ideal relationship was one which emphasised '*separateness* of personality', with neither person being subordinate to the other, and especially the woman not being subordinate to the man. He thought such separateness needed to be imposed structurally, in the sense of having separate rooms – as in a studio or office space – and perhaps even separate residences, such as his Ewenton Street studio. 'Something short of living apart,' he added.

In June 1971, Frank was approached by Gil Brealey, his contact for the Commonwealth Film Unit. Brealey had since moved to the Australia Council for the Arts, and he wanted to revive Frank's film project about psychiatry and war neurosis. Frank was not initially enthused by the notion, but he needed the money and thought he could once more spin it out to fund work on his fiction. That said, the character of the doctor had haunted him since he had abandoned the film project. He had continued to make notes about the character, with a view to using the research in his fiction.

Frank referred to this new iteration of 'The Great Warriors' as 'Doctor', which he revised from being a feature film to being a ten-part television series. The development grant was to write the scripts for the first three episodes.

Meanwhile, Frank had success with the Commonwealth Film Unit over another film project. It was for a script – 'Maurie Anderson: Printer and Pelmanist' – in which the title character was a printer, the story mapping industrial and labour changes in the printing industry, with the more recent introduction of offset printing and the deskilling of the industry rendering his job obsolete. Frank drew on his experiences at *The Riverina Express*, and the old lino-operator, Clarrie, with whom he had once had a physical altercation over an editorial he had written. The script explored the obsolescence of certain technologies and the social effects of this process.

At one stage, Frank had a 'stormy' two-hour conference with the film unit regarding this script. They had criticised his first draft as being too 'low key' and 'down beat', with no action. Frank revised the script, but was worried he had already 'sold out' and lost the original conception, along with creative control. So when he began dealing with the Australia Council for the Arts over his Doctor project, Frank stood his ground.

The protagonist of that project now had a name: Dr Trenbow. Frank wanted to map the changing mood of Australian society, between the world wars.

> The story tells of a young doctor who because of his experiences in World War I treating shell shock decides to specialise in psychiatry. It is in part a social history of psychiatry – an exploration of attitudes between the wars, to the human personality and its breakdowns. But mainly the story is about an innovator – a pioneer in a field. The story also looks at the way social and economic crises create a national 'personality'.

In one sense, Frank was transposing the discontinuous narrative form to the small screen, building each episode as he would a short story. His plan was for each episode to be structured by a single document, shown onscreen in the opening frame. The episode would then present the more complicated and messy situation otherwise hidden behind each document, and so distinguish between official and unofficial versions of reality. Frank thought this would provide the viewer access to three simultaneous layers within each story: 'an official ideology; the reality of the people handling and surviving crises; and the reality of those not surviving – those forced out by the pressures.'

The ten documents Frank chose began with a wartime medical certificate, for an undiagnosed nervous disorder, issued by a 25-year-old Captain Trenbow. This was followed in subsequent episodes by an army discharge, an admission to a mental hospital for war psychosis, a marriage certificate, a birth certificate (for Trenbow's son), a summons for an inquiry into practices in the hospital (allegations of malpractice), a bachelor of medicine degree, an eviction notice for returned soldiers squatting on government blocks, an invitation for Trenbow to address a medical conference on his psychiatric methods, and, finally, his son's enlistment notice to serve in World War II. The series would close with Trenbow visiting the hospital where he had started during the Great War (in episode one), only to find eight times the number of patients suffering from war neurosis and shell shock.

Frank worked on the drafts of the first three episodes until January 1972, submitting them to the Australia Council for the Arts shortly before he went overseas.

The last piece Frank had filed for *The Bulletin* before he left for his first trip overseas was published on 1 January 1972. 'Hello, Nineteen-Seventy Two!' outlined Frank's predictions for the coming twelve months. Such predictions were, he suggested, simply a way of trying to manipulate the future.

His first prediction was the collapse of censorship in Australia. His second was that Australians would liberate the world: Germaine Greer would liberate women, Dennis Altman would liberate gays, and Wendy Bacon would liberate children. Frank predicted the 1972 federal election would mean the end of old politics: 'The massive informal vote at the 1972 elections causes an agonising defeatism, and eventual disbanding of the parties as we know them.' But his most fanciful predictions were regarding the arts, and literature in particular:

> The most remarkable event is the re-emergence of the short story as the fashionable, feted, highest-paid art form. Badges and posters of Henry Lawson, Chekhov, O. Henry, Jack London are immensely popular as they become teenage idols. An international short story festival at Grenfell is called 'another Woodstock'. There is a move towards 'prose angst', away from mystical free-floating love. And the Film Development Corporation buys Hollywood before it is lost, and reconstructs it at Gosford under the directorship of Michael Thornhill.

In June 1971, Don Chipp had lifted the import ban on *Portnoy's Complaint*, conceding the absurdity of a censorship regime in which a publication was freely available in some states and not in others. Leonard Cohen's novel *Beautiful Losers* (1966) had been banned for import in 1967, and on appeal in 1972 the ban was upheld. Richard Walsh had recently been brought into Angus & Robertson as literary editor and publisher, in order to modernise the publishing house. One of his first moves, buoyed by the outcome of Penguin's stance on *Portnoy's Complaint*, was to publish Cohen's novel domestically and distribute it in defiance of the ban.

In between these two events, in February 1972 – while Frank was out of the country – Wendy Bacon and John Cox went to trial for their arrest in late 1970 for selling a copy of *Thorunka* to an undercover policeman in a pub. John Cox was also charged with selling a copy of the newspaper to the proprietor of the Christopher Brennan Bookshop, in Paddington. They argued that 'community standard' – the latest iteration of the householder test as a mark of obscenity – was an illusion. Germaine Greer, infamous by then for the publication of *The Female Eunuch*, appeared for the defence, arguing for the legitimate etymological roots of various four-letter words. But at the end of the trial Wendy and John were both found guilty, spending the next five nights in jail as they awaited sentencing.

Finally, at sentencing, they were fined $200 each and put on a five-year bond.

Frank landed in London on 20 January 1972, spending much of his two weeks in England catching up with Wendy Halloway. They very quickly ended up in bed together.

'I was in fact very surprised – pleasantly – that we got on so well together in and out of bed,' Wendy later wrote. 'My main fascination is which person you are,' she told him. She had heard stories of his life in Sydney, his public self, which was very different to the person she knew, his private self. 'Perhaps the riotous you is the defensive you,' she said, perceptively, adding quickly: 'it's like trying to analyse a dream, so I shouldn't go on with this line.'

While in London, Frank met with a publisher regarding a UK edition of *The Americans, Baby*, and visited the Australian writer Murray Bail. On Thursday, 3 February, Frank left England for North America, flying into Montreal, Canada, before making his way down to New York, where he stayed at the Algonquin Hotel. He felt intimidated by the famous hotel, as though he did not belong. He felt he did not know the rules. He noted in his journal how everything was sharply delineated to him, 'even the hotel room, the painting reproductions on its wall, the associations, the nature of "room service", the nature of hotel service, all so vivid . . .'

While in New York, he submitted *The Girl from the Family of Man* to a short film festival, but it was not accepted on the final bill. In late February, he travelled to New Orleans, and stayed for more than a month in a small basement flat, known as an 'efficiency apartment'. The building pipes ran through it, which 'gurgled' incessantly. But after a month of travelling Frank was happy to settle into a space of his own, where he could work and relax. He lived only a block away from the Mississippi River, where he went running along the levee each morning.

He was still filing stories for *The Bulletin*, and the first piece from New Orleans was about attending Mardi Gras. It had always been for him a symbol of debauchery and personal freedom, but the reality was disappointing. 'I got off to a bad start,' he wrote. 'I didn't have the self honesty (or the figure) to live out my deviation fantasy and go dressed as Twiggy in a satin evening dress.' He did buy a Texan-style cowboy hat, which, together with the coloured beaded necklaces, ubiquitous at Mardi Gras, had him 'looking like a camp Texan (if such a thing exists)'.

Since being in the United States, he had been trying to contact Donald Barthelme for an interview. One of the last pieces Frank had written for *The Bulletin* had been a review of Barthelme's latest book, *City Life* (1970). 'His writing makes the point that it is not, say, the short story or the novel that are dead,' Frank had written, 'but many of their practitioners.' But Barthelme remained elusive. Frank waited in New Orleans for him to reply to a letter – which he never did.

Frank made several excursions to nearby parts of the country. It was the primary season of the 1972 presidential election, and Frank travelled to Florida to attend a campaign speech by one Democratic hopeful, the Alabama governor and anti-integrationist George Wallace. 'I hope some bigot doesn't shoot me,' Frank wrote home at the time. Less than two months later, Wallace himself was shot in an attempted assassination, which ended his presidential run and left him paralysed.

'They keep saying that Wallace "doesn't matter",' Frank wrote for *The Bulletin*. 'I feel they, the men seeking the Democratic nomination, really mean that Wallace "shouldn't matter".' But at a rally in Lake City, Texas, Frank witnessed firsthand what other Democratic nominees were worried about.

When speaking to a crowd, Wallace was not flamboyant but used volume effectively – not shouting, but modulating his volume – and employed sneers and abuse and name calling to great effect. The crowd loved the sneers, and applauded each time. He attacked the press: 'Oh, we got the *New York Times* here, we got *Newsweek* here, we got *Time* here, we got the teevee networks here.' Wallace attacked the privileged rich, and when he called for higher taxes Frank thought 'he sounded like a Communist agitator from the thirties'. Wallace wanted welfare for those who needed it, but not for those whom he considered lazy. He applied a simple and rigid moralism to society, a clear sense of right and wrong, in order to distinguish himself from liberals, who, he claimed, could no longer tell the difference. He stood against a perceived American decline. 'He climaxed with the slogan: "We're saying, *Move over big government, the average man is moving in*. This is a crusade to restore this country back to what it used to be."'

Frank understood the emotional appeal. He admitted that Wallace hit at the self-doubt of somebody like Frank who otherwise questioned his own position in society, was uncertain and might be drawn to the false certainty Wallace offered. 'The arrogance of the demagogue bullying the insecurity of the rebel,' Frank observed. 'He hammers down on you. Wallace is mum, dad, the church, school, warning you of the dangers of your path which will lead to self destruction and social destruction.' But Frank understood the dangers of such demagoguery: 'But it wasn't long before I had elevated my insecurity and self-questioning into an intellectual virtue and it was only one beer, and an American Michelob beer at that, before the effect had dissipated and I saw him as the irrational long hair- and nigger-kicking conservative that he was.'

Frank spent a lot of time during this trip drinking alone in various bars. The next piece he filed for *The Bulletin* was simply titled 'American Bar'. Frank outlined his interactions with Joey, a barman at a student bar in New Orleans called Coeds. At one point, Joey asked Frank what he did and Frank told him he was a writer.

'Now if Faulkner was to come in here,' Joey said, 'he wouldn't call himself a writer. He'd call himself a farmer.'

'And he'd be lying,' Frank said, 'concealing himself.'

While in San Antonio, Texas, Frank had the opportunity to visit the set of the latest Sam Peckinpah film, *The Getaway*, starring Steve McQueen and Ali MacGraw. McQueen had Frank removed from set on the first day because he did not like strangers seeing him work. Frank asked Peckinpah about a review in the *New Yorker* calling Peckinpah's previous film, *Straw Dogs* (1971), 'the first

American film that was a fascist work of art'. Peckinpah 'snorted, and with protective arrogance said that like many other critics she had missed the point (I thought she had too)'. But this comeback let Peckinpah off the hook, so Frank persisted. After some coaxing, Peckinpah said *Straw Dogs* was about 'passive intellectuals': 'They hate to think they have it in them – they hate to admit they could be violent and like it.'

Frank was at the time reading through all of William Faulkner, in preparation for visiting his birthplace in Oxford, Mississippi. Frank drove 300 miles (480 kilometres) around Faulkner country, camping one night in a pine forest between Oxford and New Albany. He had not gone camping in Australia since 1957, and this experience reignited his passion for it. He started taking notes on camping. He was working on stories for what he was calling his 'South Coast' book, the fictional counterpart to his non-fiction 'Technological History of the South Coast'. Reading Faulkner and visiting Mississippi helped him with this. 'Maybe what I'm doing here,' he confided in his journal, 'and what I'm getting from Faulkner is a sense of "region"[,] of being able to see my home or region as vital rather than foggy.'

Writing about the South Coast brought back unbidden childhood and adolescent memories. Meeting Wendy in London only deepened this dark nostalgia. The experience of travel had already left Frank feeling vulnerable and anxious, and the lack of an external support structure exacerbated the situation. Despite what he said in his letters home, and despite his reports for *The Bulletin*, he was emotionally falling apart. 'Everything is shrunk now to my self and its habits, fears, and thinking,' he wrote in his journal. 'The USA is now something like ten feet diameter circle round me.'

Frank told Don Anderson he was drinking too much as a coping mechanism. 'The old problem of being the outsider and in my case, an outsider without highly developed social skills. But I know a hell of a lot of barmen.' He could not stomach the weak American beer over long sessions. 'The beer is everything we feared,' he reported to Don. So he turned to drinking spirits, and drinking on his own, finding himself forced by circumstance into 'the practice of solitary drinking (recalling all the Australian taboos against it)'.

He was able to confide his true psychological state, with some degree of irony, in letters to Don: 'As you have commented it is difficult, not only in Australia I might say, but in the whole world, to find a good miserable drinking companion who has proper contempt for the human condition.' And what he could not confide to Don he kept for his journal: 'I have difficulty feeling as if I am *living*. I can live retrospectively, in anticipation, but at the time I feel spasm of wanting it to be over. Rarely am I overtaken by the present.'

Later that year, for *The Bulletin*, Frank interviewed the Australian author David Ireland about his latest novel, *The Flesheaters*. In the interview Frank pointed out two scenes of castration in Ireland's first two books, *The Chantic Bird* (1968) and *The Unknown Industrial Prisoner* (1971). Ireland could not remember the scenes. 'He shook his head,' Frank wrote. 'He said he had no explanation. We didn't go into psychoanalytic interpretations and left it at that.'

But Frank had noted the scenes, and in New Orleans earlier that year, thinking about his own childhood, he wrote in his journal about the scouting accident when he was eleven years old, his falling from a tree and injuring himself. He interpreted the incident as a 'castration' that had occurred during a 'puberty ritual'. He wrote about how the consequences of this had followed him into adulthood, underpinning both his sexual and 'verbal' impotence, his fear of people generally, compounded by a fear of failure, which only spurred his attempts to gain admiration or affection, often lubricated by alcohol or, increasingly, drugs.

Sexual impotence plagued his relationships with women. He wrote about some of the reasons for this in 'The Myth of the Male Orgasm'. The previous year, Frank had written to Michael Wilding in England and told him about the end of one of his relationships: 'The Women's Liberation girl walked out on me because I couldn't fuck her anymore,' he wrote, adding: '(I guess she unconsciously frightened me).' His current relationships were not faring any better. 'My sex life is in a shocking condition . . . [it is] physically hung up.' He was taking acid 'to aggravate and disturb my guilt'. He still over-intellectualised relationships, using a rational framework to maintain emotional distance. When one relationship ended with the usual apologies, the usual regrets, Frank explained that the reason was probably because he used the word 'love' too early in the relationship, but he had later 'retracted it', hoping it would reset the relationship, as though it were some court proceeding or business transaction.

Such impotence did not seem to have affected Frank's relationships with men. He was still privately seeing John Burrows when their schedules allowed. Law reform during the 1960s was slowly moving towards decriminalising homosexuality. But initially the alternative was psychologising what was still widely considered a problem to be punished rather than cured, the more realistic view being homosexuality was within the range of normal human behaviour, requiring neither cure nor punishment. If anything, the psychological harm done to such men and women was probably a consequence of the social persecution they suffered.

Although there were already bars and clubs where same-sex communities could socialise, it was not until the Campaign Against Moral Persecution (CAMP) – which formed in July 1970 and established a headquarters in Balmain in February 1971 – that there was a public space for people to meet and politically organise. CAMP hosted nightly social events, films, discussions, and wine and cheese parties. It offered informal counselling, and had a referral service with sympathetic psychiatrists. That also worked the other way, with some psychiatrists sending their patients to CAMP events as a way of coping and finding a stable social world. CAMP ran a regular Sunday-afternoon barbeque to fundraise.

These spaces served a similar purpose to the old restrooms the CWA established in the 1920s: places for respite, where members could meet and socialise with people with similar experiences, overcome the isolation of their situation, and could plan and organise social and political activities.

In 1971 Frank attended a Sunday-afternoon gathering, reporting for *The Bulletin*. He interviewed the founders, John Ware and Christobel Poll, and their respective partners. They explained the social gatherings provided a place for individuals to 'come out' as gay or lesbian, as practice for doing so among their own social and family groups. 'Some people just come to me to talk and say "I'm a homosexual",' said John. 'They admit it to themselves through me – the letters are like that, too.'

Even though Frank intellectually accepted all of this, he was not yet emotionally able to speak publicly – to the mainstream public, at least – about the role of homosexuality in his own life. In his *Bulletin* report, he adopted his usual persona of a detached but curious outsider reporting on bohemian culture. There was no indication in this piece that he may have been part of the gay subculture. A similar resistance occurred when he discussed an affiliated subculture.

In New Orleans, Frank wrote to Don Anderson about how it was a great 'night city', with many bars open until late. 'In the Quarter there are people who do not literally come out in the day light. Some of the girls and transvestites of course shouldn't. Their whole image and survival depends on dim light.' In his journal he confided that his own survival, too, depended on keeping in the shadows. 'I have been timid about assuming insight into others,' Frank wrote. 'Except women because I think myself a woman.' This led into a series of private notes on the relationship between clothing and gender identity.

> Clothes: clothes as identity. Counter culture clothing. My David Jones clothing. Middle class with an edge of nonconformity. What about transvestism. The function of clothing. If I look ungrotesque, if I can be presentable in some aesthetic sense in girl's clothes is that enough. What is the grotesque. The breaking of set by wearing different clothes. Fancy dress. Uniforms. Clothes operate on consciousness?? Drugs, alcohol. My sexuality in female clothes not incredibly good.

The previous year, in a letter to Wendy, he suggested that his 'David Jones clothing' – meaning how he presented to the public – was probably itself a form of drag. 'So people find it hard to believe that the Frank Moorhouse in his conservative David Jones clothes is the Frank Moorhouse who writes obscene stories.'

Soon after, only a few months before he headed overseas, Frank had written a profile of Sydney's Les Girls troupe for *The Bulletin*. It opened: 'What do you do if your seventeen year old son wants to be a female impersonator?' Frank considered the history of early vaudeville acts, which satirised female stereotypes. He suggested that the development of high-quality recording technology allowed impersonators to more accurately mime female vocalists, and so the acts became more serious, the satire shifting away from the figures on stage and aimed more at the conventions of society more generally.

Frank interviewed many of the performers of Les Girls, and reported that some dressed as women offstage too, while others took female hormones. Others in the troupe did not take hormones and only dressed professionally, pointing to subcultural distinctions that were then still being drawn between transvestites and transsexuals. 'There's an obvious fascination with sexual contradiction and successful masquerade,' Frank wrote, rehearsing some of the possibilities. 'Maybe also for some men, it's another way of putting women down – men beating women at their own game. Maybe it serves as a way for the audience to flirt with other sexual roles which lie within them – maybe it arouses bisexuality, homosexuality or femininity impulses.'

It was this latter scenario, flirting with dormant sexual roles, that more accurately described Frank's situation at this stage, but his time in New Orleans proved that it was nevertheless freighted with anxiety and confusion. As in his *Bulletin* article on CAMP, Frank wrote about Les Girls as if this were his first encounter with this bohemian subculture, rather than a scene he had frequented ever since Norma Crinion took him to the Purple Onion in the early 1960s.

While Frank was overseas, Don Anderson was looking after his affairs in Australia, including shepherding *The Americans, Baby* through pre-publication. Don knew Frank was vulnerable and fragile, so he sent him only unqualified praise for the book. 'I do not exaggerate or delude myself in the least when I tell you that I am convinced it is as good as Joyce's Dubliners,' he wrote to Frank. 'And that's top flight . . . You have done for sections of Sydney in the late '60s what Joyce did for Dublin at the turn of the century.'

Frank appreciated the effort, but saw through the ruse:

> As for your praise – it came at a time when my ego was very low and was lapped up. Given discounting for friendship, I respectfully accept your praise – it's a mutual bind, you see I respect your literary judgment hence I can hardly disagree with you. But I know that you are wary of giving negative criticism after having once ventured some telling criticism, at my request, and having been brutally and drunkenly assaulted.

Frank's first thought at the prospect of his book being published was of his parents. The same night he replied to Don, he wrote a long letter home to his parents, referring to his forthcoming book:

> Again, it is likely to be a controversial book and the usual questions of obscenity will be raised. I know that it must be difficult for you to handle these sorts of things but literary fashions constantly change and what upsets some people twenty years ago goes unnoticed now. We're moving towards greater freedom of expression. As a writer, I have to react and reflect my times, and as it happens I am, for Australia, one of those breaking new ground . . . But the important thing I want you to know is that I'm trying to be an honest craftsman, working according to my own values of what is right and wrong, and working in the tradition of English literature. I suppose the tradition I am in is 'naturalism' – describing how things really are and in avoiding concealment, avoiding falsity. This is what brings about the questions of 'obscenity'. But as I've said I am not trying to be 'sensational' and it sometimes surprises me that people are upset (this is partly because as the author, I become lost in the work which sets its own rules and requirements regardless of prevailing laws).

Near the end of the letter, he added: 'Whether you read the book or not, or how different it may be from your own standards, I think that you have good reason to be satisfied with my integrity.'

A week later, he returned to Australia. Back in Sydney, Frank bided his time before publication day. He prepared a course for the WEA on the topic 'Functions of Media'. Meanwhile, in May, he gave a talk about journalism at Nowra Rotary, in which some of these ideas were aired, as well as a general discussion about his experience working in the media. His father and Owen were present. In the district 'Weekly Bulletin', Frank was referred to as 'Moorhouse Mark 3'.

> Frank's talk illustrated the difficulties in reporting – how we all tended to read into the written word the truth as we saw it individually. Returning recently from the States, Frank commented on how little news of Australia was reported in the American Press and how small was the effect of Australian activities on world Press in general.

Somebody in the audience asked Frank if he was publishing another book – a Dorothy Dixer, perhaps – to which he replied that he would be shortly. 'We'll let you know if it passes the censor,' reported the Rotary 'Weekly Bulletin', mistakenly titling Frank's forthcoming book *America's Baby*.

The final edition of *Thor* was published in June 1972, but its closing spawned a new publishing venture, Thor Publications. In 1969 Danish activists Søren Hansen and Jesper Jensen published *Den Lille Røde Bog for Skoleelever*, which in 1971 was translated into English as *The Little Red School Book* and distributed internationally. It caused some controversy. The book was basically a primer and how-to guide for political activism, but directed at school-age children. The school itself was presented as being a model for society at large, and the authors showed how to navigate its authoritarian and oppressive structures. Sections with information about sex and drugs drew the most fire.

In Australia, the National Literature Board of Review considered the book's merits, but the Department of Customs held up the final decision until April 1972, when *The Little Red School Book* was finally permitted into Australia. The Department of Education restricted its use in schools and in school libraries, arguing the material should not be made available to teenage schoolchildren – the book's intended audience. Thor Publications printed the book in a tabloid newspaper format (as with their previous publications) and organised a national campaign to have the material distributed to schoolchildren for free.

Although this episode marked the effective end of *Thor*'s years-long campaign against censorship, it was in many respects the project that cut closest to Frank's own personal concerns. Formally, *The Little Red School Book* shared its basic conceit – the school standing for society as a whole – with what Frank had attempted in his earliest juvenilia, particularly the unfinished collection of stories: 'This; the World of the Adolesense'. But substantively, *The Little Red School Book* signified everything that was not available to Frank when he grew up in Nowra in the 1940s and '50s, but which by the 1960s and '70s he felt he had desperately needed. Sexual and biological ignorance affected adolescents from that era, and this combined ignorance was the mute background to much of Frank and Wendy's relationship – especially with regards to sex, pregnancy, contraception and abortion – before, during and after their failed marriage.

The Little Red School Book would have provided context and assistance to some of Frank's formative experiences. On wet dreams: 'Boys can have orgasms while they're asleep. This is called having wet dreams. Many boys have them. They're quite normal.' On child molesters: 'If you see or meet a man like this, don't panic. Go and tell your teachers or your parents about it.' On homosexuality: 'Everybody is different – in sexual matters too. Some people are only attracted towards the opposite sex; some are attracted towards their own sex; some are attracted towards both sexes. People attracted to both sexes are called bi-sexual. People attracted to their own sex are called homosexual or queer or gay.' On being normal: 'It's normal to be different . . . You may feel you're the only person who experiences things in a "strange" way, and you may think you are abnormal. It can be a help to discover that there are many other people who are almost the same as you.'

On 5 June 1972, at about 5 pm, Frank and Sandra Levy were returning to their car on Darling Street, Balmain. As they were entering the car Sandra was stopped by two detectives, who ushered her to the footpath. They said Sandra had been identified as distributing material – copies of *Thor* and *The Little Red Schoolbook* were visible on the back seat of the car. She denied this, arguing that she had been at work all day. Frank quickly left the car to join them, asking for their identification. He took out his notebook and began documenting the exchange.

The detectives said they were going to search the car, which Frank protested, stating: 'It's been established that you cannot search the car.' He got into the car and began locking the doors from the inside, but before he could finish, a door was opened by one of the detectives and Frank was forcibly removed. His pullover was removed, and his shirt torn. He was pushed against the car and finally thrown to the ground. Frank asked if he was being charged with anything, but the detectives did not reply. They got him into a police car and returned to try to get the car keys out of Sandra's hands.

Frank got out of the police car, now stripped to the waist, and tried to defend Sandra. This time he was forced against the building and handcuffed. The detective used the police car's radio to call for a police van. Frank asked how many police were needed to restrain one man. The detectives returned to Sandra, Frank shouting all the while.

At the station, Frank and Sandra were not told what they were being charged with. They were each refused a telephone call. Finally, Frank was taken to a cell. When he asked again what he was being charged with, he was told 'assault'.

'No,' Frank said, 'I'm charging them with assault.'

'Who?' asked the policeman.

'The detectives.'

At around 9 pm, Frank was bailed for $100, after having his fingerprints taken. A few weeks later, his second book was published.

The Americans, Baby was released on 4 July 1972 – American Independence Day. The book launch was at the Balmain Volunteer, over a simple lunch and quiet drinks with a few friends and supporters. Then Gordon Barton, from Angus & Robertson, arrived and took over the bar tab. 'It was the only time in my life,' Frank said the following year, 'that people have literally ended up under the tables because of their indulgences.'

The book contained twenty stories, including 'The Story of Nature', reprinted from *Futility and Other Animals*. This acted as a bridge, bringing the two collections together, allowing some characters to cross over, while also providing a new context for that particular story. In the final edit, four stories had been cut from Frank's manuscript, as well as a mock introduction written from the perspective of an American evangelical preacher, 'Reverend Billy'. 'I first met Frank at a Rotary Conference in Ploughkeepsie, Maine,' Reverend Billy writes. 'He talked of his fascination with what he describes as the "neurotic adventure".'

The introduction parodied – without disconfirming – Michael Wilding's suggestion that Frank was a moralist, based on Frank's private claim that writing was a 'sort of religious commitment':

> This is an obscene book. You may ask why a preacher of the gospel of God aligns himself with it. I align myself with this book because it is Obscenity in the Service of Truth and Obscenity in the Service of Love and Love in the Service of Obscenity and Truth in the Service of Obscenity.

The introduction demonstrated that Frank was conscious of the comparison between writing and Rotary, as an organising principle and an ethic of social engagement: 'as I told him at Ploughkeepsie that icy day, writing, like Rotary, is an activity of the soul,' Reverend Billy says. In 1966, when Frank was going through a period of depression, his father wrote to him, explicitly connecting his own psychological difficulties with how he used Rotary as a corrective:

> So sorry to know you are still worried by emotional troubles. I can sympathise with you because I know how terrible this can be and

how difficult it is to rise above it. I think Rotary and my interest in Freemasonry has become a big help during my life because both of them offer a high standard of living without being tied to religious dogma.

The four stories omitted from *The Americans, Baby* remained unpublished. Each was paired with another story in the collection, which Frank's editor referred to as 'double-yolkers', recommending leaving one of each pair out of the book. But they are interesting stories in their own right, and throw further light on the characters and the social dynamics underlying all the stories included in the collection.

'The Colony of Two' focuses on Hugo, the Nebraskan, eight years after the events of 'The First Story of Nature'. He is planning his own utopian colony. The story goes into great detail regarding the rationale for the colony and its rules of self-government (based on the Quaker model). Hugo sends out the plan, requesting a meeting from a list of eighteen people, but only four show up: a couple with a child, and a woman named Angela. Almost immediately, they split into two factions over the question of drugs.

Afterwards, Hugo and Angela go for a drink and they end up having sex. Hugo is frustrated by the low level of interest people had shown in his utopian dream for a non-traditional, communal lifestyle. But by the end of the story it is clear, beneath the utopian dream, that Hugo harbours a yearning for more traditional domesticity with Angela alone.

Angela is the titular character from a story included in the book 'The Girl from the Family of Man'. She is the central character in a companion piece, omitted from the final list, called 'The Girl from *The Family of Man* and the Man of War'. Angela goes back to an Australian man's house after a date, only to discover his obsession with the American Civil War. 'Fanaticism . . . She'd seen it before. In the States. War crazy. He probably wore uniforms and collected firearms. She felt physically weak and nauseated.' Unable to articulate her unease, she cites her childhood portrait in *The Family of Man* collection. '*The Family of Man* means something to me.'

Angela and Kyle – the couple from 'The Girl from *The Family of Man*' – appear in another omitted story, 'The Bad Scene' (although

Angela becomes Louise partway through the typescript draft). This story reworked an earlier story, 'Some Sort of Mistake', published in *Squire* in 1967. It reworked a theme recurring in Frank's fictional imagination, starting with his unpublished 1958 story 'The Affair with Andrea'.

Futility and Other Animals had included stories with a homosexual theme. A new story, 'Carl and Paul Goodman', broadened the theme of homosexuality to include bisexuality, cross-dressing, transsexuality and the psychological ramifications of remaining in the closet. It is an episodic narrative, mapping the sexual and gender trajectory of Carl, a fourth-year university student, while having an affair with Paul Jonson, an American ten years his senior. Carl and Paul appear together for the first time in *The Americans, Baby* in the story 'The American, Paul Jonson', which details their first meeting. Carl is the narrator of the story 'The Coca Cola Kid'.

The title 'Carl and Paul Goodman' refers to a homophobic exchange between Carl (still in the closet) and a co-worker. The co-worker – Turvey, the gun-toting urban revolutionary from 'The Machine Gun' – accused another colleague of being a 'poofter'. Carl pointed out that Paul Goodman, the American radical, was a homosexual. This leads to a description of the psychological aspects of Carl still being in the closet. These include compartmentalisation ('What would Turvey say if he knew he'd had homosexual sex? – something he'd momentarily forgotten about himself. Strange.') and rationalisation, with Carl approaching the topic too academically ('He'd only been with Jonson a few times and with a couple of others, strangers. And he'd only done it because he'd been sexually frustrated – not because he was especially homosexual. Perhaps he was a little homosexual. Wasn't everyone?'). These feed into a mutual rationalisation between Carl and Paul:

'Do you think I'm homosexual?' I asked Jonson.

'We are all homosexual,' Jonson said, edgy, 'some of us just have the rare relationship which demands that it is expressed.'

Why did he sound so academic? . . .

> 'Do you think of yourself as an academ – I mean a homosexual?'
> Jonson pulled his nose. 'No, I don't – I'll marry one day.'

This story goes further than Frank's other stories in describing other aspects of a troubled sexual and gender identity:

> He lay facing the gentle fairly handsome man of about thirty who pushed his legs apart, guided them over his shoulders and then pushed his penis into him. He was surprised that it went in with so little pain and without Vaseline or anything. And it was the first time he'd been fucked facing a man, like a woman.

For Carl, such experiences raise questions of gender identity: 'Was he really a woman? – by personality, he meant. Why did he want to be fucked and didn't care to fuck?' Again: 'Why did he always want to be the woman?' At the same time, Carl is unaware how in these descriptions he is orienting the role of the woman as being subordinate to the perspective of a man.

Outside of Carl's relationship with Paul, the story explores, for the first time in Frank's fiction, the theme of cross-dressing. 'Transvestites' appeared peripherally in 'Becker and the Boys from the Band', but here Carl goes back to a male lecturer's place to have sex, and for the first time the act involves cross-dressing.

> 'Do you like dressing up?' . . .
> The lecturer took him upstairs to his bedroom, opened a wardrobe and showed him women's clothes . . .
> The lecturer undressed and changed into women's underwear. He likewise did, unable to think, ashamed, hot with excitation. He stood then in panties, step-ins, and a slip, his penis dribbling and hot. The lecturer gave him a woman's satin shift with long flared sleeves.
> 'You don't need a wig,' the lecturer said, 'your hair's a beautiful length.' . . .
> He felt totally unaware of his male body and the lecturer's male body until the caressing and fondling and the excitement of nylon and satin against his body made him come. And then he'd felt the old disgust and the intense embarrassment.

Throughout all of this, the underlying argument of the story was the vagaries of group identity, and the *anomie* of the central figure, Carl, who does not belong to any single group, and remains unrecognised.

> He'd never thought of himself as being a member of a community. Perhaps he belonged to the homosexual minority, he joked with himself. He'd never thought of it that way before.
> He would fellate men, but found he didn't have anything much in common with them beyond the sex.

The story concludes on a note of fear, with the weight of social convention crushing in: the pressure to survive, stay in the closet. 'One day they were going to discover that he was a bit of a homosexual and that would be the end. Though Paul Goodman had made it public and survived. He shuddered at the idea of Turvey and the other's knowing.'

'Carl and Paul Goodman' was the final story omitted from the line-up for *The Americans, Baby*.

The critical reception of *The Americans, Baby* initially reflected a similar divide to how *Futility and Other Animals* had been received four years earlier, hinging on whether the critic understood the discontinuous narrative form and could look past the sporadic swearing.

Marion Halligan, in *The Canberra Times*, did not appreciate the discontinuous narrative form, and was unsure whether to apply the standard of the novel or the traditional short-story collection:

> Although the stories were written at different times, one gradually realises that the same characters recur, in major and minor roles so that at times one has the feeling that one ought to be reading a rather scrappy novel. I'd have preferred more or fewer of them; as it was they had neither the fullness of characters in a novel nor the brief completeness of characters in a short story.

She found an exception in Becker, who was 'a powerful personage'. Halligan repeated a criticism levelled at Frank's previous book: 'His writing uses a lot of four letter words and what for want of a better name can be called obscenity, which in theory is a perfectly respectable literary device but which in practice tends to become boring.' Disapproval of swearing in books was still a dominant view in Australia at the time. The previous year a poll showed that 64 per cent of Australians disapproved of four-letter words in books, and 76 per cent disapproved of such language in films.

Ian Bedford, reviewing for *Nation*, understood the resonances created by the discontinuous narrative form, the cumulative effect of which was a body of fiction acting as a form of social inquiry. 'In its small compass,' Bedford wrote, 'this book of stories affords a more exact and relevant observation of peculiarly Australian social tensions than any recent work of politics or sociology that I can think of.' Bedford drew attention to the sexual ambiguity of many of the characters described:

> In a Moorhouse story the characters are not so much sexual beings, as obsessed with, or mildly interested in themselves as sexual beings. They have a sexual history, often profusely described, but for the most part an indeterminate sexual identity. Insofar as they engage in any kind of action, they are self-absorbed, if not self-aware, at least self-regarding; and they lacerate others and themselves.

Significantly, some characters avoided this ambiguity: 'An exception should be made for some of the homosexual characters.' In concluding his review, Bedford wrote: 'A number of stories in this book seem to this reader to be among the best work being produced by an Australian.'

This appeared to be the general consensus for other critics as well. Although Barbara Jefferis, in *The Sydney Morning Herald*, read the book as a novel – albeit 'not a conventional novel' – she placed it in the context of other experimental narrative forms: those deployed by John Dos Passos, Jorge Luis Borges, Donald Barthelme, Richard Brautigan and Kurt Vonnegut. 'To mention him in connection with these others is not to suggest that he is an antipodean imitator,' she wrote of Frank. 'Innovators are rare in Australian writing, but it seems very possible that Moorhouse will prove to be one. In one sense, at least, he is already that.'

In *The Australian*, Brian Kiernan built on his review of Frank's previous book: '*The Americans, Baby* is consistently better than Mr Moorhouse's first collection and establishes him as one of the most assured craftsmen and original writers of fiction in Australia today.' He added: 'Few Australian writers seem similarly to be able to draw on the immediately contemporary, and to allow current social issues to impinge on their characters' awareness in the unforced way that is found, say, in the latest novels of Bellow, Updike and Malmud.'

John Miles, in *The Advertiser*, agreed but was more effusive. 'Perhaps the great Australian contemporary novel has yet to be written, but the great Australian short story has certainly been written,' he stated. 'Frank Moorhouse is the man.' Miles appreciated, in part, the break with traditional Australian literature: 'Not a gum tree anywhere but the people are creatures of their country, their times and their attitudes.' He appreciated too the compassionate way Frank treated his characters, particularly the homosexual characters: 'In a couple of stories, "The American, Paul Jonson" and "Jonson's Letter", he tells how a man becomes a homosexual, and what it feels like to be one, with understanding.'

Ian Turner, in *The Bulletin*, claimed these 'stories by (and of) Frank Moorhouse are, I think, the best short stories we've had in Australia for a long time'. He drew comparison between Frank and 'the kind of raw-edged personal involvement that goes with Mailer and Tom Wolfe and the other exponents of the new journalism'. This elides the distinction between fiction and reality – which Frank otherwise assiduously tried to keep apart – in order to talk less about the stories as fiction than to reduce them to mere reportage: 'The place is Sydney; the time is now; the people are those who comprise the "push" . . .' In part, this was so Turner could insert an anecdote regarding his role in meeting Kenneth Rexroth in Melbourne in 1967, and persuading him to meet the Sydney libertarians, the actual party displaced by the fictional party in 'The American Poet's Visit'. That said, Turner provided a perceptive summary of the concerns and paradoxes at the heart of Frank's inquiry:

> There are three central themes in Moorhouse's stories: the contradiction between preservation of self and involvement with others; the irreconcilability of libertarian (personal) and radical (social) values; and the conflict between the demands made of the individual by the institutions of capitalist (or any other?) society and the desire for self-realisation.

On the whole, Frank's second book received broader and more positive critical praise than his first. At the end of 1972, *The Americans, Baby* was included in the 'best books of the year' lists in both *The Sydney Morning Herald* and *The Australian*.

Frank was beginning to find an independent readership beyond his own circle of acquaintances, newspaper critics and those who happened across his stories in magazines or small-circulation journals. In part, this indicated the broader marketing and distribution power of Angus & Robertson over Gareth Powell & Associates. It was also indicative of a broader shift that was slowly taking place in Australian literary culture between traditional standards and new literary forms, with some writers, and increasingly more readers, exploring new literary territory.

But Frank, always unsatisfied with the present, was already anticipating the future. On the back cover of *The Americans, Baby* was a photograph of Frank, thirty-three years old, walking barefoot in his backyard, wearing a long-sleeved turtleneck sweater and jeans. The biographical note stated: 'He is now working on a documentary-narrative of the technological history of his home region called *The Electric Experience*.'

II

'Contrary to Popular Misconception, Banned Writing Doesn't Pay'

The Americans, Baby had been published within a few months of Michael Wilding's debut collection of stories, *Aspects of the Dying Process*. Their names had become increasingly linked in public, as part of an alternative, and growing, literary scene.

When Michael reviewed Frank's first book in 1969, he had not mentioned the Push. Two years later, surveying recent Australian short stories for *Meanjin*, which included *Futility and Other Animals*, Michael revised his view regarding the general setting of the stories, placing them squarely within the Push. 'The Australian bohemia, the "modern, urban tribe" as he calls it, the Sydney push and its environs, is the basic material for Frank Moorhouse's *Futility and Other Animals*,' he wrote. This realigned the reception of Frank's writing to coincide more with Michael's own literary concerns, his own work being self-consciously positioned within the Push. So when *The Americans, Baby* and *Aspects of the Dying Process* were published a year later, *Nation Review* wrote about them together, under the heading 'Two Humble Studs from the Push'.

'Frank Moorhouse and Michael Wilding are about the same age, have published collections of prose within a few months of each other, and have drawn on the same Sydney setting and the Push crowd as the basis of many of their stories,' Irina Patsi Dunn wrote. 'But their differences are more interesting than their similarities.' Although Frank and Michael's stories tended to deal with similar characters, Frank's stories were more 'open-ended rather than inconclusive', while Michael's stories were 'discrete, self contained and tend to follow a pattern of development, with a climax (of sorts), and a literarily, if not always experientially, satisfying denouement'. Dunn speculated the difference in outlook was because Michael was an Englishman in Australia, trying to make sense of his new locality, while Frank was an Australian concerned with the encroachment of American culture.

During this period, Frank, Michael and Carmel Kelly were one day sitting on the balcony of the Balmain Volunteer, drinking and discussing the perennial 'crisis of literature'. Carmel Kelly was twenty-six years old at the time, had written for *Thor* and the previous year had had her first short story published in *Westerly*. Despite Frank and Michael both having books published that year, the general sense was that outlets for publishing their sort of new, bold fiction were narrowing. *Thor* had folded. The girlie magazines in which they had previously published – *Squire* and *Chance* – had shuttered earlier that year. *Man* still operated, but was in decline (and would close in 1974). Frank had not published a story there since 1969.

Together they concocted a beer plan for a new publication to be called *Tabloid Story*. One model for this was the special eight-page supplement of banned or problematic fiction that had appeared as an insert in *Tharunka* in April 1970. The innovation the trio came up with that day in Balmain was to solicit already established, mainstream journals and newspapers not already publishing short fiction, to host one-off supplements inserted in their pages. *Tabloid Story* would select, edit, lay out and prepare camera-ready proofs of the supplement, provided free of charge to the host, in exchange for the host covering the printing costs and including the insert in their publication. They would also provide 2000 offprints, which *Tabloid Story* would distribute locally, providing complimentary copies to their authors. The host publication would benefit by getting good quality content, basically free of charge, and *Tabloid Story* – and, more importantly, their authors – would benefit by putting new fiction in front of an established audience, without the need to cultivate and build one over time. This model also removed the pressure on editors to contend with the vagaries of distribution and sales, or to negotiate with printers.

The project became more viable when *Tabloid Story* received a $2000 subsidy from the Commonwealth Literary Fund for its first edition, which allowed the editors to pay authors industry rates, as proposed by the Australian Society of Authors – the first time a literary publication in Australia could afford to do so. *Tabloid Story* became the first publication to advertise its rates of pay, and the editors began encouraging other publications, especially literary magazines, to do likewise. This gave the three an added sense of mission. *Tabloid Story* became a vehicle to support authors and find new audiences for fiction, while at the same time advocating for fairer freelance conditions for Australian writers more generally. They even had a policy of paying on acceptance, rather than waiting until after publication, which was the industry norm – usually well after publication.

The first *Tabloid Story* was published on 20 October 1972, in *National U*, the newspaper of the Australian Union of Students, which was distributed free across all university campuses in Australia. With a circulation of 60,000, *Tabloid Story* suddenly had a far larger potential readership than any of the traditional literary magazines. Frank's inclusion, 'The Oracular Stories', came from a suite of stories he had worked on in mid-1969, when he was going through a psychologically precarious period. This was when he had broken contact with his family, and had sought, but failed to secure, psychiatric help.

The suite was not initially intended for publication. Frank had developed a character named Milton, based loosely on Michael, the name coming from Wilding's book, *Milton's Paradise Lost* (1969), an academic monograph. In 'The Oracular Stories', Milton breaks up with a woman (in the original draft her name is Wesley), who attempts suicide by swallowing thirty Nembutal capsules. The first-person narrator intervenes and revives her, but while she is unconscious, he has non-consensual sex with her. She is informed about this the next day, she is okay with it and they begin dating – much to Milton's annoyance. In the *Tabloid Story* version, the non-consensual act (Wesley's name is changed to Hestia) is precipitated by the narrator imagining Milton having sex with Hestia, and fantasising about having homosexual sex with Milton. The motif of taking pills, associated with assault or suicide, recurs in Frank's fiction, the first instance being in 'The Young Girl and the American Sailor'.

Frank probably resurrected the old draft story, rewriting it for *Tabloid Story*, because Michael's recently published collection had included 'Joe's Absence', in which Graham (a fictional Michael) and the girlfriend of Joe (a fictional Frank) have sex, while at the same time metaphorically having non-consensual sex with Joe's typescript stories – an act described as 'the rape of the stories'. In 'The Oracular Stories', this structure is inverted, with the narrator (a fictional Frank) literally having non-consensual sex with Milton's girlfriend, while metaphorically doing the same to Milton (his girlfriend being a substitute for Milton).

The absence of this underlying context, for the general reader, arguably rendered this story problematic. The Brisbane Vice Squad apparently agreed, and upon receiving a complaint regarding 'The Oracular Stories' on obscenity grounds, seized all copies of *Tabloid Story* from the campus of the University of Queensland.

On 13 November 1972, at the Blacktown Civic Centre in Sydney, Gough Whitlam, leader of the Australian Labor Party, launched his campaign for the next federal election. The ALP strategy was to build upon the gains, and the narrow loss, made at the 1969 election, and to do so through modernising how they campaigned. The 'New Politics' included opinion polls, market research, targeted messaging, impression management and consumer advertising techniques. The 'It's Time' slogan became an advertising jingle, the song performed by media and entertainment personalities – a novel practice at the time – in an effort to appeal to a new constituency: women, young people and those in the burgeoning outer suburbs.

After twenty-three years of conservative rule – Frank's entire adolescent and adult life – a generation of voters had become habituated to not placing much stock in electoral party politics as a mechanism for social change. This was one of the points of convergence between Frank and the libertarians, who were dismissive of the electoral process and had long advocated for lodging informal votes to get around Australia's compulsory voting laws. Frank was sceptical of the 'New Politics' strategy, as it relied so heavily on the communications, advertising and persuasion techniques Frank had been studying critically for more than a decade. The 'It's Time' campaign effectively promoted politics as lifestyle advocacy, geared to a television generation. On the night of the Blacktown launch, the lectern was quickly repainted and the screen behind changed, to suit the new colour resolution of television.

Frank volunteered to write a piece for *The Bulletin* about the campaign trail, albeit from the perspective of the three candidates in the seat of Macarthur. This electorate covered Nowra and much of the South Coast region Frank was then writing about for his Electric Experience project. His volunteering was more about an expenses-paid research trip for his fiction-writing than about an interest in federal politics. The article, 'Macarthur Baby', was published one week before the election. Frank spent time with each candidate as they campaigned across the district, making stump speeches, gladhanding the locals and appearing at regional events. The main hub for these events was the local community service centres Frank was already familiar with: Rotary clubs, Apex, Lions and so on. Frank recorded long conversations with the candidates on his cassette machine as they drove together from town to town.

The Liberal Party's Henry Jefferson Bate (known as Jeff) had been the sitting member in Macarthur for twenty-five years. But at sixty-six years old he failed at preselection, and chose to run anyway as an independent. The new Liberal candidate was Max Dunbier. The Labor candidate was John Kerin. Both Dunbier and Kerin were thirty-four years old, roughly the same age as Frank.

Frank focused on the continuities between each of the candidates. Coming from a farming background, each operated under what Frank called an 'ideology of self-employment'. 'They sometimes feel that they're the only people in Australia pulling their weight, keeping the country going, upholding the traditions of enterprise, initiative, community service and self-reliance,' Frank wrote. 'They cannot see that it is an economic impossibility for everyone to be self-employed. Anyone who is not self-employed is a life failure.'

Frank did not favour any candidate, but he did raise a point of concern against one of the Liberal candidate's positions: 'The Liberal Party people seemed to talk about disorder and to spread fear of disorder (in this, the most orderly of countries). There seemed to be no realisation that you achieve surface harmony only by suppressing the disagreeable.' He noted in passing that the issues which most concerned his own subculture – women's issues, homosexuality, censorship and so on – were not really on the agenda of any of the candidates. 'They are rarely raised,' Frank wrote, 'and when they are the candidates handle them gingerly, vaguely, jokingly.' Humour was used, Frank noted, not only to make light of the issues, but to maintain conformity and signal one's position within the status quo.

One week after this article was published, on 2 December, Labor took 49.6 per cent of the primary vote, gaining eight seats in the House of Representatives. Three days later, Gough Whitlam became Australia's twenty-first prime minister, the ALP forming its first federal government in twenty-three years. In Macarthur, John Kerin won with a slim majority for Labor, followed by the independent, with the Liberal candidate trailing. The former Liberal member had split the conservative vote, giving Labor the win.

The election was held the same weekend as the annual Libertarian Society conference at Minto. Frank was in attendance. The general mood was one of disinterest in the Labor victory. That same month, Frank had written a piece for *Digger*, a Melbourne-based underground newspaper. Here Frank spoke more from a counter-cultural perspective than he had in his *Bulletin* article. The various subcultures, loosely affiliated, had previously been resistant to electoral politics, but Frank noted how the recent campaign had stirred some of them into paying attention, and others into action. 'Some have even begun to believe in the ALP!' he wrote.

Frank used this piece to reorient his own position regarding the state and electoral politics, while still retaining some scepticism. He distanced himself further from the libertarians:

> The fundamental libertarian position is 'No matter whom you vote for, a politician always gets in'. I have liked it and used it to shut up people who want to discuss party politics. It works so well that it has occurred to me it must be suspect. It is after all a slogan and must contain, therefore, simple-mindedness, if not outright mystification.

Frank remained sceptical that Whitlam would effect much social change. 'You bet the ALP will keep ASIO going, along with telephone taps, dossiers and harassment of those people seen as a "threat to the system",' he noted. On arts funding: 'Some specific policies of the ALP have offered more loot to some of us, including increased grants to the arts and public lending right (yes, one day we'll all live on grants!).' But the cost was a more centralised federal arts funding body. 'So the prediction is that there will be more money in exchange for more control.' Underlying all of this was the constant concern regarding censorship: 'I doubt whether the ALP would do anything much about censorship.'

Frank used the essay to outline his general attitude to politics at this stage, even with the Whitlam victory:

> I don't find politics *immoral*; I find political activity befuddles the intellect. It is so much based on verbal formulations which will gain appeal and then power. And these formulations are distorting; they are reductions of complexity. To involve yourself in politics, except as an area of study, is to tangle yourself in a mess of illusions, mystifications and intellectual compromises.

Frank's own concerns were still with a form of human inquiry that overturned such verbal formulations, revived complexity, dispelled illusions and pressed against the contradictions of intellectual compromise.

It was a form of inquiry best characterised by literary fiction.

Frank's focus for more than a year had been on writing and revising stories for his next book, which was ostensibly concerned with the technological history of the South Coast. By late 1972, he began sending out individual stories to be published; the first two appearing over the summer.

The central figure in the stories was T. George McDowell, the father of Terri, who first appeared in 'I Saw a Child for the Three of Us', in *Futility and Other Animals*. She then became a central figure in *The Americans, Baby*, particularly in her relationship with the Coca Cola Kid, Becker. T. George McDowell made his first appearance in Frank's second book, in 'The St Louis Rotary Convention 1923, Recalled'. In that story Becker was invited to speak at McDowell's Rotary Club about soft drink manufacturing.

One of Frank's new stories, 'George McDowell Does the Job', was published in *The Bulletin* in December 1972. It introduced McDowell and his wife, Thelma, in 1938, with two daughters and a successful soft drink manufacturing business on the South Coast. 'He badly wanted a son.' The second story, 'A Black, Black Birth in 1939', appeared in *The Sun* newspaper's 'Holiday Short Story Festival' section, in January 1973. The events of this story are situated around the time of those of 'The St Louis Rotary Convention 1923, Recalled', but considered from McDowell's perspective. The original story introduced McDowell as being involved in technology, but this new story specifically describes him as being a local soft drink manufacturer. McDowell is in conversation with an unnamed 'American' – presumably Becker – voicing his concerns regarding his youngest daughter, Terri, who suffers from 'the Bohemian Problem'. McDowell tells the American about her birth in 1939, her conception having been detailed previously in 'George McDowell Does the Job'. McDowell, it seems, did not get the son he wanted.

The Electric Experience project drew heavily on Frank's research into the history of the South Coast between the world wars, a continuation of the archival research he had done for The Great Warriors and Doctor projects, as well as the recorded interviews he had done with his father. The figure of T. George McDowell was constituted of various fragments from this research and Frank Sr's memories and stories, consolidated by Frank's own imagination. McDowell was a representative of the 'ideology of self-employment' Frank had written about in his *Bulletin* article on the election in Macarthur.

As he worked through this material, history and family lore, Frank spent a great deal of time sifting through his own memories and dark imaginings from his childhood in Nowra. The title of the first story published from the project comes from a recollection of Terri being born on Black Saturday in early 1939, when bushfires engulfed the region and encircled the township. This recalled Frank's own birth in late December 1938, the historic dry spell, tinder-dry landscape, and the bushfires burning through the territory a couple of weeks later. 'It was almost as though the day had affected Terri, the new born baby. Perhaps the roaring noise of the fire, the smell of burning eucalyptus and the fear surrounding her, disturbed her forever.'

'A Black, Black Birth in 1939' contained a passing reference to a local medic who assisted during the 1939 bushfires: Dr Trenbow, the protagonist from Frank's unrealised Doctor project. Frank's growing fictional universe was singular and complex, populated with a multiplying cast of figures, coexisting in the same imaginative timeline, across generations and geographies. This was the 'continuous environment' from which his stories emerged.

Frank had submitted a draft of the first three episodes of 'Doctor' in early 1972. Since then, the governing funding body had transitioned from the Australia Council for the Arts to an Interim Council, and Frank's project had fallen through the bureaucratic cracks. The Interim Council had on file a script assessment for Frank's submission, from August 1972, but it was not until February 1973 that they finally contacted him about it. The general feeling was that the scripts were 'unsatisfactory' and required a great deal more work.

Frank waited a month before replying. He clarified that the scripts submitted were a first draft only, and were not to be considered complete, but the funds provided by the council were now depleted and so he was unable to continue working on them. Then, a month later, Frank pulled the project completely, claiming: 'I have since abandoned the idea of making the project into a television series and have converted the three episodes into a film script titled 'Between Wars' which my partner Michael Thornhill is at present trying to find backers for.'

The previous year, while his television scripts were languishing with the Interim Council, Frank had already considered the project abandoned, for the second time. But then Mike Thornhill, while visiting Frank's Ewenton Street studio one day, found the file containing the scripts and correspondence relating to the project. He saw their potential and persuaded Frank to revise the project once more, into its original feature film format. Mike secured development funding in December 1972 to allow Frank to make a first pass at a screenplay. By the time the Interim Council contacted Frank, the project had already morphed into something else.

Mike booked them into adjoining suites at the Chevron-Hilton Hotel in Surfers Paradise, Queensland, for two weeks of uninterrupted writing and revising. They stocked their hotel fridges with Carlton Draught. They had bottles of Jack Daniels, they wore Hawaiian shirts and safari suits. After a hard day's work they lounged by the pool, 'unrecognised as Scott Fitzgerald and Howard Hawkes'.

It was the longest, most sustained piece of writing Frank had ever done. A large component of the work involved archival and historical research, exploring the period before he was born. He researched the social impact of war, medicine, psychiatry and politics. He researched, for example, the Australia First Movement, the proto-fascist militias which had formed in the lead-up to World War II. He later likened it to having written a novel, while at the same time recalling why he preferred the short-story form.

Working closely with Mike made Frank aware of the differences between prose and film. In an interview with *Cinema Papers* the following year, Frank stated:

> [C]inema is much more explicit, it gives off a lot more information than prose fiction which works on the absence of detail often. Certainly the way I've been working, my style is sparse and without detailed delineation of the physical characteristics of the characters, of rooms and so on – except where necessary. When working on a script Mike will say: 'Well, what does he look like, what sort of room does he have, does he smoke, does he drink?' The film requires more data and consequently this elaboration of the original story was the bulk of the work – working out the sort of locations, movements and mannerisms and adding to the original.

By June 1973, Frank told his parents *Between Wars* was nearly ready to go into production. This was premature, and perhaps optimistic, as Mike still had to secure financing for the film. Another difference, one of which Frank would only gradually become aware, was that film production operated more slowly than book publishing.

But the money was better: the script had already earned Frank more than he had ever made from all of his other writing combined – and it was still only a work in progress. This initial windfall allowed him to pay off all his previously accrued debts.

The immediate consequences of Whitlam's election win surprised many, and even softened some hardened critics among Sydney's subcultures. Whitlam quickly ended military conscription, increased arts subsidies, began reform of the healthcare system, advocated for equal pay for women, removed race as a criterion of immigration policy, and ended literary censorship.

Senator Lionel Murphy was appointed as both attorney-general and Minister for Customs. One of his first acts was to remove the administration of censorship from the Department of Customs, relocating it in the Attorney-General's Office. By the end of 1973, all books remaining on the federal banned list were permitted into the country. Unbeknown to Frank, on 21 December 1972 – the day of his thirty-fourth birthday – Senator Murphy was sent a letter regarding *The Americans, Baby*. It had been referred to the National Literature Board of Review, where it was 'unanimously recommended' and deemed 'suitable for distribution in Australia'.

In February 1973, Wendy Bacon's and John Cox's appeal came before the court, and a retrial was ordered. Under the changing political circumstances, the prosecutor decided not to proceed, and all charges were quietly dropped. Wendy and John were notified later that year by letter. It was the last major obscenity trial in New South Wales.

Such changes were largely positive, but there were some unintended consequences and transitional problems that immediately affected Frank. In February 1972, the Australian Society of Authors, after years of lobbying the Commonwealth Literary Fund, submitted a proposal to the government for a wholesale reimagining of the fund. This was the impetus for the 1973 formation of the Literature Board of the Australia Council for the Arts. The ALP election win protracted this transition and, as a result, the funding application for the second edition of *Tabloid Story*, assigned to an intermediary body, was put on hold indefinitely. Heading into the New Year, the project was considered possibly dead in the water.

A second problem emerged around the publication of a booklet, *Illegal Relatives*, a bootleg of some of Frank's stories, released without his permission in either December 1972 or January 1973. The original impetus for the project was Wendy Bacon's trial and conviction in February 1971: *Illegal Relatives* was intended as a fundraiser towards the costs of these various trials, but publishing the stories would also be a form of protest and an attempt to subvert the Australian censorship regime.

Apparently, the plan was for Frank to supply stories and for Jenny Coopes, a cartoonist who contributed illustrations to *Tharunka*, to do accompanying drawings. But Frank seems to have lost control of the project. He was unsure about the stories from a literary perspective, and wanted to revise them. He did end up publishing one of the pieces, 'The Oracular Stories', in a revised form in late October 1972. But Whitlam's dismantling of Australia's censorship regime rendered the project moot.

The bootlegger was undeterred, however, stating in the preface:

> Shit! I can't wait any longer. Personally, I like the stories as do other friends. We all think it's good humor. To get out of the obvious ethical dilemma I'll argue the point that it's time for the 'prima donnas' to be stripped of their privileges . . . Now it's up to you to decide if it's 'ART'; if it has the necessary quota of 'Community Standards of literary value'; if FRANK is a prima donna . . .

By 'prima donna', the printer was referring to writers, and by 'stripping them of their privileges', they meant ignoring writers' copyright. This attitude rested on a long Australian tradition, from colonial times onwards, of claiming to value the work of a writer, while economically undervaluing the effort required to produce that work – or even recognising an author's moral rights over their own work. Frank was used to printers censoring or refusing to print a literary work, but this was a very different problem: a printer effectively stealing a work.

Later that year, Frank gave a WEA lecture series about how new communications technologies – offset printing, photocopying and phototransmission – could bring about the end of mass media, and effectively also end literary censorship. But, as Frank understood, the impact of new technologies on culture, when pushed far enough, tended to flip into their opposite. The same technologies that were overturning censorship could collapse an author's copyright and destroy their capacity to earn a living from their writing.

This was a possibility Frank had become aware of over the previous couple of years. In an article in *The National Times* in February 1971 – a clipping Frank kept in his files – a journalist outlined how publishers, printers and distributors in Melbourne, Sydney and Brisbane were working together to release books otherwise banned under the *Printing Act and the Obscene Publications Act*. The best-known example was *Portnoy's Complaint*. But, the article went on, the underground press was doing the same with other works, such as Henry Miller's *Tropic of Cancer* (1971) and Jerry Rubin's *Do It! Scenarios of the Revolution* (1970). One consequence was that the authors received no royalties; neither they nor their publishers had given permission for their books to be pirated in the first place. The article referred to this as the 'rip-off' press.

The effective end of censorship meant that such a trade-off was no longer justifiable, as the author's note at the end of *Illegal Relatives* – which Frank wrote when he thought the project necessary – makes clear:

> This book is published illegally and consequently the protection of the law on copyright is hardly expected, or sought. If the stories are reproduced the author would appreciate knowledge of it, and a copy. He would, of course, appreciate payment even more, since contrary to popular misconception, banned writing doesn't pay.

It is difficult to ascertain how many copies of *Illegal Relatives* were printed, how many were sold or distributed privately and where the money went. Copies were sold through Sydney bookseller Bob Gould, for example, who later paid a royalty directly to Frank for the 100 copies he handled. A further consequence was that Frank struggled to get the stories included in the bootleg published elsewhere, even in a revised form. In September 1974, one magazine editor initially rejected the story 'Alter Ego Interpretation' because it had already been 'published' in *Illegal Relatives* the year before.

A third consequence of the Whitlam election win was even more concerning. The abolition of the federal censorship regime was replaced, after negotiation between the federal and state governments, by a classification system. It was modelled on the classification system for films, which the previous federal government had introduced.

One of the first books to be given an R-rating in Victoria – restricted to those over the age of eighteen – under the *Indecent and Restricted Publications Act 1973* was *The Americans, Baby*. This severely limited its distribution and circulation. It could not be displayed on racks at motels, hotels, airports, railways or newsagents. Its sale was confined to bookshops. Even then, it could not be publicly displayed, and if somebody wanted to buy it they had to request it from the bookseller, who was required to keep it behind the counter.

This limited sales to those who already knew about the book, removing the possibility of the book being discovered serendipitously through browsing. Frank referred to this as a form of 'back-door censorship', which 'prejudices the book' and 'fouls' the relationship between books and readers, and the relationship between author and bookseller. It was effectively a form of economic censorship. 'This action makes my chances of existing as an independent self supporting writer very doubtful,' Frank wrote at the time. 'You don't put him in gaol[,] you make it impossible for him to live by his craft.' The situation was only compounded by the possibility of pirated copies being printed and distributed: the author was squeezed from both sides, by official government bureaucrats and the unofficial 'rip-off' press.

On 27 July 1973, Frank fronted the Balmain District Court, to face charges for the alleged distribution of *The Little Red Schoolbook*, and subsequently for resisting and assaulting the police. Unlike the case of Wendy Bacon and John Cox, and despite the changed political circumstances, this case proceeded. Frank was convicted, and fined $50.

The spring edition of *Overland* in 1973 contained a long essay called 'Notes on Frank Moorhouse', by Brian Kiernan. *The Americans, Baby* had been received with some critical enthusiasm. 'Partly, one suspects,' Kiernan wrote, 'this enthusiasm is a matter of general consciousness catching up with individual talent.' The essay, which drew on conversations Kiernan had with Frank, provides a useful overview of Frank's thinking about the short-story form at this stage of his career, and his role as a writer.

In many respects, the essay reinforced the view Frank had been cultivating since the early 1960s, of fiction as a form of social inquiry, and the writer as a sort of free-floating intellectual in the Mannheim tradition, one considering ideologies as obstacles to understanding individuals rather than as explanations for them. 'For someone who sees himself partly motivated as a writer by his interest in politics and social theory,' Kiernan writes, 'Moorhouse is coolly detached from his characters and their beliefs. As the author, he seems interested in ideology only as far as it affects people, and his political autobiography is relevant here.'

Frank referred to his adolescent self as being a 'socialist and an atheist'. As a cadet journalist, he met a lot of communists, and by age twenty he was a 'co-operative socialist believing in worker's control'. After Wagga and Lockhart in the late 1950s, and his return to Sydney in the early 1960s, 'demoralised after a period of social isolation and intellectual discomfort', he transposed his 'reformist zeal to change society by peaceful means' via the Workers' Educational Association. This period as organiser and publicist for the WEA helped Frank distinguish between the 'authoritarian and non-authoritarian Left', his sympathies residing with the latter. But even here his main commitment was with writing fiction: what Kiernan referred to as the 'classic morality of the writer – a concern with individuals rather than with the rigidities of any ideology'.

'Previously, when I was a socialist,' Frank told Kiernan, 'I often found that my fiction wouldn't fit the "class struggle" as expected by doctrinaire socialists. I find that at a certain stage the story takes over, and that later I can find myself agreeing with interpretations of the story which weren't consciously in my mind at the time of writing. Anyhow, when I started to see myself as a writer rather than a socialist it was a great relief.'

Frank described himself as being 'sexually recruited' into the Libertarian Society in the early 1960s, and said that within its atmosphere of free expression he developed as a writer. Frank was clear that his identity as a writer ran parallel with the libertarians and their concerns, and that he associated with them, but ultimately he did not fully identify with them. 'A lot of my writing is a natural associate of my libertarian politics but it is not intended to be their servant,' Frank said.

The difference between the consciously political writer and someone like myself is that the former would see holding of positions as central, whereas I would see them as superstructure for deeper personal dynamics. People adopt ideologies to suit their personalities, and writers who take up traditional or contemporary stances are playing personality roles, posturing, dramatizing themselves.

Kiernan pointed out that most of Frank's stories from his first two books were not so much about the various contemporary subcultures he was associated with during the 1960s and early 1970s, but rather with characters not easily belonging or fitting in comfortably with any subculture. These characters were caught between subcultures, negotiating between social changes, or else completely isolated, out of place and out of time.

Brian Kiernan's survey of Frank's work came out soon after Frank had finished editing the 1973 edition of *Coast to Coast*, published by Angus & Robertson. For the previous decade Frank had tried, and failed, to have a story included in this biennial anthology of short fiction. 'I have been rejected from every *Coast to Coast* in the last ten years,' he wrote in his editorial. 'I have never been accepted for *Coast to Coast* – except by myself. This was one of the reasons I took the editorship.'

As an author published by Angus & Robertson, Frank was given the opportunity to shape the editorial direction of the anthology, which was started in 1942 by Beatrice Davis. She was still with the firm, and frequently butted heads with Richard Walsh over changes he was trying to implement. He was aiming to modernise the publishing house, and Davis was very much part of the older institution he was looking to replace. She particularly disliked Frank's work. Walsh giving Frank the editorship of *Coast to Coast*, and Davis opposing the decision, may very well have been the final straw for Walsh. In April 1973, Beatrice Davis was sacked from Angus & Robertson, after thirty-six years' service.

Far from breaking completely with traditional writing in his role at *Coast to Coast*, Frank diplomatically included traditional, conventional stories, as well as newer, more experimental writing – including creative non-fiction: 'although new ways of handling prose narrative have developed, and [despite the fact] that different generations do do different things, and do things differently, these are by no means exclusive or open to "grading"'.

Frank included, for example, a story by Hal Porter, aged sixty-two, even though Frank had negatively reviewed Porter's latest collection of stories for *The Bulletin*. In large part, his judiciousness was because Frank considered the form of the short story itself to be under threat – part of the 'crisis of literature' – and believed there was nothing to be gained from creating schisms between its practitioners. He noted that, in the 1930s, the ABC had hosted a short-story competition which attracted 1167 entries. Ten years ago, *Coast to Coast* had 325 submissions. In 1973, Frank had only 250 submissions to choose from.

'Now I suppose there is needed a statement of faith about the "future of the short story",' Frank wrote in his editorial.

> There is no virtue in an unwanted craft, and as popular entertainment the short story is almost dead. But with small-readership short fiction there are overseas and local critics who talk of a rebirth. It seems to me that the short story is a natural form, akin to the dream, the oral tale, and the fantasy. It has all the standard technological advantages of the printed word (comparatively unrestricted distribution, can stimulate all the senses, is easily retrieved, is portable, can be consumed at a personal pace) together with special advantages. It can be specialized subculturally and regionally and, unlike the novel, it can be published outside book form. It can be an intense form which releases complex vibrations, not readily reducible to simple political or moral analysis. I can't see why it shouldn't continue.

In Kiernan's *Overland* survey, Frank reiterated these basic points, but added a further note, peculiar to his own practice: the short-story form was related to 'the episodic breaking up of life into incidents. However, the creative span is limited by the form and I like the idea of a larger unity and clusters of stories.' Later that year, when another of Frank's stories was published, it was accompanied by an artist's statement of sorts, in which Frank further developed his understanding of the form:

> It seems to me that short fiction is moving into a 'latent structure' phase where the movement, the vibrations, of the story are locked in the below-logic or non-rational, subterranean impact. That surface 'plot' can be there but it is of little consequence. It also seems to be a form which is superbly mobile and informal – not requiring book distribution, as the novel, clumsy technology, as the film. Given, also, that it can break out of the academic formality of the literary quarterlies.

Another important point from Kiernan's survey of Frank's work was its attempt to clarify a misunderstanding that dogged Frank's reception: how readers often collapsed the necessary distinction between fiction and reality, missing the degree to which fiction puts into perspective and questions certain aspects of social reality, without necessarily being autobiographical or in any way documentary.

'I find it complimentary that people are totally taken in by the performance and talk to me about the characters and the situations as though they are real,' Frank said to Kiernan. 'But they're realistic or naturalistic stories in their observed details only. There was a party for Rexroth which I attended, but that story ('The American Poet's Visit') was written long after and isn't a record of what actually happened. It's all been adjusted from a distance.'

Kiernan reiterated the point, stating: 'These are the best short stories for a long time because, first of all, they *are* stories, not raw, still-quivering slices of life.' He suggested another paired example: Frank's story 'The Jack Kerouac Wake: The True Story' and Michael Wilding's story 'Bye Bye Jack. See You Soon'. Kiernan noted how each 'claims to present the "true" account of a chaotic night'.

Jack Kerouac, the American writer, had died on 29 October 1969. When the news reached Australia, there was apparently an attempt to hold a wake for the Beat writer, but it was poorly planned, resulting in little or no attendance. The stories Kiernan referred to, by Frank and Michael, were written a few years after the supposed event – 'adjusted from a distance'.

In fact, Frank had two stories on this theme. He published the first in *Coast to Coast*. 'Wesley's Brother at the Wake for Jack Kerouac' sees the characters Milton and Wesley's (unnamed) brother in an altercation over Milton's accusation that Wesley's brother had sabotaged Kerouac's wake. Frank's second story on the theme, 'The Jack Kerouac Wake: The True Story', retells the story from the perspective of an unnamed character (presumably Wesley's brother), who answers accusations that he sabotaged the wake.

The accusation is first laid out in Michael's story, with the accused character being named Joe – the figure introduced in 'Joe's Absence'. Michael's story was first broadcast on ABC Radio in 1974, and was published the following year in his book *The West Midland Underground*. It includes references to letters Frank had written over previous years. At one point, for example, the narrator of Michael's story states: 'On the shithouse walls of California they write Ginsberg revises.' In a letter from September 1968, Frank wrote to Michael: 'I read somewhere that written on the walls of Greenwich Village pisshouses is "Ginsberg revises".'

'The Jack Kerouac Wake: The True Story' was published later that same year, in the second edition of *Tabloid Story*, which appeared as an insert in the Christmas issue of *Nation Review*. The print run of this edition was 50,000. It had been more than a year since the first edition. When the protracted transition of government funding bodies had finally settled, *Tabloid Story* received enough funding to pay its authors current industry rates, around $50 per thousand words.

Michael Wilding's contribution to this edition was 'The Nembutal Story', his response to Frank's 'The Oracular Stories'. As with the Kerouac stories, these pointed to the stark difference between Frank and Michael's approach to writing fiction. For Frank, a work of fiction was distinct from diurnal reality, while

Michael played on collapsing that distinction. As Frank said to Brian Kiernan, his stories were naturalistic or realistic only in their use of 'observed detail', which he deployed to heighten the effect of the fiction as fiction. For Michael, such 'observed detail' – which the narrator of 'The Nembutal Story' referred to as 'residual details of truth' – was used to conflate and confuse the distinctions between fiction and reality. 'The difficulty is, of course,' the narrator of this story stated, 'the mixture of these residual details of truth and the quite blatant fantasy; and my inability to decide which is which.'

In 'The Nembutal Story', Michael pushed the meta-fictional aspect of the short-story form to its limit, continuously eliding the distinction between what was fiction and what was real, to undermine the stability of reality, and so question the reliability of the fictional account. The narrator referenced internal aspects of Frank's various stories, from the unpublished first version of the 'The Oracular Stories' – where the woman character is named Wesley – to the published version – where she is named Hestia. It referenced other stories, such as 'Wesley's Brother at the Wake for Jack Kerouac', where it was first suggested that Wesley's brother had a homosexual relationship with Milton – which the narrator of 'The Nembutal Story' denies.

The meta-fictional playfulness of 'The Nembutal Story' was not enough to distract from the fact that it was premised on the possible rape of an unconscious woman. And just as 'The Oracular Stories' was, for this same reason, seized by the Vice Squad in Queensland, this time it was Michael's story causing alarm. The distributors of *Nation Review* in Queensland and Western Australia refused to handle the magazine unless the story was removed – which it was, but with blank pages kept in the printed edition, as a mark of its suppression.

Over ten weeks, from March to May 1973, Frank presented a WEA course on the topic 'End of Mass Media'. This formed the basis of his third, and final, report for *Current Affairs Bulletin*, published that October. Until now, the dominant system of the mass media – from newspapers, radio and, more recently, television – had created a centralised, relatively homogenous system, which, Frank argued, served to support 'the prevailing Order (as distinct from the government of the day) – the prevailing morality, economic system'.

It did so in three ways. First, the media provided 'a psychological railing for people to hold on to – [to] create an illusion of coherent reality'. Second, it met 'the psychological needs of the community (celebration of legends, myths, personal recognition and record)'. Third, it serviced the society by 'informing of change, new laws, regulations and procedures'. This 'Order' was reinforced by underlying social and cultural systems, both formal and informal. Frank referred, on the one hand, to the 'formalised oral systems such as churches, unions, associations, talk-clubs (Rotary, Apex and so on) with regular patterns of information-flow and reinforcement of values', and on the other hand 'the informal, decentralised circuit of the telephone-postage-spoken word'. The status quo was further maintained through allowing a certain degree of 'static', of opposition, of give, within the dominant system. The fringe supported the centre.

'But Marshall McLuhan said step back from the content and look at the "equipment" or the "system" itself,' Frank wrote. This shifted the discussion away from the content of the 'Order' itself, to reveal instead the underlying communications technologies organising and shaping the mass media, and constituting the formal cause for each of these contents to appear. The question, then, was: what are the effects of new forms of communications technology – cassette and cable telecasting, FM radio broadcasting, offset printing, photocopying and phototransmission – on the shape and content of that dominant 'Order'?

'Ten years ago Australia first saw offset printing,' Frank wrote, referring explicitly to *Oz* magazine. 'Offset makes everyone a printer.' The immediate effect of this was to slowly reconfigure the dominant structures underpinning mass media. 'The offset process has weakened, if not eliminated, control over what is printed – control both by the State, the Order and by craft traditions (value of taste and conservative typography) of the printing trade. Distribution is still controlled but seriously weakened.'

The main consequence of this was the acceleration and dissemination of unorthodox ideas, questioning and unsettling the pervasive formulations and psychological guardrails necessary to maintaining the 'Order'. This, in turn, led to the effective end of mass media, Frank argued, because the attention of the masses, previously corralled towards a narrow range of dominant media, had become fragmented across a broader range of media choices, increasingly attended by relatively smaller groups of individuals – as modern, urban tribes. More people may be engaging with media, but in more decentralised, diversified and informal ways. The centre now supported the fringe.

Offset printing, for example, saw an increase in 'little magazines'. But where older publications were predominantly 'theoretical-literary' in orientation, these newer publications were concerned more with 'life-style advocacy'. A fragmented media defined and formed various subcultures, where previously it supported a single dominant culture. 'That is,' Frank wrote, 'you find that the way you have been thinking is the way a group in another part of the city has been thinking. Or you pick up a publication which verbalises your hitherto unconscious predispositions.' These publications then worked to reinforce the boundaries of these subcultures, by 'telling adherents that they are on the right track. They also feed-in supporting material, and serve the group as a resource.'

Such subcultures would not necessarily be radical in nature. 'Inevitably there will be conservative sub-culture[s] – religious, ethnic and other – which the new technologies would permit to erect cultural palisades, or media palisades, around their values, and their children. The diversified media would work to their advantage too.' Frank questioned once more whether even the radical subcultures embedded within this media environment were really all that radical. 'The variety of the "unorthodoxies" is perhaps disappointingly limited,' he wrote. 'The formula of many of the papers is similar. Communal living – environment – sexual liberation – with or without drug evangelism – with or without mysticism – with or without conventional political action.'

The very nature of media-formed, media-defined subcultures was limited and shallow:

> Some of the Media Idealists see the diversification leading to grass-roots participation. They see the *amateurisation* as a part of the march of democracy and egalitarianism. It may lead to more people making programmes or participating in media. Offset undoubtedly did. But not on the scale which would warrant seeing it as a mass activity.

Why? Because the reconfiguration of the media which allowed such subcultures to proliferate in the first place disallowed the formation of any single subculture to coalesce and achieve dominance, to establish a new 'Order'. The broader social impact of each of these subcultures was therefore structurally limited, their ultimate effects upon society watered down, by the very conditions creating them.

In conclusion, Frank suggested that the ultimate purpose of these new, fragmented, media-formed, media-defined subcultures would increasingly become ends in themselves, and would not be useful in effecting positive change in the world beyond their own defined borders. He based this conclusion on a criticism of the speed of the new technologies. Advocates of the industrial revolution argued that the improvement of life was inseparable from the notion of progress.

'Lying behind the idea of "saving time" was the supposition that the time could be used to do other things – more leisure,' Frank wrote. 'Information technology is not quite the same. It is saving time so that the time can be spent in the same activity – time to do more of the same activity.'

By the end of 1973, two more stories from the Electric Experience project were published. 'George McDowell Delivers a Message to General Juan Garcia of the Cuban Army' appeared in *The Bulletin* in July. It is set in 1924, a year after T. George McDowell's visit to the St Louis Rotary Convention in the United States, and fifteen years before the birth of his daughter, Terri.

The story references an actual book, *A Message to Garcia* (1899), by Elbert Hubbard, which was claimed to be based on a real moment before the Spanish–American War, when President William McKinley commissioned a soldier, Andrew Rowan, with delivering a message to General Calixto Garcia, the leader of the Cuban insurgency, whereabouts unknown. The events were largely fabricated by Hubbard in order to drive home an ideological point regarding individual initiative, industriousness and self-discipline in the workplace. The phrase 'to carry a message to Garcia' became commonplace in certain early to mid-century entrepreneurial circles, as well as in Rotary and the Boy Scouts, meaning to achieve what one has set out to do.

'How has it influenced you, George?'
'Well Rowan, he did the job.'

Hemisphere, an Asian-Australian monthly culture magazine, published Frank's story 'Rules and Practices for Overcoming Shyness' in December 1973. This story was set in 1936, a dozen years on from the previous story. The story is framed by George's ten 'rules and practices', the first of which is: 'Always walk up to a man as if he owes you money.'

Not long before this story was published in *Hemisphere*, Frank signed a contract with Angus & Robertson for his third book, under the title *The Electric Experience*. But Frank was already considering a variation. A couple of months earlier, he had written to Don Anderson, testing the title *The Electrical Experience*, to distinguish it more from the 1968 book *The Electric Kool-Aid Acid Test*: 'By the way how do you react to the title – I've added "al" to Electric – it sounds less Tom Wolfe. Do you think?'

'I think you are right about "Electric<u>al</u>" in the title to the book,' Don replied dryly, 'though the only problem that suggests itself to me is: will anyone think, "He's trying to avoid it sounding like the title of a Tom Wolfe book."'

Frank had another pair of stories published, but from outside of the Electric Experience project. The first – 'The Airport, the Pizzeria, the Motel, the Rented Car and the Mysteries of Life' – was published in *Nation Review* in May 1973. It tells the story of a man meeting with his ex-wife in a foreign country, seven years after they parted. Later that year, in the issue of *Overland* containing Brian Kiernan's survey of Frank's career, was the story 'Concerning a Reunion with an Ex-wife in Portugal'. The narrative is constituted by five lettered sections (A–E), each concerned with different levels of the narrator's thinking regarding the prospect of a reunion with his ex-wife. This story appears to be related to the previous one, regarding the same fictional couple. The order of publication inverted the chronology: 'Concerning a Reunion . . .' preceded the meeting of the couple after seven years, while 'The Airport, the Pizzeria . . .' recounted the meeting itself.

An immediate reference point for these stories – although little corresponding detail exists between them – was Wendy James' return to Australia the year before, to spend Christmas with her family in Nowra. She had brought her daughters to visit Australia for the first time. After some time in New Zealand, they flew back home to England in early February 1973. She spent some time with Frank in Sydney, and regretted it was not more.

Their previous meeting in London in 1972 was accompanied – for Frank, at least – with a sense of a closure. This more recent meeting marked a transition to a new phase in their relationship. They had even omitted to address the largely bureaucratic fact that they were still legally married.

'It seems a bit odd to go all that way and still leave unfinished one of the biggest matters of my life – whether to be divorced from you,' Wendy wrote from the airplane as it was leaving Sydney, the legibility of her handwriting graphing the turbulence of flight. 'I can't see that there is any major reason why we should be but also I can't see any reason why we should remain – in law – married.'

Working on the Electric Experience material over the previous years had caused Frank to dwell more in the past, in his earlier experiences on the South Coast, in which Wendy had played, and continued to play, a dominant role in his imagination. The distance between the imagined, remembered, adolescent Wendy and the mature, independent woman and mother Frank had encountered more recently had only continued to grow. And yet, while on a camping trip with a woman during this period, Frank noted in his journal how she kept 'merging with Wendy' in his mind.

With the end of *Thor*, 'Around the Laundromats' migrated to the pages of *The Bulletin* – and became mainstream. But Frank made the move without much enthusiasm. While in the United States in early 1972, filing articles for *The Bulletin*, Frank had admitted in his private notebook that he was having difficulties working within the traditional boundaries of that publication, especially when compared to the freedom of 'writing-editing-layout' in *Thor*. Writing for *The Bulletin* 'constipate[d]' him creatively, he said. The momentum of his first year with the magazine had stalled with his trip overseas and the publication of his second book. It was a momentum he never regained.

In 1971, he had had thirty-two pieces published, but in 1972 he had only twelve. Although in 1973 he had eighteen pieces published, by the following year he had submitted only four. His relationship with the magazine was tapering off, but was never entirely severed. One important factor for this waning enthusiasm was that, during 1972, Donald Horne left the editorship. A large part of the joy of working there was due to Frank's friendship with Horne: his patronage, his expense account and their long work lunches. But the friendship continued without Frank writing for the magazine.

One important piece Frank did write for *The Bulletin* in 1973 was based on a recent visit he had made to Nowra, where he had attended a meeting convened by the local Aboriginal community.

This was the first public meeting of the Jerrinja Tribal Council of the South Coast, and took place in an old schoolhouse on the local reserve at the end of a bitumen road. 'I was told that the bitumen always runs out when it reaches an Aboriginal reserve,' Frank wrote. They all sat on old Sunday School wooden benches. The meeting was chaired by 28-year-old Burnie Longbottom, whose previous experience was on the committee of the Crookhaven Football Club. Afterwards, he told Frank he thought the meeting was a little disorganised, but Frank felt it had gone well.

The group discussed the early period of segregation in Nowra. 'At the Roxy the front stalls were marked B and that was where we had to sit,' one Aboriginal woman remembered from her childhood. 'My mother said no one told *her* where to sit and demanded her money back . . . We weren't allowed to go into the New York cafe either.' Following this was a period of failed assimilation, one-sided and paternalistic in nature. Until 1970, for example, the reserve still had a white manager, who gave permission for people to come and go. The new mood Frank wrote about was based on the assertion of a 'separate identity' against enforced assimilation. But this was a period of transition, of shaking off old imposed habits. 'The Aboriginal Welfare Board thought for us,' one of the Aboriginal men explained, referring to the Tribal Council: 'we had no mind of its own.'

Frank outlined one of the examples given of this — and the proposed solution:

> The tribal council had at first planned to ask for money to clean up the abandoned car bodies, paint the houses, and cut the grass.
>
> This sounded to me like the welfare mentality — ask the 'mission' to do it.
>
> Teddy Thomas from Wallaga Lake thought so too.
>
> 'We had grass you couldn't run through. We offered it to the dairy farmers and charged them to let their cows eat it.'

This was the new mood.

Shaking off of old habits was necessary for the local whites too, Frank argued. 'I was overwhelmed a little by the militant goodwill of Merv Nixon who as a labor activist couldn't resist left rhetoric and the temptation to keep moving resolutions,' he wrote. 'He sometimes remembered though that it was not his meeting and said embarrassingly, "put it into your own words."'

The Aboriginal woman who had spoken earlier argued that Aboriginal people had to form their own communities, in their own way. 'We are communal people,' she said, 'we are a special people; we are a people unto ourselves.'

This woman is named in Frank's article, but he does not disclose the prior and continuing relationship between her and his own family. For this was Belle McLeod, the Yuin/Wandandian woman who, in the 1940s, when she was a teenager, lived with the Moorhouse family and helped Purth take care of the infant Frank. When Purth was president of the Nowra CWA, she worked closely with Belle and others to establish the Worrigee-Wreck Bay branch in July 1961. 'Interestingly,' Frank noted in his *Bulletin* article, 'they said that the Rotary club and the Country Women's Association had helped break down the prejudice.' But this was still during the assimilation phase, and largely a part of that project.

Belle had been involved in the campaign for the 1967 referendum to change two sections of the Australian Constitution relating to Aboriginal and Torres Strait Islander peoples. In the early 1970s, she became the first Aboriginal woman to be employed by the Department of Social Security in New South Wales, based in Nowra. And by the time of this open meeting, she was working with her father, Bob Brown, to create the Aboriginal Cultural Centre in Nowra, which was completed the following year. She would go on to establish the South Coast Aboriginal Legal Service and the first Aboriginal retirement village in New South Wales.

Frank's *Bulletin* column increasingly used fictional techniques and literary devices to create fronts and facades, allowing him, in his David Jones drag, to speak through the persona of 'Frank Moorhouse, writer', without entirely revealing himself to the public.

When the first 'Around the Laundromats' column appeared in February 1973, Ward had possibly metamorphosed into a person – at least, no reference was made to Ward being a talking cat.

In one column from March 1973, titled 'How Many Sexes Are There?', Frank and Ward are conversing with a 'transvestite friend' in the laundromat, who is 'washing his female clothing but dressed in some old male clothing from before he "came out" as female'. They discuss what they call a 'theological dispute raging (again) in camp circles about whether transvestites belong in homosexual liberation movements'. The main question being: 'Is a transvestite a camp?'

The unnamed interlocutor points out that 'camp and a transvestite are similar in that we both were born male but refuse to accept traditional male role of father-husband'.

'I suppose,' Frank said, 'this goes for bachelors, too.'

They discuss how jokes against bachelors and spinsters, homosexuals and transvestites, were really about a social pressure to conform.

'We go for a female image,' the transvestite says, 'and in a rather outrageously conventional way I'm afraid – really, we out-female the women. This is why the camps feel we are outside their pressure group... Our scene becomes more complicated because as you probably know some of us are "lesbian".'

At this point, Frank brings Ward into the narrative: 'Ward[,] who was feeling quietly unwell and had so far said nothing, rolled his eyes at this.' Afterwards, Frank and Ward discuss the situation between themselves (Ward seems to speak only when they are alone together):

> 'You see Ward, we need more words for the various sexes – why there must be about nine different sexes.' I counted up – female heterosexual, male heterosexual, lesbian, male homosexual, bi-sexual, hetero-male transvestite, hetero-female transvestite, transvestites who prefer the same sex, multi-sexuals...
>
> 'And tri-sexuals,' said Ward.
>
> 'What do you mean?'

'Try anything,' he grinned weakly.

'God you're crude, Ward. You know I can't stand these sort of jokes.'

This piece of writing – representative of much of Frank's public writing during this period, especially in *The Bulletin* – was a virtuoso performance of hiding in plain sight. It used humour to maintain conformity, while explicitly stating this was the purpose of humour, under which Frank tentatively transgressed contemporary norms and raised publicly his own questions regarding sexuality and transvestism. Ward was placed in the role of the mainstream, to do the eye-rolling and crude jokes, to signal the boundary crossing and retreat back into conformity – that is, Ward represented the majority readers of *The Bulletin* – which Frank could disown and distance himself from, while at the same time presenting himself as a presumably heterosexual male columnist, equidistant from both the 'transvestite' and 'camp' figures he interacted with at the laundromat. This persona strategy is present in much of Frank's *Bulletin* writing during this period – it can be seen, for example, in his pieces on Les Girls and CAMP.

'Around the Laundromats' only lasted until June 1973; Westinghouse had complained about the use of the trademarked name 'Laundromat'. The column became 'From the Terrace'. This lasted until October, when the title was dropped altogether and became simply 'Frank Moorhouse'. During this transition, Frank would refer to himself and Ward as 'we', but quietly the figure of Ward was dropped, and by the time the column featured only Frank, the continued use of the plural pronoun became a royal 'we', behind which Frank could remain somewhat out of view.

The public persona of 'Frank Moorhouse, writer' was given a boost midyear when Angus & Robertson published a paperback edition of *Futility and Other Animals*. This introduced the book to a much larger audience than when it first came out in 1969, which allowed a fresh assessment of Frank's work.

'Moorhouse's observation, keen ear and laconic style make him one of our best short story writers,' said L.V. Kepert in *The Sydney Morning Herald*.

'Frank Moorhouse – surely the most successful Australian storywriter since Henry Lawson – became all the rage among the cognoscenti when his second collection, *The Americans, baby* was published in 1972,' wrote Thelma Forshaw, also for the *Herald*: '*Futility and Other Animals* which first appeared in 1969 and suffered a little from the nervousness of booksellers (too many four-letter words too soon?) now leaps out from under the counter to achieve just recognition of its anatomy of latterday Bloomsburyism.'

Shirley Despoja, in *The Advertiser*, opened her review by stating: 'Australian writer Frank Moorhouse has some mysterious visa which allows him to travel with perfect understanding between the sexes.'

This public presentation of Frank's own self was at the same time carried off the page and into his social relationships. It was psychologically tiring. In September, Frank wrote to Don Anderson in England, explaining how he was 'managing' his social life until after the Electric Experience project was completed:

> The random social life with its unpredictable insults and problems would probably crack me up – my psychic resources are over taxed. As for social life – as always something of a dilemma and misery. I've noted that I am on a few more cocktail party lists which I am pleased about. All I really want out of life is that I get on cocktail lists. I relish them, I really like canapés. I am a big canapé man.

He left to his notebooks the actual toll this entailed, and his reliance upon mimicry as a strategy for social survival: 'I have to mimic great people's talent perfectly because I can't do it myself – singing, laughing, etc – in fact I am a false mimic because I only do them good enough to fool people . . .'

Although Frank had a girlfriend, while at the same time maintaining peripheral 'affairs', as he described them in his notes, with other women, he had continued his sexual relationship with John Burrows. Although he had maintained contact with John, and had encounters with him for some years, they began seeing each other again more regularly during this period – a period which coincided with Wendy coming back into Frank's life. It was almost as if Frank were replaying the period in the late 1950s when he was simultaneously with both Wendy publicly – or, at this later point, with other women who kept 'merging with Wendy' in Frank's mind – and John furtively, with much the same result. '*The bi-sexual* does not have best of both worlds,' he confided in his notebooks at this time, 'he is out of full participation in either.'

This was also a period when Frank was working feverishly on his South Coast book. In the process, he was being pulled back to that early time of his life, but also, in his imagination, to the period before he was even born. It was an imaginative act guided increasingly by various archives. This had an overt creative aspect to it, putting his present life into perspective, while enabling him to write. But it also had a destructive undercurrent, when his imagination took the step from considering not existing in the past to considering the possibility of not existing at all.

> Too scared to kill myself
> don't want to live
> – Hopelessness of
> life given freedom

12

'No, That Is Called a Discontinuous Narrative'

On Friday, 28 September 1973, Paul Brennan, a young journalist and graduate of the University of New South Wales, went into the photocopy room in the library of his alma mater and made two copies of a story from the library edition of *The Americans, Baby* – 'The Machine Gun' – and two copies of a story from Morris Lurie's 1969 collection *Happy Times*. Rhonda Stockman, a student at the university, saw him make the copies. Brennan spoke with her briefly, showing her the books, which she noted were from the library. He then walked out with his four photocopies.

The next month, Frank was invited to meet with two legal officers from the Australian Copyright Council, David Catterns and Peter Banki, and its chair, Gustave 'Gus' O'Donnell. In 1964, Dal Stivens, as president of the Australian Society of Authors, suggested Australia needed a Copyright Council, modelled on the British Copyright Council. But it was Gus O'Donnell who drove the idea, and obsessively so. He understood that copyright was the foundation of a writer's economic security, the basis from which they could earn a living from their work. He saw very early how the proliferation of photocopying technology was an existential threat to that security. From 1964 until 1968, Gus led the campaign that resulted in the federal government establishing the *Copyright Act 1968*, enabling Australia to ratify the Universal Copyright Convention, 1952.

In January 1968, the Australian Copyright Council interim organisation was formed, with a staff of three: O'Donnell, Catterns and Banki. Their first challenge was to address the threat of new and developing communications technologies, such as photocopying machines and information storage and retrieval (ISR) systems, which could store and provide computer printouts of otherwise copyrighted material. They envisaged a practical licensing scheme, negotiated between copyright holders (authors and publishers) and institutions disseminating copyrighted material, while providing photocopiers to exploit such material (libraries, universities and schools). Such a scheme would require legislative amendments to the *Copyright Act*.

The need for such a scheme was underscored when the photocopier manufacturer Xerox placed a full-page advertisement in *The Australian* showcasing how easy it was to copy an entire book: the violation of copyright was actually deployed as a marketing strategy to sell photocopy machines.

Catterns and Banki developed a test case: they would argue before the courts that institutions, by providing photocopying facilities, were effectively authorising breaches of copyright. At the behest of the Copyright Council, Paul Brennan made his photocopies at UNSW – although the Copyright Council did not know in advance what books he would copy. In 1973, *The Americans, Baby* was on a reading list for an honours-level political science seminar. It was also posted on a reading list for an undergraduate political science course for 1974, so it happened to be on the shelves in the photocopy room.

Morris Lurie was approached to participate in the test case, as Brennan had made copies from his book, but he declined. Frank agreed, and he brought with him his publisher, Richard Walsh, from Angus & Robertson. Together they sued the University of New South Wales for breach of Frank's copyright, under the *Copyright Act 1968*.

That December, Frank made his affidavit, stating that he was the copyright owner of *The Americans, Baby*, and that he had not consented for his work to be copied. Rhonda Stockman also made an affidavit, stating that she witnessed Brennan making two copies of a story from Frank's book. This was crucial to the design of the case. By taking two copies of the same story, the plaintiffs ensured there was no possibility that the copying could be deemed 'fair dealing'; this meant the case would isolate the question of 'authorisation'.

One month before Paul Brennan entered the UNSW library, Catterns had presented a paper at the 17th Biennial Conference of the Library Association of Australia. What was remarkable about this paper, 'Librarians and the Law of Copyright', was that it basically outlined the Copyright Council's strategy, hinting at what they were about to do and their rationale for doing it. The *Copyright Act 1968*, Catterns explained, superseded any moral rights an author had over their works: only rights specified in the act were legally enforceable. Such copyright was a 'personal property' and an 'exclusive right', preventing others from doing certain acts with a work without prior permission. A copyright holder had two courses of legal action against a breach of copyright: the first against the individual who did the copying, and the second against a third party which authorised the copying.

Under the *Copyright Act*, acts done to 'substantial parts' of a work were deemed to have been done to the whole work. But the act did not define 'substantial parts', which referred to case law. The commonplace assumption was that 'fair dealing' would delimit what constituted 'substantial parts', but this was not necessarily the case, and was becoming less so. The reason for this, Catterns explained, was that, originally, 'fair dealing' was assumed in the absence of modern copying technology: 'when it was introduced into the law, most copying was done by hand; modern copying machines make it easy to copy beyond the limits envisaged by the phrase and very hard for a copyright owner to prove this fact'. A photocopier was an extension of the human hand, and the act of photocopying an extension of handwriting. Catterns suggested that photoduplication technology had been developed precisely to overcome the limitations of taking handwritten notes from a book or journal. In other words, breaching the limits of 'fair dealing' was the fundamental purpose of these machines. The problem was only going to be exacerbated by the development and increased use of ISR systems, the forerunners of modern computers.

'I propose to discuss in some detail the possibility that, by providing facilities for photocopying, librarians might be held to be infringing copyright by "authorizing" an infringing reproduction which might take place,' Catterns wrote. Hypothesising a test case in Australia, he continued: 'The question of authorization will be determined by the court as a question of fact, having regard to all the circumstances of the case before it. There have been no cases in which the meaning of "authorization" in relation to the provision of photocopying machines has been tested.'

In short, the conflict between copyright holders and the public need for quick and full dissemination of literary, scientific and technical literature was only going to grow. And librarians and their institutions were caught in the middle. 'The conflict is real; the solution not simple,' Catterns stated. 'Legislative guidelines seem appropriate.' Such legislative guidelines, he concluded, would also provide the framework for a practical licensing scheme to ensure that copyright holders were fairly remunerated for the distribution and dissemination of their work.

Perhaps as a reminder that librarians and their institutions were given fair and prior warning, this paper was then published in *The Australian Library Journal* in November 1973, two months after the photocopying incident and right before Frank launched his suit against the University of New South Wales.

Mike Thornhill had secured a film development grant of $2000 for the Between Wars project. Frank received $500 and Mike used the rest to travel in December 1973 to England and the United States, seeking financing for the film and scouting for actors. He was unsuccessful in raising additional funds, but while in England he secured actor Corin Redgrave to play Dr Trenbow. Corin was the son of actors Michael Redgrave and Rachel Kempson, and brother of Vanessa and Lynn Redgrave. He had come off the back of playing Octavius for a television version of Shakespeare's *Antony and Cleopatra*.

Securing Redgrave for the lead enabled Mike to raise funding back in Australia. The Australian Film Development Corporation put up half the money – $150,000 – and the other half came from private investor Parkes Development Pty Ltd. To produce the film, Thornhill and Moorhouse (T&M) Films became Edgecliff Films Pty Ltd, with the film rights agreement ensuring that it would get 25 per cent of profits from the film. Frank would receive 35 per cent of that quarter share, or 8.75 per cent of the total profits.

When Mike returned to Australia, he and Frank worked on the final draft of the screenplay. On the very day it was due at the printers, they were still unsure about the final scene. Under pressure, they realised the second-last scene was in fact the natural ending for the film, and so the final scene was dropped. Instead of the film ending with Trenbow alone in a pub near the university playing darts, it would now end with his adult son's announcement that he was going to war. This was more in line with how the original ten-part television series was supposed to end. They had come full circle.

The film was shot over six weeks, from 14 February into March. Mike had a crew of twenty-six on set, with another five maintaining the office. Judy Morris played Deborah Trenbow, Dr Trenbow's wife. The cinematographer was Russell Boyd; the following year he would shoot *Picnic at Hanging Rock*. Interiors were shot on a studio set in Bondi, while exteriors were shot in the small town of Gulgong, New South Wales, around 185 miles (300 kilometres) west of Sydney.

Mike worked quickly, but deliberately and decisively. He did not have rehearsals, explaining to *Cinema Papers*, which was reporting from set, 'I just think it makes people either (1) dry up or (2) become so overwrought in terms of performances that you gain in dramatic strength, but you lose in nuance.'

The shooting itself very nearly did not happen. In early February, Corin Redgrave's agent telephoned from England: the actor wanted to pull out of the film at the last moment. He felt Britain was on the verge of revolution, and he wanted to stay for it. That month in England, eleven people had been killed in the latest bomb attack by the Provisional Irish Republican Army, and Prime Minister Edward Heath had called for a general election in order to bring to an end a large-scale miners' strike.

Politically, Redgrave was a revolutionary, while Thornhill was an anarchist. But the director managed to convince his leading actor to come, explaining that workers in Australia would be out of a job if the film did not go ahead. Redgrave agreed, but when he was in Australia he used the car the production team hired for him to attend Trotskyite rallies around New South Wales. Despite this, Thornhill later said that working with Redgrave was the 'best professional relationship' he had yet encountered in the film industry. On set, Redgrave would do what he was told, but if he had an idea on how to make the scene better, he would share it, and Mike was willing to listen.

Mike's working relationship with Frank was 'more exotic'. One point of contention during the shooting of *Between Wars* was Frank's absence; he was at the time travelling in the United States. In part, this was a clash of schedules: the trip was already arranged when the funding for the film – and so the production schedule – was still unsettled.

'Despite the immense amount of work that I put into it as a script I still told Mike that as the scriptwriter it was my feeling that once it is handed over to the director I have no desire to exercise any proprietorship,' Frank said afterwards in *Cinema Papers*. 'If you can't trust the director you shouldn't have got into that situation in the first place. For this reason, I suppose, I don't like writing for the screen. You can't expect total ego control.'

Still, Mike was initially annoyed at Frank's unavailability on set, for the day-to-day rewriting of scenes as needed. 'I am not a good ad hoc writer,' Frank later claimed. 'I need to give thought and there has to be a sort of working continuity . . . Also, alterations you make send waves of implication back and forth through the script.'

Mike came to accept that as part of Frank's creative process, and added that, in their working together, Frank was 'fantastically generous'.

Frank travelled across the United States with Sandra Levy. Sandra visited various television broadcasting stations. Since leaving university and completing her traineeship at the ABC, she had worked for the national broadcaster, focusing mainly on children's programming. She had co-created and produced an activities program for primary schoolers called *Scan*, the individual segments framed and introduced by an animated character named Popcorn.

While in North America, Frank arranged to meet Marshall McLuhan. They discussed, among other things, how photocopying was a substitute for the act of reading. People would look at each page as they copied it, to check it had come out straight and focused, before putting it in a folder, where it remained unread. 'The photocopying machine is in fact giving them the illusion of having "read it",' Frank later reported his conversation with McLuhan, 'that it has read it for them, by scanning it electronically.'

Frank's trip overseas precipitated the end of his friendship with Michael Wilding. Although they had been moving in different directions for a while, the end still came as a shock to Frank. The previous year, after the fifth edition of *Tabloid Story* was published, Frank had withdrawn from the project. He was busy working on his next book, as well as the film project and the copyright case. Michael was working on his own projects, independently of Frank, including establishing his own press and book distribution. In 1973, Michael met Pat Woolley. An American, she had worked in the underground press in the United States before coming to Australia. They wanted to start a press called Wild & Woolley. Soon after, she returned briefly to the United States.

At the end of 1973, Michael flew to Los Angeles to meet up with Pat. Michael's trip overlapped with Frank's in early 1974. Frank tried to arrange to meet up with Michael, but Michael refused to give Frank his itinerary.

In part, Michael wanted to explore the underground scene in America on his own, guided by Pat. They were there ostensibly for work, in order to make contacts to establish Wild & Woolley. They met Lawrence Ferlinghetti at City Lights, owner of the famous San Francisco bookshop and publisher of many of the Beat Generation poets. Ferlinghetti, a poet, was associated with the Beats in their 1950s heyday. During their visit, Michael and Pat arranged to distribute City Lights books in Australia. Later in 1974, back in Australia, they published their own first titles under the Wild & Woolley colophon.

But the main reason Michael refused to give Frank his itinerary was because he felt he needed a break from the Balmain scene, and especially from Frank. Michael returned to Sydney while Frank was still overseas. Knowing Frank was coming back via England – where he and Sandra were visiting Don Anderson and the journalist Elisabeth Wynhausen – Michael wrote him a letter explaining the situation from his perspective, and posted it to England, where he knew Frank would receive it before he returned to Australia.

'Oh dear,' the letter opened. 'I suppose I shd take a carbon copy of this letter for the files, but am not. No, I have no grievance.' Michael explained why he had not given Frank his itinerary: 'With L.A., my purpose was to see LA, to see a different sort of people, to establish my own world in my own right and not be twinned in this perpetual teedledum & tweedledee.' He had grown tired of people always asking him 'how is Moorhouse'. 'I mean either we do it as a Gilbert & George double act, or we don't.' And he felt neither of them wanted to do that, or even should.

Michael went on to say how their literary work was moving in different directions: 'There were accidental similarities of milieu for our early stories. But I don't feel that's done either of us any good.' They now had their own interests, their own circles of friends. 'And, I suppose it might as well all be spelled out, the sorts of scenes we are at ease in aren't similar. God knows, I'm not at ease in many anyway, but I don't want yr anxiety making my anxiety worse.'

On a personal note, Michael felt he needed to extricate himself from Frank's influence: 'I guess when you know someone for long enough they tend to oppress you; I am very sensitive to other people's pressures; you remark on that continually . . . So I feel it is time to get out of the pressure I recognise.' He ended his explanation by stating: 'It's a sense of relief being in Sydney without you being around. I don't think we bring out desirable qualities in each other.'

For Frank, this marked the end of their friendship. When he returned to Australia, Michael telephoned him but he did not respond. Nor did he return invitations for lunch or drinks. He was deeply wounded and self-protective.

There was a final note from Michael to Frank, written on University of Sydney letterhead:

Dear Frank,
    'Dean Moriarty forgives'
    Apologies,
    Michael

But as far as Frank was concerned, it was over. In his personal notebooks for 1974, there are two entries regarding the situation, from his perspective:

Michael
    I offered everything openly & fully
    he did not – he withheld while accepting this from me.

And:

Wilding's disaffection
    now a feeling that I am *writing alone* which is the way it should be (and has been before for me)
    a false, temporary comfort to be in *alliance* or a *movement*

Their friendship had always contained an element of rivalry and competition. But that had provided the spark propelling them along the same road together, and the energy with which to overcome certain obstacles on that road. In the beginning, this was productive. In their writing they were both trying to do something new, and there was no culture in Australia to support this, no critical standards to fit their style of writing and no audience. They had to work together to create not only their own writing, but also the very conditions for its public reception. Incrementally, over years, while working with others, those conditions were finally achieved. But with those obstacles gone, so too was much of what held them together as friends.

An additional event that probably played into Frank's reaction to receiving Michael's letter in England, but which Michael would not have been aware of at the time, was that Frank was meeting Wendy to finally initiate their divorce. That prospect deeply affected him, more than he had thought it would. The impact of the symbolic ending of one relationship was compounded by the actual ending to another, forcing a retreat from both.

Three more stories from the Electric Experience project were published throughout 1974. 'The End of Ice' appeared in *The Sun*, as part of the newspaper's holiday short-story festival, on Saturday, 5 January. Its main theme was the relation between culture and technology, and the impact of technological change on individuals within that culture. Newer technologies render older technologies obsolete, but – as with Frank's unproduced screenplay on Maurie Anderson, the printer – newer technologies also render the practitioners of older technologies obsolete. 'It was not that men hate progress, but that they love inertia.'

In March 1974, the story 'Sister/Sister' was published in *Cosmopolitan*. This story was presented as a formal letter, or report, from Terri's older sister, Gweneth Mary McDowell, to Terri's psychiatrist, providing family background to assist in her care. 'I do not believe Teresa likes being alive,' Gweneth wrote.

The September edition of *Southerly* contained a third story, 'Tell Churchill that T. George McDowell Is on His Feet', an internal monologue from the perspective of McDowell himself, a stream of consciousness, but fragmented, covering observations, doubts and memories.

Moorhouse and Angus & Robertson (Publishers) Pty Ltd v University of New South Wales appeared in the Supreme Court of New South Wales in April and May 1974, presided over by Justice Frank Hutley. Frank was questioned on the first day. The purpose was to establish that he had only become aware of his book being photocopied after the fact, and so could not have given prior permission.

Q. Were you aware prior to September last year that it was proposed to have somebody go to the University of New South Wales and photocopy some book?
A. No.

It came out that Frank was a member of the Australian Society of Authors, but not of the Copyright Council. He had met Gus O'Donnell in passing a few years earlier, but had only met him formally, together with Peter Banki and David Catterns, in October 1973 – after Paul Brennan had photocopied Frank's story. Frank claimed he did not attend ASA meetings, but this was not true. The ASA had held a seminar over 9–10 March 1972, on the topic 'Australian Writers and Their Earnings', which included Frank speaking on the short-story market in Australia.

There were moments under cross-examination when Frank's testimony came under pressure, but he handled himself well. One instance focused on the photocopied story 'The Machine Gun'. It is littered with italicised paragraphs, unattributed excerpts drawn from Che Guevara's *Bolivian Diary* (1968), which had appeared in *Ramparts* magazine in July 1968. Frank was asked if this was the case, and he said yes. But when asked again, Frank clarified it was 'loose adaptation'. This was a fudge, but this line of questioning was not pursued further. Frank's use of Che Guevara's diary was permissible under the 'fair dealing' exception, but in hindsight it might have been better to have chosen another short story to build a copyright case around, one that did not itself raise questions of potential copyright violation.

Another line of questioning focused on Frank's involvement with *Thor*, referred to as 'the underground liberationist newspaper'. Frank was asked what 'liberationist' meant, but he hedged. This line of questioning clearly wanted Frank to make some statement regarding 'liberationist' as operating outside the law, or in defiance of the law, but Frank, perhaps realising this, would not be pinned down. Finally, the sought after answer was phrased as a question:

Q. Liberation from the law or from social custom?
A. I think it was used very loosely to describe attempts to change certain laws; attempts to change certain mental attitudes, and to change certain social customs.

Frank's response not only defused this line of questioning, but showed how his current position regarding copyright, and authors' rights generally, was consistent with his previous position against censorship.

There was some confusion when Frank was questioned about *Futility and Other Animals*, over the 'discontinuous narrative' form:

Q. Is that a book of stories or essays, or is that a continuous narrative?
A. No, that is called a discontinuous narrative.
Q. Was it a series of essays?
A. It is called a discontinuous narrative. *Futility and Other Animals* can, as a narrative, stand alone, but the stories are connected in a greater unity within the book. They connect to each other.

At the conclusion of the case, Justice Hutley found, first, that the university had not authorised the copyright infringement by Brennan, and, second, that it generally had 'authorised such breaches as occurred by the photocopying of the whole or part of the library copy of the said book'.

This was not the unambiguous win the Copyright Council had hoped for. In June 1974, the University of New South Wales appealed the second order, against the general infringement, while Frank and Angus & Robertson cross-appealed the first order, regarding Brennan's particular infringement.

That same month, the Copyright Agency Limited – the proposed organisation to negotiate, collect and distribute copyright fees associated with copying – was incorporated.

In the background to all of this, the federal government was moving to amend the *Copyright Act*. This was part of the broader strategy of the Copyright Council, with Gus O'Donnell leveraging his political contacts to put pressure on the Whitlam administration. Attorney-General Murphy appointed Justice Robert Franki to chair the Copyright Law Committee on Reprographic Reproduction. The terms of reference for this committee were to examine the situation of 'reprographic reproduction' – which included 'any system or technique by which facsimile reproductions are made in any size or form' – and to recommend alterations to Australian copyright law to balance the interests of the owners of copyright and the users of copyright material. This became known as the Franki Committee.

The 1974 federal election forced the Whitlam government into fulfilling one of its earlier commitments. Ever since the ASA had floated the idea for a Public Lending Right in 1966, it had tirelessly lobbied to make it a reality. In 1970 it had submitted the proposal directly to Prime Minister John Gorton and to Opposition Leader Gough Whitlam. The Library Association of Australia lobbied against the proposal. In June 1971 the Labor Party publicly stated it was in favour of the scheme. Further impetus was created when the New Zealand prime minister announced in May 1972 that a PLR scheme would be introduced there. The next month, Whitlam pledged to introduce the scheme, if elected, a pledge he repeated in November. Although work began quickly on the scheme when

Whitlam took office, it was only ready to be implemented in March 1974. But then a snap election was called for 18 May.

This coincided with Frank's copyright court case, which had not concluded when the election was held. On Monday, 13 May – the week of the election – there was a lunchtime rally at the Sydney Opera House in support of Whitlam. The Concert Hall was packed, with three-quarters of those who attended listening to the speeches outside on the square, via a public address system. Whitlam spoke and was supported by a panel of twenty writers, artists, academics and sportsmen. The main speaker was Patrick White, fresh from his recent Nobel Prize win. At the rally, Whitlam announced the government had accepted the recommendations of the PLR committee and the scheme would be implemented, retroactively, from 1 April. Its implementation was not therefore contingent on the outcome of the election. When the first-quarter payments (April to June) were calculated a few months later, $445,000 was distributed to writers (around $4.1 million in contemporary terms).

In the green room before the rally, Frank mingled briefly with White. Patrick wanted Frank's advice as a journalist, because *The Sydney Morning Herald* kept using an unflattering picture of White and he wanted to know what he could do about it. Frank's advice to the Nobel Prize–winning author was to do nothing, because if they found out he didn't like the picture, they would, out of mischief, continue to use it.

Frank also gave a speech that day. 'I speak on behalf of the anarchists of Balmain,' he said, to much applause. 'Even Balmain anarchists like myself are supporting Labor this time.' He talked in particular about Labor's already enacted policies on releasing Vietnam War conscientious objectors from jail, ending conscription, decriminalising homosexuality and abolishing national censorship. But his main focus was on Labor's ongoing arts and culture policies:

> They have let the arts get on with their work. It has to be pointed out that they are not simply grants to creative people: they are subsidies to

readers and to those who value good books, good films, good paintings, good music and good drama. The freer the creative people are to get on with their work, the more those who value the arts as consumers also benefit.

Frank even drew upon what he had learned in his 1958 agricultural course in Wagga when he declared 'the Labor Party's superphosphate for culture'.

This was the largest crowd Frank had ever spoken in front of, and the adrenaline was surging. After the event, a group went to the Journalists' Club for drinks. The inevitable adrenaline crash happened the moment Frank entered the club.

The following month – after the ALP's second election win, and after the conclusion to Frank's court case – he wrote to Wendy in England. 'Labor is back and the arts grants are safe,' he wrote. 'I even campaigned for Labor – giving a speech in the Opera House to 12,000 people. I passed out immediately after the occasion in the Journalist Club. Went straight to sleep.'

On the day of the election, 18 May, Frank had added his name to a list of dozens of writers and journalists for a full-page advertisement in *The Sydney Morning Herald*, protesting the concentration of media ownership in Australia and the conservative bias of the majority of proprietors.

From April until August 1974, Frank was involved in another court case: his appeal against his conviction the previous year for the distribution of *The Little Red Schoolbook*, and for subsequently resisting arrest and assaulting the police. On the docket were the charges: 'Malicious damage, Assault Police, Resist Police, and Exhibit restricted material.' Frank was unsuccessful in his appeal, and he owed $240 in additional costs, beyond the initial $50 fine. But as he wrote to his lawyer later that year: 'We think it was another of those small cases which hold the line against the anti-free speech people and it contained the other element of also holding the line against the police – even if we didn't win everything on this.'

In his personal notebook, Frank was more circumspect:

People in power are frightening – we are vulnerable –
there is (after court case) no defence really
I am frightened by those in power
the crime was "helping ideas escape".

In mid-1974, Frank presented a paper at a conference in Canberra. It was an excuse to get out of Sydney after the stress of his various court cases, and the federal election. Frank had rekindled his adolescent pastime, revisiting sites on the South Coast where he had hiked and camped in his youth. This coincided with a broader cultural interest in the relationship between the human and natural worlds. In his recent *CAB* report on mass media, Frank used the example of the environment as a type of peripheral concern that was tolerated in the mainstream media, as a novelty or a side issue, because it was considered unthreatening to the dominant cultural order. But, Frank argued, such concerns were reaching the mainstream: the nascent threats to the dominant 'Order' were only belatedly beginning to be recognised.

The conference in Canberra was very much a sign of this recognition. In 1971, UNESCO established an international, intergovernmental project called the Man and the Biosphere (MAB) Programme. This consisted of a rolling series of national conferences, providing a forum for experts, academics and government policymakers to receive and consider new ideas on this topic. This iteration, 'Man and Landscape in Australia', was organised by the Australian National Commission for UNESCO and held at the Academy of Science in Canberra, from 30 May to 2 June 1974.

There was a small contingent representing the arts. Frank spoke on the second day, delivering his paper, 'The Bush and the Laundromat', slotted between Leonie Kramer, a professor of English from the University of Sydney who was speaking on 'Symbolic Landscapes', and Daniel Thomas, an art historian and writer from the Art Gallery of New South Wales, who was speaking on 'Visual Images'. When Kramer finished speaking, Donald Horne stood up from the audience, said, 'Phooey!' and then sat down again.

The title of Frank's paper was a reference to his *Thorunka* and *Bulletin* column 'Around the Laundromats'. It pointed to the central schism he explored in the paper, between the bush, or rural and regional Australia, and urban centres, with their modern amenities. 'The city against the country is, of course,' Frank said, 'one of the great polarities of civilised times.' He contrasted two historical quotes. The first, from Juvenal, the second-century Roman poet, citing the problems of life in Rome, its traffic congestion, bad city planning and political corruption: 'myself, I would value a barren offshore island more than Rome's urban heart'. And then from Samuel Johnson, the eighteenth-century English writer, where Frank found a reversal of Juvenal's values: 'No, sir, when a man is tired of London, he is tired of life: for there is in London all that life can afford.'

Nature was originally considered, symbolically, as a mother, 'mother nature', and the city was a rejection of this natural order, Frank explained. The ultimate city person, in turn, had disdain for nature, and looked down on the bush. But more recently – this was the crux of Frank's paper – there had been a turn towards 'anti-urban, anti-city' values, emanating, paradoxically, from within city centres.

Frank traced the contemporary 'back-to-the-earth movement' as a slow evolution from the beatniks of the 1950s, the hippies of the 1960s, and through to the still emerging 'Greenies' of the 1970s, with their ecological action groups and campaigns against modern city developments. Frank put this movement into the category of a 'fashion', or a lifestyle advocacy group, with the caveat that this was 'not to denigrate it' but rather to consider it within the broader culture and in relation to the subcultures against which it measured itself. 'To classify as symbolic behaviour still leaves it valuable as a sign or signal of perhaps permanent changes ahead for society.' *Earth Garden*, an environmental lifestyle magazine that launched in Australia in 1972, estimated that, since 1970, some 30,000 people had returned to the earth, becoming involved in subsistence farming, bartering or alternative economies. From this, Frank stated:

> In a complicated society, in which decision-making is without consultation and often at a great distance from those affected, the new

movements are sometimes a concrete attempt to regain control of the life system – to see where the food is coming from, what is happening, how the system affects the person. A group of individuals tries to be a 'whole world'.

Ecological theories and scientific data were a major spur to such movements. 'Some of the utterances of the back-to-the-earth movement make it sound like a premature acting out of the forecasted ecological disaster,' Frank stated. 'Some talk and behave as if the breakdown of the system has occurred.'

One critical point Frank raised was how this movement appeared to be responding to urban living, rather than expressing a genuine concern for the natural world. Despite its surface rhetoric, it was more anti-urban than pro-nature. At one level, Frank was updating his earlier criticism against the Push for forming 'a gutless society', for posturing towards radicalism, while only acting in a reactionary and conservative manner. He saw similar traits within the 'back-to-the-earth movement'. 'Apart from mystical justifications and functional advantage,' he stated, 'an ideology of self-reliance, self-improvement, is also present. Although the context is fashionable and radical, its ideas are from small business and individualism – "making do with less", "testing yourself", "independence", "being your own boss", regaining control of your life".' This was the ideology Frank was exploring in his Electric Experience project.

As with much of Frank's cultural criticism, projected outward, the questions he raised were addressing otherwise inward concerns – personal dilemmas shared with others. The polarities structuring this lecture – between the bush and the laundromat, the town and the city – represented a schism Frank himself had straddled over the course of his life. It had shaped his thinking and infected his writing. Various short stories were studies of contrast, figures from regional Australia not fitting in with urban social groups, or else urban figures from such social groups yearning for something beyond the city limits.

It had been fifteen years since Frank first moved to Sydney from Nowra, feeling like Davy Crockett come in from the wilderness.

Once acclimatised, he retreated to Wagga and Lockhart, before returning to Sydney and starting over again. From the city, he criticised the small-mindedness of the towns. From the towns, he criticised the parochialism of the city. In the mid-1960s he lived during the week in Bundeena, with weekends in the city. Then he moved to Balmain, and tried to carve out a village oasis within an urban centre, but spending his weekends and vacations exploring the bushlands of his youth. In 1972, in *The Bulletin*, Frank admitted to a distrust of centralised power and authority, which he associated with the city, and a preference for small, self-governing localism, a 'lingering anti-city feeling'. Meanwhile, from his desk in his Ewenton Street studio, in his imagination he travelled back each week to the South Coast, between the wars, while working on his Electric Experience project.

Amid all of this, Frank was still trying to find his own path, a way to orient himself in the world, his own centre of gravity.

One of the ways Frank processed the end of his friendship with Michael Wilding was by writing comic fiction. He already had the character Milton, but in the act of writing, the demands of fiction, as always, overrode the initial experience that otherwise motivated the story. 'The Commune Does Not Want You', published in *Quadrant* in July/August 1974, offers a case in point. Like 'Dell Goes into Politics', this story offers a rare instance in which Frank explained the process of writing the story.

In the story, the first-person narrator goes to a share house – the eponymous 'commune' – to track down his friend Milton. Milton is not seen during the visit, the narrator engaging with other inhabitants of the commune. At the end of the story, a note is delivered from the first storey, through a hole in the floor. It is from Milton, telling the narrator to leave.

Frank later described the impetus of this story as 'pain turned to humour . . . evolved from a painful loss of a friend, a going of different ways'. But if the constituent parts of the story are measured against reality, the fiction comes into greater relief. 'Although the story is out of my life,' Frank said, 'in the sense that it expresses, in an inverted way, a condition of my being at a certain time, it is not autobiographical.' Michael Wilding did not enter a commune, for example. This simply provided a comic situation, representing their 'going in different ways'.

The story drew on other experiences unrelated to Michael. Frank had visited a commune in the United States. The house in Sydney existed, but it was not a commune. Friends of Frank's were converting their townhouse into 'a polyfunctional endospace'. The story was 'written at the time when some students, nature lovers, and bohemians, were introducing rural life into the city as a way of keeping in touch with nature'. This marked the cultural turn Frank discussed in 'The Bush and the Laundromat'. Frank had recently lost his cat, Ward, so a cat made it into an earlier draft of the story, another figure of loss. In that draft, the narrator accidently sits on a cat. In the final draft the cat becomes a pig. But it is a fictional pig. 'The commune is a site of the times in which the story was written,' Frank said, 'and represents the alien, culturally superior world where my friend was fantasised, by me, to now reside.'

But the story also demonstrates how sometimes reality was stranger than fiction, at times so implausible that it would not work in a fictional setting. The real-life friend's 'polyfunctional endospace' did, as in the story, have a hole in the ceiling of the ground floor, which was used as a 'communication hole'. One day, while Frank was visiting, a baby had fallen through that hole, onto an armchair below, and was unhurt and unfazed. Frank originally put that real experience into the story, but then removed it because, in print, 'it seemed unbelievable'. The real baby became the fictional stone lowered through the communication hole in the final story, which had a note from Milton fastened to it: 'Go away, the commune does not want you.'

The loss of Ward the cat came after Frank had dropped the character Ward from his *Bulletin* columns. In many respects the dialogue between 'Frank' and 'Ward', often disagreeable and antagonistic, was transposed from the *Bulletin* columns into Frank's stories, between a fictional narrator and the figure of Milton.

In this way, these stories became not so much about Michael Wilding, but a fictional renegotiation with Frank's own sense of self during a particular cultural period, a period of both personal and social change, and his feeling of being left behind or left out. 'I see the story as being a comic presentation of the discomfort of myself,' Frank said, 'unease of self.'

The second story Frank wrote during this period, 'Milton Turns Against Champagne', was published in *The Australian Ear* in October 1974. It drew more heavily on Michael's original letter. The title of this second story made reference to the original letter, where Michael said: 'I'm not at ease in the dinner parties & champagne & port & speeches & all that carry on.' The story also referenced two recent pieces, 'The Airport, the Pizzeria, the Motel, the Rented Car and the Mysteries of Life' and 'Concerning a Reunion with an Ex-wife in Portugal'. The narrator visits the rooms of the Jack Kerouac wake, which recalled another two earlier stories. The story even refers to Michael Wilding's version of the Jack Kerouac wake, 'Bye Bye Jack. See You Soon': the narrator in Frank's story remembers that '"Bye, bye Jack, see you soon," had been my valediction'. Michael's story has the character Joe sending postcards, following the fiasco of the wake, which read: 'DEAN MORIARTY FORGIVES.' In this referencing of earlier stories, these newer stories were taking on a fictional life of their own, thematically coalescing around one another and forming a new, nascent series of discontinuous narratives, one Frank would explore in the coming months.

In 'Milton Turns Against Champagne', the first-person narrator seeks Milton out at the university, to get an explanation for the cablegram he has been sent in Portugal ending their friendship. But Milton keeps avoiding him, refusing to explain himself. In the end, the narrator provides his own rationale for their parting of ways:

> Milton once told me he hungered for a Great Friendship or probably what he meant was a Friendship with the Great. You know, where the letters are later published and people in their memoirs recall luncheons

at which they sat spell bound while the two friends engaged in witty wisdom and whose collaboration almost resulted in the downfall of the Baldwin cabinet . . .

Well, Milton hungered for this.

If he could not have it, I realised, he wanted a dramatically broken friendship which would provoke speculation for many years after. This was to be his manoeuvre with fate. The sort of broken friendship that is written about by others in their memoirs . . .

Well, Milton had chosen the latter for the want of the former.

On 31 October 1974, Frank had a short story published in *Gayzette*, the national gay fortnightly newspaper. 'The Cup and the Wand (& the Magician)' is about a relationship between the first-person narrator and a 22-year-old man referred to as 'A'.

Frank had published stories with homosexual characters before. The triangular relationship between the narrator, his young lover and his older partner repeats the sexual geometry of an earlier story, 'Ten Years', published in *Futility and Other Animals*. But the only previous story explicitly describing gay sex – 'Carl and Paul Goodman' – was omitted by Frank from the final selection of *The Americans, Baby* and remained unpublished. So this new piece was Frank's first published story containing a description of gay sex. It was, of course, in a speciality publication largely out of sight from a mainstream audience, and indeed from many of Frank's own subculture.

A special screening of *Between Wars*, billed as the 'World Premier', was held on Friday, 8 November 1974, at the Prince of Wales Opera House in Gulgong, where much of the film had been shot. Many of the locals were in the film as extras. The following week, *Between Wars* was released in select theatres nationally. In the weeks following its release, the reviews were largely positive. Most of the popular media, such as *The Australian Women's Weekly*, which focused on the period fashions in the film, did stories on the extra-cinematic aspects of the film: behind the scenes in Gulgong, the state of the Australian film industry or the historical context of the film.

Sandra Hall, in *The Bulletin*, said: '*Between Wars* is blessed with a strong and political script by Frank Moorhouse.' Comparing it to other recent Australian films, such as *Alvin Purple*, *Petersen* and *The Cars That Ate Paris*, Mike Thornhill was quoted as saying: 'I'm not kidding myself. In this market, it's an art film.' Almost all reviews showed signs of relief there was a film produced in Australia that operated outside of this ocker milieu. The *Tribune* contrasted the film with these other 'crassly commercial' and 'frankly exploitative' films, adding: 'With *Between Wars* Michael Thornhill has dangerously defied convention and produced a sympathetic portrait of an Australian against his time.' *The Canberra Times* called it a 'turning point for our film Industry', describing *Between Wars* as 'a radical film in that it is an exploration of some of our more cherished national prejudices as they affect a symbolic Everyman'. *The Australian Jewish News* said it was 'the best Australian film produced in recent years'. Frank had produced 'an economic and articulate script', but the lion's share of the praise was for the director: 'What makes "Between Wars" such an impressive film, is the degree of control Thornhill exercises over his subject. He knows exactly what he wants from each sequence, location and situation, and he gets it just right each time.'

The *TV Times* saw the parallels between the historical context of the film and the present day: 'Rising unemployment, falling confidence, fear of socialism, and the emergence in town and country of right-wing para-military vigilantes opposed to trade-unionism – the news stories of November, 1974, but also, as a new all-Australian movie reminds us, of 1932.' Even *The Workers' News* praised the film, despite claiming it 'exhibited confusion' by failing to clearly delineate the working class or to relate any of the struggles as class struggles. *The Workers' News* appreciated the film as a departure from the Australian film industry's recent fare: '*Between Wars* is also particularly interesting because as a local product it is unselfconsciously "non-ocker".'

The most detailed and penetrating criticism of the film was done in *Cinema Papers* by John Flaus, Mike and Frank's old WEA Film Study Group colleague. '*Between Wars* is not great cinema,' Flaus opened his essay, 'but it is a nice solid little picture, and it's about time we started making them in this country.' Much of Flaus's focus was on the portrayal of the protagonist: 'Moorhouse and Thornhill set themselves a formidable task when they chose an anti-anti-hero, made him the only character in the film who is fully developed, and then cut him off from the easy devices for access to audience involvement.' This was, in part, a product of Frank's screenplay: 'the dramatic disposition of Trenbow is principally that of the reluctant participant in events, possessing neither dramatic ascendency over others nor the dramatic authority of inner strength.' This stemmed from Thornhill's decisions in executing the script: 'The director further detaches Trenbow from audience engagement: Thornhill refrains from those narrative-free one-shots which can be placed in the interstices of the action – usually between scenes – and which thereby induce a sense of being admitted to the character's inner condition.'

Flaus identified as a feature something that had become a dominant characteristic of Frank's literary fiction: its sociological imagination. 'However, the film presents an inferential kind of truth in such spectacles as the police raid of the Australia First meeting in the basement of Sydney Town Hall,' Flaus said, adding: 'With a minute of screen time we have summarized impressionistically so many observations of Australian society with such sardonic insight as our students strive and research painfully to attain after three terms in sociology or politics.'

The Electrical Experience was published in November 1974, the same week *Between Wars* was released nationally. The book contained fourteen stories – referred to as 'narratives' – accompanied by twenty-four 'fragments', listed separately. The fragments were often less than a page in length, a mere paragraph or line. These were drawn from research Frank did for the book, especially the non-fiction work he had planned but abandoned – 'The Technological History of the South Coast'. He absorbed parts of it into these fragments, some historical, some fictionalised, all based upon archival documents. Much of this material made its way into the fictional narratives themselves, as 'observed detail' to enhance the narrative effect.

The design of the book was essential to the experience of reading its contents. The stories were printed on a conventional white page with black type, but the fragments were presented on black pages with white type – one a negative of the other, all interspersed with archival photographs or advertising illustrations from the 1920s and 1930s. The font of one story, 'Gwenth McDowell's Statement Concerning Her Sister, Teresa McDowell, June 1969' – the retitled story 'Sister/Sister' from *Cosmopolitan*, with 'Gweneth' changed to 'Gwenth' – was presented as if produced on a typewriter, making it stand out from the rest of the book, a piece of 'private' correspondence interfiled with 'published' works and archival images.

The discontinuous narrative form was here enhanced to draw the reader's attention to various alternative mediums and visual structures within which it was embedded: typographic content framed by an iconic medium.

Seven of the stories had appeared in journals and newspapers since December 1972. One, 'The St Louis Rotary Convention 1923, Recalled', was previously published in *The Americans, Baby*. It acted as a bridge from that book to this, in much the same way as 'The Story of Nature' appeared in both *Futility and Other Animals* and *The Americans, Baby*, allowing characters to migrate from one to the other. This was a nod to the underlying continuous environment between the three books. An historical dimension was thereby added to that environment: the first two books were set in the 1960s and early 1970s, while *The Electrical Experience* spanned the 1930s to the 1950s, as well as the early 1970s. An additional six stories were published here for the first time, most of them filling out the life and character of McDowell.

The last story – also the final story in the collection – is only peripherally about McDowell, but it puts the whole collection into a broader generational perspective, and in doing so ties together this book with Frank's previous two, and with much else he had been concerned with over the previous decades. 'Filming the Hatted Australian' is set in the early 1970s and follows a group of young filmmakers from Sydney who have come down to the South Coast to make a documentary film, on a government grant, titled *The Australian of the First Half Century*.

The impetus for this story arguably comes from Frank satirising his previous engagement with the Commonwealth Film Unit, in their negotiations over the early treatments for what would become *Between Wars*. In 1970, Frank's initial treatment was rejected, with the note: 'I was hoping we would reveal a central character who was very much the accepted good solid Australian.' In 'Filming the Hatted Australian', the young filmmakers have a grant to make a film about precisely such an 'accepted good solid Australian'. Their attitude is the antithesis of McDowell's.

The story covers eight days of filming interviews with an older man, Frederick Victor Turner, starting slowly to gain his trust over the first couple of days, before switching tack. As the filming progresses, the older generation – Frederick's generation, McDowell's generation – is shown as small-minded, racist, sexist and violently misogynistic.

But what is remarkable about this story is the effect produced by the first-person narrator, which – while being one of the characters present, but not fully, or willingly, involved in the action – provides the reader with a critical point of entry into the story. Through this narration, the failings of the older generation might be revealed – but the tactics the filmmaker deploys to do so throw an equally critical light on the younger generation from the city, these 'university students', self-centred and self-serving. They do not so much overcome the social crimes they accuse the older generation of having committed, but they use such social concerns solely to differentiate themselves from the previous generation, and self-righteously so. In the process, they are shown as making a film for their own benefit, exploitatively and duplicitously.

In many respects, this concluding story was a capstone for Frank's three interconnected, discontinuous narrative books. It was a revision of Frank's earlier essays, 'The Gutless Society', from 1963 and 1964. The second version updated and expanded the criticisms of the first version to cover not only Frank's own generation but the generation preceding his. In 'Filming the Hatted Australian', Frank updated his argument once again, incorporating many of the experiences of the previous decade.

The story referenced Frank's ongoing concern with the relationship between technologies and cultural change, with this story of a film crew making a documentary, in a book whose previous stories – which outlined the historical development of manufacturing and electricity on the South Coast – referenced, and were, in part, structured by the parallel development of communications technology, from the letter to the telephone and then to television, across different generations of Australians.

In a sense, Frank did write 'The Technological History of the South Coast' after all.

'Well, the South Coast book is out,' Frank wrote to his parents in early December.

> I don't know whether you'll like it or not . . . The book is a gentle look at the sort of person you probably know well – who has his strengths and weaknesses – sometimes a figure of fun and sometimes a truly admirable person. I think the main character T. George McDowell is a real part of the Australian character and an important part.

Reviews had by then started appearing in the press. 'When you start out being a writer no one tells you that you have to be judged every two or so years in public by reviewers and discussed by people,' Frank told his parents. 'I find it disconcerting although I now accept it as part of the job.'

The early reviews, however, published prior to this letter being composed, had been positive. Carl Harrison-Ford, writing in

The Australian, said that this was 'probably the most assured and rounded' of Frank's books. In *The Sydney Morning Herald*, Martin Johnston wrote:

> It's tempting to call *The Electrical Experience* a completely new departure for Frank Moorhouse. But it's characteristic of his work so far as it is of Kurt Vonnegut's that each book retains a set of guy-ropes, tenuous, flexible and strong as spider-strands, linking it to the by now solid ground of the previous one. And – in a sort of personal concretisation of Eliot's 'tradition' – each book thus augments and illuminates the others.

Concerning the character of T. George McDowell, Johnston added: 'To someone like me he's a South Coast Martian. How Moorhouse makes you care so much for and about such a man is one measure of his achievement.'

Not everybody agreed. A week after Frank's letter to his parents, John Tittensor, in *Nation Review*, said of the character McDowell: 'He is, in short, a hamfisted attempt at a parody of an already parodied image, a stereotyped depiction of a stereotype, and as such is dismally boring both as a personality and as literary creation.' But this criticism was an outlier. Carl Harrison-Ford noted how such a knee-jerk reaction to Frank's previous books largely missed the underlying subtleties, which this new book made more overt, and so helped the reading public to re-evaluate what Frank was attempting in those previous books:

> Where many readers praise or condemn Moorhouse for his sexual concerns, more underlying ones that have always been there surface and deepen the picture. Where some critics see Moorhouse as two-dimensional and pre-judging, the actual structuring of the stories around questions and doubts – which once again has always been there – is more apparent in a less sensational context.

'Mr Moorhouse's best "discontinuous narrative" to date,' Brian Kiernan wrote in *The Age*, '*The Electrical Experience* is also most imaginative social history. I suspect this observation would not be unwelcome to him ... he has a tough realism that recognises, beyond the individual's attempts to come to terms with it, a world of confusing and disturbing complexity.'

It was in understanding the discontinuous narrative as a distinct literary form that these reviews displayed an advance over those for Frank's previous books. Those earlier books had often been awkwardly reviewed from the misapplied standard of either a short-story collection or a novel, but *The Electrical Experience* was assessed by its own, hard-won standard. 'The techniques, as I say, have hardly changed,' wrote Johnston. 'This book, too, is called a "discontinuous narrative." The method is one Moorhouse is getting closer to perfecting.'

Harrison-Ford wrote:

> And while the idea of the 'discontinuous narrative' has been rather vague in its application to earlier books' relationship between stories and unity as a volume, in *The Electrical Experience* this narrative is handled with a certainty and consistency that gives it viability as a literary form sitting well between stories and novels.

Brian Kiernan astutely noted the broader effect of this form in each of Frank's books to date:

> From Moorhouse's work to date is emerging the sense of a larger imaginary world lying behind the individual stories and populated by the characters who recur in them. Dr. Trenbow and Backhouse of *Between Wars*, for example, are glimpsed a number of times in this book. But as with Henry Lawson, who used many of the same characters in widely different stories, it is beside the point to speculate whether these could have been brought together in a novel. Life for Lawson did not form a novelist's coherent pattern, and similarly one feels that discontinuities are essential to Moorhouse's perception of life.

Kiernan noted Frank's long-held interest in the role of technology in cultural change, citing his previous *CAB* contributions.

These critics also observed how the form of the printed work, its design and extra-literary inclusions, enhanced the artistic unity of the discontinuous narrative form of *The Electrical Experience*. Johnston referred to this as 'a cinematic-collage approach, involving vignettes or anecdotes of his characters at different times and from different angles, miscellaneous *objets-trouvés*, scraps of jokes and songs, and letters, even, this time, period photographs. It works.'

But not every reviewer thought so. In an otherwise perfunctory review in *The Advertiser*, Anne Summers noted that the book design 'embellished the literary technique with a few graphic devices', but saw these as ornamentation only, peripheral rather than integral: 'Although they are presented quite attractively interspersed throughout the book, I do not feel that they enhance the basic literary intention in any way.' Less impressed was the *Nation Review*: 'Nor is any lift provided by the McLuhanist inanities, the old photos, the statements of Rotary policy, the tips on keeping milk fresh and on whitening black skin, which, to the naturally suspicious mind of the reviewer, are too redolent of simple self-indulgence.'

The most insightful review of *The Electrical Experience* was provided by the critic Dorothy Green in *Hemisphere*:

> Every now and then the smell of old newspaper files becomes a little obtrusive. But the final effect of such material and its deployment is not facetiousness: the characterisation and action are rooted in real experience, real observation or living memory, and the mass of historical detail is there not to fill a vacuum but to serve a dramatic purpose, chiefly the creation of the central character, T. George McDowell . . .

Regarding this character, Green wrote:

> George, at first sight, seems to owe far too much to the 'Barry Humphries' tradition, which has made it so easy to send up the suburban or small-town man in this country. But George does not stay flat on the page as a Humphries character would do. He is a multi-dimensional creation,

despicable, admirable, infuriating, endearing, dull, imaginative, cruel, terrible, pathetic, all at the same time.

Green's criticism was built upon an appreciation of the development of Frank's writing, from his earlier stories to the current collection:

> Moorhouse possesses a formidable talent, capable of helping his countrymen to understand themselves, as well as, thank God, of entertaining them. The only obstacles in his way seem to be the temptation to cleverness which mars some of the earlier stories, and a temptation which is the besetting sin of so many of his fellow fiction-writers: to use his characters for the purpose of self-glorification.

But, she added: 'The latter is very little in evidence in this latest book.'

What Green found particularly attractive about *The Electrical Experience* was the way the narrative established the characters and situations with a certain degree of detachment, which placed a greater onus on the reader. 'Moorhouse presents the evidence – it is up to the reader to judge,' she wrote. A case in point was the final story in the collection. 'Whose side is the author on – for instance, in the final story, "Filming the Hatted Australian"?' she asked. 'One statement it seems to be making is that priggishness and self-righteousness are not the monopoly of any one generation.'

The importance of this final story was also noted by Harrison-Ford: 'More complex still is the last story, "Filming the Hatted Australian" . . . It is a cold story but it clinches the volume.'

This detached perspective, which Frank had been developing over decades, was hard-earned and had not come without personal cost. As he wrote to his parents, upon publication of the book:

> The other thing I find hard is that unless you become a writer who works in total fantasy – say, writing thrillers, historical romance – you have to work with the world around you, the world you know. This is gruelling because it makes you so conscious, so much the observer, rather than the participant.

As with his previous books, Frank was most concerned about the reception among his family. But his concerns were misplaced. Purth wrote to him in early December, telling him: 'Dad is reading it and reads out parts which we can follow the characters . . .' A few days earlier, Frank Sr wrote to him, showing that he did, indeed, follow the characters well:

> Perhaps people of my generation will appreciate your book more than most. We can recognise the places and events as well as some of the personalities mentioned. To me your book demonstrates how we each effect other people's lives without realising it. Perhaps only by a thought or an expression that lives to become a guide to our behaviour.

One of the consequences of setting the book largely in the context of the previous generation, and on the South Coast, was that the stories could be read as works of fiction, rather than as veiled autobiography or some documentary of the Push. These media impositions over Frank's previous books often worked against acknowledging his skill and craftsmanship, his imaginative capacities. Martin Johnston, in *The Sydney Morning Herald*, noted this:

> Because of their subject matter, his previous books got rather a lot of snide and sniggering extra-literary attention: 'Who do you think that's supposed to be?', 'Did he really get off with her?' and the like, leading sometimes to misinterpretations almost cabbalistic in their ingenuity. This time that's just not on; no sex-and-sensation; no in-group gossip; no recognition games to play.

It was now possible to consider Frank independently from Michael Wilding, too, who had also recently published a book, *Living Together*. Johnston called this an 'extra benefit', explaining:

> [F]rom time to time Moorhouse and Michael Wilding have looked like two halves of a pantomime horse. With this book and Wilding's *Living Together* that's no longer on, either. One can read and admire each individually, which – not necessarily through any fault of theirs – has

sometimes been hard in the past. For the forking of paths may the Lord make us truly grateful.

That week in November was perhaps the biggest in Frank's professional and public career to date. Over a seven-day period, in quick succession, *Between Wars* was released in select theatres nationally, and *The Electrical Experience* was published. On the day of publication, Frank had a fish and champagne lunch with Rosemary Creswell and Murray Sime in Balmain. When Frank stood to make a speech he began to choke on a fishbone. After unsuccessfully trying to dislodge the fishbone in the restaurant, and becoming increasingly panicked, Frank was taken to the emergency room. He was released from hospital in Sydney just as, in Canberra, the High Court of Australia commenced hearing the appeal to his copyright case.

One month later, on 21 December 1974, Frank had his thirty-sixth birthday.

Coda

'Reading Biographies to Overcome Loneliness'

The publication of *Futility and Other Animals* in 1969 was something of a false start for Frank. It was reviewed, but a low print run, poor distribution and cautious booksellers operating under federal censorship meant it did not find an audience. It was with the publication of *The Americans, Baby* in 1972, after Frank had moved to Angus & Robertson, that he began to find readers. This was consolidated in 1974 with the publication of *The Electrical Experience*. But the accidental lynchpin securing this consolidation of Frank's reputation was the republication of *Futility and Other Animals* by Angus & Robertson in 1973.

For the general Australian reading public, it was as if Frank had produced three books in three years. The critical appreciation of the discontinuous narrative form that came with *The Electrical Experience*, and the realisation all three books shared a continuous imaginative background, only compounded his literary reputation. This was reinforced by Frank's increased public presence during this period, as a regular columnist for *The Bulletin*, as a participant in the dismantling of the national censorship regime and as a litigant in the process of renovating Australia's copyright legislative framework. He had even made a feature film.

For Frank, this three-year period was twenty-four years in the making. In 1950, an eleven-year-old Frank had walked out of the Roxy cinema, in Nowra, and gone home to write his first story, based on the film he had just seen. In 1974, various big screens across the country played *Between Wars*, based on an original story Frank had written. He had come full circle.

And that circle had only closed because, in the intervening years, Frank had a single-minded dedication to the craft of writing narrative fiction, and to developing a new form of that craft. But achieving this required a broadminded approach not only to the craft of writing, but also to creating the personal, social, economic and political conditions within which such writing could be pursued in Australia.

In April 1955, setting out upon this path, a sixteen-year-old Frank typed the following letter to himself, all in uppercase, to emphasise the importance of the final school year ahead, and where he wanted to go afterwards:

A LETTER TO MYSELF WRITTEN 4TH APRIL 1955
FRANK,

THE LEAVING CERTIFICATE IS A DIFFICULT EXAMINATION IN FACT IT IS THE MOST GRUELLING OF ALL EDUCATIONAL AWARDS. THE OBJECT OF THE TWO YEARS SCHOOLING IS TO ASSIMILATE AS MUCH KNOWLEDGE AS POSSIBLE SO AS TO BECOME A CITIZEN WHOSE OPINIONS ARE BACKED WITH FACTS AND UNBIASED THOUGHT. TO BECOME A WRITER OF THE HIGHEST STANDARD IT IS NECESSARY TO STUDY. STUDY IS HARD, TIRING, AND DISTASTEFUL BUT ITS REWARDS ARE GREAT. IT IS IN REALITY A FIGHT TO SUBDUE THE MIND INTO LEARNING. IT NEEDS WILL-POWER AND THIS WILL-POWER CAN ONLY BE FUELD UPON IDEALS. YOU HAVE THESE IDEALS IN THE OCCUPATION YOU HAVE CHOSEN; IN YOUR AIM TO BECOME A CREATIVE WRITER; IN YOUR AIM TO BECOME AND OBSERVER OF LIFE. REMEMBER THAT KNOWLEDGE IS POWER; IT DEMANDS RESPECT; IT IS THE NECESSARY ASSETT OF A LEADER; AND IT IS THE

ENEMY OF BIAS AND PREJUDICE – THE TWO SORES THAT HAVE FESTERED UPON THE BODY OF THE WORLD.

How far Frank had come, and the cost of getting there, can be seen in his first book, published fifteen years later.

It was evident, for example, in the 'Stories of Nature' trilogy, which was the most mature and emotionally resonant piece of fiction in the book, and perhaps Frank's most accomplished series to that date. The third story – which also closed out the book – not only offered a mature response to the futility introduced in the first story of the book, but also provided a near-perfect précis for Frank's major concerns. It demonstrates his use of literary fiction as a form of inquiry, putting into perspective many of his own experiences, from his adolescence, into his early adulthood, while at the same time putting these into a broader cultural and social context, not just of his own generation, but of the generation before, and his hopes for the generation to follow:

> Her baby would be born into a time when granddaughters would not understand their grandmothers. Already mothers and daughters were having difficulty. Perhaps we were creating an orphan generation – no parents and no god – where had she heard that – someone in the common room? She corrected herself – it was not the whole world that was alienated from its parents – only the teenagers and they for only a short time. They mostly fell back and went about imitating their parents. It was the intellectually rebellious and the neurotics who went on feeding and nursing their alienation – proceeding further in the direction away from their parents. But her daughter would be freer. Her daughter would be offered more alternatives with less censure. The following of strange paths would be easier for her and she would have a mother who – if she had not gone far along the strange paths – at least understood why some people did. Or did she understand? What was so great about non-conformity? What was great about independence? What was so good about strange paths? Perhaps her daughter wanted a familiar path? But whatever, her daughter would not have to live with the emotionally gruelling voice which said, 'Do you

really think you are doing a wise thing?' whenever she deviated from the normal.

In the Christmas edition of *The Bulletin* in 1974, Frank had a new short story published. 'The Chain Letter Story' is based on a ubiquitous phenomenon: something good, or sometimes the forestalling of something bad, is supposed to happen to the recipient if they send the letter on, to keep the chain going. There were different forms of such chain letters: some were financial scams (effectively pyramid schemes, sending cash through the mail), or religious (saying and passing on prayers), or superstitious (good luck will come if you continue the chain, bad luck will come if you break the chain) and so on. Frank converted this social phenomenon into a story.

'This is a chain letter story,' the narrator stated. 'Send a copy of this story to two friends (2). Do not break the chain. If you do not wish to join the chain DO NOT READ THIS STORY. THIS IS NOT A JOKE.'

The chain letter in the story was supposed to have been started in 1953 by Antoine de Sedi, in South America. The narrator of the story had recently broken the chain and had a string of bad luck. Although ostensibly a comic story, suitable for holiday readers of *The Bulletin*, it allowed Frank to play out some of his broader concerns. The story satisfied Frank's penchant for formal procedures and protocols, outlining the rules and rituals of chain letters. It touched on communications technology, and his thoughts regarding photocopy machines and their social impact. 'And the copy I received this time is photocopied,' the narrator stated. 'For Chrissakes, chain letters have either to be written in your own handwriting or typed out personally ... The luck accumulates through the undertaking of the ritualistic chore – monk-like, dutiful repetition.'

The story also parodied the call and response of Frank and Michael Wilding's back-and-forth story writing over the previous years, a metaphorical chain letter that had started in 1968. This process was previously parodied in Frank's story 'Wesley's Brother at the Wake for Jack Kerouac', in which he called this a form of 'communal literature'.

Finally, 'The Chain Letter Story' allowed Frank to bring together the imaginative threads of his characters, from his various discontinuous narratives, each of which was itself a form of chain letter story, this latest story being yet another link:

> This is a rotten luck chain. Send it to a person who often has rotten luck. This is a chain of commiseration. Nothing very good has ever happened to any of us in this chain. Becker had good luck with a girl in a lavatory but nine minutes later lost his job with Coca Cola. T. George McDowell lost his factory and his daughter is now into films. Milton was hijacked by a New Life Style and four days later became an enemy. Cindy failed to get a guarantee of permanent love and nine months later had a baby. I myself am not feeling too hot. THIS IS NOT A JOKE.

This story was a way for Frank to survey the past and consider a new way forward – to seek out the next chain in his own story.

Considering the future, Frank's immediate concerns, heading into 1975, were that the Franki Committee and the High Court decision – both related to the question of photocopying and copyright in Australia – were going to hand down their findings. That December, Frank's publisher, Richard Walsh, informed him that Angus & Robertson had submitted *The Electrical Experience* into the Miles Franklin Literary Award. The Whitlam Labor Party had only several months earlier been elected to a second term of three years – what could possibly go wrong? Regarding his own writing and future projects, despite his public success, by the end of 1974 Frank found himself constricted by the circle within which he had found himself. He was trying both to widen the circle, by moving forward with new writing and film projects, and to deepen it, by looking back to the period before he was born. It was an era he had started researching for *Between Wars* and *The Electrical Experience*, but felt he had not yet exhausted. He still felt its pull. In the years to come he would frequently reflect on his own prehistory. 'I am bit & pieces of "generations" of Australians,' he noted on one index card: '– an Australian of the past, of the country town, yet of the future'. Another card reads: 'piece together my customs traditions trace back before parents -> NSW rural convict peasants -> British -> Yorkshire -> London working class'.

In October 1975, Frank gave a lecture at Wollongong University on his film *Between Wars*. After screening the film, Frank discussed at length the pre-production creative process of researching and writing, as well as the production of the film itself. Frank referred to his view concerning the 'accidental nature of most human destiny (how little control we have over our lives)', but he conceded he also 'ascribes slightly to circularity of history'. Frank listed some of the characteristics of the immediate period following the Great War he had become interested in while working on the film and his subsequent book, *The Electrical Experience*. Near top of his list he wrote: 'new world status League of Nations Peace Talks'.

This referred back to something he had read in the book *Psychiatric Aspects of Modern Warfare*, by Dr Reginald Ellery, the model for the protagonist of *Between Wars*, Dr Edward Trenbow. Ellery concluded that efforts to overcome the 'larger lunacy' of war needed to be political, and ambitiously so. He cited the League of Nations as one such effort. 'A League of Nations was formed and intended to function as an international police force; but certain countries did not join and other countries deserted the League, which feared to exercise its power,' he wrote in the final chapter of his book. 'Here again, capitalist interests defeated a logical and well-intentioned plan for preserving peace.'

During this period, Frank felt lost. 'Reading biographies to overcome loneliness', he wrote in his personal notebook for 1974. A couple of years later, he noted: 'I dont know if my life is in its greatest mess or simply faultering before significant takeoff.' He had the vague idea he wanted to write about the League of Nations, but he was busy working on other book and film projects. And yet the idea continued to develop, with the immediate model for its execution being *The Electrical Experience*: a single volume of discontinuous narratives, set between the wars, historically grounded, imaginatively rendered. But he did not want to lean too heavily on past successes. He wanted to find new forms, and establish new standards by which to measure those forms.

During that period of gestation, he received a letter from his father, as if responding to Frank's private concerns. 'It is always difficult, in life, to know when you achieve success,' Frank Sr wrote to his youngest son, 'it is slow in coming – but what looks like success today might be only a minor achievement compared with the success you are yet to attain.'

Sources

The Frank Moorhouse Papers (UQFL231) are held at the Fryer Library, part of the University of Queensland. Over the course of my research, I have consulted this material when it has been processed and unprocessed, housed and rehoused in variously numbered boxes, and when new material has been incorporated into the collection. This included a tranche of material submitted in 2022, which remained unprocessed at the time I consulted it in March 2023.

This extensive archive covers the years 1957 to 2022, and includes Frank's literary and essay drafts, lectures notes, personal papers, an extensive private and business correspondence, research notes and index cards, newspaper cuttings, and financial and medical records.

Additional archival material is held by the National Library of Australia. The Papers of Frank Moorhouse, 1951–1970 (MS 5798) contains juvenilia (1951–1957), drafts of short stories and essays (1960–1969), notes and journals, scrapbooks containing clippings from Frank's work as a journalist (1957–1959), and professional correspondence with publishers and editors, up to and including the publication of *Futility and Other Animals* (1969).

The State Library of New South Wales holds the archives of various people associated with Frank Moorhouse. This includes the Don Anderson Papers 1969–1990 (MLMSS 5449), the Clive Hamer Papers (MLMSS 9374), the Donald Horne Papers 1960–1992 (MLMSS 3525), and the Michael Wilding Papers (MLMSS 7973).

Special Collections at the University of New South Wales, Canberra, holds the Papers of Jennifer Rankin (MSS 348).

Private Moorhouse family archives were provided by Arthur Moorhouse of Nowra.

Interviews and correspondence were conducted with Don Anderson, Paul Coombes, Wendy James, Helen Laidlaw, Arthur Moorhouse, Frank Moorhouse, Owen Moorhouse and Keith Paterson.

Newspapers and journals consulted
Australian Highway (1965–1967)
The Australian Worker (1962–1963)
Broadsheet (1960–1979)
The Bulletin (1880–1974)
City Voices (1965)
Current Affairs Bulletin (1947–1974)
The Lockhart Review (1962)
The Riverina Express (1958–1963)
The Shoalhaven News (1914–1947)
The Shoalhaven and Nowra News (1948–1959)
Tharunka (1962–1974)
Thor (1971–1972)
Thorunka (1970–1971)

Bibliography of published material referenced and consulted
1: A Prehistory of Frank Thomas Moorhouse Jr
Ailwood, Sarah & Sainsbury, Maree, 'The Imperial Effect: Literary Copyright Law in Colonial Australia', *Law, Culture and the Humanities*, vol. 12, no. 3, 2016.

Arnold, Rollo, 'Henry Lawson: The New Zealand Visits', *Australian Literary Studies*, vol. 3, no. 3, 1968, pp. 163–89.

Barnes, John (ed.), *The Writer in Australia: A Collection of Literary Documents*, Oxford University Press, 1969.

Becke, Louis & Jeffery, Walter, *Admiral Phillip: The Founding of New South Wales*, T. Fisher Unwin, 1899.

Bond, Catherine, '"Curse the Law!": Unravelling the Copyright Complexities in Marcus Clarke's *His Natural Life*', *Media and Arts Law Review*, vol. 15, no. 4, 2010, pp. 452–77.

Clark, Alan, *Cordial Making in the Nowra District*, Shoalhaven Historical Society, 1999.

Coleman, Peter, *Obscenity, Blasphemy, Sedition: Censorship in Australia*, Jacaranda, 1962.

Cousins, Arthur, *The Garden of New South Wales: A History of Illawarra & Shoalhaven Districts, 1770–1900*, Illawarra Historical Society, 1994.
Dutton, Geoffrey (ed.), *The Literature of Australia*, Penguin, 1964.
Dymock, Darryl, *'A Special and Distinctive Role' in Adult Education: W.E.A. Sydney 1953–2000*, Allen & Unwin, 2001.
French, Robert, 'Australia's Queer History', *LGBTQIA*, vol. 20, no. 4, 2018, pp. 47–9.
Godfrey, G.F. (ed.), *Fifty Years Ago: A.J.A. N.S.W. District 1911–1961*, Australian Journalists' Association, 1961.
Green, H.M. (revised and edited by Dorothy Green), *A History of Australian Literature: Pure and Applied*, volumes 1 and 2, Angus & Robertson, 1984.
Hancock, Bill, *The Year Dot to the Arrival of Alexander Berry in the Shoalhaven: The Early Shoalhaven Aboriginals*, Shoalhaven Historical Society, 2013.
Harrison, Kay, *A Nursery for Cattle*, Shoalhaven Historical Society, 1988.
Inglis, K.S., *This is the ABC: The Australian Broadcasting Commission 1932–1983*, Black Inc., 2006.
Johanson, Graeme, *A Study of Colonial Editions in Australia, 1843–1972*, Elibank Press, 2000.
Jones, Jennifer, *Country Women and the Colour Bar: Grassroots Activism and the Country Women's Association*, Aboriginal Studies Press, 2015.
Kent, Jacqueline, *A Certain Style: Beatrice Davis, a Literary Life*, Viking, 2001.
King, Arthur H. (ed.), *The First Seventy-Five Years of the Rotary Club of Nowra: A Collection of Reports and Activities Recorded in Newspaper and Rotary Bulletins from 1935 to 2010*, The Rotary Club of Nowra, 2010.
Langshaw, Elaine (ed.), *Nowra Public School, 1862–2012*, 2013.
Lawson, Henry, '"Pursuing Literature" in Australia' (1899), in John Barnes (ed.), *The Writer in Australia*, Oxford University Press, 1969, pp. 71–9.
Livingstone, K.T., *The Wired Nation Continent: The Communication Revolution Federating Australia*, Oxford University Press, 1996.
Lyons, Martyn & Arnold, John (eds), *A History of the Book in Australia 1891–1945: A National Culture in a Colonised Market*, University of Queensland Press, 2001.
Macmahon Ball, W., 'The Australian Censorship', *The Australian Quarterly*, vol. 7, no. 26, 1935, pp. 9–14.
Maddrall, Roslyn Helen, 'Braidwood Goldfields, 1850–1860s: History of Goldfields, Braidwood District', *Tallaganda Times*, 1978.
Moore, Nicole, *The Censor's Library*, University of Queensland Press, 2012.
Moorhouse, Frank (ed.), *Moorhouse the Machinery Man: Fifty Years in Australia 1925–1975*, 1975.
Moorhouse, Frank Osborne, *The Story of Mechanised Farming in the Shoalhaven – Being Researches and Recollections of Frank Osborne Moorhouse*, Shoalhaven Historical Society, 1986.
Mullin, Katherine, 'Poison More Deadly than Prussic Acid: Defining Obscenity after the 1857 *Obscene Publications Act* (1850–1885)', in David Bradshaw & Rachel Potter (eds), *Prudes on the Prowl: Fiction and Obscenity in England, 1850 to Present Day*, Oxford University Press, 2013, pp. 11–29.
——, 'Pernicious Literature: Vigilance in the Age of Zola (1886–1899)', in David Bradshaw & Rachel Potter (eds), *Prudes on the Prowl: Fiction and Obscenity in England, 1850 to Present Day*, Oxford University Press, 2013, pp. 30–51.

Nowra CWA, *Gateway to Service: Country Women's Association, N.S.W., Nowra Branch, 1924–1984*, CWA, Nowra Branch, 1984.
Palmer, Nettie, *Modern Australian Literature 1900–1923*, Lothian Book Publishing Company, 1924.
Palmer, Nettie (ed.), *An Australian Story Book*, Angus & Robertson, 1928.
Parkinson, Robert James, *Silver Screen in the Shoalhaven*, Robert James Parkinson, 2005.
Paterson, Keith, *The Circus and Other Travelling Tent Shows in Shoalhaven, 1855–1955*, Shoalhaven Historical Society, 2008.
Roberts, M.J.D., 'Morals, Art, and the Law: The Passing of the *Obscene Publications Act, 1857*', *Victorian Studies*, vol. 28, no. 4, 1985, pp. 609–29.
Shoalhaven Historical Society, *Living Echoes: A History of the Shoalhaven*, Shoalhaven Historical Society, 1996.
Smith, Babette, *A Cargo of Women: Susannah Watson and the Convicts of the Princess Royal*, Allen & Unwin, 2008.
Stafford, Jane & Williams, Mark, *Maoriland: New Zealand Literature, 1872–1914*, Victoria University Press, 2006.
Stephens, A.G., 'Introduction to *The Bulletin Story Book* (1901)', in John Barnes (ed.), *The Writer in Australia*, Oxford University Press, 1969, pp. 106–10.
Townsend, Helen, *Serving the Country: The History of the Country Women's Association of New South Wales*, Doubleday, 1988.
Wilding, Michael, *The Radical Tradition: Lawson, Furphy, Stead*, Foundation for Australian Literary Studies, 1993.
Wotherspoon, Garry, *Gay Sydney: A History*, NewSouth Publishing, 2016.
Young, Sally, *Paper Emperors: The Rise of Australia's Newspaper Empires*, NewSouth Publishing, 2018.

2: 'Fuck Father Christmas!'
Coleman, Peter, *Obscenity, Blasphemy, Sedition: Censorship in Australia*, Jacaranda, 1962.
Jones, Jennifer, *Country Women and the Colour Bar: Grassroots Activism and the Country Women's Association*, Aboriginal Studies Press, 2015.
Kiernan, Brian, 'Notes on Frank Moorhouse', *Overland*, no. 56, 1973, pp. 9–11.
Moore, Nicole, *The Censor's Library*, University of Queensland Press, 2012.

3: 'This is it; This Is Failure or Success in Life!'
Dorsey, George A., *Why We Behave Like Human Beings*, Harper & Brothers, 1925.
Eysenck, H.J., *Uses and Abuses of Psychology*, Penguin, 1953.
Gellert, Leon, 'The Short-story Market', *The Sydney Morning Herald*, 4 June 1955.
——, 'The Structure of Censorship', *The Sydney Morning Herald*, 26 November 1955.
Halloway, Wendy, 'Terror by Night' and 'The Sun Came Up', *Platypus: Nowra Intermediate High School Magazine*, no. 9, 1955.
Quiller-Couch, Sir Arthur, *On the Art of Writing: Lectures Delivered in the University of Cambridge, 1913–1914*, Cambridge University Press, 1916.

4: 'I Feel Like Some Other Species Looking at Humans'
Abercrombie, M., Hickman, C.J. & Johnson, M.L., *A Dictionary of Biology*, Penguin, 1954.

Bongiorno, Frank, *The Sex Lives of Australians: A History*, Black Inc., 2015.
McRae, William A., *About Ourselves and Others*, Oxford University Press, 1941.
Steichen, Edward, *The Family of Man*, Simon & Schuster, 1956.
Walker, Kenneth & Fletcher, Peter, *Sex and Society*, Penguin, 1955.

5: 'Is This You, Moorhouse?'
Moore, Nicole, *The Censor's Library*, University of Queensland Press, 2012.
Moorhouse, Frank, 'The Young Girl and the American Sailor', *Southerly*, vol. 18, no. 4, 1957, pp. 114–17.
——, 'I Saw It from a Double Decker Bus', *Southerly*, vol. 20, no. 1, 1959, p. 23.
——, 'One Night in Bed', *Westerly*, vol. 5, no. 1, 1960, pp. 23–25.
Sawer, Geoffrey, *A Guide to Australian Law for Journalists, Authors, Printers and Publishers*, Melbourne University Press, 1949.

6: 'There Are Those Who Kick, Those Who Get Kicked and Those Who Kick Back'
Bongiorno, Frank, *The Sex Lives of Australians: A History*, Black Inc., 2015.
Brown, Ian 'Charlie', 'The Societyless Gut', *Broadsheet*, no. 32, 1963, pp. 1–3.
Coleman, Peter, *Obscenity, Blasphemy, Sedition: Censorship in Australia*, Jacaranda, 1962.
Coombs, Anne, *Sex and Anarchy: The Life and Death of the Sydney Push*, Viking, 1996.
Hiatt, Les, 'A Reply to Charlie Brown', *Broadsheet*, no. 33, 1963, pp. 3–4.
Hill, Deirdre, *A Writer's Rights: The Story of the Australian Society of Authors, 1963–1983*, Australia & New Zealand Book Company, 1983.
Horne, Donald, *The Lucky Country: Australia in the Sixties*, Penguin, 1964.
Mannheim, Karl, *Ideology and Utopia: An Introduction to the Sociology of Knowledge*, Kegan Paul, Trench, Trubner, 1936.
Moore, Nicole, *The Censor's Library*, University of Queensland Press, 2012.
Moorhouse, Frank, 'The Uniformed Stray', *Meanjin Quarterly*, vol. 21, no. 3, 1962, pp. 321–26.
——, 'The Gutless Society', *Broadsheet*, no. 30, 1963, pp. 4–6.
——, 'Spider Town', *Overland*, no. 29, 1964, pp. 4–10.
——, 'The Respectable Deviant', *Westerly*, vol. 9, no. 1, 1964, pp. 20–5.
——, 'The Gutless Society', *Oz*, no. 10, 1964, pp. 13–14.
Stratton, David, *The Last New Wave: The Australian Film Revival*, Angus & Robertson, 1980.
Sweeney, 'Activism versus Oblomovism', *Broadsheet*, no. 34, 1963, pp. 3–4.
Wesker, Arnold, 'O, Mother, Is It Worth It?', *Overland*, no. 19, 1960, pp. 17–18, 27.
——, 'The Secret Reins', *Encounter*, March 1962, pp. 3–6.

7: 'I Am More Confused Now'
Anderson, Don, 'James Baldwin: Banned Novelist', *The Australian Highway*, vol. 45, no. 3, 1965, pp. 5–7.
Coombs, Anne, *Sex and Anarchy: The Life and Death of the Sydney Push*, Viking, 1996.
Hill, Deirdre, *A Writer's Rights: The story of the Australian Society of Authors, 1963–1983*, Australia & New Zealand Book Company, 1983.
Horne, Donald, *Time of Hope: Australia 1966–72*, Angus & Robertson, 1980.
Moorhouse, Frank, 'Where Do You Stand?', *The Australian Highway*, 44:4, 1964, p. 4.

———, 'Of Ova Seize', *The Australian Highway*, vol. 45, no. 1, 1965, p. 4.
———, 'Nish', *Pluralist*, vol. 4, no. 1, 1965, pp. 18–19.
———, 'What Can You Say?', *Red and Black*, no. 1, 1965, pp. 21–5.
———, 'Dead', *Australian Letters*, vol. 7, no. 1, 1965, pp. 32–4.
———, 'Apples and Babies', *Squire*, vol. 2, no. 5, 1965, pp. 41–4.
———, 'Honey-comb Is My Favourite Sweet', *Squire*, vol. 2, no. 6, 1966, pp. 7, 34.
———, 'The Falling of the Star', *The Bridge*, vol. 2, no. 2, 1966, pp. 33–6.
———, 'Sing a Song of Sex', *SCJ: The Sydney Cinema Journal*, no. 1, spring 1966, pp. 10–14.
———, 'Teaching the Masses Their Media', *SCJ: The Sydney Cinema Journal*, no. 2, winter 1966, pp. 3–8.
———, 'The Importance of the Word "Berkeley"', *Broadsheet*, no. 50, 1966, pp. 1–6.
———, 'Futility and Other Animals', *Summer's Tales 3*, Macmillan, 1966, pp. 35–40.
———, 'O.K., O.K.', *Oz*, no. 32, 1967, pp. 16–17.
———, 'A Barmaid, a Prostitute, a Landlady', *Squire*, vol. 3, no. 5, 1967, pp. 42–3, 46.
———, 'The Nature of Demonstrations', *Noise*, 1967, pp. 14–17.
Rodriguez, Judith (ed.), *Jennifer Rankin: Collected Poems*, University of Queensland Press, 1990.
Wilding, Michael, 'Joe's Absence', *Southerly*, vol. 28, no. 1, 1968.

8: 'Writes Short Stories and Does Not Intend to Write a Conventional Novel'

Burns, Robert, 'At the Royal George', *Nation*, 12 July 1969.
Coombs, Anne, *Sex and Anarchy: The Life and Death of the Sydney Push*, Viking, 1996.
Cowan, Peter, 'Frank Moorhouse, Futility and Other Animals', *Westerly*, vol. 14, no. 3, 1969, pp. 48–9.
England, Katherine, 'Anguished Egos on the Couch', *The Advertiser*, 23 August 1969.
Hall, James, 'What Makes Gareth Powell Run', *The Australian*, 13 September 1967.
Hill, Deirdre, *A Writer's Rights: The Story of the Australian Society of Authors, 1963–1983*, Australia & New Zealand Book Company, 1983.
Keesing, Nancy, 'The New Guilt', *The Bulletin*, 12 July 1969.
Kiernan, Brian, 'Sex and the Urban Tribe', *The Australian*, 5 July 1969.
McLaren, John, 'Harvest of Stories', *Overland*, no. 44, 1970, pp. 52–3.
McLuhan, Marshall, *The Mechanical Bride: Folklore of Industrial Man*, Vanguard Press, 1951.
———, *The Gutenberg Galaxy: The Making of Typographic Man*, University of Toronto Press, 1962.
———, *Understanding Media: The Extensions of Man*, Routledge & K. Paul, 1964.
———, 'John Dos Passos: Technique vs. Sensibility', in H.C. Gardiner (ed.), *Fifty Years of the American Novel: A Christian Appraisal*, Scribner, 1951, pp. 151–64.
Moorhouse, Frank, 'Girls Galore', *Dissent*, no. 20, 1967, pp. 13–16.
———, 'Some Sort of Mistake', *Squire*, vol. 4, no. 2, 1968, pp. 6–8.
———, 'Something About Marshall McLuhan', *The Australian Highway*, vol. 47, no. 2, 1967, pp. 6–7.
———, 'The Crying Pain', *Squire*, vol. 3, no. 11, 1967, pp. 8–10.
———, 'The Dirty Girl', *Stand*, vol. 8, no. 4, 1967, pp. 4–11.
———, 'Her Mother's Visit', *Westerly*, vol. 12, no. 3, 1967, pp. 10–15.
———, 'No Birds Were Flying', *Chance*, December 1967, pp. 30–3.

———, 'Alphaville and Irony', *SCJ: The Sydney Cinema Journal*, no. 4, 1968, pp. 3–6.
———, *Futility and Other Animals*, Gareth Powell & Associates, 1969.
Wilding, Michael, 'Joe's Absence', *Southerly*, vol. 28, no. 1, 1968, pp. 37–53.
———, 'Living in the Inner City', *Southerly*, vol. 29, no. 3, 1969, pp. 231–6.

9: 'The Stories Aren't Dirty Enough'
Bowes, Dominic, *Exposing Indecency: Censorship and Sydney's Alternative Press 1963–1973*, Honours Thesis, University of Sydney, 2012.
Ellery, Reginald Spencer, *Psychiatric Aspects of Modern Warfare*, Reed & Harris, 1945.
———, *The Cow Jumped Over the Moon*, F.W. Cheshire, 1956.
Hill, Deirdre, *A Writer's Rights: The Story of the Australian Society of Authors, 1963–1983*, Australia & New Zealand Book Company, 1983.
Horne, Donald, *The Lucky Country: Australia in the Sixties*, Penguin, 1964.
———, *Time of Hope: Australia 1966–72*, Angus & Robertson, 1980.
Moorhouse, Frank, 'The American Poet's Visit', *Southerly*, vol. 28, no. 4, 1968, pp. 275–85.
———, 'The Supersonic Coward', *Man*, vol. 65, no. 3, 1969, pp. 58–64, 97–101.
———, 'The Dirty Girl', *Man*, vol. 65, no. 4, 1969, pp. 91–5.
———, 'The Coca Cola Kid', *Chance*, June 1969, pp. 8–10.
———, 'Now Here Is the News . . .', *Current Affairs Bulletin*, vol. 44, no. 12, 1969, pp. 178–91.
———, 'Becker and the Moon', *Southerly*, vol. 30, no. 1, 1970, pp. 57–63.
———, 'The Girl from the Family of Man', *Westerly*, vol. 15, no. 2, 1970, pp. 25–31.
———, 'The Machine Gun', *The Bulletin*, 18 July 1970, pp. 44–6.
———, 'Skillful Dislike', *The Bulletin*, 12 December 1970, pp. 54–5.
Powles, John, 'A White Man's Blindness', *The Australian Highway*, vol. 46, no. 1, 1965, pp. 9–11.
Quinan, John, *Frank Moorhouse and the Discontinuous Narrative*, Honours Thesis, University of Queensland, 1979.
Quinnell, Ken, 'Frank Moorhouse', *Cinema Papers: Australian Film Quarterly*, April 1974, pp. 138–140.
Scott, Natalie, '"Bull" It Seems Is Quite an Improper Word', *The Australian*, 24 May 1969.
Thornhill, Michael, 'The American Poet's Visit 1: Mike Thornhill Explains Why He Made His "Mini-Movie"', *Masque*, no. 10, 1969.

10: 'But the Important Thing I Want You to Know Is That I'm Trying to Be an Honest Craftsman'
Bedford, Ian, 'By the Waters of Balmain', *Nation*, 22 July 1972.
Bowes, Dominic, *Exposing Indecency: Censorship and Sydney's Alternative Press 1963–1973*, Honours Thesis, University of Sydney, 2012.
Hall, Richard, 'The Australian Books of the Year', *The Australian*, 15 December 1972.
Halligan, Marion, 'Opening Up Vistas', *The Canberra Times*, 14 October 1972.
Hill, Deirdre, *A Writer's Rights: The Story of the Australian Society of Authors, 1963–1983*, Australia & New Zealand Book Company, 1983.
Horne, Donald, *Time of Hope: Australia 1966–72*, Angus & Robertson, 1980.
Jefferis, Barbara, 'Riotous City Life', *The Sydney Morning Herald*, 22 July 1972.

Jost, John, 'A Rosy Future for the Miracle Worker', *The Age*, 22 December 1973.
Kent, Jacqueline, *A Certain Style: Beatrice Davis, a Literary Life*, Viking, 2001.
Kiernan, Brian, 'Moorhouse Territory', *The Australian*, 29 July 1972.
Moorhouse, Frank, 'The ABC's Search for Identity', *Current Affairs Bulletin*, vol. 46, no. 10, 1970, pp. 147–59.
——, 'Anti-Bureaucratisation & the Apparatchiki', *Thorunka*, no. 2, 1970, pp. 16–17.
——, 'One All Draw and Forty to Go', *The Bulletin*, 13 February 1971.
——, 'The Myth of the Male Orgasm', *Thor*, 1971, pp. 8–10.
——, 'The Mystique of Rotary', *The Bulletin*, 29 May 1971.
——, 'Camping in Balmain', *The Bulletin*, 19 June 1971.
——, 'Getting Up in Drag', *The Bulletin*, 20 October 1971.
——, 'Language, Arranged and Deranged', *The Bulletin*, 11 December 1971.
——, 'Hello, Nineteen-Seventy Two!', *The Bulletin*, 1 January 1972.
——, 'Mardi Gras in New Orleans', *The Bulletin*, 18 March 1972.
——, 'American Bar', *The Bulletin*, 22 April 1972.
——, 'Violence Is All?', *The Bulletin*, 6 May 1972.
——, 'Asylums and Prisons', *The Bulletin*, 22 July 1972.
——, *The Americans, Baby*, Angus & Robertson, 1972.
——, *Days of Wine and Rage*, Penguin, 1980.
Munro, Craig & Sheahan-Bright, Robyn (eds), *Paper Empires: A History of the Book in Australia, 1946–2005*, University of Queensland Press, 2006.
Perlez, Jane, 'Letters to Twiggy – Favourable Reply', *The Australian*, 27 November 1971.
Pringle, John, 'Books of the Year', *The Sydney Morning Herald*, 9 December 1972.
Quinan, John, *Frank Moorhouse and the Discontinuous Narrative*, Honours Thesis, University of Queensland, 1979.
Quinnell, Ken, 'Frank Moorhouse', *Cinema Papers: Australian Film Quarterly*, April 1974, pp. 138–40.
Turner, Ian, 'Just How Free Is Free?', *The Bulletin*, 19 August 1972.

11: 'Contrary to Popular Misconception, Banned Writing Doesn't Pay'

Despoja, Shirley, 'The Modern Urban Tribe', *The Advertiser*, 14 July 1973.
Dunn, Irina Patsi, 'Two Humble Studs from the Push', *Nation Review*, 14–20 October 1972.
Edwards, John, 'A Thriving Underground Press Is Defying Australian Censorship', *The National Times*, February 1971.
Forshaw, Thelma, 'Better Class of Ghetto', *The Sydney Morning Herald*, 4 August 1973.
Hill, Deirdre, *A Writer's Rights: The Story of the Australian Society of Authors, 1963–1983*, Australia & New Zealand Book Company, 1983.
Jones, Jennifer, *Country Women and the Colour Bar: Grassroots Activism and the Country Women's Association*, Aboriginal Studies Press, 2015.
Kelpert, L.V., 'Australian Cry from the Underground', *The Sydney Morning Herald*, 13 May 1973.
Kent, Jacqueline, *A Certain Style: Beatrice Davis, a Literary Life*, Viking, 2001.
Kiernan, Brian, 'Notes on Frank Moorhouse', *Overland*, no. 56, 1973, pp. 9–11.
Long, Jessica, 'South Coast to Farewell Aboriginal Elder Aunty Belle McLeod', *South Coast Register*, 23 March 2015.
Moorhouse, Frank, 'Macarthur, Baby', *The Bulletin*, 25 November 1972.

——, 'I Say Whitlam Doesn't Matter', *Digger*, December 1972, p. 7.
——, 'George McDowell Does the Job', *The Bulletin*, 30 December 1972.
——, 'A Black, Black Birth in 1939', *The Sun*, 10 January 1972.
——, (ed.), *Coast to Coast*, Angus & Robertson, 1973.
——, 'End of Mass Media?', *Current Affairs Bulletin*, vol. 50, no. 5, 1973, pp. 26–31.
——, 'George McDowell Delivers a Message to General Juan Garcia of the Cuban Army', *The Bulletin*, 28 July 1973.
——, 'The Airport, the Pizzeria, the Motel, the Rented Car and the Mysteries of Life', *Nation Review*, 18–24 May 1973.
——, 'Concerning a Reunion with an Ex-wife in Portugal', *Overland*, no. 56, 1973, pp. 2–8.
——, 'The New Black Mood', *The Bulletin*, 26 May 1973.
——, 'How Many Sexes Are There?', *The Bulletin*, 31 March 1973.
——, *Futility and Other Animals*, Angus & Robertson, 1973.
Quinan, John, *Frank Moorhouse and the Discontinuous Narrative*, Honours Thesis, The University of Queensland, 1979.
Wilding, Michael, *Aspects of the Dying Process*, University of Queensland Press, 1972.
——, 'Short Story Chronicle', *Meanjin Quarterly*, no. 30, 1971, pp. 255–67.

12: 'No, That Is Called a Discontinuous Narrative'

Catterns, David, 'Librarians and the Law of Copyright', *The Australian Library Journal*, November 1973, pp. 408–15.
Cohen, Lysbeth, 'Year Without End', *Australian Jewish Times*, 20 May 1976.
Davison, Mark J., Monotti, Ann L. & Wiseman, Leanne, *Australian Intellectual Property Law*, Cambridge University Press, 2008.
Flaus, John, 'Between Wars', *Cinema Papers: Australian Film Quarterly*, December 1974, pp. 1–4.
Green, Dorothy, 'Short Circuit', *Hemisphere*, vol. XIX, no. 5, 1975, pp. 38–9.
Hall, Sandra, 'Arty – but the Plot's Solid', *The Bulletin*, 16 November 1974.
Harrison-Ford, Carl, 'The Universe in a Small Town', *The Australian*, 23 November 1974.
Hill, Deirdre, *A Writer's Rights: The Story of the Australian Society of Authors, 1963–1983*, Australia & New Zealand Book Company, 1983.
Howard, John, 'A Battle Rages Between Wars', *TV Times*, 23 November 1974.
Johnston, Martin, 'Overcome by Softdrinks', *The Sydney Morning Herald*, 30 November 1974.
Kiernan, Brian, 'On Social Change and Shifting Values', *The Age*, 7 December 1974.
——, 'Notes on Frank Moorhouse', *Overland*, no. 56, 1973, pp. 9–11.
Macdonald, Dougal, 'Between Wars Explores Country's Ideas', *The Canberra Times*, 19 November 1974.
Moorhouse, Frank, 'The End of Ice', *The Sun*, 5 January 1974.
——, 'Sister/Sister', *Cosmopolitan*, March 1974, pp. 88–9.
——, 'Tell Churchill that T. George McDowell Is on His Feet', *Southerly*, vol. 34, no. 3, 1974, pp. 237–43.
——, *Days of Wine and Rage*, Penguin, 1980.
——, 'The Commune Does Not Want You', *Quadrant*, vol. 18, no. 4, 1974, pp. 25–8.
——, 'Milton Turns Against Champagne', *The Australian Ear*, no. 10, 1974.

——, 'Wesley's Brother at the Wake for Jack Kerouac', *Coast to Coast*, Angus & Robertson, 1973, pp. 67–71.
——, 'The Jack Kerouac Wake: The True Story', *Tabloid Story*, no. 2, 1973, pp. 6–7.
——, 'The Cup and the Wand (& The Magician)', *Gayzette*, no. 20, 1974, pp. 16–17.
——, *The Electrical Experience*, Angus & Robertson, 1974.
Musgrove, Nan, 'Learning Equals Fun Plus Games', *The Australian Women's Weekly*, 11 December 1974.
Summers, Anne, 'Some Small Town Traumas', *The Advertiser*, 15 March 1975.
Tittensor, John, 'Fiction', *Nation Review*, 6–12 December 1974.
Weiniger, Peter, 'Local Ability', *The Australian Jewish News*, 21 March 1975.
Wilding, Michael, *Wild & Woolley: A Publishing Memoir*, Giramondo, 2011.
——, 'Bye, Bye Jack, See You Soon', ABC Radio, 22 December 1973.
——, *Living Together*, University of Queensland Press, 1974.

Coda
Ellery, Reginald Spencer, *Psychiatric Aspects of Modern Warfare*, Reed & Harris, 1945.
Moorhouse, Frank, 'The Chain Letter Story', *The Bulletin*, 32 December 1974.
——, *Futility and Other Animals*, Gareth Powell & Associates, 1969.

Acknowledgements

Many thanks to those who assisted me in researching and writing this book, including: Don Anderson, Peter Banki, Reuben Bolt, Michelle Boulous Walker, Angela Carr, Paul Coombes, Megan Crook, Ryan Cropp, Sophie Cunningham, Carol Dettman, Nick Dettman, Jude Dodd, Kate Evans, Stuart Glover, Rohan Haslam, Sarah Holland-Batt, Wendy James, Amanda Lohrey, Jennifer Mills, Ryan O'Neill, Keith Paterson, James Tierney, Michael Wilding, Geordie Williamson and Desiree Wellins.

Special thanks to Arthur and Rhonda Moorhouse, Owen Moorhouse, and the Moorhouse family.

And to the following researchers and authors who provided access to their raw research materials: Anne Coombs, Don Graham, Jennifer Jones, Judith Rodriguez and Babette Smith.

The following institutions and their staff provided assistance and archival material: National Library of Australia, National Archives of Australia, State Library New South Wales, University of New South Wales Canberra, University of Queensland Library, the Workers' Educational Association Sydney, Shoalhaven Historical Society, Shoalhaven Libraries, and especially the Fryer Library at the University of Queensland.

Lisa Featherstone and the School of Historical and Philosophical Inquiry, University of Queensland, where I am an Honorary Fellow.

This project has been assisted by the Australian Government through the Australia Council for the Arts, its arts funding and advisory body. Additional funding was provided by the Council of Australian University Librarians (CAUL) in partnership with the Australian Society of Authors (the CAUL/ASA Fellowship), and the Hazel Rowley Literary Fellowship.

Thanks also to Meredith Curnow and the team at Penguin Random House Australia.

Frank Moorhouse, for his support and encouragement – and continuing example.

And Tess – this is not only for you, this is because of you.

ALSO PUBLISHED BY PENGUIN RANDOM HOUSE

In some ways, the people in these stories are a tribe – a modern, urban tribe – which does not fully recognise itself as such. Some of the people are central members of the tribe while others are hermits who live on the fringe. The shared environment is both internal – anxieties, pleasures and confusions – and external – the houses, streets, hotels and experiences. The central dilemma is that of giving birth, of creating new life.

The experiences of the inner-city ambience are shown through stories of growing up, leaving home, coming to the city from the country, or returning there; first love affairs, hetero- or homosexual; and finding a peer group, a life style, an ideology, and the anti-ideology of Libertarianism.

ALSO PUBLISHED BY PENGUIN RANDOM HOUSE

A timeless collection of stories exploring physical and psychological boundaries, some tentatively and others with vigour.

In *The Americans, Baby* the milieu is a Sydney under-40 population who, hoping that being earnest or outrageous will make them feel real, are left saturated with anxiety instead. An inherent resistance to American cultural intrusions and the risks that those from a great powerful land such as the US take when they meddle in another culture (they can be snared, seduced, destroyed) are explored with traditional Moorhouse flair and wit.

These stories are timeless in their concerns, and explore ideology, idealism, conflict, relationships and sex.

ALSO PUBLISHED BY PENGUIN RANDOM HOUSE

T. George McDowell believes in getting the job done.

'I do not care for words in top hats. I believe in shirt-sleeve words. I believe in getting the job done. We're like that on the coast.'

T. George McDowell, a manufacturer of soft drinks on the south coast of New South Wales, prides himself on extolling the virtues of progress. He is a Rotarian and exponent of wireless, refrigeration and electricity. He is a Realist and a Rationalist – 'fair man but hard as nails' according to his staff – but trouble in the shape of his youngest daughter, Terri, tests his values and beliefs, and he finds that his own sexual longings begin to intrude in his dreams.

First published in 1974, *The Electrical Experience* is an at times humorous examination of the Australian soul, and won the National Book Council Award for Fiction.

Discover a new favourite

Visit **penguin.com.au/readmore**